The

CHALLENGE

the

BOOK OF MORMON

MAKES TO THE WORLD

THE

CHALLENGE

THE

BOOK OF MORMON

MAKES TO THE WORLD

THIRTY CONDITIONS ANY WRITER MUST MEET
TO PRODUCE A COMPARABLE BOOK

GRACE GUYMON JONES

Rock Canyon Publishing
Provo, Utah

ISBN # 9781790130665

Rock Canyon Publishing, Provo, Utah

To order this book go to:
www.challengetotheworld.com

Front cover design by Morgan Crockett
Book design by Design Type Service, Salt Lake City, Utah

Printed in the United States of America

10 9 8 7 6 5 4 3 2 1

Contents

To all the honest in heart
who seek truth wherever it may be found

Preface

Sometime in 1966, a friend gave me a copy of a two-page typewritten document that upon first glance is merely a list, but I soon found it to be much more. Titled "The Challenge the Book of Mormon Makes to the World," the document in reality is a powerful declaration of belief which outlines thirty conditions any writer would need to meet to produce a book comparable to the Book of Mormon. I was profoundly impressed with the apparent impossibility of duplicating the Prophet Joseph Smith's accomplishment it describes.

As this declaration has circulated among Latter-day Saints and others, its authorship remained unknown for many decades. Since I was considering writing a book based on the thirty conditions, I began an informal search to find the author.

An obvious early candidate was the late BYU Professor Hugh W. Nibley, considered by many the world's leading authority on the Book of Mormon. Nibley was known to have used a modified version of this challenge to "test" his students by inviting them to attempt to write a book like the Book of Mormon in one semester. Dr. Nibley described the outcome in every class he gave the assignment:

> To date no student has carried out this assignment, which, of course, was not meant seriously. But why not? If anybody could write the Book of Mormon, as we have been so often assured, it is high time that somebody, some devoted and learned minister of the gospel, let us say, performed the invaluable public service of showing the world that it can be done.

When I called Professor Nibley and asked him if he had written the original version, he said that he had not, nor did he know who authored it.

I next called the FARMS (now the Maxwell Institute), the Missionary Department at Church headquarters, and anybody else I could think of but no one knew the answer. A secretary at the Missionary Department said she hoped someone would "do something with [what she called] the list," which gave me encouragement.

In time, I came upon a copy of Hugh B. Brown's "Profile of a Prophet," a long-remembered BYU devotional address given on October 4, 1955, about two and a half years before he was ordained an apostle. Several direct quotes from the thirty conditions appeared in that address. Then I discovered that one of my neighbors in Provo, Utah, is the daughter of one of Elder Brown's former secretaries, Mary Lou Taylor. With this fortunate circumstance, I asked the neighbor to inquire of her mother about The Challenge. She agreed to call her and learned that even though her mother could not definitively settle the authorship question, she said Elder Brown was always exacting in attributing sources and would not have quoted material that was not his own without citing it. Based on this circumstantial evidence, it appears that Elder Brown, later a member of the First Presidency, is the author.

Some years after my introduction to this declaration and after our children were grown, I began collecting material for this book. My motivation to undertake such a big project was so that my children, grandchildren and other descendants, would know of my strong testimony of the Book of Mormon, and of my conviction that it originated in the way the Prophet said it did—from a record written on golden plates given to him by an angel that he then translated "by the gift and power of God."

Life being what it is, it has been many years since I began this work, but providentially much new evidence is now available that would have been absent from the book had it been finished earlier.

As I began writing, I realized there are others beyond our family circle whose knowledge and testimonies could benefit from this book's many "infallible proofs" of the Book of Mormon, as Elder Jeffrey R. Holland calls them, from the extensive historical and doctrinal evidences, and from the many beautiful stories of conversion I have been fortunate to find. *The Challenge* is written to brighten the flame of testimony in everyday Latter-day Saints, in those in which it may have dimmed, and in sincere investigators of the restored gospel.

Grace Guymon Jones
Provo, Utah
November 2018

Acknowledgments

I am indebted to the many who have helped make this book possible by their valuable contributions of time and talent.

Among these are Suzy Bills and Debby Harrison, BYU professors and editors, for their skillful editing of the early manuscript; and Marian Spencer of the More Good Foundation for her attentive care in checking the many scriptures cited in the book.

Several family members have provided necessary and much appreciated assistance. These include: son Richard Jones for legal counsel; son-in-law Jim Engebretsen, for his business acumen and crucial contacts; daughter Tammy Engebretsen, grandsons Parker Jones and Jay Drennan, and grandson-in-law Matthew Larson, for helping with images and finalizing agreements with the many talented artists who contributed to the book; grandson Nathan Jones for website design and development; granddaughter Michelle Drennan for graphic design direction, and to daughter Sheri Drennan and sister Joyce Hamilton for many hours of proofing.

Heartfelt thanks to Dr. Ted Dee Stoddard, professor emeritus of management communication at BYU, who provided significant content, organization, and style editing of the manuscript; and to Don Norton, retired BYU English professor and master editor, for his superb final edit of the book.

Special recognition and gratitude to Book of Mormon Central's Executive Director Kirk Magleby. His encouragement, immense subject knowledge, and hundreds of hours of extra mile editing and revising the manuscript, are truly appreciated.

Finally, to son Milt Jones, Jr., whose insights, writing and editing expertise were invaluable. And for the support of my understanding husband Milt Sr., and the mountains of dishes and other household tasks he uncomplainingly tackled while I researched and wrote.

Introduction

The transcendent events surrounding the coming forth of the Book of Mormon—its translation, publication, and central role in the establishment and growth of The Church of Jesus Christ of Latter-day Saints—comprise a story of faith, testimony, and conversion repeated for millions the world over since the book was first published in 1830. The Prophet Joseph Smith, translator of the book, and those who assisted him in the early days of the Restoration, made bold and unapologetic claims concerning the book's origin and power to transform the hearts and lives of sincere seekers of truth throughout the earth.

Among these was Elder Orson Pratt, who proclaimed: "God Himself is the author of the Book of Mormon. He inspired the ideas it contains. . . . He sent forth His angels from heaven, clothed in brightness and glory, to chosen witnesses, commanding them to declare to all nations, kindreds, tongues, and people, that this precious book [is] divine revelation."[1] The Book of Mormon is a witness that God has power to speak to His children in our day by any means agreeable with his omnipotent will, including through a sacred record kept by ancient American prophets and translated by a modern American prophet. Additionally, the book is a faithful companion, defender and champion of the Bible, and restorer of much lost truth.

The Challenge the Book of Mormon Makes to the World presents Elder Hugh B. Brown's thirty conditions or limitations any would-be writer must meet to produce a book comparable to the Book of Mormon. Using these conditions as a framework, *The Challenge* provides extensive evidence in support of the assertion that neither Joseph Smith, an unlearned farm boy, nor the most celebrated of scholars, or anyone else, could have produced the Book of Mormon without divine aid. (We have found it necessary to update the original conditions due to anachronistic language or advancements in Book of Mormon scholarship. The table of contents consists of short versions of the conditions with the full versions found under these chapter titles at the beginning of each chapter.)

Dr. Hugh Nibley provides an apt analogy as to why authoring a book like the Book of Mormon is such a daunting task:

Where else [but in the Book of Mormon] will one find such inexhaustible invention combined with such unerring accuracy and consistency? To put it facetiously but not unfairly, the artist must not only balance a bowl of goldfish and three lighted candles on the end of a broomstick while fighting off a swarm of gadflies, but he must at the same time be carving an immortal piece of statuary from a lump of solid diorite.

In an undertaking like this, merely to avoid total confusion and complete disaster would be a superhuman achievement. But that is not the assignment; that is only a coincidental detail to the main business at hand, which is, with all this consummately skillful handling of mere technical detail, to have something significant to say; not merely significant, but profound and moving, and so relevant to the peculiar conditions of our own day as to speak to our ears with a voice of thunder.[2]

Accordingly, one of the first challenges for a potential author of a book comparable to the Book of Mormon is the actuality of its existence. Regardless of how improbable it may seem to some that a book, engraved on plates of gold in a language called "reformed Egyptian," revealed by an angel of God, and translated in the way Joseph Smith said it was, "by the gift and power of God," this long and complex book does exist. With that reality and the book's ever-growing, worldwide influence, skeptics are finding it increasingly difficult to simply dismiss it as unworthy of examination, as has been the practice. The book is filled with too many powerful evidences of its divinity for such easy disregard.

President Gordon B. Hinckley, the fifteenth President of the Church, has written:

Unbelievers may doubt [Joseph Smith's] First Vision and say there were no witnesses to prove it. Critics may scorn every divine manifestation incident to the coming forth of this work as being of such an intangible nature as to be unprovable to the pragmatic mind, as if the things of God could be understood other than by the Spirit of God. They may discount our theology. But they cannot in honesty dismiss the Book of Mormon. It is here. They can feel it. They can read it. They can weigh its substance and its content. They can witness its influence.[3]

The challenge, therefore, the Book of Mormon makes to every writer in the world is one of replication—that is, to produce a book comparable to the one that came to us through the Prophet Joseph Smith. Such a book about ancient Tibet, for example, or any other little-known civilization, must provide a detailed description of countless aspects of that society, fulfill Bible prophecy, and change writing styles many times while using language that can be traced to that civilization's beginnings. Further, many historical, linguistic and archaeological evidences must validate the book.

When we think about even a few of the conditions Joseph Smith faced as he dictated the words of the Book of Mormon to his scribes, we realize that those who dismiss the book without a sincere and deep examination of its message, risk rejecting a modern revelation from God, with eternal outcomes to follow that choice.

Among the conditions examined in *The Challenge* are these: Joseph Smith had little formal education. During the period of translation work he could read but not write well enough to compose an adequate letter, and he was only twenty-three years old (Chapter 3); he did no research—library or other resources available to the prophet were decidedly limited (Chapter 4); the book is long, 531 pages of small text, composed of 239 chapters, and 6,604 verses (Chapter 5); one hundred and eighty-eight new names appear in the book (Chapter 14); the English translation of the Book of Mormon exhibits unmistakable characteristics of ancient Hebrew (Chapter 15); the book fulfills Bible prophecy unlike any other book in the world (Chapter 21); the manuscript was completed in about 74 working days (Chapter 30); and Joseph gained no wealth from the book but voluntarily died a martyr to seal his testimony of the book and his mission with his own blood (Chapter 29).

Although *The Challenge* presents much evidence supporting the truth of the Book of Mormon and Joseph Smith's calling as a prophet of God, it does not, and cannot, provide absolute proof of these things. "The origin, preparation, translation, and verification of the truth of the Book of Mormon," declared President Ezra Taft Benson, "have all been retained in the hands of the Lord, and the Lord makes no mistakes. You can be assured of that."[4] As Elder Neal A. Maxwell has written, "The scriptures . . . will remain in the realm of faith. Science will not be able to prove or disprove holy writ. However, enough plausible evidence will come forth to prevent scoffers from having a field day—but not enough to remove the requirement of faith."[5]

Thus, *The Challenge* is written in the spirit of Austin Farrer's observation that "though argument does not create conviction, the lack of it destroys belief. What seems to be proved may not be embraced; but what no one shows the ability to defend is quickly abandoned. Rational argument does not create belief, but it maintains a climate in which belief may flourish."[6]

Ultimately, such a climate of belief can help a person, hungering for truth and righteousness, come to his or her own inspired testimony of the book's divine truth, which will come as a fruit of faith and reason, after honest inquiry, diligent study, and sincere prayer (see Moroni 10:3–5). Regarding faith and reason, and the important role of evidence in strengthening conviction, Elder Jeffrey R. Holland, speaking at Book of Mormon Central's 50th anniversary commemoration of the discovery of chiasmus in the Book of Mormon, noted that

> truly rock-ribbed faith and uncompromised conviction comes with its most complete power when it engages our head as well as our heart. . . . I believe God intends us to find and use the evidence He has given— reasons, if you will—which affirm the truthfulness of His work. . . . My testimony . . . is that the gospel is infallibly true and that a variety of infallible proofs supporting that assertion will continue to come until Jesus descends as the ultimate infallible truth of all. Our testimonies aren't dependent on evidence—we still need spiritual confirmation in the heart . . . but not to seek for and not to acknowledge intellectual,

documentable support for our belief when it is available is to needlessly limit an otherwise incomparably strong theological position and deny us a unique, persuasive vocabulary in the latter-day arena of religious investigation and sectarian debate.[7]

Hugh Nibley suggests only three possible explanations for the origin of the Book of Mormon: 1) spontaneous generation; 2) Joseph Smith's account—"by special messengers and gifts from God," or 3) that Joseph Smith or someone else simply created it out of thin air. "No experiments have been carried out," he observes, "for testing any of these theories." No one has considered the first, the second is widely dismissed with contempt, and the third is accepted "without question or hesitation."

And yet the third theory is quite as extravagant as the other two, demanding unlimited gullibility and the suspension of all critical judgment in any who would accept it. It is based on the simple proposition that since people have written books, somebody, namely Smith or a contemporary, wrote this one. But to make this thesis stick is to show not only that people have written big books, but that somebody has been able to produce a big book like this one. But no other such book exists. . . .

We respectfully solicit the name of any student or professor in the world who could come within ten thousand miles of such a performance. As a sheer tour-de-force there is nothing like it. The theory that Joseph Smith wrote the Book of Mormon simply will not stand examination.[8]

Milt Jones, Jr.

Chapter 1

Write a
Sacred History
of Ancient Tibet

You must write a sacred history of ancient Tibet covering a period from 2200 BC to AD 400. Why Tibet? Because you likely know no more about ancient Tibet than Joseph Smith, or anyone else, knew about ancient America in 1829.

Suppose you were to sit down to write a history of ancient Tibet. What details would you include? You would probably mention mountains. Tibet is famous for the snow-capped Himalayas. Yaks may appear in your book. These shaggy beasts have been an important part of Tibetan life for centuries. You should say something about Tibetan Buddhism with its monks and monasteries. Religious influence is strong in contemporary Tibet as it was anciently. But how much do you really know about ancient Tibet? Could you write biographical sketches of important people? Would you include accurate geographic descriptions of cities and lands? Could you write extensively about wars? And then weave the whole thing into a coherent narrative that will captivate readers for generations ever after?

A Remarkably Complex Book

The description of ancient America in the Book of Mormon contains all of these historical elements and many more. Joseph Smith was divinely inspired as he dictated details of agriculture, hunting, mining, warfare, and destructive natural disasters. The Book of Mormon contains long genealogies and short annual summaries. We read of noble heroes and base villains. Topographical details are interwoven with scenes of religious rituals and trans-oceanic migrations. There is shipbuilding and commerce. We read of architecture, textiles, and jewelry. Monetary systems of exchange and judicial proceedings are described in considerable detail. The Book of Mormon contains notable stories of dynasties, palace intrigues and hardy explorers tramping through uncharted wilderness. Human slavery and governmental systems are discussed along with astronomical observations correlated with sophisticated calendars. People, places, things and ideas—the stuff of history—all feature prominently in the pages of the Book of Mormon.

How many nuances would you get right if you wrote in detail about ancient Tibet or ancient America? Could you call people by their right names? The Book of Mormon has nearly 200 proper names that impress modern scholars.[1] Could you correctly place dozens of battles in appropriate seasons of the year based on climate and planting/harvest cycles? The Book of Mormon times war episodes precisely to coincide with agricultural requirements in rainy and dry seasons.[2] Could you accurately describe a calendar system that measures time in base 20 numbers? Fractions and multiples of 20 are prominent throughout the Nephite text. (See Helaman 14:2, Mormon 3:1, 3 Nephi 5:7-8, 2 Nephi 5:34, 4 Nephi 1:22, Mormon 8:6.) The Book of Mormon consistently gets so many little details right that bright, well-informed readers are awed by its uncanny historical accuracy.

In addition to minute details, the Book of Mormon paints the big picture precisely. It tells the story of four nations, three of whom left the Near East during the axial period ca. 600 BC and sailed to the New World. Two of the nations amalgamated ca. 200 BC but only one remained intact after ca. 400 AD amidst constant warfare. The nations inhabited a land with northward and southward components. The southward part was nearly surrounded by water and had a narrow east-west strip running coast to coast separating contentious rivals north and south of the line. Ca. 50 BC large scale migrations began moving northward. The Book of Mormon describes advanced societies with city states constantly shifting alliances. Ca. 30 AD the text describes failed governments deteriorating into tribalism. All of this fits comfortably into what we now know about ancient America.

Sixty Things No Longer Preposterous

Eminent anthropologist John E. Clark gave a powerful presentation at the Library of Congress in 2005 as part of the celebration of Joseph Smith's 200th birthday. Clark called his presentation "Joseph Smith, Archaeology, and the Book of Mormon." In it, he lists 60 things described in the Book of Mormon that most people found preposterous when the book first appeared for sale on March 26, 1830. Things like highways, buildings of cement, thrones, and Egyptian-like script evoked howls of laughter from critics. No one could have written accurately about these kinds of things in Joseph Smith's day when Native Americans were generally considered barbaric tepee dwellers living on the frontier. Fast forward to our day when archaeology reveals exactly what the Book of Mormon describes. Clark explains that historical forgeries are disproven over time, while authentic ancient documents such as the Book of Mormon have their contextual details confirmed by future scholarship.

Here is a good example of historical confirmation at work. The Book of Mormon contains the curious idea that trees can grow in and from humans (see Alma 32:28, 41; 33:23). Page 3 of the pre-Columbian Dresden Codex shows a tree of life growing from the cleft heart of the Mayan maize god spread across a sacrificial altar. So, a notion totally alien to the world of Joseph Smith turns out to be an authentic belief in ancient America. And when a copy of page 3 of the Dresden Codex, published in 1831 by Lord Kingsborough, in his *Antiquities of Mexico*, The Book of Mormon, published in 1830, was corroborated on this point the very next year, but only in a very expensive limited-edition book published in London.

A Monumental Challenge

The Book of Mormon has hundreds of points that have been and can be verified by archaeologists, botanists, geographers, geologists, linguists, paleontologists, etc. The more time one spends in its inspired pages the more one stands in awe of its magnificence. Hugh Nibley as a US Army Intelligence Officer with a fluent command of German was in the first wave of Allied troops wading ashore on Utah Beach on D-Day. In the autobiographical film *Faith of an Observer* Nibley talks about what was going through his mind on that fateful day surrounded by battlefield commotion. All he could think about was how marvelous the Book of Mormon is.

Later, while spending much of his remarkable scholarly life studying and writing about this new American scripture, Nibley summarizes the unimaginable challenge of producing a book comparable to the Book of Mormon:

> Where will you find another work remotely approaching the Book of Mormon in scope and daring? It appears suddenly out of nothing—not an accumulation of twenty-five years like the Koran, but a single staggering performance, bursting on a shocked and scandalized world like an explosion, the full-blown history of an ancient people, following them through all the trials, triumphs, and vicissitudes of a thousand years without a break, telling how a civilization originated, rose to momentary greatness, and passed away, giving due attention to every phase of civilized history in a densely compact and rapidly moving story that interweaves dozens of plots with an inexhaustible fertility of invention and an uncanny consistency that is never caught in a slip or contradiction.[3]

Could you create a history of ancient Tibet containing hundreds of accurate contextual details interwoven with a compelling story line? Joseph Smith did it for ancient America as a 21 to 23-year-old in 1827–1829. The young prophet translated authentic ancient records by the gift and power of God. The Book of Mormon is still in print almost 200 years after its first press run of 5,000 books. Good first edition copies are currently worth well over one hundred thousand dollars on the rare book market. The book has been translated into 110 languages making it available to about 89% of the world's population in their native tongue. Four and a half million copies are published annually with many more copies distributed digitally.

Filled with the Savior's Love

The Book of Mormon is a manifestation of the love of God for His children no matter their nation, kindred, or tongue. Reading and praying about the Book of Mormon causes people's lives to change. Its power to teach the gospel in plainness and assist in freeing the sin-bound soul through the Savior's atonement is inexhaustible. One way of understanding the efficacy of a written work is known as reception history. This discipline is not concerned with whether a particular individual or group correctly interprets a given text, but rather focuses on the influence of that text over time without judgment. The Book of Mormon has its own rich reception history, as the following brief accounts illustrate: first, how the book affected members of the Church in the Baltics when it became available to them in their own language, and second, how it was received by three non-Latter-day Saints, each on different continents.

R. L. and Evelyn Benson were serving as missionaries for the Church in Lithuania in 2001 when the Book of Mormon was published in Lithuanian. Previously, the only edition available to the people was in Russian, a language many could not read. At a special meeting the Lithuanian edition of the book was distributed to Church members. "It is difficult to express the feelings and emotions of the evening," Evelyn recalls. "There were tears and smiles and more tears and more smiles. Church members were so busy leafing through their newfound treasure that they did not want to stop for refreshments. No one wanted to leave the building. What a night—one never to be forgotten!"[4]

In the early 1970s, the Church determined that the Book of Mormon needed to be translated into Afrikaans, and approached Felix Mynhardt, a language professor at Pretoria University, South Africa, and a non-Latter-day Saint, to do the translation. Professor Mynhardt, who had undoubtedly been given the gift of languages in his youth and was fluent in more than sixty languages, agreed to take on the project. Commenting on this experience, Mynhardt said he "didn't know who Joseph Smith was before he translated this book, but while he translated it, he was a prophet of God! He could have been nothing else! No person in 1827 could have done what he did. The science did not exist. The knowledge of ancient Egyptian did not exist. The knowledge of these ancient times and ancient peoples did not exist. The Book of Mormon is scripture." He further testified that "it is scripture of the same caliber as the Old Testament, or for that matter, the New Testament."[5]

Southern Baptist minister Lynn Ridenhour agrees: "Reared in a small conservative Baptist church back in the hills of the Ozarks, I was taught with strong convictions that [Latter-day Saints] were . . . [not Christians] and to believe that the Book of Mormon was a lie. We have the Bible and no man was to add to the scriptures lest his soul be damned." But when Ridenhour gave the Book of Mormon a try, he couldn't deny its truth. He found "the central message of the

Book of Mormon is—to repent and come unto Christ, which means to establish a covenant with Him. And that message is coming to light in these latter days. And that's why I embrace the Book of Mormon. Our generation knows very little, if anything, about establishing a covenant with Christ." Ridenhour believes the whole Book of Mormon, finding that "there is absolutely nothing in it that contradicts the Bible."[6]

Alfred R. Young (1919–2012) was introduced to the Book of Mormon by a fellow prisoner while enduring hellish years of captivity in a Japanese prisoner of war camp during World War II. His posterity are now members of the Church. Many times, he repeated his testimony that if enduring incarceration and torture was the only way he could receive the Book of Mormon, he would do it all again because the book brought light into his world of darkness.[7]

An Overview of the Challenge

A brief summary of the scope and structure of the Book of Mormon should help you determine if writing a similar book is something you are ready to attempt. For starters, the Book of Mormon is an abridgment by Mormon of the writings of many prophet-historians compiled over more than a thousand years on many metal plates.

The Book of Mormon consists of 15 books beginning with the writings of Nephi, who tells of keeping two records: the small plates of Nephi, devoted to spiritual matters, focuses on the ministry and teachings of ancient American prophets, and the large plates of Nephi contain the secular history of his people. The narrative begins with the prophet Lehi (Nephi's father and a contemporary of Jeremiah) leading his family and others on a flight from Jerusalem in approximately 600 B.C. to escape the impending destruction of the city by the Babylonians in 586 B.C. After a difficult eight-year passage through the Arabian wilderness, the group reaches the shore of the Arabian Sea where Nephi is commanded by the Lord to build a ship to carry them to their Promised Land in the Western Hemisphere.

Upon arriving in the New World, and with the death of Lehi, Nephi's brothers Laman and Lemuel rebel against him, threatening to kill both him and his followers who are compelled to flee. This division establishes the setting for much of the book's future history in which two distinct nations, the Nephites and the Lamanites, will often be at war. At Nephi's death, his younger brother Jacob takes up the story and the plates. Other prophets follow Jacob, faithfully maintaining the written records. The small plates are the source of the books of 1st and 2nd Nephi, Jacob, Enos, Jarom, and Omni, comprising the first 142 pages of our present-day Book of Mormon.

Throughout the following centuries, in the pattern of the Old Testament, the people prosper when they are obedient to the Lord and suffer chastisement and affliction when they rebel—the book is a testament of the temporal

"Christ Blesses the Nephite Children"

and spiritual blessings of righteousness. It tells of evil kings, corrupt judges, secret combinations, famine, war, pestilence, persecution of the righteous, the tender mercies of the Lord, faith in God, miracles, repentance, and hope through the Atonement of Christ, among other vital doctrines and instruction. The crowning event of the sacred record is found in 3rd Nephi with the appearance and ministry of the Savior to the Nephites following His resurrection in Judea. The account of the Savior's visitation to ancient America was taken from the Plates of Mormon, an abridgment by Mormon of the large plates of Nephi that includes many commentaries by both Mormon and his son Moroni. After the book of Omni, the Words of Mormon, a short editorial insert, appears, followed by Mormon's extract from the large plates containing the books of Mosiah, Alma, Helaman, and 3rd and 4th Nephi, consisting of 324 pages, the heart of the book.

Near the end of the Book of Mormon we find the Book of Ether, which is the record of a people known as the Jaredites, who, led by their prophet-leader, the brother of Jared, journeyed from the Tower of Babel and were shown how to build barges. The Jaredites were driven on the sea by God to a Promised Land in the New World, many centuries before Lehi's arrival. The Jaredites eventually self-destructed in a brutal civil war.

After the Nephites and Lamanites descended into utter depravity, the Book of Mormon story ends early in the fifth century AD with a final battle between the two great nations. Even though the Nephites gathered hundreds of thousands of warriors, they were annihilated by an even larger army of Lamanites. Moroni was the only Nephite survivor. After wandering for about 21 years, adding a few concluding chapters, he buried the gold plates in a stone box in the Hill Cumorah sometime about 421 AD near present-day Palmyra, New York. Moroni would return as a resurrected being to deliver the plates to the Prophet Joseph Smith for translation in 1827. The final three books are: Mormon, Ether, and Moroni, consisting of 63 pages. The Book of Mormon in its current edition totals 531 pages.

Joseph Smith could not have produced the Book of Mormon without divine aid. Could you?

Chapter 2

Your Education
Is Limited and You
Have Been Raised
in Rural Isolation

You have no more than three years of formal education and have spent your early years in backwoods farming communities.

Joseph Smith Jr., born December 23, 1805, in the village of Sharon, Vermont, to Joseph and Lucy Mack Smith, was the fifth of eleven children. Joseph's formal schooling consisted of about three years.[1]

After repeated crop failures, the Smith family sought to improve their circumstances by moving several times. When Joseph was ten, the family moved to Palmyra, New York. His father went ahead and later sent for his family, hiring a man and a team of horses to transport them. The man turned out to be an unprincipled person who let others ride with him and made Joseph walk, even though it was in the dead of winter and the boy was still lame from an operation on his leg and had been on crutches for three years. Joseph said he "suffered the most excruciating weariness and pain." Another family traveling with them had sleighs, and Joseph was eventually allowed to ride in the last sleigh for a time. But as they neared Palmyra, the driver, a member of the other family, knocked Joseph down, left him bleeding in the snow, and drove off. Joseph thought he was going to lie there and die, but a stranger came along, picked him up, and carried him to Palmyra. This episode makes it clear that even though Joseph was mistreated, the Lord was looking out for his young prophet-to-be.[2]

These incidents also demonstrate how the Lord positioned Joseph and his family in the area where the gold plates were buried from which Joseph would translate the Book of Mormon. Four years after moving to Palmyra, the family purchased a farm in nearby Manchester and lived there until after 1830.[3] Farm work left little time for schooling during Joseph's youth as he was occupied, along with his father and brothers, in clearing sixty acres of heavily wooded land, fencing, gathering sap from their fifteen hundred trees, and making maple syrup from them.[4]

Eber D. Howe's 1834 *Mormonism Unveiled*, includes affidavits gathered from some of the Smith's neighbors. The documents labeled the Smiths as "lazy" and "indolent." These events occurred after Joseph's First Vision during a time when persecution became common for the once highly respected Smith family. However, tax records regarding the Smith family's assets contradict Howe's accusations.[5]

"If Any of You Lack Wisdom"

The Smiths were a religious family who read the Bible and had family prayer, but like many of that time, they belonged to no church, at least for a time. Joseph was fourteen when contentious religious revivals commenced that caused him "serious reflection and great uneasiness" (Joseph Smith—History 1:8). Four members of his family decided to join a church,[6] but the more Joseph read the Bible and listened to the contradictory positions taught by the various preachers, the more bewildered he became. "So great were the confusion and strife among the different denominations," Joseph later wrote, "that it was impossible for a person young as I was, and so unacquainted with men and things, to come to any certain conclusions who was right and who was wrong" (Joseph Smith—History 1:8). Ultimately, he found guidance in the scriptures:

> I was one day reading the Epistle of James 1:5, which reads, "If any of you lack wisdom, let him ask of God, that giveth to all men liberally, and upbraideth not; and it shall be given him." Never did any passage of scripture come with more power to the heart of man than this did at this time to mine. It seemed to enter with great force into every feeling of my heart. I reflected on it again and again, knowing that if any person needed wisdom from God, I did; for how to act I did not know, and unless I could get more wisdom than I then had, I would never know; for the teachers of religion of the different sects understood the same passages of scripture so differently as to destroy all confidence in settling the question by an appeal to the Bible[7] (Joseph Smith—History 1:11–12).

Joseph's Prayer Is Answered

Joseph decided he would ask God which church was right and which one he should join. He retired to the nearby woods and knelt to pray:

> So, in accordance with this, my determination to ask of God, I retired to the woods to make the attempt. It was on the morning of a beautiful, clear day, early in the spring of eighteen hundred and twenty. It was the first time in my life that I had made such an attempt, for amidst all my anxieties I had never as yet made the attempt to pray vocally.
>
> After I had retired to the place where I had previously designed to go, having looked around me, and finding myself alone, I kneeled down and began to offer up the desires of my heart to God. I had scarcely done so, when immediately I was seized upon by some power which

Joseph Smith's First Visitation

entirely overcame me and had such an astonishing influence over me as to bind my tongue so that I could not speak. Thick darkness gathered around me, and it seemed to me for a time as if I were doomed to sudden destruction.

But, exerting all my powers to call upon God to deliver me out of the power of this enemy which had seized upon me, and at the very moment when I was ready to sink into despair and abandon myself to destruction . . . I saw a pillar of light exactly over my head, above the brightness of the sun, which descended gradually until it fell upon me.

It no sooner appeared than I found myself delivered from the enemy. . . . I saw two Personages, whose brightness and glory defy all description, standing above me in the air. One of them spake unto me, calling me by name and said, pointing to the other—*This is my Beloved Son. Hear Him!*

My object in going to inquire of the Lord was to know which of all the sects was right, that I might know which to join. . . . No sooner, therefore, did I get possession of myself, so as to be able to speak, than I asked the Personages, who stood above me in the light, which of all the sects was right, (for at this time it had never entered into my heart that all were wrong)—and which I should join.

I was answered that I must join none of them, for they were all wrong . . . that all their creeds were an abomination in his sight, that those professors were all corrupt; that: they draw near to me with their lips, but their hearts are far from me, they teach for doctrines the commandments of men, having a form of godliness, but they deny the power thereof (Joseph Smith—History 1:16–19).

As difficult as it might be for an unbelieving world to accept this as the answer Joseph received, God is not a God of confusion. We read in Ephesians 4:5 that there is but "one lord, one faith, one baptism," which makes it clear that if all the churches were teaching different doctrines and interpretations of the Bible, they could not all be correct. However, Joseph thought one might be true and was eager to know which one, so he could become a part of it.

From the early days of Christianity, various creeds were written and rewritten by hundreds of churches to the point that they have made God incomprehensible, while bearing little resemblance to Christ's original church or teachings. Clearly, this is not pleasing to the Lord.

B. H. Roberts, an early twentieth-century Latter-day Saint leader, comments:

It should be observed that Joseph Smith, then but a boy, scarcely removed from childhood, was not himself pronouncing judgment upon the status of Christendom. It was not he who declared the sects to be all wrong, their creeds an abomination, and the professors thereof corrupt. He . . . on account of his extreme youthfulness and his lack of general information, was among the least qualified to pronounce upon such a question. . . . No human wisdom was sufficient to answer that question. . . . God had been the judge of "fallen Christendom." Joseph Smith was but his messenger, to herald that judgment to the world.[8]

God Can Reveal Himself to Man

Following this "First Vision," Joseph said, "I had now got my mind satisfied so far as the sectarian world was concerned—that it was not my duty to join with any of them, but to continue as I was until further directed" (Joseph Smith—History 1:26).

There are those who contend that Joseph Smith could not have seen God, and they often base their belief on such scriptures as John 1:18 and 1 John 4:12 that say, "No man hath seen God at any time." However, the full text of John 1:18 reads: "No man hath seen God at any time; the only begotten Son, which is in the bosom of the Father, he hath declared him." Irenaeus, an early Christian author, wrote in 180 AD that this scripture should be read as follows: "For no man hath seen God at any time" unless "the only-begotten Son of God, which is in the bosom of the Father, He hath declared [Him]." Irenaeus was well aware that righteous men had seen God in the past.[9]

Furthermore, "an Early Christian document called the Clementine Homilies portrays the apostle Peter as agreeing with Irenaeus' view. 'For I maintain that the eyes of mortals cannot see the incorporeal form of the Father or [His] son because it is illuminated by exceeding great light. . . . For he who sees God cannot live, for the excess of light dissolves the flesh of him who sees; unless by the secret power of God the flesh be changed into the nature of light, so that it can see light."[10] Joseph Smith revealed the same essential truth in Doctrine and Covenants 67:11: "For no man has seen God at any time in the flesh except quickened by the Spirit of God."

Joseph Smith's later inspired translation of the Bible, undertaken at the Lord's command, states that the original rendering reads no "sinful" man has ever seen God and that Jesus Christ is the only way to God. Christ taught, "Blessed are the pure in heart: for *they shall see* God" (Matthew 5:8; emphasis added). And John 6:46 tells us: "Not that any man hath seen the Father, save he which is of God, he hath seen the Father" (see also 3 John 1:11). These scriptures tell us that the righteous can see, have seen, and will see God.

Regarding the marvelous manifestation to Joseph by the Father and the Son, Gordon B. Hinckley, President of The Church of Jesus Christ of Latter-day Saints at the time, declared:

> Two beings of substance were before him. He saw them. They were in form like men, only much more glorious in their appearance. He spoke to them. They spoke to him. They were not amorphous spirits. . . . They were beings of flesh and bone whose nature was reaffirmed in later revelations which came to the Prophet. Our entire case as members of The Church of Jesus Christ of Latter-day Saints rests on the validity of this glorious First Vision. . . . Nothing on which we base our doctrine, nothing we teach, nothing we live by, is of greater importance than this initial declaration.[11]

President Ezra Taft Benson writes: "The visitation of God the Father and Jesus Christ to Joseph Smith . . . is fundamental to the theology of the Church. Upon the reality of the First Vision rests the Church's claim to divine authority. . . . It is bedrock theology to the Church. The adversary knows this and has attacked Joseph Smith's credibility from the day he announced the visitation of the Father and the Son."[12]

Why "A Boy of No Consequence" Was Chosen

It is not a mystery why the Lord would choose a young fourteen-year-old farm boy for such a monumental work. "Here was a clean, pure, unsophisticated mind," says President Hinckley, "that could be made the recipient of truth without any clouding of any preconceived ideas or notions."[13]

President Spencer W. Kimball adds, "[Joseph] was not steeped in the traditions and legends and superstitions and fables of the centuries. He had nothing to unlearn. He prayed for knowledge and direction. The powers of darkness preceded the light. When he knelt in solitude in the silent forest, his earnest prayer brought on a battle royal that threatened his destruction. For centuries, Lucifer with unlimited dominion had fettered men's minds and could ill-afford to lose his satanic hold."[14]

The Lord needed someone who was humble, teachable, courageous, and obedient. Joseph was all of these, and through him the Lord was able to bring forth the Book of Mormon and restore His church once more to the earth.

Joseph exhibited great courage even as a child. At the age of seven, he was stricken with typhus fever that left him with a horribly painful sore in his leg. The doctors were not able to successfully treat him and were afraid it would be necessary to amputate his leg. After Joseph experienced several weeks of severe pain, the doctors decided to try a new operation and remove the affected parts of bone from his leg. As there was no anesthesia in those days, they planned to tie him to the bedstead. Joseph objected. They then proposed he drink some brandy. He refused, saying, "I will not touch one particle of liquor, neither will I

"If Father Will Hold Me"

be tied down, but I will tell you what I will do—I will have my father sit on the bed and hold me in his arms, and then I will do whatever is necessary."

He insisted that his mother not be present to watch him suffer. During the agonizing operation, the doctors removed nine large pieces of the bone. (Fourteen additional pieces of bone afterwards worked their way out while his leg was healing.) The surgery was successful, but Joseph was on crutches for over three years and had a slight limp the rest of his life.[15] This event in itself was a miracle. Dartmouth University surgeon, Dr. Nathan Smith, who performed the surgery, was the only physician in the United States who knew how to successfully operate for osteomyelitis, Joseph's ailment, and it was many years before this procedure was known and practiced by others.[16]

In an 1831 revelation to Joseph, the Lord said He would use "the weak things of the world" to do His work (Doctrine and Covenants 1:23). The Book of Mormon itself records these words from the Lord: "The learned shall not read them, for they have rejected them. . . . I will show unto the children of men that I am able to do mine own work" (2 Nephi 27:20–21). Elder Neal A. Maxwell writes: "Young Joseph Smith went into the grove merely wanting to know which church to join—not seeking to be a seer, revelator, a translator, and prophet."[17] He could not have imagined the challenges and persecutions that lay ahead as a result of his earnest prayer or the great work the Lord had for this "weak" servant to accomplish in restoring the gospel of Jesus Christ.

Knowing that Joseph had always been a truthful boy, his family did not hesitate to believe his account of the visit from the Father and the Son. However, that was not the case with many others. Joseph was "greatly surprised" at the reaction of the Methodist minister to whom he related his vision. The minister treated Joseph's account "with great contempt, saying it was all of the devil, that there were no such things as visions or revelations in these days; that all such things had ceased with the apostles and there would never be any more of them" (Joseph Smith—History 1:21). The minister repeated Joseph's account to others, and thereafter he suffered continuous ridicule and persecution.

Joseph writes of these events: "And though I was an obscure boy, only between fourteen and fifteen years of age, and my circumstances in life such as to make a boy of no consequence in the world, yet men of high standing would take notice sufficient to excite the public mind against me, and create a bitter persecution; and this was common among all the sects—all united to persecute me" (Joseph Smith—History 1:22).

"Why persecute me for telling the truth?" he asked. "For I had seen a vision; I knew it, and I knew that God knew it, and I could not deny it, neither dared I do it; at least I knew that by so doing I would offend God and come under condemnation" (Joseph Smith—History 1:25).

Though modern-day revelations and visions were not accepted by most churches at the time, the Book of Mormon is particularly clear on the subject:

> I speak unto you who deny the revelations of God, and say that they are done away, that there are no revelations, nor prophecies, nor gifts, nor healing, nor speaking with tongues, and the interpretation of tongues; Behold I say unto you, he that denieth these things knoweth not the gospel of Christ; yea, he has not read the scriptures; if so, he does not understand them. For do we not read that God is the same yesterday, today, and forever, and in him there is no variableness neither shadow of changing. And now, if ye have imagined up unto yourselves a god who doth vary, and in whom there is shadow of changing, then have ye imagined up unto yourselves a god who is not a God of miracles (Mormon 9:7–10).

Joseph's Annual Instruction from Moroni

Three years after receiving this First Vision, while Joseph was praying for further direction, a heavenly messenger appeared to him. The angel said his name was Moroni, and he told Joseph that God had a work for him to do. He further said that Joseph's "name should be had for good and evil among all nations, kindreds, and tongues, or that it should be both good and evil spoken of among all people" (Joseph Smith—History 1:33). Elder Neal A. Maxwell comments on this prophecy, "Except from a divine source, how audacious a statement! Yet his contemporary religious leaders, then much better known than Joseph, have faded into the footnotes of history, while the work of Joseph Smith grows constantly and globally."[18]

An example of Joseph's name being "had for evil" was witnessed by John Groberg as a young missionary serving in the islands of Tonga during the 1950s. One location he and his companion visited was the small volcanic island of Tafahi. Only eighty people lived there. There were two churches on the island, neither of which was a Latter-day Saint Church. A family of six invited them in, and Elder Groberg eventually asked, "Have you ever heard of President Eisenhower?"

"No, who is he?"

"He's the president of the United States."

"Where is the United States?"

The conversation continued about Khrushchev, Charles De Gaulle, the Great Depression, famous movie stars, the Korean War, etc. The island residents had heard of none of these people or events. Then Elder Groberg asked if they had heard of Joseph Smith. Their faces suddenly showed recognition and the father said, "Don't talk to us about that false prophet! Not in our house! We know all about him. Our minister has told us!" After learning the truth about Joseph Smith, a few people from Tafahi did join the Church. [19]

Hundreds of books have been written about Joseph Smith—those that condemn and say only evil about him and those that praise and recognize him as one of the great men of the age and a prophet of God. Elder Neal A. Maxwell writes that it is safe to say that "no prophet has been scrutinized in such an intense way, on as wide a scale, or for so long a period of time as Joseph Smith, Jr."[20]

Regarding Moroni's visit, Joseph writes: "He said there was a book deposited, written upon gold plates, giving an account of the former inhabitants of this continent, and the source from whence they sprang. He also said that the fulness of the everlasting Gospel was contained in it, as delivered by the Savior to the ancient inhabitants." The messenger further told Joseph that an instrument known as the Urim and Thummim was deposited with the plates. He described it as two stones in silver bows—and these stones were fastened to a breastplate. He said that "the possession and use of these stones were what constituted 'seers' in ancient or former times; and that God had prepared them for the purpose of translating the book" (Joseph Smith—History 1:34–35).

The Urim and Thummim was used in biblical times and is mentioned seven times in the Old Testament[21] and is mentioned in the Book of Mormon in Mosiah 8:13. It was prepared by God and used by righteous persons to reveal truths to mankind. The Lord further explains the Urim and Thummim's necessity in Mormon 9:34: "The Lord knoweth the things which we have written, and also that none other people knoweth our language; therefore, he hath prepared means for the interpretation thereof."

Moroni instructed Joseph during the rest of the night and again the following morning. He cited several passages from the Bible and quoted prophets such as Malachi, Isaiah, Joel, and Peter concerning the preparations to be made in the last days for the millennial reign of Christ. Through a vision, Joseph was shown the location of the plates (Joseph Smith—History 1:36, 40, 41, 50).

On the following day, Joseph went to the Hill Cumorah as instructed by Moroni. Joseph writes the following about the experience:

On the west side of this hill, not far from the top, under a stone of considerable size, lay the plates, deposited in a stone box. This stone was thick and rounding in the middle on the upper side, and thinner toward the edges, so that the middle part of it was visible above the ground, but the edge all around was covered with earth. Having removed the earth, I obtained a lever, which I got fixed under the edge of the stone, and with a little exertion raised it up. I looked in, and there indeed did I behold the plates, the Urim and Thummim, and the breastplate, as stated by the messenger. The box in which they lay was formed by laying stones together in some kind of cement. In the bottom of the box were laid two stones crossways of the box, and on these stones lay the plates and the other things with them (Joseph Smith—History 1:51–52).

Many of the numerous metallic records discovered to date have been found in foundation deposits, often in stone boxes, as were the Book of Mormon plates.[22]

Joseph attempted to take the plates from the box but "was forbidden by the messenger, and was again informed that the time for bringing them forth had not yet arrived, neither would it, until four years from that time; but he told me that I should come to that place precisely in one year from that time, and that he would there meet with me, and that I should continue to do so until the time should come for obtaining the plates" (Joseph Smith—History 1:53).

Each year, for four years, Joseph returned and was tutored by Moroni concerning the Lord's plans and how and in what manner His kingdom was to be conducted in the last days. Moroni visited Joseph, and others, twenty-two known times during the seven years after his first visit. Joseph was shown many things concerning both heaven and earth. Additionally, he was tutored by others besides Moroni. Joseph writes: "After having received many visits from the angels of God unfolding the majesty and glory of the events that should transpire in the last days, on the morning of the 22 of September, 1827, the angel of the Lord delivered the record into my hands."[23]

As noted, Joseph's family had no difficulty in accepting his heavenly visitations, knowing he had always been honest and trustworthy. According to his mother, Joseph reported these experiences as follows: "All seated in a circle, father, mother, sons and daughters, and giving the most profound attention to a boy, eighteen years of age, who had never read the Bible through by course in his life, . . . the sweetest union and happiness pervaded our house. . . . Joseph . . . would describe the ancient inhabitants of this continent, their dress, mode of traveling, and the animals upon which they rode; their cities, their buildings, with every particular; their mode of warfare; and also, their religious worship. This he would do with as much ease, seemingly, as if he had spent his whole life among them." Joseph warned his family that they were not to tell other people about the plates because such individuals would seek to kill him for the sake of the gold after he got the plates.[24]

A Matter-of-fact Account

Although it was many years later, British-born literary scholar Arthur Henry King was another one who had no difficulty believing Joseph Smith's account:

When I was first brought to read Joseph Smith's story, I was deeply impressed. I wasn't inclined to be impressed. As a stylistician, I have spent my life being disinclined to be impressed. So when I read his story, I thought to myself, this is an extraordinary thing. This is an astonishingly matter-of-fact and cool account. This man is not trying to persuade me of anything. He doesn't feel the need to. He is stating what happened to him, and he is stating it, not enthusiastically, but in quite a matter-of-fact way. He is not trying to make me cry or feel ecstatic. That struck me, and that began to build my testimony, for I could see that this man was telling the truth.[25]

John Taylor, a close friend of the Prophet, writes that Joseph "was uneducated when he was a boy. . . . The Lord took him into His school and He taught him things that I have seen puzzle many of the wisest scientists, profoundest thinkers, and the most learned men that I have met within this world. Why? Because he was taught of God. . . . And he sought to teach others."[26]

The Prophet Given Power from God

One who has studied the life of Joseph Smith could not help but be impressed that although he lived "without the advantages of a formal education he gained a fair knowledge of five languages, became a master of the contents of the Bible, became conversant with general history and developed into an interesting conversationalist upon any common subject."[27] His journal has been printed with annotations in six large volumes, and many hundreds of outstanding books and articles have been written about him.

President Harold B. Lee says the following about Joseph's background and accomplishments:

Joseph Smith, the young man not schooled in the theologies of the day, not schooled in the high schools of learning of his day . . . [was] one who could be submissive to the teachings and whisperings of the Spirit. Joseph Smith could not have established this Church. He could not have brought forth the work of the Lord, the Book of Mormon. They may scoff at the Prophet Joseph Smith as a man. They may question how this Church began, but here the thing stands as a monument—the Book of Mormon itself. Joseph, the man, could not have done this, but Joseph, actuated by the power of Almighty God, could and did perform the miraculous service of bringing forth the kingdom out of obscurity in the restored gospel of Jesus Christ.[28]

Joseph's lack of education did not hinder him being worthy and capable of doing the Lord's work.

Chapter 3

You Are Young
with Virtually No
Literary Skills

*You are twenty-three years old and are unable to compose
even an acceptable letter.*

Great authors are usually much older than Joseph Smith who was only 23 when he translated the Book of Mormon. Victor Hugo was sixty when he wrote *Les Miserables,* George Bernard Shaw was fifty-six when he penned *Pygmalion,* and Lloyd C. Douglas was fifty-two when he composed *The Robe.* All had considerably more education than young Joseph. However, age and education played no part in the coming forth of the Book of Mormon: Joseph was not the author, but rather was the Lord's instrument through whom the book was translated.

Early Employment and Courtship

The economic circumstances of the Smith family made it necessary for Joseph and his brothers to hire out as farm laborers or find other available work. For a few months, Joseph worked for Josiah Stowell, who was searching for a lost silver mine thought to have been excavated by the Spaniards. During these early times, it was not uncommon for men of character to seek buried treasure. After about a month of work, in October 1825, Joseph persuaded Stowell that the effort was futile, and the hunt was abandoned.[1] Joseph wrote in his history that this episode was the source of the later circulated derogatory stories claiming that he was a "money digger."

While employed by Mr. Stowell, Joseph boarded for a short time at the home of Isaac and Elizabeth Hale in Harmony, Pennsylvania. There, he met and took a romantic interest in the Hales' schoolteacher daughter, Emma, who reciprocated Joseph's feelings. Her father, troubled by Joseph's lack of education, opposed the relationship. However, the couple continued courting, and their affection blossomed. Emma was twenty-two and therefore did not need her father's consent to marry, though both she and Joseph sought it.[2] After failing to gain his approval, they eloped on January 18, 1827. Joseph moved his new bride to the Smith family home in Manchester where she was welcomed

Joseph Smith receives the plates at the Hill Cumorah

by Joseph's family, and a close relationship developed between Emma and her mother-in-law, Lucy Mack Smith. Joseph farmed with his father the following summer.[3]

Joseph Receives the Golden Plates

In the fall of 1827, after instruction from the angel Moroni during each of the four previous years to prepare Joseph for his mission as translator of the Book of Mormon, the time finally arrived for the twenty-one-year-old prophet to obtain the gold plates.[4] Long before sunrise on September 22, Joseph and Emma hooked up a wagon and drove the three miles to the Hill Cumorah. Emma waited while Joseph climbed the hill for his fifth and culminating meeting with the angel.[5]

Moroni gave Joseph the plates and other ancient artifacts that would aid in the translation process—the Urim and Thummim and the breastplate—along with a charge regarding the great responsibility that rested upon him. Moroni warned Joseph to be diligent in protecting the plates, or his enemies would be able to steal them and he would be "cut off" from the Lord. Joseph hid the plates in a hollow log near his home and soon learned why Moroni had given him such a strict charge. "'Every stratagem that could be invented' was used to get them from him." He shortly became aware of a plot that would-be thieves had devised to obtain them. Fearing the plates might be discovered in the log, Joseph returned to retrieve them, wrapped them in a linen frock, and started through the woods. As he jumped a log, he was struck from behind with the stock of a gun. He was able to knock his assailant down and flee but was assaulted again a half mile later and then a third time before arriving home. When Joseph arrived home with the plates, his mother described him as "altogether speechless from the fright and the fatigue of running." From that time until he returned the plates to Moroni, after their translation, enemies attempting to steal them hounded the Smiths.[6]

What Is Known about the Plates

Joseph described the plates as eight inches long, six inches wide, and six inches thick, with leaves slightly thinner than common tin. If they had been made of pure twenty-four-karat gold, their weight would have been about two hundred pounds. Pure gold would be too soft to make useful plates, but if the plates had been made of an alloy named tumbaga, known to be widely used in pre-Columbian Mesoamerica, composed mostly of eight-karat gold and copper, they would have weighed about fifty-three pounds—a more reasonable weight for Joseph to carry, although it still required great strength and endurance to carry them while being attacked and chased by multiple assailants.[7]

Book of Mormon Artifacts (facsimiles)

The text of the Book of Mormon supports the conclusion that the golden plates were probably not made of pure gold. In fact, they were made of "ore" (see 1 Nephi 19:1 and Mormon 8:5). The Eight Witnesses reported that the plates had "the appearance of gold" (see "The Testimony of Eight Witnesses"). Metallurgist Read H. Putnam explained that "[the plates] would need to be soft enough at the surface to accept the engraver's tool, yet firm enough in the center to keep the plate from distortion under the pressure; it would also have to be smooth enough for the lines and figures to retain their proportions." Thus, according to Putnam, the plates had to be an alloy.[8] William Smith, brother of the Prophet, lifted the plates while they were in a pillowcase, estimated that they weighed sixty pounds, and said he thought they were a mixture of gold and copper. Martin Harris, a prosperous Palmyra, New York farmer who was one of the Three Witnesses to the Book of Mormon and was able to see and hold the plates, estimated they weighed forty to fifty pounds (see Chapter 22).[9]

Histories kept on metal plates were virtually unknown in 1829, but hundreds of such plates have been found throughout the world since that time. A 1963 article, "Gold Plates Used Anciently," by Franklin S. Harris, lists sixty-three individual sets of metal plates on display in various museums.[10] Dr. Paul R. Cheesman spent years compiling extensive evidence that ancient cultures wrote on and kept metal records like the plates from which Joseph translated. Cheesman wrote *Ancient Writing on Metal Plates,* which includes photographs of engravings and other writings found in the Americas.[11]

Attempts to steal the gold plates, along with ongoing intense persecution that threatened Joseph's life, made the work of translation almost impossible in Palmyra. At the invitation of Emma's father, who had made peace with Joseph, the couple moved to Harmony, Pennsylvania. Following a brief stay with the Hale family, they purchased a house from Emma's eldest brother, Jesse, also in Harmony. The small, two-story home sat on a thirteen-acre farm bordering the Susquehanna River. Martin Harris acted as scribe for the translation during a short period in 1828. Later, a young schoolteacher, Oliver Cowdery, arrived at Joseph's door. Cowdery learned of Joseph's visions while boarding with Joseph's family and received confirmation through prayer that Joseph was engaged in the work of God. Oliver acted as scribe for nearly all of the translation.[12]

A pageant, "America's Witness for Christ," showing the coming forth of the Book of Mormon, has been presented nearly every summer since 1937 at the Hill Cumorah in New York State. Recognized as one of America's largest and most spectacular outdoor theatrical events, it attracts an audience of thousands to its July performances. It dramatizes how Joseph Smith acquired the plates

Hill Cumorah Pageant

from which the Book of Mormon was translated and presents a dramatic portrayal of some of the epic events and prophecies found in the book.

Joseph was only twenty-four years of age when the Book of Mormon, now subtitled "Another Testament of Jesus Christ," was published and introduced to the world.[13] Eventually many millions of copies would flood the Earth.

Chapter 4

Do No Research
of Any Kind

Your book must be written on the basis of what you now know. There were no libraries available that held information Joseph Smith could have used. Likewise, you can do no research of any kind.

Research Resources Were Not Available to the Prophet

Most writers would find it difficult—if not impossible—to construct an accurate history as relatively simple as one about their own hometown without prolonged, in-depth research. How accurate would such a history be if an author were limited to only what he or she already knows? As Book of Mormon scholar John W. Welch observes,

> Even if Joseph had wanted to pause to check his details against reputable sources, to scrutinize the latest theories, to learn about scholarly Biblical interpretations or Jewish customs, or to verify any Book of Mormon claims against the wisdom or theologies of his day—even if he had wanted to go to a library to check such things (something he showed no inclination to do until later)—there simply was no library anywhere nearby for him to use.[1]

Dr. Welch is referring to Harmony, Pennsylvania, where most of the translating of the Book of Mormon took place. Some have suggested Harmony, which was within 50 miles of the library at Allegheny College at Meadville, Pennsylvania. There were two Harmonys at the time, and that college library was 50 miles from the other Harmony Township, but 235 miles from the rural Harmony (now called Oakland) where the Smiths lived.

Before moving to western New York and later Pennsylvania, young Joseph lived with his family in Sharon and Norwich Vermont, just across the river from Dartmouth College in Hanover, New Hampshire. Dartmouth had an excellent library but Joseph and his family left Vermont and moved to western New York when the prophet was only ten years old. There was a library in Palmyra and another in Manchester five miles from the Smith Family farm.

These were subscription libraries used by people who could afford membership. The Smiths were not people of means and there is no evidence they ever used either library.[2] Additionally, these libraries were limited in their holdings and likely would have had little or no information about ancient America.

Joseph's wife, Emma, who acted as a scribe for a small portion of the book, confirms the fact that Joseph did not do research: "The larger part of the labor [of translation] was done [in] my presence. . . . During no part of it did Joseph Smith have any [manuscripts] or book of any kind from which to read or dictate except the metallic plates which I knew he had. If he had had anything of the kind he could not have concealed it from me."[3]

Emma further recalled that during the translation, Joseph "could neither write nor dictate a well-worded letter let alone dictate a book like the Book of Mormon. And, though I was an active participate in the scenes that transpired and was present during the translation of the plates . . . [Joseph's ability to translate was] marvelous to me, 'a marvel and a wonder,' as much as to anyone else."[4] This obscure young man once paused while translating and dictating to Emma—probably from the fourth chapter of 1 Nephi—concerning the "wall of Jerusalem"—and said, in effect, "Emma, I didn't know there was a wall around Jerusalem."[4] The Smith family regularly read the Bible together, but apparently information about a wall around Jerusalem had not registered with Joseph.

Evidences of Lehi's Arabian Peninsula Exodus

An impressive example of the book's uncanny accuracy is found in the detailed account of the terrain traveled by Lehi and his group from Jerusalem down through the Arabian Peninsula before they sailed to the Promised Land in the New World. This route matches the ancient Frankincense Trail, which, according to Dr. Eugene England, was unknown in the West until the twentieth century. After thoroughly studying the journey of Lehi from Jerusalem, England reports that "the details that we know now, through direct, modern observation and research into ancient sources unknown to Joseph Smith, correspond to what the Book of Mormon describes" regarding this route. "There is a piling up of parallel detail after detail, with no contradictions."[5] Not only did Joseph do no research, but these details were simply not known in Joseph Smith's world.

These Book of Mormon verses describing Lehi's route are now corroborated: "he traveled in the wilderness in the borders which are nearer the Red Sea" (1 Nephi 2:5); "waters of the river that emptied into the . . . Red Sea . . . [were] continually running" (1 Nephi 2:9); "we traveled for the space of four days, nearly a south-southeast direction" (1 Nephi 16:13); "we did travel nearly eastward from that time forth" (1 Nephi 17:1); "and we did come to the place which we called Bountiful, because of its much fruit and also wild honey" (1 Nephi 17:5).

George Potter and Richard Wellington, who lived in Saudi Arabia for ten and eighteen years respectively, agree with England's conclusion. They spent six years documenting what they believe to be the route of Lehi's journey from Jerusalem to Bountiful. They found 81 geographical details in the Book of Mormon regarding the journey that match and support Lehi's likely route. Joseph Smith's odds of having guessed the details and gotten them in the correct order and direction in relation to each other would be one in over trillions.[6] "At the time Joseph Smith translated the Book of Mormon, only twenty-four percent of the seventeen-hundred-mile course that we believe Lehi took through Arabia had been seen and subsequently described in writing by westerners," say the researchers.[7] It would be necessary for a person to actually travel the route to be able to correctly describe the terrain, something impossible for Joseph to have done.

An ancient custom of the desert is the naming of places after people, a custom observed by Father Lehi. After the group had traveled three days in the wilderness, near the borders of the Red Sea, they pitched their tents in a valley by the side of a stream of water (1 Nephi 2:5–6). Lehi named the river after his oldest son Laman, saying, "O that thou mightest be like unto this river, *continually running* into the fountain of all righteousness" (1 Nephi 2:8–9; see also Alma 8:7).

A Continuously Running River

Critics considered the Book of Mormon's description of a continuously running river of water in this dry desert area to be preposterous. They were sure they had found the book's fatal flaw. Besides the water that was continually flowing, Lehi mentions a fertile valley with plentiful seeds, grains, and fruits (1 Nephi 8:1) which he named after his son Lemuel, saying, "O that thou mightest be like unto this valley, firm and steadfast, and immovable in keeping the commandments of the Lord" (1 Nephi 2:10). Researchers have found that the wadi Tayyip al-Ism in northwest Arabia matches all these characteristics perfectly.

Potter and Wellington visited the proposed site many times at different times of the year and found that even after a seven-month dry spell, the stream was still flowing. Erosion in the canyon shows that a substantial river has flowed in the chasm for a very long time.[8] In addition, the site is the right distance and at a place Lehi's caravan could have traveled in the three-day time period described in the text. Although it cannot be proven that this is the exact stream of water mentioned in 1 Nephi, we now know that such a place does exist and very well could be the river of Laman.

One of three altars found at Nahom

A Place Called Shazer

Another significant detail in the Book of Mormon involves another place named by the Lehites. "The first important stop after Lehi's party had left their base camp (the valley of Lamuel) was at a place they called Shazer (1 Nephi 16:13–14). The combination *shajer* is a common Palestinian place-name. Its collective meaning is 'trees,' and many Arabs (especially in Egypt) pronounce it shazher." Various spellings of the word are found throughout the area, all in one form or other denoting a weak but reliable water supply or a clump of trees.[9] This name could not have been just a lucky guess on Joseph's part.

The Altars at Nahom

The Book of Mormon further records that after Lehi and his family, along with the family of Ishmael, had traveled extensively, "Ishmael died and was buried in the place which was *called* Nahom" (1 Nephi 16:34; emphasis added). This wording tells us that Lehi was not the originator of the name; they apparently encountered other people who gave them this information. Their trip was an eight-year journey.

An altar inscribed with the name of *Nahom (NHM)* and dated to at least 700 BC, a hundred years before Lehi's family left Jerusalem, was found in the year 2000 in the southwest corner of the Arabian Peninsula, the route that Lehi and his group are believed to have traveled. We also learn that "the origin of the name Nahom is connected to a place of burial" and that "the Semitic roots of the name *Nahom* closely relate to sorrow, hunger, consoling, and mourning" and may, therefore, reflect the origin of the Hebrew name used by Nephi. Since the discovery of the first altar at the Bar'an temple site, two other altars bearing the name *Nihm* have been identified at the same location. Further, an archaeological examination of the area has uncovered a vast cemetery "covering many square miles and numbering many thousands of tombs—the largest burial area known anywhere in Arabia."[10] This discovery demonstrates the existence of a Book of Mormon place-name other than Jerusalem or the Red Sea in the right place at the right time.[11]

Researchers maintain the following: "It is important to emphasize that in the world of archaeology, written inscriptions are the evidence most sought after because they often establish names and dates, key ingredients for interpreting the past. The inscription on the three altars from the seventh and sixth centuries BC, all mentioning the NHM (Nahom) tribe, establish clearly the existence of this name in that region of Yemen during the first half of the first millennium BC when Lehi's party was on the move."[12]

Likely Site of Bountiful Found

Australian explorers Warren and Michaela Aston are pioneers in Lehi trail research whose many trips to the region have yielded a ground survey of the entire east coast of the Arabian peninsula and, among other major discoveries, the identification of the two most significant locations mentioned by Nephi— Nahom and Bountiful. Of Bountiful, Warren Aston has written: "In Joseph Smith's day, and for more than a century after, it seemed impossible that such a place could exist in seemingly barren Arabia. However, a beautiful, wooded valley that fits Nephi's description of the place in detail after detail has been identified on the remote southern coast of the country of Oman." Some of the details that match this land Bountiful include its location "nearly eastward," as recorded by Nephi; the possibility of overland access from the interior desert; the fertility of the area (fruits and honey); the suitability of the area for a long encampment and for shipbuilding; the ready availability of timber; year-round freshwater; a prominent mountain, which Nephi mentioned, with cliffs overlooking the ocean; and a source of ore, which was needed to make tools to build their ship (very few places in the Arabian Peninsula have ore). There are also suitable winds and currents to carry their ship out to sea and on their journey to the Promised Land.[13]

The accuracy of the Book of Mormon's description of places in southern Arabia has prompted one skeptic of the book to declare that Joseph Smith must have had access to several important documents on southern Arabia, particularly from the Dartmouth College library in Hanover, New Hampshire, several miles north of Lebanon, New Hampshire, where the Smith family resided at one time. The problem with this theory is that the Smith family moved from this area when Joseph was a mere child. In addition, Dartmouth did not acquire books on the subject until the twentieth century. The Book of Mormon was published in 1830. There may have been a few books describing Arabian geography in libraries in the United States before and during the time Joseph Smith translated the Book of Mormon, but there is no evidence he ever visited such a library or knew of its existence.[14] And, as noted earlier, only about a quarter of Lehi's travel route had been explored by 1829 so no written information would have been available even if Joseph had tried to find it.

It is known that Joseph briefly attended schools in Palmyra in 1818 and that he used several elementary textbooks in arithmetic and reading. There is little direct evidence that his literary skills extended much beyond a cursory acquaintance with a few books. As Joseph's mother, Lucy Mack Smith, wrote in her biography of the Prophet, Joseph was a "remarkably quiet, well-disposed child." He "seemed much less inclined to the perusal of books than any of the rest of our children, but far more given to meditation and deep study."[15]

Nephi's account of Lehi's journey along the Frankincense Trail provides dozens of details that are corroborated by the work of modern researchers. Many other evidences are discussed in other chapters in this book—things that no one could have known in 1829 but that subsequent research has established as factually accurate. Joseph had no need for a library to facilitate research. The Book of Mormon was revealed to him as he translated it through the gift and power of God. When Joseph Smith was asked by United States President Martin Van Buren how the Church differed from other religions of the day, Joseph responded, in part, that the distinction lay in the gift of the Holy Ghost, which the Lord bestowed upon him, and that all other considerations were contained in that gift.[16]

When we examine the entire book and consider the abundance of information it contains on many aspects of ancient life, "Was it sheer bluff and luck that 23-year-old Smith dictated to his scribes hundreds of statements in the scriptures that involve geographical matters while staying consistent in them all?" asks professor John L. Sorenson who has spent considerable years studying many aspects of the Book of Mormon.[17] A more plausible explanation is that Joseph correctly translated ancient eyewitness accounts from the plates.

Chapter 5

It Will Be a Big,
Singular Book
Never to Be Replicated
(Except by a Prophet)

Your book must be more than five hundred pages and more than three hundred thousand words in length.

Remember what a challenge it often was, or perhaps still is, to write an assigned school paper of even three pages—or about five hundred words? Writing more than five hundred *pages* containing 200,068 words of sacred history without research would be quite an undertaking. "There are many great, massive, impressive works in English literature," writes Hugh Nibley, [including] "the *History of England, Frederick the Great,* [and] *The Decline and Fall [of the Roman Empire],* but these authors were paraphrasing large historical works. They had all the records in front of them. They simply retold the story with their materials provided them."[1] Joseph Smith's lengthy history is unprecedented.

The book itself declares that it is an authentic product of the Near East. It gives a full and circumstantial account of its own origin. It declares that it is but one of many, many such books that have been produced in the course of history and may be hidden in sundry places at this day. It places itself in about the middle of a long list of sacred writings, beginning with the patriarchs and continuing down to the end of human history. It cites now-lost prophetic writings of prime importance, giving the names of their authors. It traces its own cultural roots in all directions, emphasizing the immense breadth and complexity of such connections in the world. It belongs to the same class of literature as the Bible, but, along with a sharper and clearer statement of biblical teachings, it contains a formidable mass of historical material unknown to biblical writers but well within the range of modern comparative study, since it insists on deriving its whole cultural tradition, even in details, directly from a specific time and place in the Old World.

The Book of Mormon is God's challenge to the world. It was given to the world not as a sign to convert it, but as a testimony to convict it. In every dispensation the world must be left without excuse. It is given without reservation or qualification as a true history and the word of God.[2]

Isaiah in the Book of Mormon

Prophets commonly quote the writings of earlier prophets. The Book of Mormon contains quotations from Biblical prophets, particularly Isaiah. About one-third of Isaiah's writings in the Bible are found in the Book of Mormon, with variations in many verses. The Book of Mormon follows the "accepted ancient procedure, in which 'holy men of God,' when they quote earlier scriptures, favor not the original language or their own translation, but whatever version of scriptures is most familiar to the people they are addressing. The Book of Mormon addressed a society which knew primarily the King James Version."[3]

The Lord knew the importance of Isaiah's teachings and wanted to make sure they were preserved and made available in the Americas. During His appearance to the Nephites, as He referred to the writings of Isaiah, the Savior said, "And now, behold, I say unto you, that ye ought to search these things. Yea, a commandment I give unto you that ye search these things diligently; *for great are the words of Isaiah*" (3 Nephi 23:1; emphasis added).

A comparison of texts reveals the significant fact that in a few cases the words of Isaiah in the Book of Mormon more nearly match Isaiah's text found in the Dead Sea Scrolls (discovered in 1947, 117 years after the Book of Mormon was published) than those of the Bible. For instance, in the King James Version, Isaiah 48:11 reads, "for how should my name be polluted?" The same verse in the Isaiah scroll, Isaiah 14:32, says, "for I will not suffer my name to be polluted." The Book of Mormon also reads, "for I will not suffer my name to be polluted" (1 Nephi 20:11).[4]

The Book of Mormon restores and clarifies many Bible verses, often adding inspired commentary. Perhaps there is no better example of this than a comparison of KJV Isaiah 29 with 2 Nephi 26:14–18 and 2 Nephi 27. Chapter 29 is Isaiah's vision of the spiritual conditions in the last days and some specifics of the coming forth of the Book of Mormon (see chapter 16). Isaiah 29:10 reads: "For the Lord hath poured out upon you the spirit of deep sleep, and hath closed your eyes: the prophets and your rulers, the seers hath he covered." In contrast, 2 Nephi 27:5 reads: "For *behold,* the Lord hath poured out upon you the spirit of deep sleep. *For behold, ye have* closed your eyes, *and ye have rejected* the prophets; and your rulers, and the seers hath he covered *because of your iniquity*" (emphasis added). The KJV version of the verse seems to say that the Lord arbitrarily acted against the people, but Nephi's version provides a perfect rationale for the punishment (the people rejected the prophets, rulers, and seers whom the Lord covers because of the people's wickedness).

Mormon the Abridger

Even though the Book of Mormon is more than five hundred pages long, it does not try to be comprehensive because it is an abridgement. The book's abridger, Mormon, repeatedly reminds us that he had to drastically condense his sources: "This book cannot contain even a hundredth part of what was done among so many people. . . . But behold there are records which do contain all the proceedings of this people" (3 Nephi 5:8–9). Thus, "Mormon's concern over what to leave out must have been as great as his anxiety over what to include. On every page, he was making choices. Two major tendencies are evident: he interpreted political events in spiritual terms, and he highlighted the distinction between the obedient and the disobedient. Mormon's editing was the way he shaped his history to make it the bearer of God's word."[5]

The Four Standard Works of the Church

As a prophet, Joseph Smith's sacred writings are not limited to the Book of Mormon. Through his instrumentality, we now enjoy the Inspired Version of the King James Bible, The Doctrine and Covenants, and the Pearl of Great Price. The Old and New Testaments, Book of Mormon, Doctrine and Covenants, and Pearl of Great Price are accepted as scripture and comprise the Standard Works of The Church of Jesus Christ of Latter-day Saints.

Other Scripture—The Joseph Smith Translation of the Bible

On March 7, 1831, Joseph Smith was instructed in a revelation from the Lord (Doctrine and Covenants 45:60–62) to begin translating the New

Joseph Translating the Bible

Testament.[6] Joseph "made his translation of the Bible as a prophet, not as a scholar; he used neither ancient manuscript nor a knowledge of biblical languages."[7] The Book of Mormon revealed that many plain and precious truths respecting the gospel—and, also many covenants of the Lord—had been taken out of the Bible. In some cases, whole books mentioned in the Bible are missing from the collection in the Old and the New Testaments and are "lost books" so far as our knowledge of them is concerned.

The Sermon on the Mount has been called the "Constitution of Christianity." We are grateful that Joseph Smith restored meaning that was lost in the King James Version (KJV). The following examples show Joseph's prophetic revision in the Inspired Version, now known as the Joseph Smith Translation (JST) and the Book of Mormon.

KJV: "Blessed are the poor in spirit: for theirs is the kingdom of heaven" (Matthew 5:3). JST and Book of Mormon: "Blessed are the poor in spirit *who come unto me,* for theirs is the kingdom of heaven" (Matthew 5:5 and 3 Nephi 12:3).

KJV: "Blessed are they which do hunger and thirst after righteousness: for they shall be filled" (Matthew 5:6). JST and Book of Mormon: "And blessed are all they who do hunger and thirst after righteousness, for they shall be filled *with the Holy Ghost*" (Matthew 5:8 and 3 Nephi 12:6).

Modern Bible translations sometimes render poor readings. For example, The Good News Bible, Luke 2:33, reads, "The child's father and mother were amazed." The King James Bible states, "And Joseph and his mother marveled." Joseph was not Jesus' father. Thus, the Good News Bible takes away the Savior's divine sonship.

The King James Version, despite its imperfections, is the rendering accepted by The Church of Jesus Christ of Latter-day Saints as its canonical English version of the Bible. A Latter-day Saint edition of the King James Bible was published in 1979 after seven years of labor by dedicated scholars, hundreds of professors, former missionaries, and seminary and institute teachers. The actual text was not changed, but it contains helps and scriptural references unavailable in any previous edition. Roger Coleman of the Cambridge University Press, which took on the complex, difficult work of typesetting so that the verses on each page fit with their exact cross-references on the same page, made the following comment after the completion of this landmark edition: "Nothing is perfect in the world . . . but *this* Bible is as nearly perfect as human beings can manage."[8]

The Greek Translation of the Old Testament is known as the Septuagint.[9] The forward to the 1611 King James Bible states that the Septuagint translators "were Interpreters, they were not prophets; they did many things well, as learned men; but yet as men they stumbled and fell, once while through oversight, another while through ignorance, yea, sometimes they may be noted to add to the original, and sometimes to take from it."

Joseph Smith explained, "I believe the Bible as it read when it came from the pen of the original writers. Ignorant translators, careless transcribers, or designing and corrupt priests have committed many errors." However, the Prophet Joseph loved the Bible and included biblical passages in the sermons he gave during his life. When asked, "Wherein do you differ from other sects?" he answered, "In that we believe the Bible, and all other sects profess to believe their interpretations of the Bible, and their creeds."[10]

In the Book of Mormon, an angel tells the prophet Nephi that the Apostle John's words would be plain and pure and easy to understand: "Wherefore the things which he shall write are just and true; and behold they are written in the book which thou beheld proceeding out of the mouth of the Jew; and at the time they proceeded out of the mouth of the Jew, the things which were written were plain and pure, and most precious and easy to the understanding of all men" (1 Nephi 14:23).

Though the Bible was altered and the Book of Mormon was needed, "Joseph Smith regularly testified of the truthfulness of the Bible," writes Jeffery Marsh, "and he encouraged the Saints to study it. He bore witness of the Bible's ability to help us recognize the language and spirit of inspiration from the Almighty: 'He that can mark the power of Omnipotence, inscribed upon the heavens, can also see God's own handwriting in the sacred volume: and he who reads it oftenest will like it best, and he who is acquainted with it, will know the hand [of God or recognize the Spirit] wherever he can see it.'"[11]

Other Scripture—The Doctrine and Covenants

The Explanatory Introduction to the Doctrine and Covenants describes it as "a collection of divine revelations and inspired declarations [nearly all through Joseph Smith] given for the establishment and regulation of the kingdom of God on the earth in the last days. The revelations were received in answer to prayer, in times of need, and came out of real-life situations involving real people."[12] Several early revelations in the Doctrine and Covenants pertain to the translation and publishing of the Book of Mormon.

President Ezra Taft Benson provides a brief introduction to this volume of scripture:

Section 1 of the Doctrine and Covenants is the Lord's preface to the book. The Doctrine and Covenants is the only book in the world that has a preface written by the Lord Himself. In that preface He declares to the world that His voice is unto all men (see D&C 1:2), that the coming of the Lord is nigh (see D&C 1:12), and that the truths found in the Doctrine and Covenants will all be fulfilled (see D&C 1:37–38).[13]

President Gordon B. Hinckley speaks of the wide range of important topics found in the Doctrine and Covenants:

> Some is direct revelation, with the Lord dictating to His prophet. Some is the language of Joseph Smith, written or spoken as he was moved upon by the Holy Ghost. Also, included is his narrative of events that occurred in various circumstances. All brought together, they constitute in very substantial measure the doctrine and practices of The Church of Jesus Christ of Latter-day Saints . . . and procedure concerning the governance of the Church . . . [as well as] unique and remarkable rules of health. . . . The covenant of the eternal priesthood is described in a manner not found elsewhere in scripture. The privileges and blessing of the three degrees of glory [are included]. . . . Repentance is proclaimed in language clear and compelling. The nature of the Godhead, which has troubled theologians for centuries, is described in language understandable to all. The Lord's law of finance is pronounced, mandating how funds for the operation of the Church are to be acquired and disbursed. Work for the dead is revealed to bless the sons and daughters of God of all Generations.[14]

Other Scripture—The Pearl of Great Price

The "Introductory Note" to the Pearl of Great Price says the book "is a selection of choice materials touching many significant aspects of the faith and doctrine of The Church of Jesus Christ of Latter-day Saints." The book includes selections from the book of Moses (from the Joseph Smith Translation of the Bible), the book of Abraham (from Egyptian papyri that came into the possession of the Prophet), extracts from Matthew 23–24 (also from Joseph's translation of the Bible), excerpts from Joseph Smith's official testimony and history, and "The Articles of Faith of The Church of Jesus Christ of Latter-day Saints,"[15] authored by the Prophet.

The papyri that inspired the book of Abraham, came into Joseph's possession in 1835. The Church purchased two or more other Egyptian papyri and four mummies from a man named Michael Chandler in Kirtland, Ohio. The mummies came from the catacombs of Egypt. Joseph translated some of the papyri into English and was pleased to find that one of the rolls contained Abrahamic material.[16]

John Tvedtnes, former associate director of the Neal A. Maxwell Institute for Religious Scholarship at Brigham Young University, identifies two examples of ancient traditions that support nonbiblical aspects of the book of Abraham. The Pearl of Great Price tells of a famine in Abraham's homeland of Ur (Abraham

1:29–30; 2:1), and although the Bible does not mention the famine, a number of early Jewish and Muslim texts do. Scientific investigations confirm there was indeed a drought during Abraham's time—and in a region that included his homeland. Many other early sources say that Abraham wrote about astronomy. Abrahamic astronomical material is not found in the Bible but a great deal of it is found in the book of Abraham (Abraham 2).[17]

Other significant historical and doctrinal details not found in the Bible, but found in the book of Abraham, include incidents in Abraham's early life; a concise explanation of the Abrahamic covenant; the vastness of God's creations and how they are governed; the doctrine of our premortal existence and of God's eternal nature; the doctrine of foreordination; and the earth as a testing ground for God's children. The last two chapters contribute greatly to our knowledge of the creation of the earth. They reveal that this world was created out of existing materials rather than from nothing, that a plurality of gods participated in the creation, and that the creation was carefully planned in a heavenly council before it was carried out (Abraham 5:1–3).[18]

The Pearl of Great Price mentions a person named Mahijah who lived at the time of Enoch (Moses 6:40). Mahijah is not mentioned in the Bible but is found several times in the Dead Sea Scrolls. The Bible says that "Moses died there in the land of Moab" (Deuteronomy 34:5); however, the Book of Mormon says he was "translated" (Alma 45:19). A Dead Sea Scroll called "The Ascension of Moses" speaks of this translation of Moses. "There is little in the Bible about the prophet Enoch (Genesis 5:18–24) or about a city named after him. The Pearl of Great Price states that the City of Enoch was translated—or taken up into heaven (Moses 7:69). The Dead Sea Scrolls describe in detail the translation of the city of Enoch."[19] Additional scripture found in the Pearl of Great Price is a blessing to people throughout the earth, because it helps validate the Book of Mormon, and Joseph's calling as a Prophet.

The Prophet's Greatest Contributions Are Doctrinal and Spiritual

Joseph Smith brought forth more pages of holy sacred scripture than any other prophet in the Judeo-Christian tradition. We certainly can be thankful for the many added truths he brought to the world. And as impressive as the quantity of the Prophet's scriptural contribution may be, the depth of doctrinal and spiritual insight is even greater. As Finnish religious scholar Helkki Raisanen has observed, "Theologians must take the teachings of Joseph Smith seriously, since the founder of the Church of Jesus Christ of Latter-day Saints had recognized and dealt with problems that have puzzled Christian theologians for generations."[20]

One of the chief purposes of the Book of Mormon is to be an additional testament of the Savior. The book supports the Bible in its mission. It was never financially profitable. If Joseph's goal had been to write a book as a money-making scheme, there would certainly have been an easier way than writing a lengthy, complicated religious history of unknown civilizations.

Author and scholar Gerald N. Lund writes, "I have studied the writings of some of the world's most learned men and women, people with enough letters behind their names to provide a serious game of Scrabble. They are brilliant, erudite, scholarly, and articulate—but compared to Joseph Smith, they are like children beginning a study of the alphabet."[21]

Chapter 6

Do No Content-Editing of Your First and Only Draft

Other than corrections for spelling, punctuation, grammar, capitalization and typographical errors, you must make no changes to the text of your book.

The first draft of most writers' compositions rarely approaches the quality of the final product. Write and rewrite is the process by which the conscientious author works.

Richard Paul Evans, author of *The Christmas Box* and other bestselling novels, tells of the enormous research that goes into one of his books. "Whenever one of my novels is released, I am sure to hear within a few days about the errors in it. In spite of my seemingly endless hours of research and rewrites, and the fact that I work with some of the most respected and relentless editors in America, errors are still made by me and missed by my editors." He is convinced that the unschooled Joseph Smith could not have invented such a complex work as the Book of Mormon. "It would have been so fraught with errors that today's readers would have found it absurd. . . . Were the Book of Mormon not true it would not have withstood the test of time."[1]

Translation Required Prophet's Full Concentration

Near the end of her life, Emma Smith, Joseph's wife, wrote about the process of translating the Book of Mormon: "I am satisfied that no man could have dictated the writing of the manuscripts unless he was inspired; for, when [I was] acting as his scribe, your father would dictate to me hour after hour; and when returning after meals, or after interruptions, he could at once begin where he had left off, without either seeing the manuscript or having any portion of it read to him. This was a usual thing for him to do. It would have been improbable that a learned man could do this; and, for one so ignorant and unlearned as he was, it was simply impossible."[2]

Elder B. H. Roberts tells us that the translation was not a mere mechanical process: "It required the utmost concentration of mental and spiritual force possessed by the Prophet, to be able to exercise the gift of translation through the means of the sacred instruments provided for that work."[3] To accomplish the work, Joseph had to be humble and faithful. One morning the young Prophet was upset about something Emma had done. David Whitmer refers to the incident noting that Joseph "could not translate a single syllable." Joseph went outside into the orchard "and made supplication to the Lord; [he] was gone about an hour—came back to the house, and asked Emma's forgiveness . . . and then the translation went on all right."[4]

Insights from First Manuscripts

Royal Skousen, BYU professor of Linguistics and English Language and leading expert on the Book of Mormon text writes, "An examination of the original Manuscript of the Book of Mormon reveals that during the translation process Joseph never went back to cross out, revise, or to modify." Oliver Cowdery copied the entire Book of Mormon onto a second manuscript known as the Printer's Manuscript, of which all but one line has survived. "Only about 28 percent of the Original Manuscript still exists. The remainder was either destroyed as it rested in the cornerstone of the Nauvoo House or was lost during the nineteenth century after being taken from the cornerstone."[5]

A study of the "original manuscript also supports the traditional belief that Joseph received a revealed text through the interpreters [Urim and Thummim or seer stone][6] . . . . All the evidence (from the original manuscript, witnesses' statements, and from the text itself) is consistent with the hypothesis that Joseph Smith could actually see . . . word for word and letter for letter—and that he read off this revealed text to his scribe." Joseph had the scribe read back what was written so he could check it for correctness (however, his scribes still made some errors). He sometimes spelled out the words, such as *Coriantumr*, which has an unusual word-ending in English, but which Oliver Cowdery wrote as *Coriantumer*, but later, as directed, changed to Coriantumr. The evidence points to the conclusion that Joseph was not the author of the Book of Mormon but that "it was revealed spiritually through him and in his own language."[7].

Skousen has spent many years, since 1988, on a "Critical Text Project," whose aim has been to document every change the Book of Mormon has undergone from the original and printer's manuscripts through its various editions since 1830. A computerized collation of the twenty past editions revealed that "scribal and printer's errors, as well as Joseph Smith's editing for the 1837 edition, account for the majority of those changes, most of which are minor, and do not affect meaning." Skousen's research shows that five-sixths of the Book of Mormon was typeset from the printer's manuscript and that nearly all of the printer's manuscript still exists.[8]

"Changes in the Book of Mormon text," explains Skousen, "fall into three categories: (1) the referencing system (chapters and verses); (2) accidentals, such as paragraphing, spelling, and punctuation; and (3) substantives, which are changes in words, forms of words, phrases, and sentences—including removal of archaic King James Version language and inclusion of text clarifications. 'In every case, the original text could be restored without any problem, or Joseph Smith's clarifications [in later editions] could be kept.'[9] Skousen further notes "that textual evidence shows the original text to be more systematic than initially thought." He found "astonishing consistency" in the original text.[10]

Full Details of Translation Process Not Revealed

Although several eyewitnesses to the translation process left statements describing what they observed of the mechanics of the translation, the Prophet remained silent on how the interpretation of the Egyptian-like characters was actually transmitted. When questioned on the subject, he replied only that the translation was done "by the gift and power of God." The translation was revealed to him by divine revelation. It involved a revelatory experience—one he chose to put into words.[11]

Today, for someone to attempt to explain how the Book of Mormon was translated from reformed Egyptian into English in the late 1820s—that is, to say that Joseph Smith read the words of the text on a seer stone that was usually put in a hat to shut out the light for easier reading—is naturally improbable to many. If someone in that time period had forecast that in the future, people could look into a small, handheld device (for example, a cell phone) and read any of thousands of books, that too would have been unbelievable. And what

would have been even more unbelievable would have been for a person to predict that if a book were printed in, say, Spanish, but the reader needed English, with the tap of a finger, the book would appear in English. People would have considered a person out of his or her mind to predict such a phenomenon.

However, to the Lord, such a feat was certainly not a problem. His early American prophets wrote the Book of Mormon, which was scripture written for our day, and to have the words appear on the Urim and Thummim or on a seer stone now seems to have been an efficient and exact method for the

"By the Gift and Power of God"

translation. From Joseph's background, we know he did not have the knowledge or skill to write the incredible information contained in the Book of Mormon, but the Lord prepared a way for the translation to take place. Thus, no one should feel concerned about the method of translation.

Dictation versus Translation

Donald B. Doty, author of three textbooks and many scientific articles, writes: "I am amazed that the Prophet produced the manuscript from dictation. Dictation is a rapid way of getting ideas onto paper, but it is one of the most difficult methods of composition. Words are often repeated, phrases may be trite or redundant, and the finished product is usually unstructured; it is more conversational than readable. Yet the Book of Mormon is intense prose, filled with complex, highly developed philosophical concepts that are presented extensively, logically, and coherently."[12] Such outcomes provide powerful evidence that Joseph Smith was not composing; he was translating, which is a very different process.

Yet some errors appeared. An example of a typographical error is found in the book of Alma. The original edition of Alma 57:25 reads, "and also the *foes* of our whole army." An examination of the printer's manuscript shows that the correct word should have been *joy*, thus reading, "according to the goodness of God, and to our great astonishment, and also the *joy* of our whole army, there was not one soul of them who did perish." The meaning of the original version is clear within the context of the verse.[13]

Additionally, the spellings of some words that were acceptable in 1828 are not in common use today. Only six English language dictionaries were available in 1828 (among them Noah Webster's 1828 dictionary). All list numerous variant spellings for words. Words that Oliver Cowdery used in the original manuscript, such as *adhear, ancles, befal, journied,* and *writen*, were legitimate spellings. In one instance, Oliver used the word *strait* (narrow, tight) over *straight* (free from curves) nineteen out of twenty-two times. The original typesetter changed them all to *straight*. The 1981 edition changed them back to *strait*.[14] Oliver was taking rapid dictation, with punctuation rarely dictated by Joseph. The printer inserted most of the punctuation and made a few grammatical corrections. These account for many of the changes.[15]

Helps for the Reader

Over time, changes were made to the layout of the book, along with other improvements. The 1879 edition was the first to be divided into chapters and verses, making it easier for the reader to locate references in the book. The first edition—with double-column pages, chapter headings, chronological data, revised footnote references, a pronouncing vocabulary, and an index—was published in 1920.[16] The 1981 edition includes expanded footnotes and chapter headings.

The 1981 edition also added an introduction and chapter-heading summaries written by Elder Bruce R. McConkie. At the time, it was presumed that the American Indians were all descendants of Lehi, but that theory was abandoned as more scientific information was gathered and numerous others were identified in the Americas long before Lehi's time. The 1981 McConkie introduction reads, "After thousands of years, all were destroyed except the Lamanites, and they are the *principal* ancestors of the American Indians." In 2007, this was revised to read "and they are *among* the ancestors of the American Indians."[17]

Revisions in the Bible

As noted in chapter 5, attempted corrections and revisions of the Bible have been going on for centuries. Many changes and omissions occurred during the development of modern Bible texts. The number of revisions in the King James Version of Matthew alone increased from 43 in 1611 to 583 in 1870.[18] "There are many more variants per word in the New Testament text—and many more highly debated variants, than in the Book of Mormon text. Does this variation mean that the New Testament is false, that it is not God's word because humans have made errors in its transmission? The word of God still comes through [in] the Book of Mormon despite the occasional errors in transmission."[19] Revisions of the Bible are still going on today.

One especially interesting instance of revisions involves modern Bible translations that have removed the word *begotten* from "For God so loved the world, that he gave his only *begotten* Son" (John 3:16; emphasis added). Some modern translations now read, "For God so loved the world, that he gave his only Son." If He is the "only Son," then who is *our* father? The rest of us are disinherited in these versions. Both the KJV and JST retain "begotten." Great truths have been lost and are still being lost through such revisions. The Book of Mormon restores lost truths![20] In this instance, Alma calls Christ "the only begotten son of the Father" six times.

The Most Correct Book

The Book of Mormon's title page explains, "And now, if there are faults they are the mistakes of men; condemn not the things of God, that ye may be found spotless at the judgment-seat of Christ." [21] Significantly, Joseph Smith "told the brethren that the Book of Mormon was the most correct of any book on earth, and the keystone of our religion, and a man would get nearer to God by abiding by its precepts, than by any other book."[22]

Correctness does not need to refer only to the translation, grammar, or spelling. Alluding to the meaning of correctness in the Book of Mormon,

Donald B. Doty says: "Above all other considerations, it is the *doctrine* contained in the Book of Mormon that makes it the most correct of books. The Book of Mormon establishes better than any other book the plain and precious truths of the gospel." Doty further observes "that since the plates of Mormon and their English translation did not suffer the many editorial changes most other scriptures experienced over the centuries as they were translated and transcribed, the Book of Mormon is closer to the source of its inspiration."[23]

The Savior was the overseer of the book's compilation. An example of His involvement is found in 3 Nephi 23:9–14 during His visit to the New World after His resurrection. He chastised the record keeper for not writing those things He had commanded to be written.[24] Thus, even though there have been minor revisions in the Book of Mormon, the message as dictated remains the same and still stands—revealed sacred scripture to bless the world.

Chapter 7

Tell the Histories of Previously Unknown Nations and Peoples

Your book must contain the histories of two distinct and separate nations, along with the histories of other contemporary nations or groups of people.

The Book of Mormon does not claim to be the history of all the peoples who have lived in the Americas, nor does it claim to account for their beginnings.[1] The book is primarily a record of two great nations in ancient America. The major part of the book tells of Lehi and his descendants, known as the Nephites and the Lamanites. Additionally, the Book of Mormon references a group known as the Mulekites and includes an account of an earlier major civilization known as the Jaredites. Over time, other groups may have immigrated to the New World.

The Jaredites and Wicked Kings

The Jaredites left the Old World when the Lord confounded the tongues at the Tower of Babel centuries earlier than Lehi and his group. The estimated date for Babel is between 3100 BC and 2200 BC.[2] The Jaredite record was abridged by Moroni from twenty-four plates of gold written by the last great Jaredite prophet, Ether. The record tells how the Lord led the Jaredites to a "choice land" (Ether 1:42) and gives a brief overview of their history and eventual destruction because of wickedness.

Jared and his brother, who lived near the Tower of Babel, were righteous individuals who prayed to the Lord that their language might not be confounded. The Lord answered their prayers by sending them and their friends to a choice land protected by a divine covenant. They would always be free as long as they were righteous, but if they became wicked and refused to repent, they would ultimately be destroyed. The Jaredites traveled through the wilderness to the seashore where the Lord instructed them to build eight barges to carry them to the promised land. After crossing the ocean, they settled in their new land, built homes, developed farms, and were blessed by the Lord. In time, they spread to other areas of the land.

Unfortunately the Jaredite people wanted a king—against Jared's and his brother's counsel. This unrighteous desire of the people ultimately prevailed, and, as foretold by the prophets, many of the subsequent kings were wicked. There were many wars, often between a king and his son. Periods of righteousness were followed by rebellion and misery. Prophets usually labored in vain to persuade the people to repent. King Coriantumr was the lone survivor after he killed his last remaining foe, Shiz,[3] in a final civil war.

Coriantumr wandered southward, eventually coming to the city of Zarahemla where he lived among the Mulekites for the final nine months of his life (Omni 1:21). The non-combatant prophet, Ether, hiding in a cave, witnessed the results of the final battle and added his account to the records that were written upon the twenty-four plates of gold, which he then hid. Years later, about 121 BC, the plates were found by the people of Limhi, who were Nephites. The prophet Mosiah translated them by the gift of God. Moroni abridged them and included them with the records in his possession. Their history is found in the book of Ether, the next-to-last book in the Book of Mormon.

The history of the Jaredites appears to match closely that of the Olmec culture of Central America. Research has shown that the primary Olmec centers disappeared near the same time as the Jaredite nation, between 400 and 300 BC. We now have evidence that there were Olmec/Jaredite survivors.[4] One Maya archaeologist, Michael Coe, who has done early excavation work at LaVenta, an ancient Olmec city in southern Mexico, describes a great civil war that took place—a war that apparently brought an end to the Olmec civilization. LaVenta is in the same area as possibly the city of Lib, a Jaredite city in the Book of Mormon that collapsed during the same time period when the Jaredites were annihilated by war.[5]

Early History of Mexico Parallels the Jaredite Record

The Book of Mormon is not the only written account of the migration of early settlers who left the Tower of Babel at the time of the confusion of tongues. Mariano Veytia (1720–1778), who learned to read the paintings, charts, monuments, and diagrams of the early Mexican records, presented his findings in *Historia Antigua de Mexico* (Ancient History of Mexico) first published in 1836. Veytia's history tells of seven families who had the same language and who migrated at the estimated date of 2133 BC to "New Spain," where the Creator God commanded them to come. Unable to explain their seagoing vessels, as their drawings showed no way to control them—no oars and so forth—he thought it was "not credible that they would throw themselves to the whim of the waters."

The record keeper of the book of Ether in the Book of Mormon describes in some detail the eight "barges" the Lord commanded the Jaredites to build, along with instructions on how to build them (Ether 2:16–25). They were "tight like unto a dish," and there was no way to guide them, which did put them at the mercy of the Lord, who would drive them by the wind on the water to "a land choice above all other lands" (Ether 2:10). The Book of Mormon tells how the finger of the Lord touched sixteen small stones, making them glow to provide light inside the barges (Ether 3:1–6).

Veytia recounts: "I say that the origin and first parents of all of them [the nations populating the Americas] were seven families who, in the scattering of peoples because of the confusion of tongues at the Tower of Babel, joined together because of finding themselves of one language that they called Nahuatl, which is known as the Mexican language, and they traveled to these parts, where they established themselves and multiplied, and went on dividing into towns and nations."[6]

The Book of Ether records God's merciful warning to the Jaredites when "many prophets, [who] prophesied of great and marvelous things, and cried repentance unto the people, and except they should repent the Lord God would execute judgment against them to their utter destruction" (Ether 11:20). The prophet Ether "did cry from the morning, even until the going down of the sun exhorting the people to believe in God unto repentance lest they should be destroyed" (Ether 12:2–3). The people rejected the words of Ether, who lived to see the total destruction of this once great civilization whose people never accepted the truth of Ether's dire warning, "Repent or perish."[7]

The Mulekites and Their Little King

The Book of Mormon also briefly mentions the Mulekites, a group who, like Lehi's party, fled to the New World, leaving Jerusalem at approximately 588 BC before the Babylonians destroyed the city. Mulek (Hebrew meaning "king"), who escaped with the group, was the young son of King Zedekiah, is known as the "Little King." The Bible records that "the king of Babylon slew the sons of Zedekiah before his eyes" (Jeremiah 52:10), but it does not say "all" the sons of Zedekiah; and the young son, Mulek, escaped and made his way to the western hemisphere (Helaman 8:21). "Biblical scholarship now bears out this Book of Mormon detail: King Zedekiah had a son named Mulek."[8] The Mulekites who eventually became more numerous than the Nephites, later made contact with the Nephites, and joined with them at approximately 200 BC. Subsequently, both groups were referred to as "Nephites."

Ancient Sea Travel Viable

All of these migrant groups traveled by sea. Shortly after Lehi's group arrived at the seashore in southern Arabia, the Lord, as mentioned in Chapter 1, commanded Nephi to build a ship "after the manner which I shall show thee; that I may carry thy people across these waters" (21 Nephi 17:8). The Lord showed him where to find ore to make tools to construct the ship. Nephi struck rocks (flint) together to start a fire, made bellows from animal skins to blow the fire, and, with much effort, built the ship.

If these travelers to the Americas recorded the routes of their sea voyages, those routes were not included in the abridgement. Thus, it is not known if Lehi and his group traveled east across the Indian Ocean and then across the Pacific to South or Central America or if they went a westerly route. What is known is that either route would have been possible, depending on the combination of winds, currents, season, and distances. Nephi could not have mapped out such a complicated voyage, but he testified that his group was guided by God. According to research by John L. Sorenson, "Divine knowledge of wind and sea conditions, within the range we now know to have existed, could indeed have permitted the successful crossing of two oceans . . . in a plausible period of time." This crossing may have included stopping from time to time at various islands for supplies.[9]

In 1947, Norwegian explorer Thor Heyerdahl made his famous voyage, crossing the Pacific in his balsa log raft *Kon-Tiki*. He wanted to prove his theory that the South Sea Islands were settled by explorers from pre-Inca South America. He followed that trip with expeditions on reed rafts to show that ancient people could have sailed from the Old World to the New.[10] At a pre-Columbian transatlantic crossing seminar held at Lumpkin, Georgia, in 1973, participants agreed that Africans, Mediterranean's, and Orientals all may have sailed to America before Columbus.[11]

Kon-Tiki raft

Destruction of Nephite Civilization a Warning to Modern America

After many hundreds of years of wars and bloodshed between the two great civilizations of the Nephites and Lamanites, the Nephites were destroyed, and any remaining Lamanite survivors were scattered over the face of the land. Moroni, the last Nephite prophet, took the records his father Mormon had abridged, added a few additional important teachings, and roamed alone for approximately 36 years. "I make not myself known to the Lamanites lest they should destroy me," he wrote. "And because of their hatred they put to death every Nephite that will not deny the Christ" (Moroni 1:1–2). Moroni recorded fierce battles among the Lamanites themselves (Mormon 8:8).

The people had been warned many years before by the Prophet Lehi, "If the day shall come that they will reject the Holy One of Israel, the true Messiah, their Redeemer and their God, behold, the judgements of him that is just shall rest upon them. Yea he will bring other nations upon them, and he will give unto them power, and he will take away from them power, and he will take away from them the lands of their possessions, and he will cause them to be scattered and smitten" (2 Nephi 1:10-11).

How did the plates end up in the Hill Cumorah? One obvious possibility is that Moroni himself may have carried the records to New York during his years of wandering between the extermination of the Nephites and his last writings on the plates (see Mormon 6:6 and Moroni 1:1–4). Or he may have taken them there as a resurrected being. We know only that, whatever the means, in 1827 the plates were in a "hill of considerable size" close to the home of young Joseph Smith near Palmyra, New York, where Moroni delivered the sacred record to him.[12] The hill has since been known to Latter-day Saints as the Hill Cumorah.

Chapter 8

Accurately Portray the Cultures and Institutions of These Peoples

Your book must describe these peoples' religious, economic, political, and social cultures and institutions. Additionally, you will present many specifics about their society, including the names of their standardized system of weights and measures.

Book of Mormon peoples were not illiterate heathens merely subsisting from day to day; rather, they were impressively advanced in spiritual, economic, political, and social matters. Daniel C. Peterson who has spent years studying their cultures writes that "The founding leaders of the migrations [to the Americas] were definitely literate, and the Nephites in their middle era are said to have produced 'many books and many records of every kind'"[1] (see Helaman 3:15).

What language did they use? Moroni said "the characters which are called among us the reformed Egyptian" had been "handed down and altered by us, according to our manner of speech" (Mormon 9:32). Through their scriptures and prophets, they knew much about Christ, and He was of great importance in their lives. The prophet Jacob records, "For this intent have we written these things, that [our beloved brethren and our children] may know that we knew of Christ, and we had a hope of his glory many hundred years before his coming; and not only we ourselves had a hope of his glory, but also all the holy prophets which were before us" (Jacob 4:4).

Religious Freedom and Prosperity

Religious traditions varied depending upon the righteousness of the people, with the faithful having a strong belief in Christ: "And we talk of Christ, we rejoice in Christ, we preach of Christ, we prophesy of Christ, and we write according to our prophecies, that our children may know to what source they may look for a remission of their sins"(2 Nephi 25:26).

Religious freedom was generally upheld: "Now there was a strict law among the people of the church, that there should not any man, belonging to the church, arise and persecute those that did not belong to the church, and that there should be no persecution among themselves" (Alma 1:21).

When the people were righteous, they prospered, and the Lord aided them in their battles. Wickedness invariably brought hardships and war time losses: "And we did observe to keep the judgments, and the statutes, and the commandments of the Lord in all things, according to the law of Moses. And the Lord was with us; and we did prosper exceedingly; for we did sow seed, and we did reap again in abundance. And we began to raise flocks, and herds, and animals of every kind" (2 Nephi 5:10–11).

"Behold Your Little Ones"

An Agrarian Society

"Making a living" for the Nephites and the Lamanites differed greatly from what we mean today by that expression. The Nephite men did "till the ground, and raise all manner of grain and all manner of fruit of every kind." The women did "spin, and toil, and work all manner of fine linen, yea, and cloth of every kind." As a result, they "did prosper in the land" (Mosiah 10:4–5). Most people farmed and kept "flocks and herds" (2 Nephi 5:11).

They had to produce, not only to provide for their families but also to provide for the "thousands . . . yea, and tens of thousands, who [did] sit in idleness" (Alma 60:22). These elite people consisted of priests, record keepers, architects, merchants, artists, and judges, who seemed idle to the hard-working farmers. However, we can be sure that most of the people in these ancient times "simply toiled daily at the hard work in front of them without the complex structure of jobs or 'careers' that organize the lives of many of us today."[2]

And there were those who "harkened not unto the voice of the Lord, because of their wicked combinations; wherefore, there began to be wars and contentions in all the land, and also many famines and pestilences, insomuch that there was a great destruction, such an one as never had been known upon the face of the earth" (Ether 11:7).

Care for the Poor

Some groups cared for the poor—an ancient welfare system: "And they did impart of their substance, every man according to that which he had, to the poor, and the needy, and the sick, and the afflicted; and they did not wear costly apparel, yet they were neat and comely" (Alma 1:27). Mosiah describes a welfare program for widows and their children: "Now there was a great number of women, more than there was of men; therefore, King Limhi commanded that every man should impart to the support of the widows and their children, that they might not perish with hunger; and this they did because of the greatness of their number that had been slain [in wars]" (Mosiah 21:17).

Medicinal Customs

The people were familiar with and used medicinal herbs: "There were some who died with fevers, which at some seasons of the year were very frequent in the land—but not so much so with fevers, because of the excellent qualities of the many plants and roots which God had prepared to remove the cause of diseases, to which men were subject by the nature of the climate" (Alma 46:40).

The Legal System

Some of their situations have a familiar ring today: "Now these lawyers were learned in all the arts and cunning of the people; and this was to enable them that they might be skillful in their profession" (Alma 10:15). The legal concepts and procedures found in various trials in the Book of Mormon indicate that the writers of the text were "thoroughly immersed in the social context and jurisprudence of early biblical time"—specialized knowledge that Joseph Smith did not possess.[3]

The Burden of Unjust Taxes

And, yes, there were usually taxes, often extracted by wicked leaders. King Noah taxed the people "one fifth part of all they possessed, a fifth part of their gold and of their silver, and a fifth part of their ziff, and of their copper, and of their brass, and their iron; and a fifth part of their fatlings; and also, a fifth part of all their grain" (Mosiah 11:3). At one point, the Lamanites were even greedier than King Noah in the tribute they demanded from their conquered subjects. The Nephites had to "deliver up their property, even one half of all they possessed, one half of their gold, and their silver, and all their precious things" (Mosiah 19:15). King Riplakish "did tax them with heavy taxes; and with the taxes he did build many spacious buildings. And he did erect him an exceedingly beautiful throne; and he did build many prisons, and whoso would not be subject unto taxes he did cast into prison"(Ether 10:5-6). By contrast, righteous King Benjamin was benevolent in his reign: he labored to support himself "that [his people] should not be laden with taxes"(Mosiah 2:14).

A System of Laws

As in our day, a system of laws regulated the affairs of the people in Book of Mormon times. A few examples: "Now there was no law against a man's belief; for it was strictly contrary to the commands of God that there should be a law which should bring men on to unequal grounds" (Alma 30:7). Further, it was against the Nephite law to have slaves. Ammon proclaimed, "It is against the law of our brethren, which was established by my father, that there should be any slaves among them" (Alma 27:9). "And they durst not steal, for fear of the law, for such were punished; neither durst they rob, nor murder, for he that murdered was punished unto death" (Alma 1:18).

Some punishments for breaking the laws were swift and severe. Third Nephi 4:28 describes the hanging of the captured leader of the wicked Gadianton robbers. After he was dead, "they did fell the tree to the earth," an act that followed an ancient Israelite law and practice of public execution.[4] And, as in old world laws, a distinction was made between a common thief and a robber in the Book of Mormon. The Gadianton robbers were always called robbers and never thieves, and their behavior and treatment were comparable to that of ancient Near Eastern robbers.[5]

Coronation Ceremonies

Some other noteworthy customs are mentioned in the Book of Mormon. "The book of Mosiah describes a coronation rite in all its details and presents extensive religious and political histories mixed in with a complicated background of exploration and colonization."[6] When the sons of King Mosiah declined their privilege of inheriting kingly office, their father abolished the monarchy and had judges elected by popular vote. His justification was "that it is not common that the voice of the people desireth anything contrary to that which is right" (Mosiah 29:26). He knew of the wickedness of King Noah that had caused the people to be taken into bondage, and he feared it would be repeated (Mosiah 29:18–19). At that time, King Mosiah had already established a system of laws that were still in effect (Alma 1:1).

The Wicked Oppose Freedom

The book of Alma contains "a remarkably full and circumstantial military history. The main theme of the book of Helaman is the undermining of society through moral decay and criminal conspiracy; the powerful essay on crime is carried into the next book, where the ultimate dissolution of the Nephite government is described."[7]

Usually, the majority ruled, but there were various treasons, dissents, rebellions, and revolts through the years as the wicked attempted to take away the rights of the people and destroy the Church. In Alma 51, we read about a conspiracy to deprive the people of their freedoms. Those who wanted a civil government under judges so they could freely practice their religion were called Freemen. Suspense and intrigue prevailed as these dangerous times unfolded.

An Ingenious Monetary System

The Book of Mormon does not mention coins but does use the word "money." In Alma 11:3–19, the names, weights, and values of their pieces of gold and silver are listed when Alma discusses judicial wages.: "And the judge received for his wages according to his time—a senine of gold for a day, or a senum of silver, which is equal to a senine of gold." Alma goes into great detail regarding their different pieces of gold and silver, their relative values and their commodity equivalents: "A senum of silver was equal to a senine of gold, and either for a measure of barley, and also for a measure for every kind of grain."

The names of the different pieces of gold and silver were senine, seon, shum, or limnah of gold and senum, amnor, ezrom, or onti of silver. The lesser pieces were called shiblon, leah, shiblum, and antion. "Clear evidence of [name] borrowing by the Nephites can be seen in the words. The proper names of Shiblon and Shiblum are found among Jaredites and Nephites. There is a remarkable and natural consistency in the picture which the most cunning calculations of a forger could not hope to achieve."[8]

Nephites monetary units of 1, 2, 4, and 7, have been shown by mathematicians to be the most efficient system possible for carrying out business transactions. This scheme requires fewer "coins," weights or measures or monetary units, than any other system devisable. This standard, writes researcher Richard P. Smith, is an "ingenious system which an intelligent group of people with a willingness to change their system as improvements suggested themselves, should be expected to develop. The probability is low that the monetary description could have been a lucky accident on Joseph Smith's part."[9]

Nephite and Lamanite societies were clearly advanced civilizations.

Chapter 9

Use Many Different
Writing Styles

Because many ancient authors contributed to the Book of Mormon, each with his own distinctive writing style, you must change your style many times.

T he alert reader would have little difficulty distinguishing among the writings of Henry David Thoreau, James Joyce and Leo Tolstoy, since each author has his own distinctive writing style. The Book of Mormon was written by many authors, most of whom were ancient American prophets. Multiple authors' styles can be clearly demonstrated through a method known as *stylometry*—computer-aided statistical analysis of writing style—also known as *computational stylistics* or *wordprint*.[1]

Wordprint and Author Identification

In 1980, Wayne A. Larson, Alvin C. Rencher, and Tim Layton published the first rigorous analysis of Book of Mormon authorship using wordprint. Their research revealed that each Book of Mormon writer left a pattern that is not easily altered, which creates a unique "linguistic fingerprint," as one author calls it.[2] The researchers used three basic statistical techniques: (1) Multivariate Analysis of Variance (MANOVA); (2) frequency of commonly occurring non-contextual words; and (3) frequency of rarely occurring non-contextual words.[3]

Wordprint analysis was performed on twenty-one Book of Mormon authors, including the four major authors—Mormon, Nephi, Alma, and Moroni. More than one hundred authors contributed to the Book of Mormon, but most have too few words to support statistically significant analysis. Tests were made to compare Book of Mormon authors' writing styles with nineteenth-century authors and to compare the nineteenth-century authors with each other. The Book of Mormon authors, taken individually or collectively, did not resemble any of the nineteenth-century writers, including Joseph Smith and contemporaries such as Sidney Rigdon or Solomon Spaulding. Skeptics had proposed both Rigdon and Spaulding as possible Book of Mormon ghost writers. The nineteenth-century writers could be differentiated from each other, and their variation pattern is similar to the variation pattern among Book of Mormon authors.[4]

Each author's style in the Book of Mormon was preserved by Joseph Smith's formal translation in which meaning was transferred while the imprint of the original language remained. Based on wordprint research, the odds against the Book of Mormon having a single author have been calculated 100 billion to one![5] Neither Joseph Smith, nor any other writer, no matter how educated or talented, could have fabricated a work with so many discernible authorship styles.

After the Larson-Rencher-Layton studies were published, wordprinting continued to undergo critical evaluation. In the early 1980s, John L. Hilton joined forces with a small group of statisticians ("The Berkeley Group") who attempted to verify the accuracy of wordprinting in general and to corroborate the Larson-Rencher-Layton results. Hilton summed up the group's work: "After seven years of study and development, we concluded that wordprinting measurements are now at the stage where scholars can use such tests confidently and without personal bias to analyze contested authorship in many literary works, including the Book of Mormon."[6]

Identifying Isaiah's Writings

As discussed in chapter 5, about one-third of the book of Isaiah is included in the Book of Mormon. Taken from the Brass Plates of Laban, these passages include many clarifications and some variations from the KJV Isaiah

A Book of Mormon prophet engraving on metal plates

text. Some of the most significant wordprint research has been done on Isaiah because of the centuries-old controversy whether Isaiah wrote all of the book or whether others wrote much of it after the prophet's martyrdom. Unbelieving biblical scholars as early as AD 1100 claimed that it was beyond the capacity of any person, even the prophet Isaiah, to correctly name Cyrus of Persia as the king who decades later would free the Israelites from Babylon.[7] As Professor L. LaMar Adams has written, "To a person with a testimony of prophecy, such a pronouncement isn't astonishing. But to a person who lacks that testimony, it's impossible. Those who reject the existence of prophecy as we know it have no choice but to conclude that the book of Isaiah must have been written by more than one man."[8]

Against this backdrop, a group of thirty-five scholars in Semitic languages, statistics, and computer science at BYU formulated a "literary style analysis" project to put the Isaiah multi-author claims to the test. The study, conducted over several years, examined Isaiah in the original Hebrew. The group used "more than 300 computer programs, analyzed several hundred stylistic variables, and obtained more than 4800 statistical comparisons."[9] Multi authors are easier to identify in Hebrew than they are in English. The BYU team was confident they had found

> a unique authorship style throughout the various sections of Isaiah. The rates of usage for the elements of this particular style are more consistent within the book of Isaiah, regardless of the section, than in any other book in the study. This statistical evidence led us to a single conclusion: based on style alone, the book of Isaiah definitely appears to be the work of one man. The two parts of Isaiah most often claimed to have been written by different authors, chapters 1–39 and 40–66, were found to be more similar to each other in style than to any of the other eleven Old Testament books examined.[10]

Larson, Rencher and Layton found that Isaiah was a separate recognizable writer among Book of Mormon authors, "yet none of the statistical tests showed Isaiah to particularly stand out. That is, Mormon, Nephi, and the others appeared to be as distinctively individual as Isaiah. If Joseph Smith or any other nineteenth-century author had written the book, this would not be expected."[11]

Stylometry can build confidence, but "while [wordprint analysis] can measure certain facts objectively, it cannot prove the holiness of the Book of Mormon. . . . [Its] divine origin is obtainable only by developing faith. . . . Wordprinting can, nevertheless, bolster the establishment of faith by rigorously demonstrating factual information about the book."[12]

Common Experiences of Book of Mormon Writers

Dr. Daniel Ludlow identified five experiences common to the ancient major authors of the Book of Mormon: "(1) the writers are all witnesses of Jesus Christ—that is, they saw him in vision or in person; (2) they were all tutored by supernatural beings—angels or translated beings; (3) they all had visions of our day and wrote especially for us; (4) they all received heavenly counsel regarding what they should include in their writings; and (5) they all warned us that we will be held accountable for what we do with their words."[13]

Joseph Smith could not have mimicked the different writing styles of the many Book of Mormon authors. His account of how he received and translated it through the gift and power of God is the only viable explanation of its authorship.

Chapter 10

Weave into Your Book
the Pure Gospel of Jesus Christ

You must weave into your book the pure Gospel of Jesus Christ and His pattern of Christian living.

In a time when many doubt Christ's resurrection—or even His existence—a book has appeared that, along with the Bible, testifies not only that He lived but that He did in reality rise from the tomb and lives today. Prophets in the Book of Mormon knew of Him, knew He would be born, and knew of the prophecy that He would be crucified and resurrected, and would visit His "other sheep" in ancient America (3 Nephi 15:17).

These New World prophets knew of the Savior's resurrection and that all mankind would be resurrected because of His redeeming mission.[1] The Introduction to the Book of Mormon proclaims that "the crowning event recorded in the Book of Mormon is the personal ministry of the Lord Jesus Christ among the Nephites soon after his resurrection. The book puts forth the doctrines of the gospel, outlines the plan of salvation, and tells humankind what they must do to gain peace in this life and eternal salvation in the life to come."

What follows is an overview of the religion of Jesus Christ as found in the Book of Mormon, along with His comparable teachings in the Bible.

God Speaks through Prophets

The Lord has always worked through prophets. As Amos 3:7 declares, "Surely the Lord God will do nothing, but he revealeth his secret unto his servants the prophets." The Book of Mormon, which was written by many prophets, makes a similar statement: "Behold they [the prophecies] were manifest unto the prophet by the voice of the Spirit; for by the Spirit are all things made known unto the prophets" (1 Nephi 22:2). Author Sheri Dew describes the essential role and mission of prophets:

> Christ's church, which is 'built upon the foundation of the apostles and prophets, Jesus Christ himself being the chief corner stone' (Ephesians 2:20), cannot exist without prophets and apostles. In all of scripture there is no evidence of the Lord identifying a people as his own and

57

then failing to provide them with a prophet to communicate his will. Prophets are not motivated by money or power. Their words haven't been polluted by the philosophies of men or by self-interest. Their objective is to take the gospel of Jesus Christ to every person who will listen, and then to help them live it. And their mission is to testify and bear witness of Christ. There is no source of information on earth as pure and unsullied.[2]

The Lord has provided prophets for His Church on the earth in modern times, beginning with Joseph Smith, who spoke many latter-day prophecies. For example, on December 25, 1832, Joseph foretold the American Civil War—more than twenty-eight years before the first shot was fired on April 12, 1861. He prophesied that the war would begin at the rebellion of South Carolina, "which will eventually terminate in the death and misery of many souls." He said that it would be between the northern states and the southern states, that the southern states would call on other nations, particularly Great Britain, to defend them, and that slaves would rise up against their masters. This prophecy can be found in Doctrine and Covenants, Section 87.[3] Joseph Smith's successors have continued to receive guidance, and the Church of Jesus Christ is led by a prophet today. It is through prophets that revelation is given by the Lord to direct the work of His Church on the earth.

The Lord's Plan for His Children

Through the Book of Mormon, the Bible, and additional latter-day scripture, all of which have come to us through prophets, we learn where we came from, why we are here, and where we are going when we die. Before the world was created, we were all present at a great council in heaven where we learned the possibility of taking on mortal bodies through birth on Earth, to be tried and tested so we could become perfected like our Father. We shouted for joy over this announcement (Job 38:7), but this meant we would need to leave heaven. Two distinguished sons of God presented their plans for our lives in our new surroundings. Our Heavenly Father knew that we would make mistakes, but He presented a plan whereby all could be forgiven of these sins and become spotless. Jesus agreed with His Father's plan: "Father, thy will be done, and the glory be thine forever" (Moses 4:2). The other son, Lucifer, said, "Behold, here am I. Send me, I will be thy son and will redeem all mankind that one soul shall not be lost and surely I will do it; wherefore give me thine honor" (Moses 4:1).

Thus, in our premortal existence, we had agency to choose whom we would follow. Two-thirds of the hosts of heaven followed Christ's plan, which included all those to be born into mortality; one-third followed Lucifer and were cast down to Earth without receiving a mortal body. Adam and Eve were chosen as our first parents. In the Garden of Eden, they partook of the forbidden fruit, making them mortal with the ability to have mortal children and descendants. For their transgression, they were driven from the Garden of Eden to be tested in this fallen world. In the Book of Mormon, we read, "Adam fell that men might be; and men are, that they might have joy" (2 Nephi 2:25).

So what was the result? The Book of Mormon prophet Nephi answers: "Men are free according to the flesh; and all things are given them which are expedient unto man. And they are free to choose liberty and eternal life, through the great Mediator of all men, or to choose captivity and death, according to the captivity and the power of the devil, for he seeketh that all men might be miserable like unto himself" (2 Nephi 2:27).

Because our Heavenly Father loves his children, He sent His Only Begotten Son, Jesus Christ, to atone for our sins "that whosoever believeth in him should not perish but have everlasting life" (John 3:16). "Remember that there is no other way nor means whereby man can be saved, only through the atoning blood of Jesus Christ, who shall come; yea, remember that he cometh to redeem the world" (Helaman 5:9). And since Heavenly Father is not a respecter of persons all those who don't have the opportunity to learn about His Son while on Earth will learn about Him and have a chance to accept Him in the spirit world after their time on Earth.

The Book of Mormon makes a significant, unique contribution to our understanding of the gospel with its descriptions of plans. The word *plan* does not appear in the Bible. It appears in the Book of Mormon many times, all pertaining to the great plan of salvation (Alma 42:5). A few of the variants listed are: plan of redemption (Alma 12:31-33); plan of mercy, (Alma 42:15); plan of restoration (Alma 41:2); and plan of happiness (Alma 42:8). Additionally, we are warned of the cunning plan of the devil (Alma 28:13).

Baptism Necessary for Entrance into the Kingdom of God

One of the hallmarks of Christianity is the ordinance of baptism, which was practiced and taught by believers in both the Bible and the Book of Mormon. The Bible shows how Christ set the example being baptized by John in the River Jordan. Jesus taught, "Except a man be born of water [baptism] and of the Spirit [the Holy Ghost], he cannot enter into the kingdom of God" (John 3:5). "He that believeth in me and is baptized shall be saved; but he that believeth not shall be damned" (Mark 16:16). Many say they believe in Christ, but do they really believe Him when He says we must repent and be baptized to be saved?

When the Savior appeared to the Nephites in the western hemisphere, He taught them the necessity of this essential ordinance: "And whoso believeth in me, and is baptized, the same shall be saved; and they are they who shall inherit the kingdom of God. And whoso believeth not in me, and is not baptized, shall be damned" (3 Nephi 11:33–34).

Baptisms in the Waters of Mormon

The ordinance of baptism is not complete without the further ordinance of confirmation. Those with priesthood authority lay their hands upon the head of the one baptized and confer the gift of the Holy Ghost. This third member of the Godhead will act as a guide and comforter after confirmation as long as the recipient of this gift abides by the principles of the gospel. The Holy Ghost can temporarily come upon a person before baptism as a convincing witness that the gospel is true.

When a person seeks baptism, it is necessary that she or he have faith in the Lord Jesus Christ. Desire should be strong enough that the person is willing to repent of his or her sins, make restitution for sins where possible, and vow to live a righteous life. Because no unclean thing can dwell with God in His kingdom, baptism provides a spiritual cleansing and is the first step to becoming eligible to return and live with God in the kingdom of heaven. In the Book of Mormon, Christ said, "Repent all ye ends of the earth, and come unto me, and be baptized in my name, and have faith in me, that ye may be saved" (Moroni 7:34).

Essential Priesthood Authority Restored

The authority to baptize and perform other sacred ordinances must come from God. He gives His priesthood authority to worthy men who may then bestow this authority on others. This point is mentioned frequently in the Book of Mormon: "I Jacob, having been called of God, and ordained after the manner of his holy order, and having been consecrated by my brother Nephi . . . behold ye know that I have spoken unto you exceedingly many things" (2 Nephi 6:2). "They were baptized by the hand of Alma, who had been consecrated the high priest over the people of the church, by the hand of his father Alma" (Alma 4:4). "And he began to teach the people in the land of Melek according to the holy order of God, by which he had been called" (Alma 8:4).

When Christ visited the Americas after His resurrection, He chose twelve disciples and gave them the authority to act in His name: "He touched with his hand the disciples whom he had chosen, one by one, even until he had touched them all, and spake unto them as he touched them. . . . The disciples bare record that he gave them power to give the Holy Ghost" (3 Nephi 18:36–37).

The Bible further teaches that for a baptism to be valid, a person performing the ordinance must have the proper authority. Hebrews 5:4 says, "And no man taketh this honor unto himself, but he that is called of God, as was Aaron"[4] (see Exodus 28:1–3). Jesus taught, "Ye have not chosen me, but I have chosen you, and ordained you" (John 15:16). Paul taught Timothy, "Neglect not the gift that is in thee, which was given thee by prophecy, with the laying on of the hands of the presbytery" (1 Timothy 4:14). Book of Mormon people realized the importance of authority: "And it came to pass that Limhi and many of his people were desirous to be baptized; but there was none in the land that had authority from God" (Mosiah 21:33).

John the Baptist confers the Aaronic Priesthood upon Joseph Smith and Oliver Cowdery

Neither divinity school training with a diploma nor a mere belief in the Bible can give anyone the authority to baptize any more than a person without proper authority can swear in a new citizen of a country. The fifth Article of Faith of The Church of Jesus Christ of Latter-day Saints reads, "We believe that a man must be called of God, by prophecy, and by the laying on of hands by those who are in authority, to preach the Gospel and administer in the ordinances thereof."

While translating the Book of Mormon, Joseph Smith and Oliver Cowdery, his scribe, learned about baptism for the remission of sins.

Wanting to know how they could receive this blessing, they went to the nearby woods and prayed. An angel, who identified himself as John (the resurrected John the Baptist of the New Testament) appeared, saying he had come under the authority of Peter, James, and John (Apostles whom Christ had ordained). Laying his hands upon their heads, the angel conferred the lesser priesthood of Aaron, known as the Aaronic Priesthood, upon them. They were then instructed to baptize each other

Not long thereafter, Peter, James, and John appeared to Joseph and Oliver and conferred upon them the higher Melchizedek Priesthood, thus

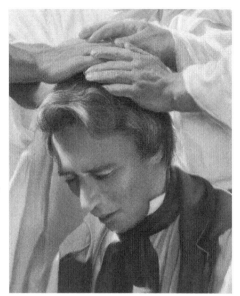

Peter, James and John confer the Melchizedek Priesthood upon Joseph Smith

giving them the keys to the apostleship and the authority to restore and organize Christ's church upon the earth.[5]

Just as Christ called and ordained Twelve Apostles in Jerusalem (Luke 6:13) and twelve disciples in the Americas (3 Nephi 12:1), The Church of Jesus Christ of Latter-day Saints also has Twelve Apostles. They are called and ordained by those having authority that has been passed down from Joseph Smith through his successors.

The sixth Article of Faith of The Church of Jesus Christ of Latter-day Saints reads: "We believe in the same organization that existed in the Primitive Church, namely, apostles, prophets, pastors, teachers, evangelists, and so forth."

Proper Mode of Baptism Taught

As in our day, the mode of baptism was debated during Book of Mormon times. When the Savior appeared to the Nephites, He taught the correct baptismal procedure: "Whoso repenteth of his sins . . . and desireth to be baptized in my name, on this wise shall ye baptize them—Behold, ye shall go down and stand in the water, and in my name shall ye baptize them. And now behold, these are the words which ye shall say, calling them by name, saying: Having authority given me of Jesus Christ I baptize you in the name of the Father, and of the Son, and of the Holy Ghost, Amen. And then shall ye immerse them in the water, and come forth again out of the water" (3 Nephi 11:23–25). The word *baptism*, coming from a Greek word meaning to dip or immerse, symbolizes death, burial, and resurrection, and is properly done by immersion. Any other method is not baptism. (Baptism is discussed more fully in Chapter 12.)

Little Children Are Innocent before God

In the Book of Mormon, Christ teaches that infant baptism, which had crept into the early New World church, is erroneous and hence unnecessary. "Listen to the words of Christ, your Redeemer, your Lord and your God. Behold, I came into the world not to call the righteous but sinners to repentance; the whole need no physician, but they that are sick; wherefore, little children are whole, for they are not capable of committing sin" (Moroni 8:8). Further, "Little children cannot repent; wherefore, it is awful wickedness to deny the pure mercies of God unto them, for they are all alive in him because of his mercy" (Moroni 8:19).

The belief that little children need baptism has brought heartache to untold numbers of parents whose children die without baptism. Some religions teach that innocent, unbaptized children suffer eternal torment in hell and can never enter the kingdom of heaven.

Such was the agony of the parents of a little six-year-old boy who had fallen into a well in a southern State in the United States when this false doctrine was preached at his funeral. Adding to the parents' grief was the regret that the boy's eternal damnation was their fault because they failed to have him baptized. Fortunately, as they mourned at their child's grave, Latter-day Saint missionaries lifted their burden by teaching them true doctrine regarding the baptism of little children.[6]

No verses in the Bible sanction infant baptism, and perhaps not surprisingly, the practice of baptizing little children is controversial among ministers and has caused some to leave the ministry, either by choice or involuntary termination.

An example of this conflict occurred in Brazil with three Methodist seminary students: Helio da Rocha Camargo, Saul Messias de Oliveira, and Walter Guedes de Queiroz. They, along with a large group of other seminary students, questioned the practice of infant baptism. The students were "inclined to see in that ceremony an anti-biblical practice created by the Roman Church in the first centuries of Christianity, and felt that it should be eliminated from the Protestant churches because of its incompatibility with the scriptures." (Infant baptism was inaugurated into the Roman Catholic Church at the Council of Carthage XVI AD in 418[7] and afterwards adopted by many other churches.) Their superiors disagreed, and the students had their choice to accept this teaching of the church or withdraw. All three left the seminary, and later, after studying other churches, each independently found and joined The Church of Jesus Christ of Latter-day Saints.[8]

Harvard University's first president, Henry Dunster, lost his position and his home in 1654 because of his rejection of the Puritan practice of infant baptism. He believed that to baptize infants was an affront to the Lord, and he demanded scriptures showing that children needed baptism. None exist.[9] Joseph Smith was given a vision on January 21, 1836, on the topic of infant baptism in which it was revealed to him that "children who die before they arrive at the years of accountability are saved in the celestial kingdom of heaven" (Doctrine and Covenants 137:10). Further, the age of accountability revealed to the Prophet was eight years (D&C 68:27).

The Sacrament Provides Access to the Atonement

The Savior introduced the ordinance of the sacrament into His Church so that His people would remember Him and His infinite Atonement in the Garden of Gethsemane and on the cross. He first inaugurated this ordinance at the Last Supper with His Twelve Apostles in Jerusalem immediately before His crucifixion. Later, after His resurrection and during His visit to the western hemisphere, He introduced the sacrament to the Nephites. The Savior then spoke of the need for proper authority to administer the sacrament: "Behold there shall one be ordained among you, and to him will I give power that he shall break bread and bless it and give it unto the people of my church. . . . And this shall ye do in remembrance of my body, which I have shown unto you. And it shall be a testimony unto the Father that ye do always remember me. And if ye do always remember me ye shall have my Spirit to be with you" (3 Nephi 18:5, 7).

The Savior then commanded that they take wine, drink of it, and give it unto the multitude. "And ye shall do it in remembrance of my blood, which I have shed for you, that ye may witness unto the Father that ye do always remember me, and if ye do always remember me ye shall have my Spirit to be with you" (3 Nephi 18:11). These prayers, given when the sacrament is blessed, are found in Moroni chapters 4 and 5.

Other instructions regarding the sacrament were given to Joseph Smith in August 1830 when the Prophet received the following revelation: "It mattereth not what ye shall eat or what ye shall drink when ye partake of the sacrament, if it so be that ye do it with an eye single to my glory—remembering unto the Father my body which was laid down for you, and my blood which was shed for the remission of your sins" (Doctrine and Covenants 27:2).

During World War II, the Saints in Freiburg, Germany, had a great desire to partake of the sacrament, but they had not had bread for weeks. They were finally able to purchase some potato peelings for the equivalent of $50, and they used them in place of bread. That action was no doubt acceptable to the Lord.[10] Since its early beginning, The Church of Jesus Christ of Latter-day Saints has used water instead of wine for the sacrament.

Temples Necessary to Redeem the Dead

If baptism is a prerequisite for entering into the kingdom of God, what is to become of the billions of people who either never heard of Christ or never had the opportunity for baptism during their mortal lives? Would a kind Heavenly Father present a set of conditions His children must follow to return to live with Him and not provide a way for them to fulfill those conditions? Because God is a loving and just Father, He has made provision for all His children to have the opportunity to accept (or reject) the mercy of the Atonement and, upon conditions of repentance, receive the saving ordinances, either personally in mortality or vicariously in the spirit world prior to the resurrection. Vicarious ordinances on behalf of the deceased are performed in latter-day temples.

After the Savior was crucified, Peter tells us that He "went and preached unto the spirits in prison" (1 Peter 3:19). The Apostle further says, "For this cause was the gospel preached also to them that are dead, that they might be judged according to men in the flesh, but live according to God in the spirit" (1 Peter 4:6). This does not imply that these dead are given a "second chance," it is actually a "first chance" for all those who do not have the opportunity to hear the gospel while on the earth and thus receive a fair judgment. Baptism and other vicarious ordinances are valid only when the deceased, now in the spirit world, accepts them.

The story is told of a heathen king who was converting to Christianity. He was pleased with the blessings his newfound religion offered, but he was concerned about his ancestors who had gone to their graves unsaved. When informed that they "had surely gone to hell," he adamantly replied, "Then to hell I will go with them." Elder James E. Talmage observed the following about the king: "Had he been correctly informed he would have known . . . that the spirits of his noble dead would have the opportunity of learning the saving truths which in the flesh had never saluted their ears. The Gospel is being preached to the dead. Missionary service in the spirit world has been in progress since its inauguration by the disembodied Christ while His crucified body lay in the tomb."[11]

The 1 Corinthians 15:29 scripture has puzzled both Bible scholars and lay people alike: "Else what shall they do which are baptized for the dead, if the dead rise not at all? why are they then baptized for the dead?" Baptism for the dead was practiced in Paul's day and afterwards. In the second century, there were groups such "as the Montanists and Marcionites—who are invariably referred to as Christians—[who] practiced a similar rite. It was practiced for more than 300 years before the practice was condemned in AD 393 by the Council of Hippo, which certainly implies that it was still a vital issue."[12] In rejecting this practice, what remained of the original Church moved further away from original Christian practices and teachings. Baptism for the dead was restored through Joseph Smith.

Unfortunately, this vicarious ordinance for persons who are deceased, is considered false doctrine by most Christian churches today—condemning countless millions to "burn in hell" because they never heard of Christ and were never baptized.

Moses built a type of portable temple to travel with the children of Israel in the wilderness, and much has been written about the elegance of Solomon's temple and the vastness and beauty of the Temple of Herod. Christ's life was linked to the temple from the ritual of purification given after His birth, to His teaching in the temple at twelve years of age, and to the many instances of people approaching Him at the temple to be healed or to be taught by Him.

Temples have always played an important role in Christianity. They are connectors between heaven and Earth. Temples also played an important part in Book of Mormon society. Nephi writes of building a temple "after the manner of the temple of Solomon save it were not built of so many precious things" (2 Nephi 5:16). Christ descended from heaven near "the temple which was in the Land Bountiful" (3 Nephi 11:1). The Nephites offered sacrifices (Mosiah 2:3) and received instructions (Mosiah 2:9) in their temples.

The Lord commanded Joseph Smith and the early Latter-day Saints to build temples.[13] The first one in modern times was built in Kirtland, Ohio. Shortly after the dedication of the Kirtland Temple, the Prophet Elijah appeared to Joseph Smith and Oliver Cowdery in this temple. Elijah came in fulfillment of the words of Malachi: "And he shall turn the heart of the fathers to the children, and the heart of the children to their fathers" (Malachi 4:6).

For centuries, Jewish people have looked forward to the return of Elijah. During Passover feasts, they leave an empty chair to welcome him to celebrate with them at their table. On April 3, 1836, during Passover feast time, Elijah did return—to the temple in Kirtland, Ohio, where he restored the keys of the sealing power (temple marriage ordinances). Elijah conferred upon Joseph and Oliver the power to bind, or seal, on Earth and in heaven all the ordinances pertaining to the fullness of salvation. "Joseph Smith said that Elijah was the last prophet that held the keys of this priesthood; he was to come and restore this authority in the last dispensation."[14] Thus, the great genealogical work of seeking out the names of deceased ancestors began.

Many great visions and revelations were received in the Kirtland Temple. The Savior appeared and proclaimed His acceptance of the temple and of the Saints as His people; Moses appeared and restored the keys of the gathering of Israel; Elias appeared and committed the dispensation of the gospel of Abraham; and Elijah came preparatory to the "coming of the great and dreadful day of the Lord" (Malachi 4:5). Genealogy has since become one of the most popular activities in the world.

Not only can vicarious baptisms take place for those who have passed on but men and women, both living and deceased, can be sealed together as husband and wife for eternity in the temples.[15] The ceremony for living couples does not marry them and then pronounce a divorce, "until death do ye part," as do other marriage rituals. Families are sealed together eternally in the Lord's holy temples, fulfilling Christ's promise in Matthew 16:19: "And I will give unto thee the keys of the kingdom of heaven [authority]: and whatsoever thou shalt bind on earth shall be bound in heaven."

Temples, now located in many countries around the world, offer these holy saving and binding ordinances. Some 160 temples were in operation in 2018 with 10 more under construction and 31 more announced, only two of which will be in the U.S. The most famous is no doubt the Salt Lake Temple in Salt Lake City, Utah, which fulfills Isaiah's prophecy: "And it shall come to pass in the last days, that the mountain of the Lord's house shall be established in the top of the mountains, and shall be exalted above the hills, and all nations shall flow unto it" (Isaiah 2:2). Millions from all nations have visited this magnificent edifice.

The importance of temple work is shown in an event that occurred in early 1877 when the founding fathers of the United States, led by George Washington, appeared to President Wilford Woodruff in the St. George, Utah Temple, demanding that their temple ordinances be performed. The group included the signers of the Declaration of Independence and the United States Constitution. President Woodruff was promptly baptized for these men and for fifty

American Founding Fathers appear to Wilford Woodruff in St. George Temple

other eminent men. He afterwards told several brethren who were serving in the temple "that it was their duty to . . . labor until they got endowments[16] for all of them."[17] Baptisms were later performed for their wives and family members.

Many who have passed to the "other side" have helped people find genealogical information through various miraculous means, enabling their temple ordinances to be performed. One such incident occurred in May 1884 in Logan, Utah. The nine-year-old daughter of Bishop Henry Ballard was outdoors playing with friends when two elderly men called to her, handed her a newspaper, and told her to take it to her father and no one else. She did as she was instructed. Bishop Ballard was preparing for the dedication of the Logan Temple. After he received the paper, he discovered it had been published in England, and the date of publication was three days earlier. Everyone was astonished, for there was no earthly way it could have reached Logan in so short a time in the year 1884. The newspaper contained the names of more than sixty of Bishop Ballard's immediate relatives and other intimate friends, along with genealogical information. There were no temples in the British Isles at the time where the ordinances could have been performed. This newspaper, a miraculous artifact, is preserved in the Church History Museum in Salt Lake City.[18]

Joanna Lucas of Ukiah, California, was involved in another such miraculous incident at the Family History Library in Salt Lake City where she was attempting to find information regarding her Great-great-grandfather Ernst Otto von Damitz. The book with the information she was seeking was missing from its assigned shelf space and could not be located. In frustration, she dropped her research materials on a library table. An elderly bearded man then approached her and asked if he could help. Lucas explained her problem and showed him the genealogical information she had gathered. The man said his name was also Ernst, and he led her to another location. After a short search, she found the book she needed so she could do temple work for her ancestor. Lucas wanted to thank Ernst, but he had disappeared. She asked the library personnel about him, but they said no one by that name worked there. Later, as she looked through the photos in the newly found book, she discovered a picture of an elderly bearded man who she was certain was the man who had shown her where to find the missing book. The photo caption identified the man as her deceased great-great-grandfather Ernst von Damitz.[19] Incidents like this are not uncommon.

The Fall of Adam and "Original Sin"

"One of the strongest points of doctrine of the original Christians," observes Elder Robert E. Wells, "was the concept that Christ atoned for the sins of Adam, just as He has atoned for our sins. It should therefore follow that we are not jeopardized or prejudged because of anything that Adam did. . . . The transgression of Adam and Eve in the Garden of Eden was not an accident nor was it even a surprise to our Heavenly Father."[20] Adam and Eve were commanded to: "Be fruitful, and multiply, and replenish the earth." (Genesis 1:28). For our first parents to be able to obey this commandment, it was necessary that there be a fall so they could have children.

Adam and Eve recognized that their choice was part of God's plan. In the book of Moses, Adam says: "Blessed be the name of God, for because of my transgression my eyes are opened, and in this life I shall have joy." Eve also understood that the fall was necessary and good: "Were it not for our transgression we never should have had seed, and never should have known good and evil and the joy of our redemption" (Moses 5:10–11).

The Book of Mormon further explains this most consequential event: "If Adam had not transgressed he would not have fallen. . . . And all things which were created must have remained in the same state in which they were after they were created; and they must have remained forever, and had no end. And they would have had no children; wherefore they would have remained in a state of innocence, having no joy, for they knew no misery; doing no good, for they knew no sin. But behold, all things have been done in the wisdom of him who knoweth all things. Adam fell that men might be; and men are, that they might have joy" (2 Nephi 2:22–25).

In 1 Corinthians 15:22, we read: "For as in Adam all die, even so in Christ shall all be made alive." The second of the thirteen Articles of Faith, authored by the Prophet Joseph Smith, says: "We believe that men will be punished for their own sins, and not for Adam's transgression."

Why Latter-day Saints Do Not Use the Cross

Book of Mormon prophets knew that the Savior would die on the cross. The prophet Jacob wrote: "We would to God that we could persuade all men not to rebel against God, to provoke him to anger, but that all men would believe in Christ, and view his death, and suffer his cross and bear the shame of the world" (Jacob 1:8).

Many churches adorn their buildings with a cross, and members of these churches sometimes ask why The Church of Jesus Christ of Latter-day Saints and its members do not worship, wear, or decorate their churches with this symbol. "To [Latter-day Saints], the cross is a symbol of his passion, his agony," explains Elder Robert E. Wells. "Our preference is to remember his resurrection. We seek to honor the living Christ who was brought forth in glory from the tomb on the third day."[21] If the Savior had died by some other means, such as a dagger or sword, would it not be thought strange if Christians wore a replica of one of these instruments simply because it was used as the means of putting the Lord to death?[22] The Church, however, recognizes and respects the rights of others to use the cross as a religious symbol.

No Paid Ministry in the Restored Church

Neither Christ nor His disciples received compensation for teaching the gospel to the people. The elders are told in 1 Peter 5:2 to "Feed the flock of God which is among you . . . not by constraint, but willingly; not for filthy lucre, but of a ready mind." Micah 3:11–12 teaches that priests who teach for hire and prophets who divine for money bring a curse upon the people. And in Matthew 10:8, Christ instructs His Apostles with these words: "Freely ye have received, freely give." And Paul teaches, "What is my reward then? Verily that, when I preach the gospel, I may make the gospel of Christ without charge, that I abuse not my power in the gospel" (1 Corinthians 9:18).

If a person is paid for services, it is her or his vocation. The Book of Mormon tells us that "priestcrafts are that men preach and set themselves up for a light unto the world, that they may get gain and praise of the world; but they seek not the welfare of Zion" (2 Nephi 26:29). Further, "But the laborer in Zion shall labor for Zion; for if they labor for money they shall perish" (2 Nephi 26:31). Such scriptures do not say that there are not some sincere ministers who serve for their love of Christ and their fellowmen. However, other churches' "loss of gain" (either of members and/or money) as a result of the popularity and rapid growth of The Church of Jesus Christ of Latter-day Saints in some areas causes persecution. It occurred in the early days of the Church, and it occurs in modern times.

One such case occurred in Ghana, Africa: "During the 1980s there was a growing opposition to the Church by religious leaders who felt threatened by the Church's growth." Many false accusations were made regarding the Church's doctrines and practices, even charging that it was a front for the U.S. Central Intelligence Agency. "There was evidently great concern among leaders of the other churches who realized that [this 'American'] Church was growing rapidly at their expense." Enough lies and false propaganda were dispersed to persuade the government to ban the Church from operating in Ghana and to seize its church buildings, locking them and placing them under guard. Gatherings of members were banned, arrests were made, and members were "imprisoned for administering to the sick or other activities perceived to be in violation of the ban." Thanks to some of the larger churches, particularly the Roman Catholic Church, which charged the Ghanaian government with violating religious freedom, and through external pressure, the "freeze" was ended after nearly eighteen months. The Church then grew even more rapidly—fueled by the curiosity about the actual beliefs of the Church.[23]

The Church of Jesus Christ of Latter-day Saints relies on a lay ministry, such as bishops, branch presidents, stake and district leaders, who receive no salary for their Church service. In fact, they donate to the Church a tenth of their earnings as tithing from their regular paid employment. The tens of thousands of missionaries who serve the Church receive no wages for their service. Neither are choir directors, organists, secretaries, Sunday School teachers, nor other members, who serve in the Church, paid for their service. There are no seminaries to train and grant degrees preparing one to become a bishop or other leader in the Church. Those called to positions of leadership may have spent two years serving as a missionary for the Church, could have attended religion classes during high school, and perhaps participated in religion or institute classes in college for four years or more. But whether they have spent several years learning Church teachings and doctrine, or are fairly new converts, leaders depend on the Spirit of the Lord to guide them in their callings.

The bishop's paid profession might be as a farmer, a doctor, or any other honorable vocation, but his worthiness and leadership abilities are essential to his call to serve. Having no paid local ministry creates a climate in which all need to study, learn, teach, and serve others. Volunteer Church leaders have great love for those whom they serve. Church leaders, such as the First Presidency and the Quorum of the Twelve, who spend full-time in church service do receive a living allowance.

The Church does not attempt to build massive congregations. In fact, when congregations grow to several hundred members, they are divided into two groups and new leaders are called as necessary to lead both groups. It is common for three congregations to share the same building, rotating the use of the chapel, classrooms, and cultural hall during the Sabbath Day and for weekday activities. Smaller groups create a closeness and unity among the members that can be difficult to achieve in larger congregations.

A Correct Understanding of the Godhead

To truly worship God, a person needs to understand the nature of the Father and the Son and their relationship to each other. Most Christian churches teach that the Godhead consists of three personages in one—or the "Holy Trinity"—whereas the scriptures, when rightly understood, teach that the Godhead consists of three separate personages who are one in purpose. In the Book of Mormon, we read "that the grace of God the Father, and also the Lord Jesus Christ, and the Holy Ghost, which beareth record of *them,* may be and abide in you forever" (Ether 12:41 (emphasis added).

Moroni 7:27 tells us that "Christ hath ascended into heaven, and hath sat down on the right hand of God." In Mark, we read, "After the Lord had spoken to them, he was received up into heaven, and sat on the right hand of God" (Mark 16:19). Neither scripture suggests that Christ sat down beside Himself. Similarly, regarding the need to repent and be baptized, Christ taught the Nephites, "This is my doctrine, and I bear record of it from the Father; and whoso believeth in me believeth in the Father also; and unto him will the Father bear record of me, for he will visit him with fire and with the Holy Ghost" (3 Nephi 11:35). Why would the Savior go to such lengths to define this relationship if He and the Father and the Holy Ghost were one person?

Some professors of religion accuse members of The Church of Jesus Christ of Latter-day Saints of being non-Christian. One major reason for this misconception is the Church's belief in the nature of the Godhead—consisting of three personages. Others hold that members of the Church of Jesus Christ of Latter-day Saints worship a different Jesus. Latter-day Saints worship the biblical Jesus, whereas those who believe in the three-in-one Nicaean Creed follow a philosopher's Jesus. "For over eighteen hundred years 'orthodox Christianity' has been so affected by Greek philosophy that its doctrines now include many concepts believed to be biblical which in reality have no scriptural basis whatsoever. . . . Close, honest research would show a departure from the Bible and that The Church of Jesus Christ of Latter-day Saints teaches true biblical Christianity."[24] C. S. Lewis wisely stated, "It is not for us to say who, in the deepest sense, is or is not close to the spirit of Christ. We do not see into men's hearts. We cannot judge, and are indeed forbidden to judge. It would be wicked arrogance for us to say that any man is, or is not, a Christian in this refined sense."[25]

Dictionaries define a Christian as a follower of Jesus Christ, "one who believes in or professes belief in Jesus as the Christ" and one whose "life conforms to the example and teaching of Jesus."[26] Those who formulate their own definition of the word *Christian* sometimes manipulate that definition to purposely exclude Latter-day Saints.

Latter-day Saints maintain that the Godhood consists of *three distinct personages*, that the Father and Son have bodies of flesh and bone, and that the Holy Ghost is a spirit. Members adamantly affirm that this belief follows the Bible. For instance, Genesis 1:26 reads, "Let *us* make man in *our* image" (emphasis added). This verse reveals God in the plural, so with whom was God speaking? Joseph Smith's Inspired Version of the Bible for Genesis 1:27 reads: "And I, God, said unto mine Only Begotten, which was with me from the beginning, Let us make man in our image, after our likeness; and it was so." Members of The Church of Jesus Christ of Latter-day Saints believe this is the correct reading of the original Genesis text. When Jesus was giving His great intercessory prayer (John 17:5), He said, "And now O Father, glorify, thou me with thine own self with the glory which I had with thee before the world was." His words offer simple, further evidence that He was with the Father in the premortal world and was a separate being from the Father.

The Bible does say that the Father and the Son are one, although the word "one" refers to both God the Father and Jesus the Son. For example, Christ, in John 10:30 says, "I and my Father are one." He later clarifies this statement while praying for His disciples and all believers as He petitions His Father, "That they all may be one; as thou, Father, art in me, and I in thee, that they also may be one in us; that the world may believe that thou hast sent me. And the glory which thou gavest me I have given them; that they may be one, *even as we are one*" (John 17:21–22); emphasis added). Christ continually talks about His Father in John 17, which does not make much sense if we suppose that the Father and the Son are one person.

As reported in Acts 7:55–56, Stephen saw "Jesus standing on the right hand of God." Jesus prayed to His Father and admonished others to do likewise. Paul, in Hebrews 1:3, called Christ the "express image" of the Father's "person." "There are more than five hundred passages of scriptures in the Bible that can be used to argue that God has a body."[27] Is it not possible that the Bible, in Genesis 1:26, actually means what it says when it states, "Let us make man in our image"? Using the Bible as our guide, do we have any reason to believe other than that Christ is literally the Son of His Father? Shortly before Christ descended from the heavens to the Nephites (3 Nephi 11:7), they heard a voice out of the heavens saying, "Behold my Beloved Son, in whom I am well pleased, in whom I have glorified my name—hear ye him."

After the baptism of Christ, there was heard "a voice from heaven, saying, "This is my beloved Son, in whom I am well pleased" (Matthew 3:17). At Christ's transfiguration before Peter, James, and John, a voice out of the cloud said, "This is my beloved Son, in whom I am well pleased; hear ye him" (Matthew 17:5). To whom is Christ pleading in Gethsemane when He says, "O my Father, if it be possible let this cup pass from me?" (Matthew 26:39). His last words upon the cross were to His father: "Father, into thy hands I commend my spirit" (Luke 23:46). And after His resurrection, He said to Mary, "Touch me not; for I am not yet ascended to my Father" (John 20:17). Latter-day Saints believe the scriptures clearly proclaim that the Father and the Son are separate personages.

Constantine Re-defined the Godhead as a Mystery

Disagreement among early Church leaders about the relationship between the Father and the Son was so great that in the year AD 325, Constantine, the pagan emperor of Rome, summoned an ecumenical council to Nice to resolve this dispute. "He was not seeking the truth, but to resolve a controversy that threatened to split his kingdom." Greek philosophy was the only acceptable mode of thinking for intellectuals at the time, and intense Roman persecution had made martyrs of many knowledgeable Christians. The conclusion reached after lengthy and heated debate was that the Godhead were "of the same substance," or *one*, without body, parts, or passions. Constantine chose the twenty-seven books now in our New Testament and had all other books, with which he did not agree, burned. Did the three hundred or so bishops at the council actually read the chosen scriptures and agree on such a conclusion?[28] "Constantine was forced to replace dissenting bishops with ones willing to support the new Creed." Thus, did the early Church, not through scriptures or prophets but through philosophy, render God utterly "incomprehensible," in its creeds? The Godhead is now, not surprisingly, referred to regularly as "a mystery" by much of Christendom.[29]

Elder Bruce R. McConkie writes that "Eternal life is reserved for those who know God and the One whom he sent to work out the infinite and eternal atonement. . . . It follows that the devil would rather spread false doctrine about God and the Godhead, and induce false feeling with reference to any one of them, than almost any other thing he could do. "The creeds of Christendom illustrate perfectly what Lucifer wants so-called Christian people to believe about Deity in order to be damned," continues Elder McConkie. "They say he is a spirit, without body, parts, or passions. They say he is everywhere and nowhere in particular present, that he fills the immensity of space and yet dwells in the hearts of men, and that he is an immaterial, incorporeal nothingness." Elder McConkie concludes, "They say he is a one-god-in-three, and three-gods-in-one who neither hears, nor sees, nor speaks. Some even say he is dead, which he might as well be if their descriptions identify his being."[30]

Sir Isaac Newton took it upon himself to search many facets of Christianity, including early church history and writings of the fathers. He was especially interested in the "Trinity," which was then—and is now, as noted—considered by many a mystery. After serious investigation, he concluded that fraud had been imposed upon the church, that the word "trinity" is not found in the New Testament, and that original texts had been altered in support of a false doctrine. "These three are one" is found *only* in the King James Version (1 John 5:7), and Newton's studies persuaded him that the original texts had been deliberately debased. Scholars agree that no ancient Greek texts include the wording "these three are one." Modern English translations now typically read "the three are in agreement."[31]

Edith Counsell and her husband, Thomas, of Manchester, England, were members of the Church of England but were dissatisfied with its teachings. Edith had long refused to accept the Trinity doctrine. At the age of seventeen, she had inquired of the vicar of St. Bartholomew's Church, where she attended, for a clearer explanation. She was ridiculed and told that she was an "imbecile" for trying to imagine God the Father, but that if she must imagine Him, she could note a "puff of smoke" from a chimney and liken Him to that. When Missionaries from the Church of Jesus Christ of Latter-day Saints knocked at the Counsells' door, Edith and Thomas were very receptive to the missionaries' teachings about the true nature of God and were baptized into The Church of Jesus Christ of Latter-day Saints.[32]

Members of The Church of Jesus Christ of Latter-day Saints accept the true doctrine that three separate personages constitute the Godhead. Latter-day Saints further believe that the Father and the Son appeared to Joseph Smith. Perhaps Joseph's greatest contribution to the world is the knowledge he revealed regarding the nature of deity. How can we worship that which we do not know or understand? In the Sermon on the Mount (Matthew 7:23), the Lord, speaking about false prophets standing before him on judgment day, states that He will say, "I never knew you." But in the Joseph Smith Translation, the Lord says, "*You* never knew *me*" (Matthew 7:30; emphasis added). Most Christian churches throughout the world today preach of a mysterious, incomprehensible deity.

The Eternal Potential and Destiny of God's Children

Members of The Church of Jesus Christ of Latter-day Saints believe that the Father and the Son have resurrected, exalted bodies of flesh and bone, and as children of a Celestial Father, they can become like them. In the Book of Mormon, Christ says: "Therefore I would that ye should be perfect even as I, or your Father who is in heaven is perfect" (3 Nephi 12:48). The Bible teaches this same doctrine: "Be ye therefore perfect, even as your Father which is in heaven is perfect" (Matthew 5:48).

The Bible further tells us, "I have said, ye are gods; all of you are children of the most high" (Psalms 82:6; see also John 10:34). In Romans 8:16–17, we read: "The Spirit beareth witness . . . that we are the children of God. And if children, then heirs; heirs of God, and joint heirs with Christ." Joseph Smith taught, "God himself was once as we are now, and is an exalted man, and sits enthroned in yonder heavens! That is the great secret."[33]

C. S. Lewis, in *Mere Christianity*, wrote "that we were 'gods' and He is going to make good His words. If we let Him—for we can prevent Him, if we choose—He will make the feeblest and filthiest of us into a god or goddess, dazzling, radiant, immortal creature, pulsating all through with such energy and joy and wisdom and love as we cannot now imagine."[34]

The fifth president of the Church, Lorenzo Snow, penned a couplet, "As man now is, God once was: As God now is, man may become."[35] This is not a new doctrine conceived by Joseph Smith. This truth is found in many of the earliest Christian writings and is in harmony with scripture.

In 1998, Catholic Priest Jordan Vajda was pursuing his graduate studies at the Dominican School of Philosophy and Theology at Berkeley, California. Aware that The Church of Jesus Christ of Latter-day Saints was receiving criticism for its teachings about becoming like God, he decided to discover for himself what the original Church of Jesus Christ actually taught on this subject, so he chose the concept as the subject of his master's thesis.

He found that this doctrine, not taught by present-day Catholics and Protestants, was, in reality, part of the heritage of the Christian Church in the first millennium. Members in that period believed that salvation meant "becoming a god." Vajda further discovered that Roman Christianity, from about the second century on, apostatized and had gotten it wrong on this issue. He concluded that "the Latter-day Saints are owed a debt of gratitude by other Christians because the Saints remind us all of our divine potential. The historic Christian doctrine of salvation—theosis, i.e., human divinization—for too long has been forgotten by too many Christians." Father Vajda continues: "Indeed, if the Latter-day Saints were inclined to do so, they could point out that they alone, among contemporary followers of Jesus, seem to possess the ancient Christian doctrine of *theosis* (Divinization)."

Describing the adversarial film *The God Makers,* Vajda writes: "What was meant to be a term of ridicule has turned out to be a term of approbation, for the witness of the Greek Fathers of the Church . . . [is] that they also believed that salvation meant 'becoming a god.'" Vajda further observes, "It seems that if one's soteriology [belief in salvation by Jesus Christ] cannot accommodate a doctrine of human Divinization, then it has . . . rejected the heritage of the early Christian church and departed from the faith of first millennium Christianity. . . . And the supreme irony is that such persons should probably investigate the claims of [this] Church, which proclaims that within itself is to be found the 'restoration of all things.'"

Vajda took his own advice and investigated the claims of the church that teaches this doctrine. He is no longer Father Vajda; rather, he is Brother Vajda, a member of The Church of Jesus Christ of Latter-day Saints.[36]

"The idea that man might become as God—known in Greek as *theosis* or *theopoiesis*—may be found virtually everywhere, from the New Testament through the writings of the first four centuries." "Church [of Jesus Christ of Latter-day Saints] members take seriously such passages as Psalm 82:6, John 10:33–36, and Philippians 2:5–6 in which a plurality of gods and the idea of becoming like God are mentioned. The notion of *theosis* is characteristic of church fathers Irenaeus (second century AD), Clement of Alexandria (third century AD), and Athanasius (fourth century AD). Indeed, so pervasive was the doctrine in the fourth century that Athanasius's arch-enemies, the Arians, also held the belief and the Origenist monks at Jerusalem heatedly debated 'whether all men would finally become like Christ or whether Christ was really a different creature.' According to an ancient formula, 'God became man that man might become God.' . . . Early Christians 'were invited to study to become gods.'"[37]

Latter-day Saints do not believe they will ever be independent of God or no longer subject to Him. He will always be their Father and God. They do not believe anything will take away His glory; rather, they believe that true knowledge about God will only add to God's glory as His children follow Christ.

Miracles in the Restored Church

Christ's many miracles, such as healing the sick, raising the dead, and causing the blind to see, the deaf to hear, and the lame to walk, are well known to students of the Bible. The Savior performed comparable miracles in the Americas when He appeared after His resurrection, and they are recorded in the Book of Mormon. Jesus said to the assembled Nephites, "Have ye any that are sick among you? Bring them hither. Have ye any that are lame, or blind, or halt, or maimed, or leprous, or that are withered, or that are deaf, or that are afflicted in any manner? Bring them hither and I will heal them, for I have compassion upon you. . . . For I perceive that ye desire that I should show unto you what I have done unto your brethren at Jerusalem, for I see that your faith is sufficient that I should heal you. . . . And he did heal them every one as they were brought forth unto him (3 Nephi 17:7–9).

The Book of Mormon further tells of His disciples' labors and miracles among the Nephites: "And there were great and marvelous works wrought by the disciples of Jesus, insomuch that they did heal the sick, and raise the dead, and cause the lame to walk, and the blind to receive their sight, and the deaf to hear; and all manner of miracles did they work among the children of men; and in nothing did they work miracles save it were in the name of Jesus" (4 Nephi 1:5).

Why do some people today say there are no more miracles? The prophet Mormon's answer: "By the power of his word have miracles been wrought. . . . And if there were miracles then, why has God ceased to be a God of miracles and yet be an unchangeable Being? . . . The reason why he ceaseth to do miracles among the children of men is because that they dwindle in unbelief, and depart from the right way, and know not the God in whom they should trust" (Mormon 9:17, 19, 20). The Lord taught the Nephites, "I am a God of miracles. . . . I work not among the children of men save it be according to their faith" (2 Nephi 27:23).

By this same power, miracles still occur within The Church of Jesus Christ of Latter-day Saints.[38] One early example occurred in 1839 when the Saints arrived to settle the swampy, mosquito-infested area that would soon become Nauvoo, Illinois. As might be expected, many contracted malaria, including Joseph Smith and several of the Quorum of the Twelve. What followed was one of the greatest days of faith and healing in modern Church history.

According to an account in Joseph Smith's history, he was ill for several days but eventually rose from his bed and went about healing those in his own house, including the many his wife Emma had taken in. He then moved from tent to tent, and, among those camped along the banks of both sides of the river and healed all who were ill. Some were close to death, but they arose and were made well. Elijah Fordham, who was "about breathing his last" and "unable to speak, his eyes were set in his head like glass, and he seemed entirely unconscious of all around him." Joseph held his hand and looked into his eyes in silence for a length of time. Elijah began to be aware of his surroundings. Joseph asked if he had the faith to be healed. Elijah felt it was too late. Joseph asked him if he believed in Jesus Christ. His answer was a feeble, "I do."

"Joseph then stood erect. . . . He spoke in a very loud voice, saying, 'Brother Fordham, I command you, in the name of Jesus Christ, to arise from this bed and be made whole.' . . . Fordham arose from his bed, and was immediately made whole. His feet were bound in poultices which he kicked off; then putting on his clothes he ate a bowl of bread and milk and followed the Prophet into the street." Joseph healed dozens, but there were too many for him to administer to by himself. Therefore, he requested members of the Quorum of the Twelve—several of whom he had healed—to go and visit the others and heal them. Many, including those a mile or two along the river, were also healed under their hands.[39]

Another large miraculous healing event occurred forty years later, in 1877, among the Zuni Indians in New Mexico. Elder Llewellyn Harris, who was serving there as a missionary, was staying with a Zuni family and was awakened in the night by the father who told him that their daughter was dying. She was gasping for breath and then appeared not to be breathing. Elder Harris administered to (blessed) her, and she revived and slept through the night. He soon learned that a smallpox epidemic was sweeping through the Zuni villages, and he found himself blessing ten to twenty families a day. The word spread, but the disease was spreading so rapidly that he couldn't visit all the afflicted. At that point, the Zunis brought all their sick to one place, a large room. Elder Harris called on the Lord to strengthen him, and he blessed all of them as they were brought to him. His interpreter kept a count and informed Elder Harris he had blessed 406 souls. Elder Harris said the power of the Lord was made manifest to such a degree that nearly all recovered.

A postscript to this event occurred in 1970. Dale Tingey was a mission president in the Southwest, which included the Zuni pueblo where he met a Sister Martinez, a Latter-day Saint who was celebrating her 114th birthday. Tingey, being aware of the healing miracle years earlier, asked Martinez if she knew about it. She pointed to the pox marks on her face and said her parents had taken her to a large room, but while they waited, the father thought she was dead and wanted to leave and bury her. Her mother refused and later told her that she revived immediately after the blessing and was healed. She then smiled and said, "I haven't been sick in a hundred years."[40] Miracles have been an ongoing part of the restored Church and continue today. (Latter-day Saints recognize that there are healings and diverse miracles among others who have the faith to receive these gifts.)

The Law of Tithing

The payment of tithes and offerings is stressed in the Bible and emphasized in the Book of Mormon. The Savior quoted Malachi as He taught the Nephites:

> Will a man rob God? Yet ye have robbed me. But ye say: Wherein have we robbed thee? In tithes and offerings. Ye are cursed with a curse, for ye have robbed me, even this whole nation. Bring ye all the tithes into the storehouse, that there may be meat in my house; and prove me now herewith, saith the Lord of Hosts, if I will not open you the windows of heaven, and pour you out a blessing that there shall not be room enough to receive it. (3 Nephi 24:8–10)

Tithing is a basic tenet of the restored Church, which teaches that one-tenth of each member's increase belongs to the Lord. No one is exempt, including the bishop and other leaders in the Church. No collection plates are ever passed in Church services, and no bills are sent to the members. A person wishing to donate fills out a donation slip and either mails it, gives it with the contribution to the bishop or one of his counselors, or pays the donation electronically online.

Evidence that members of The Church of Jesus Christ of Latter-day Saints believe in the principle of tithing and "put their money where their mouths are" can be found in a study conducted by the *Chronicle of Philanthropy,* published in April 2003. Analyzing the 1997 tax data for households that earn more than $50,000 a year and that itemized donations to charity, the researchers found that the Salt Lake City-Ogden areas of Utah ranked first among the fifty largest metropolitan areas as the most generous donors in the United States. The study further noted that much of the giving was tithing to the Church, with donors on average giving 15 percent of their discretionary income to religious and nonprofit causes.[41]

Additionally, a 2017 survey found that "Latter-day Saints contribute more financially than do other denominations, but feel the least pressure to donate." The survey was conducted by LendEDU, a financial resource website, which "polled 1,000 religiously affiliated Americans 'who indicated they . . . contribute financially to their respective religions.' Patrick Mason, dean of the School of Arts and Humanities at Claremont Graduate University, believes that "one of the reasons for the . . . Church's success over the past 100 years has been its financial stability . . . because it was able to instill in its members a belief that tithing was not . . . simply a voluntary offering that you gave after all your other expenses were paid but (the) consistent refrain that tithing is the first thing you pay."[42] Members who do not pay tithing do not lose membership in the Church, but they do lose blessings.

Church members may donate to other Church funds, which include fast offerings, missionary work, humanitarian aid, or "other." Strict accounting is made of all donated funds, and receipts are given to the donor. In the United States, the funds are deposited in a local bank and sent electronically to the Church account in Salt Lake City. The Church returns the amount needed to fund the local congregation for building upkeep, utilities, landscape services, etc. Study manuals, hymnals, and so forth, are provided to each congregation from these funds. Affluent congregations thus help those in less-prosperous situations.

A Council on the Disposition of the Tithes at Church headquarters in Salt Lake City, consisting of Church leaders, determines how tithing money will be used.[43] Their decisions fund construction of thousands of Church meeting houses throughout the world; maintenance of these and other buildings; support for higher education such as the three Brigham Young University campuses; Seminary and Institute of Religion buildings; construction and maintenance of temples, worldwide missionary work, including living allowances for mission presidents; expenses for more than four hundred mission homes; cars for some missionaries; administration of the world's largest family history program; support for the Church's worldwide self-reliance programs; humanitarian aid for members and non-members; and other needs of the global Church.

Those in full time church leadership positions, such as the First Presidency and the Quorum of the Twelve, receive an allowance for their living expenses. Most have been successful in their professions—heart surgeons, lawyers, college presidents, business executives, etc., so the amount they receive is often well below what they would have been earning in their pre-church occupations. None applied for or sought their full-time calling but humbly accept their new work for the Church. There are no earthly mansions offered for their service. Those from the Salt Lake area continue to live in the homes they occupied before their Church call. Others might live in unpretentious apartments close to Church headquarters in Salt Lake City. Their living expenses are taken from tithing funds and from Church owned business investments.

These leaders teach that "the Church exists to improve the lives of people across the world by bringing them closer to Jesus Christ. The assets of the Church are used in ways to support that mission. Those who attempt to define the Church as an institution devoted to amassing monetary wealth miss the entire point. . . . The key to understanding the Church is to see it not as a worldwide corporation, but as millions of faithful members in thousands of congregations across the world following Christ and caring for each other and their neighbors."[44] Tithing is a primary vehicle for doing this. The Lord has promised great blessings to those who tithe. "Would any of us intentionally reject an outpouring of blessings from the Lord? Sadly, that is what we do when we fail to pay our tithing."[45]

The Fourth Article of Faith provides the basis for the doctrine of Christ as taught and practiced in the Church: "We believe that the first principles and ordinances of the Gospel are: first, Faith in the Lord Jesus Christ; second, Repentance; third, Baptism by immersion for the remission of sins; fourth, Laying on of hands for the gift of the Holy Ghost." These doctrines are embraced by members and reinforced by teachings in the Book of Mormon and other church scriptures. Following these teachings brings peace and happiness to Latter-day Saints throughout the world.

Chapter 11

The Book Will Not
Be Fiction but a True
and Sacred History

Your book must not be mere fiction with moral value. Rather,
it must be true and sacred history.

Edward Blass, who warned any would-be forger against writing a long book, also warned against writing a historical book: "Don't write a historical document! They are by far the easiest of all to expose, being full of things too trifling, too inconspicuous, and too troublesome for the forger to check up on."[1] An example is found in the film version of Lloyd C. Douglas's novel *The Robe*. A voice from the deck warns two lovers waiting at the dock with, "The tide, sir! The tide!" There are only low tides in the Mediterranean where this scene took place and they would not be dangerous.

The Robe and other literary masterpieces are filled with such slips.[2] But what if an inaccuracy of this kind had appeared in the Book of Mormon? It is one thing to write a long, historical novel; however, to produce a book and claim it to be factual, *sacred* history, even scripture, and have every incident and detail subject to the ongoing scrutiny of both scholars and laymen alike is quite another matter.

Hugh W. Nibley comments on the wide latitude granted fiction writers: "In our time we have epics produced by C. S. Lewis and J.R.R.Tolkien who have invented cultures and worlds all of their own. They are free to do this. . . . Lewis mixed his religion in with a sort of science fiction theme . . . but these people were not held to historic accuracy."[3] The events and claims surrounding the coming forth of the Book of Mormon of necessity require it be held to the demanding standard of nonfiction.

The Historicity of the Book of Mormon

The preface to the Book of Mormon, written by the book's last prophet-historian, Moroni, declares it to be a "record of the people of Nephi, and also of the Lamanites". . . and also "a record of the people of Jared." Joseph Smith knew that he was translating an ancient record, not writing fiction, and to the end never wavered in his assertion that the book is a true sacred scriptural history. Had he claimed otherwise, he might have received awards in the field of literature for producing a great work—and avoided all the persecution that followed his startling claim that he received the plates from an angel of God. However, he was not writing for prestige, power, or wealth. He translated the sacred record because he was duty-bound as commanded by the Lord.

Latter-day Saint author Robert Detweiler lists seven traits that define a sacred text which are in stark contrast with works of fiction: 1) Sacred texts claim to be divinely inspired. 2) They reveal sacred messages from deity or deities. 3) They have veiled or hidden messages in the form of mysteries, parables, and so on. 4) They require an authoritative interpreter. 5) They effect the transformation of lives. 6) They serve as the foundation of religious ritual. 7) And they are evocative of divine presence.[4] The Book of Mormon exhibits all seven of these traits. The fifth trait is perhaps the most important because the book continues to change the lives of millions of people for the better as it brings them to, or closer to, Jesus Christ.

Things Pleasing unto God

From the beginning, the prophets who authored the sacred New World history were commanded by God to fulfill His purposes as they wrote. Nephi explained to his descendants why he and the prophets who followed him would write the things of God and not the things of the world:

> For the fullness of mine intent is that I may persuade men to come unto the God of Abraham, and the God of Isaac, and the God of Jacob, and be saved. Wherefore, the things which are pleasing unto the world I do not write, but the things which are pleasing unto God and unto those who are not of the world. Wherefore, I shall give commandment unto my seed, that they shall not occupy these plates with things which are not of worth unto the children of men. (1 Nephi 6:4–6)

The Savior confirmed the value of sacred records when He ministered among the Nephites:

> After he had expounded all the scripture unto them which they had received, he said unto them: Behold, other scriptures I would that ye should write, that ye have not. And it came to pass that he said unto Nephi: bring forth the record which ye have kept. . . . I commanded my servant Samuel, the Lamanite, that he should testify unto this people, that at the day that the Father should glorify his name in me that there were many saints who should arise from the dead, and should appear unto many, and should minister unto them. And he said unto them: Was it not so?
>
> And his disciples answered him and said: Yea, Lord, Samuel did prophesy according to thy words, and they were all fulfilled. . . . Nephi remembered that this thing had not been written. . . . Jesus commanded

"Bring Forth the Records"

that it should be written; therefore it was written according as he commanded." (3 Nephi 23:6–7, 9, 12–13)

Earlier, in 2 Nephi: 29:12, Christ emphasized the importance of keeping records: "For behold, I shall speak unto the Jews and they shall write it, and I shall also speak unto the Nephites and they shall write it; and I shall also speak unto the other tribes of the house of Israel, which I have led away, and they shall write it." The Jews did write the words of the Lord (the Old Testament); early Christians wrote a record (the New Testament); and the Nephites wrote what the Lord commanded them (the Book of Mormon). We are now blessed to have all these sacred records. In addition, at some future time, we will have the records of other scattered tribes of the house of Israel.

> The early writers of the Nephite records have made no attempt to relate an exhaustive history, or to acquaint future readers with the details of their civilization, or the geography of their land. Rather, the object has been to preserve a religious philosophy of life, to convince the reader as to the reality of God, and to establish the certainty that Jesus is the Christ. The reader who searches for these things will find them in rich abundance.[5]

Words of the Prophets Bring Souls unto God

The Book of Mormon makes it clear that the Nephite records were preserved to bring souls to salvation. Regarding the brass plates that were painstakingly recovered from Jerusalem by Nephi and his brothers, Alma charged his son Helaman: "I command you that ye take the records which have been entrusted with me; And I also command you that ye keep a record of this people" (Alma 37:1–2). "For he promised unto them that he would preserve these things for a wise purpose in him, that he might show forth his power unto future generations" (Alma 37:18).

Elder Bruce R. McConkie wrote:

The Book of Mormon is a history of God's dealings with the ancient inhabitants of the Americas. It is a history of fallen peoples. As with the Bible in the Old World, so with the Book of Mormon in the New. Both record the teachings of holy men of God who spake as they were moved upon by the power of the Holy Ghost. Thus, this is a volume of holy scripture. It speaks of God, of Christ, and of the gospel. It records the terms and conditions whereby salvation comes. The Bible of the New World,[6] as I choose to designate the Book of Mormon, has been preserved for us by a divine providence which kept the ancient record in prophetic hands. It is Another Testament of Jesus Christ.[7]

The Doctrine and Covenants declares that this sacred history, the Book of Mormon, contains the fullness of the gospel—that is, the knowledge a person needs to come unto Christ and be saved. The fullness of the gospel includes repentance, baptism, the gift of the Holy Ghost, faith in Jesus Christ, endurance to the end, and the potential reality of eternal life. The book repeatedly teaches that after the believer has come to Christ and received the Holy Ghost, further revelations will follow conditioned upon obedience and diligence.

"Another important new idea about the Book of Mormon," writes John L. Sorenson, "is that it is not a history in the sense of the word often used today. Rather than being a narrative of what happened in a particular territory, it is like the Old Testament, primarily a family chronicle written by prophets under the Lord's inspiration. . . . Moroni . . . concluded and buried the record not because there was no more history being made around him (see Mormon 8:1–9 and Moroni 1:1–2). Those happenings were simply not part of his group's history."[8]

Book of Mormon Prophets Saw Our Day

"The book was prepared by men with seeric vision who saw our day and addressed specific issues we would confront," writes Robert W. Millet. For instance, as Moroni finishes his father's records, he concludes, "Behold, I speak unto you as if ye were present, and yet ye are not. But behold, Jesus Christ hath shown you unto me, and I know your doing" (Mormon 8:35).[9] "What Moroni saw was a day of wickedness, degeneracy, and apostasy," says Millet. "We need, and can greatly benefit from the prophetic teachings and warnings found within the pages of the Book of Mormon to guide us through the trying days in which we live." Millet continues, "The Book of Mormon is not just a book that helps us feel good; it is a heavenly document that helps us *be* good. It is not only an invitation to come unto Christ; it is a pattern for accomplishing that consummate privilege."[10]

Professor William E. Berrett provides further insight: "The volume abounds with striking examples of the rewards of righteousness or unrighteousness, especially as it affects the life and prosperity of a whole nation. A world in turmoil could learn much from its pages. . . . The great pity is that so many become too lost in debate over the origin of the book to see clearly its message."[11]

The Fullness of the Gospel

The introduction to the Book of Mormon declares that it contains "the fullness of the everlasting gospel." Monte S. Nyman discusses this phrase's meaning:

> Some have wondered how the Lord and his prophets could state this, when in fact the Book of Mormon contains no specific reference to such matters as eternal marriage, degrees of glory in the resurrection, vicarious work for the dead, and so forth. Again, let us focus upon what the gospel is. The Book of Mormon contains the fullness of the gospel in the sense that it teaches the doctrine of redemption—that salvation is in Christ and in him alone—and the principles of the gospel (faith, repentance, rebirth, enduring, resurrection, and judgment) more plainly and persuasively than any other book of scripture. The Book of Mormon does not necessarily contain the fullness of gospel doctrine. Rather, it is a sacred repository of eternal truth relative to the most fundamental and far-reaching doctrine of all—the doctrine of Christ.[12]

The word *gospel* when translated from the Greek word *evangelion* literally means "good news," which the Book of Mormon contains in abundance. Michael B. Parker provides additional insight into the meaning of "the gospel":

> In the Book of Mormon, 3 Nephi 27:13–19, when Jesus was teaching the Nephites he explained what is meant by 'the gospel': He said he came into the world to do the Father's will; the Father sent him to be crucified; because of his atonement, all men will be judged by him according to their works; those who repent and are baptized will be filled with the Holy Ghost; if they endure to the end they will be found guiltless before the Father when he (Jesus) stands to judge the world; if they don't endure to the end they will be cast out; the Father's words will all be fulfilled; because no unclean thing can enter the Father's kingdom, only those who rely in faith on the atonement of Christ, repent, and are faithful to the end can be saved.[13]

What did Joseph Smith teach about the Book of Mormon? He knew it to be a true and sacred history and declared as much to the Twelve Apostles on

Sunday, November 28, 1841, and then recorded his words in his journal: "I told the brethren that the Book of Mormon was the most correct of any book on earth, and the keystone of our religion, and a man would get nearer to God by abiding by its precepts, than by any other book."[14] Millions of Latter-day Saints have found this prophecy true in their own lives.

You Will Fill the Book with 239 Chapters of Prophecy, Doctrine, Exhortation, and Profound Wisdom

You must include in your book 54 chapters dealing with wars, 21 historical chapters, and 55 chapters on visions and prophecies; and these must not contradict the Bible. You must write 71 chapters on doctrine and exhortation, and here, too, every statement must agree with the Bible, or your book will be proven to be a hoax. Finally, you must write 21 chapters on the ministry of Christ, and they will not only agree with the New Testament but will strengthen and enhance it.

Wickedness and War

Nearly a third of the Book of Mormon is devoted directly or indirectly to war. The wars and battles described include some of the most detailed and intriguing narratives in the book. The weapons are not those commonly used in Joseph Smith's day but rather are of ancient vintage. The Book of Mormon mentions bows, arrows, swords, cimeters, clubs, stones, and slings. Nephite battle gear includes breastplates, arm shields, "and shields to defend their heads" (Alma 43:19). Historian William J. Hamblin finds that "The warfare tactics not only differ from modern day methods, but also differ from what we read in the Bible regarding Biblical warfare."[1]

The Lamanites instigated most of the wars throughout the years, believing they had been wronged: the Nephites "did rob them of their right to the government when it rightly belonged unto them" (Alma 54:17). As a result, the Nephites were compelled to protect themselves according to God's command: "Ye shall defend your families even unto bloodshed. Therefore, for this cause were the Nephites contending with the Lamanites, to defend themselves, and their families, and their lands, their country, and their rights" (Alma 43:47). Thus, "the design of the Nephites was to support their lands, and their houses, and their wives, and their children, that they might preserve them from the hands of their enemies; and also that they might preserve their rights and their privileges, yea, and also their liberty, that they might worship God according to their desires" (Alma 43:9).

At times, it was necessary for the Nephites to build fortifications around their cities to protect themselves from invading Lamanites, who often greatly outnumbered them. For example, Alma 48:8 reads: "Yea, he [Moroni] had been strengthening the armies of the Nephites, and erecting small forts, or places of resort; throwing up banks of earth around about to enclose his armies, and also building walls of stone to encircle them about, round about their cities and the borders of their lands; yea, all round about the land."

Even after the Lamanites had virtually destroyed the Nephites, wars continued. Mormon, who abridged the records that became the Book of Mormon, recorded, "The Lamanites are at war one with another; and the whole face of the land is one continual round of murder and bloodshed; and no one knoweth the end of the war" (Mormon 8:8).

"Nearly all ancient war was connected with religion and was carried out through a complex series of religious ritual, law, and beliefs," writes William J. Hamblin. "In numerous details the Book of Mormon unintentionally reveals the close ties between war and religion. Activities such as consulting prophets before battle are often mentioned in the Book of Mormon."[2]

Nephite missionaries converted large numbers of Lamanites to Christ during one period of their history (see Alma 25). Many of these Lamanite converts were persecuted and killed by nonbelieving Lamanites, but so great was their conversion and desire not to shed blood that they took an oath to never again take up arms. They buried their weapons of war and refused to defend themselves, willing to suffer death if necessary. The Nephites took compassion on these faithful converted Lamanites and made arrangements for them to relocate in Nephite territory where they were given the land of Jershon, and then Melek for their inheritance (Alma 27:22, 35:13.). These people dwelt there in peace for some time until bitter fighting resumed between the Nephites and the Lamanites. The converted Lamanites wanted to break their oath and help their Nephite brothers, but they were dissuaded by the prophet Helaman.

In the next conflict the converted Lamanites had sons, two thousand young men, who had *not* taken the oath against war. Choosing to fight for the liberty of the Nephites and their own families, they asked Helaman to be their leader. These young men, referred to as "the sons of Helaman," or his two thousand "stripling warriors," engaged in furious fighting, and although many were wounded, none were killed. They emerged victorious because of their great faith: "Now they never had fought, yet they did not fear death; and they did think more upon the liberty of their fathers than they did upon their lives, yea, they had been taught by their mothers, that if they did not doubt, God would deliver them," writes Helaman. "And they rehearsed unto me the words of their mothers, saying: We do not doubt our mothers knew it" (Alma 56:47–48).

On one occasion, when war was raging and some Nephites refused to take up arms, Moroni tore his coat and made a "title of liberty" banner upon which he wrote, "In memory of our God, our religion, and freedom, and our peace, our wives, and our children." He then placed the banner upon a pole and "prayed mightily unto his God for the blessings of liberty to rest upon his brethren" (Alma 46:12–13). Afterwards, Moroni rode throughout the land to gather freedom-loving people to support him and this hallowed cause (Alma 46:19–20). Moroni and the Nephites were eventually victorious.

"Some might feel there is too much about wars in the Book of Mormon," notes Elder Neal A. Maxwell, "but if one gets too concerned about the warfare in the book, great truths can be overlooked. By including the numerous wars in his abridgment of the plates, Mormon was able to teach powerful religious lessons: The value of freedom, God's role in preserving it, the moral justifications for waging war to uphold freedom, and the moral limitations on bloodshed, even for freedom's sake."[3] When the people were righteous, the Lord blessed them, and they prospered. Riches led to pride, then covetousness, and finally to a society dominated by powerful evil combinations, which inevitably led to armed conflict and finally extermination—a theme that is repeated again and again in their history, observes Hugh Nibley.[4] The material in the Book of Mormon was selected with scrupulous care and with particular readers in mind. It was written for our day so we would learn and benefit from the mistakes of the Book of Mormon people.

The Book of Mormon describes three groups who arrived in the New World at different times and covers more than two thousand years of religious history with a central message that Jesus is the Christ. The principal narrative concerns the Nephites and follows them from righteous living to their eventual destruction because of their great wickedness. They ignored the Lord's warning to repent. We can and should learn from their sobering history.

Visions and Prophecies

Visions and prophecies abound in the Book of Mormon. The first two pages of the book recount Lehi's vision of the coming of Christ and the destruction of Jerusalem because of the wickedness of its inhabitants (1 Nephi 1:9, 13). Nephi prophesies concerning the coming of a "Messiah, a Savior of the world"; the crucifixion of Christ six hundred years from the time Lehi and his family left Jerusalem; the great destruction that would take place in the New World at that time; and the dispersion and scattering of the Old World Jews who in the latter days would be "gathered together again . . . [and] come to a knowledge of the true Messiah" (1 Nephi 10:4, 13–14).

Another significant prophecy foretells the Spirit of God coming down upon a man who would go "forth upon the many waters, even unto the seed of my brethren, who were in the promised land" (1 Nephi 13:12). This verse has long been understood by Book of Mormon believers to refer to Christopher Columbus.

Research reveals that "Columbus came increasingly to see himself as a divinely inspired fulfiller of prophecy . . . with the conversion of all races. He came to believe that he was predestined to fulfill a number of prophecies in preparation for the coming of the Anti-Christ and the end of the world. . . . 'God made me the messenger of the new heaven and the new earth. . . . He showed me the spot where to find it.'"[5] This is consistent with Nephi's prophecies in 1 Nephi 13:12. Columbus was writing a book, which he did not complete, called *Book of Prophecies*. In it, he saw himself as the fulfiller of biblical prophecies. Columbus *was* fulfilling prophecy more precisely than even he imagined.[6]

President N. Eldon Tanner affirmed that "the Latter-day Saints believe Columbus was inspired to discover this land in order that a free nation, dedicated to the maintenance and preservation of the rights of man, including his right to worship God according to the dictates of his own conscience, might arise here; a nation founded upon the proposition that all men have equal rights to life, liberty and the pursuit of happiness, and that governments derive their just powers from the consent of the governed."[7]

Book of Mormon prophecies describe North, Central, and South American settlers' battles for freedom against "their mother Gentiles" and their delivery out of captivity "by the power of God" (1 Nephi 13:17–19). Who can doubt that this did happen, resulting in eventual freedom from foreign rule?

Nephi was shown a vision of the Bible being brought to America. He learned why we respect the Bible: "The book that thou beholdest is a record of the Jews, which contains the covenants of the Lord, which he hath made unto the house of Israel; and it also containeth many of the prophecies of the holy prophets." Further, "[the book contains] the covenants of the Lord, which he hath made unto the house of Israel; wherefore, they are of great worth unto the Gentiles" (1 Nephi 13:23).

Doctrine and Exhortation

It would take another complete book to cover the many doctrines and exhortations included in the Book of Mormon; only a few will be discussed in this part of this chapter.

The Atonement

The Atonement of Christ, His supreme accomplishment to set men and women free from the effects of death and sin, making possible a reconciliation of humans and God, is the major focus of the Book of Mormon. It teaches that

"He is Risen"

we must "remember that there is no other way nor means whereby man can be saved, only through the atoning blood of Jesus Christ. . . . Yea, remember that he cometh to redeem the world" (Helaman 5:9). The King James Version of the Bible likewise declares that Christ "gave himself a ransom for all" (1 Timothy 2:5–6).

"Jesus Christ, as the Only Begotten Son of God and the only sinless person to live on this earth, was the only one capable of making an atonement for mankind. . . . The Atonement is conditional, however, so far as each person's individual sins are concerned, and touches everyone to the degree that he has faith in Jesus Christ, repents of his sins, and obeys the gospel."[8]

As Elder Spencer J. Condie points out, "By atoning for our sins as our Father planned, the Savior stands 'betwixt' all of us sinners and the demands of justice, 'having . . . taken upon himself [our] iniquity and [our] transgressions' (Mosiah 15:8–9). An atonement which could satisfy justice required the sacrifice of an innocent person who would vicariously suffer the punishment for the sins of others (see Alma 34:8–16). Justice demanded death, and the Redeemer died that he might become the first fruits of the Resurrection and overcome the bonds of death. Mercy opened the way for the resurrection of all."[9]

The third Article of Faith of The Church of Jesus Christ of Latter-day Saints states: "We believe that through the Atonement of Christ, all mankind may be saved, by obedience to the laws and ordinances of the Gospel."

Baptism Is Essential

That baptism is an ordinance necessary for salvation is repeatedly emphasized in the Book of Mormon. Christ taught the Nephites the importance of baptism: "I bear record that the Father commandeth all men, everywhere, to repent and believe in me. And whoso believeth in me and is baptized, the same shall be saved; and they are they who shall inherit the kingdom of God. And whoso believeth not in me, and is not baptized, shall be damned" (see 3 Nephi 11:32–35). The Savior repeated this same message three times in this discourse to emphasize its importance, and it is stressed in other places in the Book of Mormon—along with the need for the person performing the baptismal ordinance to have proper authority.

Is this compatible with Bible teachings? In the Bible, Christ taught: "He that believeth and is baptized shall be saved; but he that believeth not shall be damned" (Mark:16:16). Jesus felt baptism so important that he set the example, being baptized Himself by the hand of John in the River Jordan (Mark 1:9). Jesus taught that baptism is part of the process of being "born again" (see John 3:3).

Great debates about "grace versus works" divide Christians and splinter churches. The Book of Mormon clearly resolves this doctrine, showing the need for both components. Critics of The Church of Jesus Christ of Latter-day Saints charge that its members believe they are saved by good works, that they can "work" their way to heaven. This judgment is a great fallacy. Latter-day Saints agree with the prophet Jacob in the Book of Mormon: "It is only in and through the grace of God that ye are saved" (2 Nephi 10:24). But they also believe they have some responsibilities. Those who say women and men are "saved by grace only" tend to quote only selected verses in the Bible, such as, "For God so loved the world that he gave his only begotten Son, that whosoever believeth in him should not perish, but have everlasting life" (John 3:16). Bible readers should be certain they don't ignore the *numerous* other scriptures stating that more than mere belief *is* expected of the believer—most notably, good works and righteousness.

Probably the most often cited scripture, erroneously used to eliminate the need for "good works," is found in Ephesians 2:8–9: "For by grace are ye saved through faith and that not of yourselves; it is the gift of God: Not of works, lest any man should boast." However, the next verse puts a different light on "works": "For we are his workmanship, created in Christ Jesus unto *good works* which God hath before ordained that we should walk in them" (Ephesians 2:10).

We are expected to do good works! The Book of Mormon brilliantly declares "for we know that is it by grace that we are saved, after all we can do" (2 Nephi 85:23).

"The day cometh that all shall rise from the dead and stand before God, and be judged according to their works" (Alma 11:41). "For our words will condemn us, yea, all our works will condemn us. . . . And our thoughts will also condemn us" (Alma 12:14). James clearly taught: "What doth it profit . . . though a man say he hath faith and have not works? Can faith save him?" (James 2:14). "Faith, if it hath not works, is dead" (James 2:17.) The devils believe. Are they saved? "Thou believest that there is one God; thou doest well; the devils also believe, and tremble" (James 2:19). Abraham was willing to sacrifice his son because of his faith in God: "Seest thou how faith wrought with his works and by works was faith made perfect. . . . Ye see then how that by works a man is justified and not by faith only" (James 2:21–24).

Is it possible that the Lord gave us the Ten Commandments (Exodus 20:3–17) but did not expect us to *do* anything regarding them? Does the Sermon on the Mount matter (Matthew 5–7)? Why would He bother to teach all these principles, along with "by their fruits ye shall know them," if we weren't expected to do some works to produce the resulting "fruits"? (see Matthew 7:20). Members of the Church of Jesus Christ grasp the fact that Jesus is the vine and that His followers are the ones who should bring forth the good fruit: "He that abideth in me, and I in him, the same bringeth forth much fruit: for without me ye can do nothing" (John 15:5). More teachings in the Bible include Ecclesiastes 12:13–14; Matthew16:27; Matthew 7:21; 1 Peter 1:17; John 14:12, 15; Isaiah 3:10–11; Luke 6:46; and Revelation 20:12. Why are all these scriptures ignored by so many Christian churches? If anyone genuinely believes the scriptures, then the Latter-day Saints are clearly justified in accepting the Book of Mormon teaching that grace and works are both necessary for salvation.

"For millions of us, Christianity has been dumbed down into a bumper-sticker religion," concludes journalist David Kupelian. "Simply by mouthing, one time a single phrase—'I accept Jesus Christ as my savior'—we somehow believe we're guaranteed eternal life in heaven, no matter how insincere or selfish or shallow our motives for doing so, no matter how corrupt and unrepentant a life we live after our 'conversion.'"[10] The Book of Mormon teaches: "And if he [an individual who repents and is baptized] endureth to the end, behold, him will I hold guiltless before my Father at that day when I shall stand to judge the world" (3 Nephi 27:16). C. S. Lewis found that attempting to determine which is the more important, faith or works, is like asking which blade of a pair of scissors is the more important.[11]

Martin Luther expressed his feelings about the importance of good works as follows: "Where there are no good works, there is no faith. If works and love do not blossom forth, it is not genuine faith, the Gospel has not yet gained a foothold, and Christ is not yet rightly known."

The Ministry of Christ in Ancient America

After Christ was crucified and resurrected, He appeared to the Nephites and taught them His doctrine (3 Nephi 9–28). His teachings are found throughout the Book of Mormon. The prophets in the Book of Mormon gave details of Christ's birth and sacred calling. About eighty-three years before Christ's birth, Alma prophesied: "And behold, he shall be born of Mary, at Jerusalem which is the land of our forefathers, she being a virgin, a precious and chosen vessel, who shall be overshadowed and conceive by the power of the Holy Ghost, and bring forth a son, yea, even the Son of God" (Alma 7:10). Christ knew that the Nephites already had the Ten Commandments (contained on the records they brought with them from Jerusalem)—but not the "Sermon on the Mount," which He had given during his mortal ministry to the Jews. Therefore, that sermon, with some variations from the Bible version, is among the teachings He delivered to them (as pointed out in chapter 5).

Jesus Christ "is the same yesterday, and today, and forever," as recorded in 1 Nephi 10:18 and Hebrews 13:8, it follows that His teachings will endure forever. There are no contradictions between the teachings of Christ found in the Book of Mormon and the Bible. Christ's words are elaborated upon, corrected (such as the Sermon on the Mount, 3 Nephi 12:3–12), and clarified in the Book of Mormon. We are doubly blessed.

Chapter 13

You Must Swim against the Prevailing Tide of Worldly Belief

Many of the claims, ideas, principles, and statements pre-sented in your book must be fundamentally inconsistent with many of the prevailing worldly beliefs of your day.

When Thomas Hoving, director of the Metropolitan Museum of Art, New York City, was considering purchasing the Bury St. Edmunds Cross for the museum's collection, he had to determine if the two-foot-high carved ivory cross was genuine before agreeing to the seller's $600,000 price. The cross was inscribed "Jesus of Nazareth, King of the Confessors"—not the usual "King of the Jews." "The cross could not be a fake," he said. "It struck me as though my brain actually shifted within my skull! Fakers want to do what everyone else has done. No forger would have made up the peculiar inscription, 'King of the Confessors.'"[1]

If Joseph Smith had been trying to perpetuate a fraud, he would not have included so many statements and accounts in the Book of Mormon that seemed so implausible at the time of its publication. Many of these claims, which were inconsistent with prevailing opinions in 1830, have since been proven very likely true.

Several miraculous events in the Bible are difficult for the unbeliever to accept: Noah and the ark, the parting of the Red Sea, Jonah and the whale, the Savior's many miracles, and His resurrection. There is little or no tangible evidence to support these events, yet believers accept them on faith. Although true religion will always require faith, a growing body of evidence supports the historicity of the Book of Mormon.

The Savior's Appearance in the Americas

When the Book of Mormon was first published in 1830, its critics imme-diately cried "Fake!" "Fraud!" "Deceiver!" Why? Not only did the book record God's dealings with some of the ancient inhabitants of the Americas—people with ancestry from the Eastern Hemisphere—but it provided an account of Christ's personal visit and teachings among them after His crucifixion and resurrection! "Blasphemy!" cried the Book of Mormon critics. "If these things are true, where is the evidence?"[2]

Scant information regarding Christ's appearance to the Nephites was available when the Book of Mormon was published, but since that time material has been uncovered and many books have been written about the "Indian" legends of North, Central, and South America and their traditions of a "White God" who visited their ancient ancestors and taught them His gospel.[3] These legends are now so well known that even supermarket tabloids blast forth with headlines such as "Jesus Walked in America!"[4]

For more than twenty-four years, antiquarian L. Taylor Hansen researched legends from numerous Native American tribes all over the Americas. Hansen compiled her findings in a book titled *He Walked the Americas*. The book jacket reads, in part: "Almost two thousand years ago a mysterious white man walked from tribe to tribe among the American Nations. . . . Who was this white Prophet who spoke a thousand languages, healed the sick, raised the dead and taught in the same words as Jesus himself?"[5]

In 1541, Francisco Hernandez, who was known as a brilliant and honorable man, arrived in Yucatan, one of the first Catholic priests to reach the Americas. He was of the strong opinion that Christianity was known by the natives many centuries before the coming of the Spaniards. He found they believed in the Father, the Son, and the Holy Ghost and knew of Christ's crucifixion on the cross and that He was dead for three days before His resurrection. Asked how they knew these things, Hernandez was told that the lords (chiefs) taught these things to their children, and the stories were passed down from generation to generation.[6]

"In 1980, an entire Nivacle native tribe of 200 people [in Paraguay] converted to the gospel when [Latter-day Saint] missionaries told them the story of the Savior visiting the Americas. The leader of the tribe recognized the story as one passed down from their ancestors and knew he was hearing restored truths."[7] The Church has continued to grow in all parts of Paraguay since then, and there are now more than 90.000 members and 136 congregations. In 2002, when the Paraguay Asunción Temple was built, there were three missions within the country's borders.[8]

Mariano Fernandez Veytia, who lived in Europe most of his life (1718-1780), traveled to Mexico where he learned to read the native records that were in the form of paintings, charts, monuments, and diagrams. He later wrote a history of Mexico in which he told "of the coming to New Spain of a great teacher of religion whom the natives called Quetzalcoatl. [Veytia] transcribed many of the teachings of Quetzalcoatl, recognizing similarities to his own Christian doctrines and practices."[9] Hernan Cortez conquered the mighty Aztec nation, in part, because they believed he was the White God whom their forefathers had promised would one day return to them.[10] Dr. Joseph Allen finds the tradition of a white god named Quetzalcoatl "is strong and repetitive. Every school child in Mexico studies Quetzalcoatl and knows the importance of his role."[11]

Allen further points out that "in the Aztec language, the word *coatl* means serpent. The word *quetzal* comes from the quetzal bird, which has long, beautiful feathers. By placing the Aztec word *quetzal* in front of the word *coatl*, we have the word *Quetzalcoatl*. Quetzalcoatl, therefore, means 'feathered serpent'—or quetzal bird serpent or serpent with precious feathers."[12] In addition, "the deity Quetzalcoatl apparently had its origin in the visit of Jesus Christ to the American continent." Similarities between Christ and Quetzalcoatl are found in that each "were recognized as creator of all things;" "were born of virgins;" "were described as being white or as wearing a white robe;" "performed miracles;" "taught the ordinance of baptism;" "prophesied of future events;" were associated with a great destruction "at exactly the same time period in history;" were associated with the symbol of the cross; "sent out disciples to preach their word;" "promised they would come a second time;" and are associated with a new star.[13]

Perhaps the most striking commonality between the Savior and Quetzalcoatl is the serpent. Dr. Andrew Skinner has written: "From the beginning the true Messiah was legitimately represented by the image of the serpent, but that symbol was usurped and perverted by the quintessential false messiah, Satan." Among ancient Egyptians, serpent imagery was incontrovertibly associated with the afterlife, resurrection, and eternity. The snake was an apt representation of regeneration and immortality because it sheds its skin every season. The serpent in the Garden of Eden (Genesis 3:1) clearly symbolized evil, as it was in league with the devil except when God told Moses to "make thee a fiery serpent, and set it upon a pole: and it shall come to pass, that everyone that is bitten, when he looketh upon it, shall live" (Numbers 21:4–9.) It became an agent of life and salvation for God's covenant people. Moses lifted up the serpent in the wilderness, and even so was the Savior "lifted up" that "whoever believeth in him should not perish, but have eternal life" (John 3:14–15).[14] Moses' brazen serpent narrative appears frequently in the Book of Mormon (2 Nephi 25: 20, Helaman 8: 14-15), sometimes with avian motifs (1 Nephi 17: 41, 2 Nephi 25: 3).

The Land of Jerusalem

The Book of Mormon twice states that Jesus was to be born at Jerusalem, a fact that critics like to cite as clear evidence that the book is false. Joseph Smith no doubt knew that the Bible reports Jesus's birth in Bethlehem, but the plates from which he was translating read "land of Jerusalem." Therefore, that is how he transcribed it. Bethlehem is in close proximity to metropolitan Jerusalem and was considered to be in the land of Jerusalem, as other documents have since confirmed. In fact, there is "a striking disagreement between the canon and the apocryphal literature" regarding the exact birthplace of Jesus.

The latter sources, which are often very old, place it at a point halfway between Jerusalem and Bethlehem.[15] "[Some say] that the disagreements are so clear, so persistent and so old that the misunderstanding on the subject goes right back to the beginning: for example, some sources favor a cave, others a stall. The only thing that sources agree on is that the birth took place 'in the land of Jerusalem.'"[16] The "city of Jerusalem" is referred to many times in the Book of Mormon and the "land of Jerusalem" several times, with clear distinctions between the two. However, "land of Jerusalem" is not found in the Bible, so Joseph Smith did not get the term from that source. But its usage is accurate for Book of Mormon time.

It has been "documented beyond any doubt that in ancient Israel, the term *land* was often used to indicate the rural area and villages associated with a larger city with the same name. Bethlehem, only five miles from Jerusalem, would certainly fall in its economic sphere as a smaller village at the time Christ was born. Furthermore, scholars have actually found ancient textual references to Bethlehem 'in the land of Jerusalem.'"[17] "No one in modern times would have known for sure (before the 1887 discovery of the Tell El-Amarna Tablets) that Bethlehem was also part of an area anciently called the land of Jerusalem."[18] Thus, what some supposed was an error in the Book of Mormon ends up as one more piece of evidence of its validity.

A Land Choice above All Others

In the Book of Mormon, the Lord often tells the people they "shall be led to a land of promise; yea, even a land which I have prepared for you; yea, a land which is choice above all other lands." He declared this to the Nephites as well as to the Jaredites, and He continued to call it "a land choice above all other lands," even after their arrival in the New World. In 1830, many readers had reason to challenge this statement. Did any place in the western hemisphere qualify as a "choice land" at that point in time? But who could deny the promise in the years that followed? America became one of the most powerful nations in the world, and its inhabitants were blessed with abundance, freedom, and especially religious liberty.

One critic thought he had struck gold when he pointed out that the Book of Mormon tells how Moroni "went forth among the people, waving the *rent part* of his garment in the air, that all might see the writing which he had written upon the *rent part*" (Alma 46:19; emphasis added). The antagonist boasted that no one could write upon the *rent,* for the word implies an absence of cloth. That's true, and it is bad English. However, that verse rendered in the 1830 edition represents perfectly acceptable Hebrew usage. And because the Book of Mormon was written originally by people with ancient Hebrew background (Mormon 9:33), the term *rent part* is actually more evidence for the authenticity of the book.[19]

Salt Lake City

Are eccentric statements a deterrent to a book? Hugh Nibley explains that a flawless document is more suspect than one that has odd, strange, or unusual items in it. "Copyists have a weakness for correcting texts they don't understand, so they write it so they can understand. But if you have one that is full of the weirdest stuff, there you have a real gem, because that stuff came from somewhere."[20]

"Joseph Smith's feat in creating the Book of Mormon, had he done so, would be comparable to an archer's shooting at the broad side of a barn and thinking he had hit it, while referees later discovered that his arrow had hit the center of a small target that he did not even know existed!"[21] These many years later, the "referees" are discovering truths about many facts and claims in the Book of Mormon that were inconsistent with contemporary beliefs when it was first published. Joseph Smith was seemingly unaware of the powerful evidence that would later come forth to support the book. And many more powerful vindications are bound to surface with the passage of time. (Other alleged inconsistencies in the book are discussed in chapters 14, 17, and 19).

Chapter 14

Do the Impossible—
Get the Details Right

Your book will feature authentic modes of travel, a description of clothing, crops, mourning customs, and types of government. You must introduce about 200 new names that will stand the test of time as to their correct geographical, historical, and linguistic derivations.

Those conditions are quite an order! You will need to be well acquainted with those about whom you write. Joseph Smith certainly knew the people of the Book of Mormon, not only from translating the book, but also from heavenly manifestations and tutoring by heavenly messengers sent from God. His mother, Lucy Mack Smith, wrote that "he would describe the ancient inhabitants of this continent, their dress, their manner of traveling, the animals which they rode, the cities that they built, and the structure of their buildings with every particular, their mode of warfare, and their religious worship as specifically as though he had spent his life with them."[1] A great deal about their lifestyle and customs is found in the Book of Mormon.

Modes of Travel

How did Book of Mormon people travel? An account in the book of Alma tells of the great missionary Ammon journeying to the Lamanite city, Ishmael, where he becomes a servant of King Lamoni. After Ammon saves the king's flocks from robbers, he prepares the king's horses and chariots (Alma 18:10). From this, we can deduce that the Lamanites had wheeled transportation. Ancient highways have been found in areas where the Book of Mormon civilizations might have existed.[2] Horses are mentioned nine times in the book and may have been used for travel.

Clothing

The Book of Mormon has many descriptions of clothing. About 421 BC, the Lamanites are described as wearing "a short skin girdle about their loins and their heads shaven" (Enos 1:20). However, about 90 BC, Alma tells a different story regarding Nephite clothing: "And they did not wear costly apparel, yet they were neat and comely" (Alma 1:27). He further notes they had an "abundance of silk and fine-twined linen, and all manner of good homely cloth" (Alma 1:29).

Where did they get their silk and linen? "Although the flax plant was apparently not known in pre-Spanish America, several fabrics were made from vegetable fabrics that look and feel much like European linen. One was made from fibers (called *henequen*) of the leaf of the ixtle (maguey or agave) plant, but fibers from the yucca and other plants produced similar results. Conquistador Bernal Diaz said of *henequen* garments that they were 'like linen.' Silk from cocoons gathered from the wild in Mexico and spun into expensive cloth at the time of the Spanish conquest provides the most literal parallel to Asiatic 'silk.'" Other fabrics with silk-like properties were made from kapok, the pod of the Ceiba, or a fiber from the wild pineapple plant, and even from fine rabbit hair.[3]

A Variety of Grains and Fruits

In the book of Mosiah, Zeniff gives an account of his people during a period from about 200 to 187 BC and mentions their crops: "And we began to till the ground, yea, even with all manner of seeds, with seeds of corn, and of wheat, and of barley, and with neas, and with sheum, and with seeds of all manner of fruits, and we did begin to multiply and prosper in the land" (Mosiah 9:9).

Use of the term *sheum* in the Book of Mormon is itself significant, because the Semitic Akkadian language could not be read (and hence the term *sheum* was not known) until decades after the Book of Mormon was published. In 1973, Robert F. Smith, an authority on ancient Near Eastern languages, observes that *sheum* is "a precise match for Akkadian [she'um], (old Assyrian wheat), the most popular ancient Mesopotamian cereal-name." What is now known about pre–Columbian barley in the Americas should caution readers of the Book of Mormon not to quickly dismiss the reference to pre–Columbian wheat as anachronistic—being placed in the wrong place at the wrong time.[4]

Crops are mentioned in other places in the Book of Mormon. As tribute to the king of the Lamanites, the Nephites were compelled to give "one half of our corn, and our barley, and even all our grain of every kind" (Mosiah 7:22). Barley is one of the most frequently mentioned grains in the Book of Mormon. "The December 1983 issue of *Science 83* reported the discovery in Phoenix, Arizona, by professional archaeologists of what they supposed to be pre–Columbian domesticated barley. . . . This Arizona find is the first direct New World evidence of cultivated pre–Columbian barley in support of the Book of Mormon."[5] Since then, archaeologists have found barley in several states all over North America—Arkansas, Iowa, Illinois, Missouri, North Carolina, Oklahoma, Wisconsin, and New Mexico. It is also now being found in Mexico and the Southwest.[67] Corn "was the most important cultivated plant in ancient times in America," found even "in the high valleys of the Andes in South America."[8]

Mourning Customs

Book of Mormon mourning customs included fasting and prayers. After one of their many wars, in which thousands were killed, Alma writes it "was a time . . . [of] great mourning and lamentation heard throughout all the land, among all the people of Nephi—Yea, the cry of widows mourning for their husbands, and also of fathers mourning for their sons, the daughter for the brother, yea, the brother for the father, and thus the cry of mourning was heard among all of them, mourning for their kindred who had been slain" (Alma 28:4–6).

Following the murder of one of their leaders, "the people did assemble themselves together to mourn and to fast, at the burial of the great chief judge who had been slain" (Helaman 9:10). These mourning customs likely originated with the ancient Hebrews, as 2 Samuel 1:12 describes: "And they mourned and wept, and fasted until even . . ." Alma wrote that those who are willing to take upon them the name of God are "willing to mourn with those that mourn" (Mosiah 18:9).

The mourning practices of the wicked did not include fasting and prayer. Ether 15:16 describes the Jaredites who had become fully ripened in iniquity in their final battle: "After they retired to their camps they took up a howling and a lamentation for the loss of the slain of their people, and so great were their cries, their howlings and lamentations, that they did rend the air exceedingly."

Forms of Government

There were various types of government during the many centuries of Book of Mormon history. The people were ruled by kings, both righteous and wicked, and by judges, again both righteous and wicked.

For five centuries, they "lived under a monarchial form of government. King Mosiah II warned the people regarding the dire consequences of a wicked king, and created a government based on principles of legal equality for citizens. . . . This era of 'democracy' is described in the books of Mosiah, Alma, Helaman, and 3 Nephi." It was a system based on judges, with ultimate authority vested in the people. "For the first time in America, elections were held to select leaders of the people" (Mosiah 29:25).[9] Checks and balances were part of the system: "If your higher judges do not judge righteous judg-ments, ye shall cause that a small number of your lower judges should be gathered together, and they shall judge your higher judges, according to the voice of the people" (Mosiah 29:29).

Some governmental positions bestowed significant power: "Now, Moroni being a man who was appointed by the chief judges and the voice of the people,

King Benjamin confers Priesthood on Mosiah

therefore he had power according to his will with the armies of the Nephites to establish and to exercise authority over them" (Alma 46:34).

Civil law among the Nephites emphasized honesty. "They durst not lie, if it were known, for fear of the law, for liars were punished; [but] . . . the law could have no power on any man for his belief. And they durst not steal, for fear of the law, for such were punished; neither durst they rob, nor murder, for he that murdered was punished unto death" (Alma 1:17–18). "Now there was no law against a man's belief; for it was strictly contrary to the commands of God that there should be a law which should bring men on to unequal grounds" (Alma 30:7). The Nephites had a unique way of rehabilitating offenders. After they had defeated the Gadianton robbers following years of bloody battles, they "did cast their prisoners into prison, and did cause the word of God to be preached unto them; and as many as would repent of their sins and enter into a covenant that they would murder no more were set at liberty" (3 Nephi 5:4).

At one point, shortly before the Savior appeared on the American continent after His resurrection, the people became exceedingly wicked, which resulted in the murder of their chief judge, followed by a collapse of the government. The people broke up into tribes of families and friends, each led by a chief (3 Nephi 7:2-3). "And the regulations of the government were destroyed because of the secret combinations of the friends and kindreds of those who murdered the prophets" (2 Nephi 7:6).

The Nephites were taught to keep the law of Moses until it was fulfilled (Alma 30:3), which happened when Christ appeared to them. They had different laws at various times, and Nephite laws were different from those among the warring Lamanites. Alma's record, which covers the period from approximately 91 BC to 52 BC, states that "there was a law that men should be judged according to their crimes. Nevertheless, there was no law against a man's belief; therefore, a man was punished only for the crimes which he had done; therefore all men were on equal grounds" (Alma 30:11). Individual freedom was the rule, as the record states: "It is against the law of our brethren, which was established by my father, that there should be any slaves among them" (Alma 27:9).

We learn from the different types of sovereignty in the Book of Mormon that some forms of government provide more possibility of spiritual progress and less threat of spiritual regress than others, and "perhaps the riskiest form of government, from a spiritual perspective, is mortal autocracy, or supreme rule by one man over all others."[10]

Many New Names

Perhaps there are some who could coin 188 new proper names, as are found in the Book of Mormon, but would their names be in harmony with the language and writing of the historical setting of that day? "Though most of the names in the Book of Mormon are Lehite-Mulekite (descended from Lehi's colony and the people of Zarahemla/Mulek), a sizeable number are Jaredite [the first inhabitants]. Of the 188 names unique to the Book of Mormon 142 are Lehite-Mulekite, 41 are Jaredite, and 5 are common to both groups."[11]

Among these new names, not one of them starts with the letter "w."[12] And in no instance are the letters "q," "x," or "w" found in an uncorrupted proper name in the translated Nephite records (nor in the Bible). None of these letters occur in any name based on the Hebrew alphabet, and the Nephites, as Israel-ites, would, therefore, have not used any of them.[13] How would Joseph Smith have known this if he were authoring the Book of Mormon?

The name, *Sariah*, Lehi's wife, was previously unknown outside the Book of Mormon, although a version of it appeared as a male name, Seraiah, in the Bible. However, at about the turn of the twentieth century, it was found as a woman's name on a papyrus from Egypt and on a number of seals and bullae (seal-impressions) from Israel dating to Lehi's time.[14] Additionally, the non-biblical name of Sariah's son, *Nephi,* has been attested to the very time and place of the first Book of Mormon figure who bears it.[15] A name with a very unconventional spelling, "*Paanchi*," (double a's), introduced in Helaman (1:3), was found in Egyptian records a generation after the publication of the Book of Mormon and turned out to be a rather prominent and important name.[16]

Hebrew names often have peculiar nonbiblical forms; highly characteristic is the ending "iah" (for example, Amalickiah, Jeremiah, Remaliah, Zechariah, and Zedekiah). Lehi, as a traveling merchant, would have had frequent contacts with Arabs, and his elder sons have good Arab names, Laman and Lemuel. "It was not until 1940 that the name Lehi itself started turning up as a personal name, first in the old Hebrew settlement at Elath."[17]

Since the 1960s, researchers have found fourteen more Book of Mormon names not present in the Bible but which have come to light on arrowheads, seals, and bullae with Hebrew inscriptions. They are Abish, Aha, Ammonihah,

Chemish, Hagoth, Himni, Isabel, Jarom, Josh, Juram, Mathoni, Mathonihah, Muloki and Sam.[18] Most are not the common names with which Joseph Smith would have been familiar.

Chapter 15

Expertly Use Many Literary Devices, Including the Infallible Proof of Chiasmus

You must correctly use figures of speech and other literary devices—chiasmus, simile, metaphor, narration, parable, exposition, description, oratory, and lyric.

"One of the interesting complexities of the original English-language text of the Book of Mormon is that it contains expressions that appear to be uncharacteristic of English in all of its dialects and historical stages," declares Royal Skousen. "These structures also support the notion that Joseph Smith's translation is a literal one and not simply a reflection of either his own dialect or the style of early modern English found in the King James Version of the Bible."[1]

Hebraisms in the Book of Mormon

Nephi described his writing system as combining "the learning of the Jews and the language of the Egyptians" (1 Nephi 1:2). A thousand years later, the last Book of Mormon prophet, Moroni, called it "reformed Egyptian" (see Mormon 9:32–34). Hebrew was the Semitic language of Jerusalem where Lehi and his family lived before their long journey to the New World. Moroni indicated that Nephi knew Hebrew (Mormon 9:32–34); thus, we would expect to find *Hebraisms* in the Book of Mormon—and we do. Some Hebraisms were unfortunately edited out of the 1830 edition by the printer to improve what was considered awkwardness in English, but the book still has many examples that are preserved in the English language translation.[2] For instance, there are a total of eighteen *ands* in one verse in Helaman 3:14. Critics of the Book of Mormon have cited the stylistic awkwardness of the verse, and an English teacher would likely mark down the composition of the sentence. However, when this verse is expressed in Hebrew, it is essential that every one of the *ands* be present—an important element in the construction of that sentence.[3] Here is Helaman 3:14 with every *and* in italics:

> But behold, a hundredth part of the proceedings of this people, yea, the account of the Lamanites *and* of the Nephites, *and* their wars, *and*

contentions, *and* dissensions, *and* their preaching, *and* their prophecies, *and* their shipping *and* their building of ships, *and* their building of temples, *and* of synagogues *and* their sanctuaries, *and* their righteousness, *and* their wickedness, *and* their murders, *and* their robbings, *and* their plundering, *and* all manner of abominations *and* whoredoms, cannot be contained in this work.

Hebrew language forms found in the Book of Mormon include expressions such as *It must needs be, did go, did eat,* and *did smite*—all awkward in English but classic and correct grammar in Semitic languages.

The Book of Mormon often refers to the *stiffneckedness* of the people. English speakers would likely prefer an adjective such as *stubborn* or *inflexible,* but in the Hebrew language, *stiffnecked* is an adjective used to describe an obstinate person.

In Alma 63:11, reference is made to "the son of Helaman, who was called Helaman." It might have been more logical for Joseph Smith *Jr.* to have added a *Jr.* to Helaman the son of Helaman, but there is no word for the English *junior* in Hebrew.

In the Book of Mormon, the numbering system always places an *and* between the numbers, such as "forty *and* six," "two hundred *and* seventy *and* six years," etc.—examples that are precisely correct in Hebrew. The numbers, as in all Hebrew, read from right to left, and readers recite the numbers with an *and* to separate the columns.[4]

Other linguistic evidences of Hebraisms in the Book of Mormon have been noted by scholar John A. Tvedtnes.[5] "In contrast to typical English grammatical structure, Hebrew places the *possessive noun* second, making it necessary to add the preposition *of* before the noun, such as in

"plates *of* brass" (1 Nephi 3:24)

"works *of* righteousness" (Alma 5:16)

"words *of* plainness" ((Jacob 4:14)

"Because Hebrew has fewer adverbs than English, it often uses prepositional phrases with the preposition meaning *in* or *with.*" Examples include

"*with* patience" (Mosiah 24:15)

"*in* righteousness" (1 Nephi 20:1)

"*with* joy" (Jacob 4:3)

"Hebrew uses *conjunctions* much more frequently than does English:

'in all manner of wood, *and of* iron, *and of* copper, *and of* brass, *and of* steel, *and of* gold, *and of* silver, *and of* precious ores'" (2 Nephi: 5:15)

"The city of Laman, *and the city of* Josh, *and the city of* Josh, *and the city of* Gad, *and the city* of Kishkumen, have I caused to be burned with fire. (3 Nephi 9:10)

"In Hebrew a verb is sometimes followed by a cognate, a word that comes from the same root, such as

'I have *dreamed a dream*" (1 Nephi 8:2)

"and he did *judge righteous judgements*" (Mosiah 29:43)

"*taxed* with a *tax*" (Mosiah 7:15)

"Hebrew language often uses *compound prepositions*, made up of a preposition plus a noun, in places where English would normally use just a preposition:

"ye shall be taken *by the hand of* your enemies" (Mosiah 17:18)

"the words which have been spoken *by the mouth of* all the holy prophets" (1 Nephi 3:20)

"*by the mouth of* angels, doth he declare it" (Alma 13:22)

"Both the Bible and the Book of Mormon begin subordinate clauses with prepositions and a word that translates as *that*:

"And *because that* they are redeemed from the fall" (2 Nephi 2:26)

"*because that* my heart is broken" (2 Nephi 4:32)

"*because that* ye shall receive more of my word" (2 Nephi 29:8)

Examples could also be given with *relative clauses, extra positional nouns and pronouns, interchangeable prepositions, naming conventions, and possessive pronouns.* Getting all these Hebraisms correct was an impossibility for the unschooled Joseph Smith without divine help, but he did get them correct,[6] which is strong evidence that he received and translated the Book of Mormon precisely as he claimed.

The Book of Mormon features *colophons*, which are usually synopses used by publishers at the beginning or end of their books. The book "starts out with a colophon telling us whose hand wrote it, what his sources were, and what it is about."[7] Mormon follows Nephi's pattern in his editorial labors. Words of Mormon acts as a colophon as he explains how he selected and edited the records. The book of Alma begins with a *preface* and ends with a *summary* in the last verse. The book of Helaman begins with a lengthy preface, 3 Nephi provides a brief genealogical sketch going back to Lehi, and 4 Nephi begins with a long explanatory title and concludes with words that signal its end. There are other colophons throughout the book. "Considering the way Joseph dictated the book to scribes, for the most part in a matter of weeks, we should realize that he could not himself have come up with this complicated set of prefaces and summaries. . . . It is most unlikely that he could have kept in mind what he had promised in the prefaces and then remembered to close off so many sections neatly with summaries."[8]

A Most Significant Discovery

Chiasmus is a complex, inverted form of parallelism. In 1967, while attending a lecture at a Catholic seminary in Germany, John W. Welch, a young Latter-day Saint missionary, learned about this form of writing found in the New Testament. He was understandably excited when he soon discovered that many writers in the Book of Mormon employed this literary device as well.

Chiasmus was frequently used in the ancient Near East and was highly developed in Hebrew. It is found in the oldest sections of the Hebrew Bible and earlier. Instead of simply saying something twice in direct parallel form (a-b-c/a-b-c), a chiastic text repeats itself the second time in opposite order (a-b-c/c-b-a), same meanings with varying words.

"Although knowledge of this literary form lay dormant for centuries, it was rediscovered in the Bible in the nineteenth century. . . . By the time the concept of chiasmus received recognition, or was re-detected, the Book of Mormon had long been in print," and Joseph Smith had been dead for ten years. The possibility of Joseph noticing this form of writing accidentally is very remote, and even if he had, the challenge of writing original, artistic chiastic sentences would have been overwhelming.[9]

Chiasmus is found in lengthy Book of Mormon passages. For example, all of Alma 36 is in chiastic format. Other times, it is found in a few verses or even in one verse. A short example is found in Mosiah 3:18–19:

A. But men drink damnation to their own souls except they *humble* themselves

    B. and become as little *children,*

        C. and believe that salvation . . . is in and through the *atoning blood of Christ, the Lord*

            D. For the *natural man*

                E. is an enemy to *God,*

                    F. and *has been* from the fall of Adam,

                    F. and *will be,* forever and ever,

                E. unless he yields to the enticings of the *Holy Spirit*

            D. and putteth off the *natural man*

        C. and becometh a saint through the *atonement of Christ the Lord,*

    B. and becometh as a *child,*

A. submissive, meek, *humble*

According to scholar H. Clay Gorton, "The entire book of First Nephi is a chiastic masterpiece with layer upon layer of chiastic structure within it. In the literal category, 165 chiastic elements are in the first half of the book and

165 corresponding words or phrases lead away from the central element in identical reverse order. The central theme of the literal chiasm is the 'coming to the Lamb of God.'" Gorton found that 961 chiasms have been identified in the Book of Mormon, 53 percent of the verses are chiastic, and thirty-three different authors in the Book of Mormon used chiasms.[10]

Other Literary Features

Other examples further illustrate the high degree of literary skill that would be necessary to produce the Book of Mormon:

Similes, which express a comparison of two different things or ideas:

"A tree springing up unto everlasting life" (Alma 32:41)

'They who do wickedly shall be as stubble to be burned." (1 Nephi 22:15)

"even as a goat fleeth with her young from two lions." (Alma 14:29)

Metaphors are figures of speech in which a word or phrase that ordinarily means one thing is used as another thing to suggest a likeness between the two:

"Fountain of all righteousness." (Ether 12:28)

"They were stiff necks and high heads." (2 Nephi 28:14)

"Puffed up in the pride of their hearts." (2 Nephi 28:15)

Narration is a form of composition that tells an event or a story. The Book of Mormon is filled with informative and exciting narratives. Here are brief summaries of two:

Nephi with his broken bow

1 Nephi 16, tells of Nephi breaking his bow and thus being unable to obtain food for his family, dealing with the conflict that arose as a result, making a bow of wood and asking for guidance from the Lord about where to go to find beasts to hunt, receiving an answer through the Liahona in which he was led to the top of a mountain where he was successful in obtaining meat that saved his father's family from starvation, and, finally, the group continuing on their journey.

Alma 55 tells the suspenseful story of Moroni refusing to exchange prisoners with the Lamanite leader, Ammoron; outwitting Ammoron by smuggling weapons to the Nephite people who were prisoners in the city of Gid, then surrounding the city and taking possession of it.

Exposition is speech or writing that explains a process, thing, or idea. Alma's comparison of the word to a seed is a good example of this type of writing:

> Now, we will compare the word unto a seed. Now, if ye give place, that a seed may be planted in your heart, behold, if it be a true seed, or a good seed, if ye do not cast it out by your unbelief, that ye will resist the Spirit of the Lord, behold, it will begin to swell within your breast; and when you feel these swelling motions, ye will begin to say within yourselves—It must needs be that this is a good seed, or that the word is good, for it beginneth to enlarge my soul; yea, it beginneth to enlighten my understanding, yea, it beginneth to be delicious to me. (Alma 32:28).

Description is common in the Book of Mormon. This is how Nephi describes the events that took place in the New World immediately following Christ's crucifixion:

> There arose a great storm, such an one as never had been known in all the land. And there was also a great and terrible tempest; and there was terrible thunder, insomuch that it did shake the whole earth as if it was about to divide asunder. And there were exceedingly sharp lightnings, such as never had been known in all the land. . . . And many great and notable cities were sunk and many were burned and many were shaken till the buildings thereof had fallen to the earth and the inhabitants thereof were slain, and the places were left desolate . . . there was thick darkness upon all the face of the land . . . the inhabitants . . . could feel the vapor of darkness . . . and it lasted for the space of three days. (3 Nephi 8:5–7, 20, 23).

Oration is skilled public speaking, as in Mosiah 1–5 when King Benjamin gave an eloquent farewell address to his people. Among other things, he counseled them to serve God, foretold the fate of the wicked, taught about salvation through the Atonement, and explained the necessity of good works. Here is an excerpt from the speech:

> Believe in God; believe that he is, and that he created all things, both in heaven and in earth; believe that he has all wisdom, and all power, both in heaven and in earth; believe that man doth not comprehend all the things which the Lord can comprehend. And, believe that ye must repent of your sins and forsake them, and humble yourselves before God and ask in sincerity of heart that he would forgive you; and now, if you believe all these things see that ye do them (Mosiah 4:9–10).

Biblical scholars have identified twenty distinguishing elements of farewell speeches of ancient religious and political leaders that are consistent in these addresses. Benjamin's speech contains more of these elements than most fare-well addresses, validating it as a traditional Israelite farewell sermon.[11]

Lyric or *poetry* in general is verse artfully expressing the author's per-sonal emotions or sentiments. There are numerous beautiful poetic passages throughout the Book of Mormon, although they are often unrecognized as poetry because they appear as prose in the book. Short poems include:

Nephi's heartfelt words:

Adam fell
That men might be;
And men are,
That they might have joy. (2 Nephi 2:25)

Nephi's testimony of Christ:

I glory in plainness
I glory in truth;
I glory in my Jesus,
For he hath redeemed my soul from hell. (2 Nephi 33:6)

And Abinidi's testimony:

He is the light and the life of the world;
Yea, a light that is endless,
That can never be darkened;
Yea, and also a life which is endless,
That there can be no more death. (Mosiah 16:9)[12]

One of the most impressive types of Hebrew poetry is called *parallelism*. The Book of Mormon contains about a dozen different styles of parallelism. *Poetic parallelisms* are words, phrases, or sentences that correspond, compare, contrast, or repeat. For example, in a simple *synonymous parallelism*, the second phrase repeats or echoes the idea of the first, as in Mosiah 16:10:

Even this mortal shall put on immortality,

and this corruption shall put on incorruption.

An antithetical parallelism, giving opposite aspects of the same idea, is found in Alma 5:40:

Whatsoever is good cometh from God,

and whatsoever is evil cometh from the devil.

Other forms of parallelism are much longer and more complex. "Only the Book of Mormon prophets, who used the structural forms of ancient Hebrew poetry and who were inspired from on high, could have written such beautiful poetic structures," writes Professor Donald W. Parry.[13]

Hyperbole exaggerates language for emphasis. An example of this writing style is found in Alma 29:1: "O that I were an angel and could have the wish of mine heart, that I might go forth and speak with the trump of God, with a voice to shake the earth, and cry repentance unto every people!"[14]

Parables are most often short stories used to teach a truth or moral lesson. One exception is the long and detailed "allegory of the tame and wild olive trees" found in Jacob 5. Recognized as "one of the greatest parables ever recorded. It records the history of Israel down through the ages, the scattering of the tribes to all parts of the earth, their mingling with, or being grafted in, the wild olive trees, or in other words the mixing of the blood of Israel among the Gentiles by which the great blessings and promises of the Lord to Abraham are fulfilled. No mortal man, without the inspiration of the Lord, could have written such a parable."[15]

It is significant that Joseph Smith had never seen an olive tree. The first publication in English on olive tree cultivation and horticulture appeared in 1852. Yet the Book of Mormon, published in 1830, correctly describes the cultivation, grafting, dunging, and pruning of olive trees. Additionally, the allegory correctly refers to olives in a *vineyard* instead of an orchard. *Vineyard* is a term used in the Near East to designate an orchard of olive or fig trees or grapes.[16]

Another figure of speech in the Book of Mormon is known as *antenantiosis,* the practice of stating a proposition in terms of its opposite. For instance, this happens when Jacob counsels to "despise not the revelations of God" (Jacob 4:8), and it occurs in the promise, "if ye do this, and endure to the end, ye will in nowise be cast out" (Mormon 9:29). This form is found in several places in the Book of Mormon as well as in the Bible; and it helps make prophetic messages more forceful.[17]

A literary device known as *epanalepsis* is another feature of the Book of Mormon. "It occurs where an author repeats certain words in the course of a lengthy sentence, to pick up a previous train of thought after a parenthetical aside, to remind the reader of the original idea of the sentence. A good illustration is in Alma 3:1: "And it came to pass that the Nephites who were not slain by the weapons of war, *after having buried those who had been slain*—now the number of the slain were not numbered, because of the greatness of their number—*after they had finished burying their dead* they all returned to their lands, and to their houses, and their wives, and their children.' Some authors in the Book of Mormon use the device more frequently than others. Mormon uses it forty-nine times, whereas Nephi uses it only seven. Eighty-four occurrences have been identified [in the Book of Mormon]."[18]

It is impossible that Joseph Smith could have known all these language complexities.

Chapter 16

Your Book Must Withstand Unceasing Attacks until the End of the World

Your book must withstand many decades of examination by the ablest of scholars and unrelenting attacks by its severest of critics, those most eager to prove it a forgery, and those most competent to expose its every potential flaw.

"From the day [the Book of Mormon] appeared, important persons, at the urgent demand of an impatient public, did everything they could to show it a forgery," wrote Hugh Nibley. "And Joseph Smith, far from keeping it out of the hands of unsympathetic critics, did everything he could to put it into those hands."[1] Notwithstanding the long odds against success, any astute forger would likely agree with German scholar Friedrich W. Blass, who noted: "There is no such thing as a clever forgery. No forger can escape detection if somebody really wants to expose him." If a person were attempting such a deception, the advice would be to "keep your document as short as possible. The longer a forgery is the more easily it may be exposed, the danger increasing geometrically with the length of the writing."[2]

But the Book of Mormon is a long, complex work. Hugh Nibley adds:

It is a surprisingly big book, supplying quite enough rope for a char-latan to hang himself a hundred times. As the work of an imposter it must unavoidably bear all the marks of fraud. It should be poorly organized, shallow, artificial, patchy, and unoriginal. It should display a pretentious vocabulary (the Book of Mormon uses only 3,000 words), overdrawn stock characters, melodramatic situations, gaudy and over-done descriptions, and bombastic diction. . . . Whether one believes its story or not, the severest critic of the Book of Mormon, if he reads it with care at all, must admit that it is the exact opposite. . . . It is carefully organized, specific, sober, factual, and perfectly consistent.[3]

The Prophet knew his translation was not a forgery that would soon be exposed and forgotten. However, the book's publication galvanized intense opposition and persecution against Joseph and the fledgling church he founded, without bringing him monetary reward. Clearly money was not his motive.

The Meyer Paradox

Eduard Meyer, considered the preeminent 19th century scholar of ancient civilization, is a textbook example of the way the learned world normally treats the Book of Mormon. Commenting on Meyer, the classical scholar Werner Jaeger, observed "that the only time the lectures of the immortal . . . Meyer were really interesting and the only time he was ever able to fill his lecture hall at the University of Berlin was when he talked about the [Latter-day Saints]." Meyer, who moved from Germany to Utah for a year to study the Church, believed that Joseph Smith and the system he founded provided a clear window to understand the founding of Islam and its prophet:

> Among the religious innovations of our time, [this new faith] excited my interest at an early age, before all else because . . . here one might hope to discover significant clues for a proper understanding of Mohammed and his religion. . . . [Its] uniqueness . . . is . . . that it is NOT just another of countless sects, but a new revealed religion. . . . We can study its origin and history from an exceptionally rich contemporary store of documents both by its members and their enemies. . . . What in the study of other revealed religions can only be surmised after painful research is here directly accessible in reliable witnesses. Hence, the origin and history of [the restored Church] possesses great and unusual value for the student of religious history.[4]

Meyers sees in the Book of Mormon "nothing but religion; remove the religious parts of it and the whole book collapses. The very skeleton of the narrative is full of religious tendencies and associations . . . In other words: if we remove from it what certainly comes from Joseph Smith, as good as nothing remains."[5] And yet, despite his esteem for the religion's "great and unusual value" in the study of religious history, Meyer all but ignores the Book of Mormon with a "remarkably superficial and disappointing" dismissal of the text, admitting he had "not been able to read the complete Book of Mormon."[6] Meyer leads a long line of non-Latter-day Saint scholars, who upon cursory examination of the book, declare it unworthy of study, since, as Meyer explains in excusing himself, "no human except a believer could find the strength to read the whole thing."[7]

Meyer's summary rejection of the book is typical of the incredulity most scholars show when they refuse to engage with the Book of Mormon. As soon as a serious examination of the text is undertaken the reluctant detective begins to find a complexity and depth which can only be accounted for by Joseph Smith's story. At this point, the sophisticated move is to disengage, since the wary scholar already knows enough to suspect where more digging will lead, so he denounces the book as dull, unliterary, dogmatic, etc. Thus marginalized, the book can safely be given the silent treatment, denigrated, and ignored forevermore. "Antagonists of the Book of Mormon," wrote Dr. Richard Cracroft, "have always considered the book fair game for easy cheap shots, slurs, and slipshod generalizations—most of which reveal . . . a basic ignorance of the book's origins and contents. Indeed, historian Thomas O'Dea correctly asserts that 'the Book of Mormon has not been universally considered by its critics as one of those books that must be read in order to have an opinion of it.'"[8]

Early Opposition to the Book

In January 1831, Abner Cole was the first antagonistic writer "to characterize the Book of Mormon for the public in the first few months after publication" by portraying the book "scornfully and humorously," in an attempt to blunt the growth of the new Church in Ohio.[9]

> Cole undertook to discredit Joseph Smith and his book in a six-part "Gold Bible" newspaper series, written under the pseudonym of Dogberry. Rejecting Joseph Smith's attribution of authorship and editorship of the Book to Mormon, Cole proclaimed the book a fraud, launched ad hominem attacks on Joseph and the Smith family, and suggested that Smith's whole design was to make money. Cole became the first to assert in print the short-lived theory that Joseph Smith was the book's author and that he had lifted its contents "almost entirely . . . from the Bible," its stories being "chiefly garbled from the Old and New Testaments.[10] . . . . Although others voiced their criticism in letters, sermons, and newspaper articles,[11] it was Abner Cole, asserts Terryl L. Givens, who "did as much to inflame and shape public reaction to the Book of Mormon as any (hostile) person of his generation.[12]

Soon thereafter, others began to write in opposition to the book. Alexander Campbell, an influential theologian and founder of the Disciples of Christ was losing followers to the new movement, including Sidney Rigdon. In February 1831, Campbell responded by publishing the first significant commentary on the Book of Mormon in his newspaper, the *Millennial Harbinger*.[13] Campbell described Joseph Smith, "as ignorant and as impudent a knave as ever wrote a book," and said was the book's sole author 'as certainly . . . as Satan is the father of lies.'"[14] However, Cracroft adds, Campbell's

> most significant—and enduring—contribution to future Book of Mormon criticism . . . is the "environmental" theory: that Joseph Smith introduced 19th-century elements into his story, incorporating "every error and almost every truth discussed in N. York for the last ten years."[15] By 1844, the year of Joseph Smith's death, however, Campbell had changed his mind about Smith's sole authorship of the book—the

claim simply had not stood up—and accepted the Spalding-Rigdon hypothesis for the book's authorship, despite the contradiction of his earlier arguments that the hypothesis raised.[16]

Eber D. Howe might qualify as the "most dedicated early critic" of the Book of Mormon. In 1833 Howe collaborated with Philastus Hurlbut, an excommunicated former member, to promote the idea, "in *Mormonism Unvailed*, that Solomon Spalding's unpublished novel manuscript had been acquired and religionized by Sidney Rigdon as the Book of Mormon and that Rigdon was the Iago, the prime mover of the whole conspiracy."[17] The Spalding-Rigdon hypothesis never gained acceptance in Palmyra, but nevertheless, "remained the standard explanation of non-Latter-day Saint critics well into the twentieth century," until Woodbridge Riley, a non-Latter-day Saint, published a refutation of the Spalding-Rigdon hypothesis in *The Founder of Mormonism: A Psychological Study of Joseph Smith, Jr. (1902)."*[18]

The most effective 19th century critic of the Book of Mormon is easily its most famous:

> Unquestionably . . . it is Mark Twain's treatment of [the Church] and the Book of Mormon in his best-selling travel narrative, *Roughing It* (1872), that has become the most important single factor in forging the popular perception of the book of Mark Twain's dismissive treatment of the Book of Mormon helped forge lasting popular misconceptions of the Book of Mormon in the 19th century—or, for that matter, the 20th century. *Roughing It*, which also sold well in Great Britain and Germany, provided the literate world with its first popular critique of the book and, unfortunately for the book's reputation, remains the best-known and most widely cited non-[Latter-day Saint] treatment of the Book of Mormon.[19]

Twain concludes his enormously influential treatment of the Book of Mormon patronizingly and damningly: "The Mormon Bible is rather stupid and tiresome to read, but there is nothing vicious in its teachings. Its code of morals is unobjectionable—it is "smouched" from the New Testament and no credit given."[20] . . . . Uneven and stumbling as it is, Mark Twain's comic handling of the [subject] has given generations of readers an authoritative reason to slight the Book of Mormon, dismiss its claims, and ignore its message.[21]

Fawn Brodie, Archetypal Antagonist

When Fawn Brodie's *No Man Knows My History—The Life of Joseph Smith* was first published in 1945, it was celebrated as the definitive work on the life of the Prophet and is still considered authoritative today by some who don't bother to check the author's footnotes. The first paragraph of a later edition is the Preface to Hugh Nibley's 1946 reply to Brodie, *No Ma'am That's Not History*, a short book he calls "a review," provides a revealing glimpse into Brodie's method:

> When the writer first read Mrs. Brodie's book . . . he was struck by the brazen inconsistencies that swarm in its pages, and so wrote this hasty review. At that time he had no means of knowing that inconsistency was the least of the author's vices, and assumed with other reviewers that when she cited a work in her footnotes, she had actually read it, that when she quoted she was quoting correctly, and that she was familiar with the works in her bibliography. Only when other investigations led the reviewer to the same sources in ensuing years did the extent of Mrs. Brodie's irresponsibility become apparent. While a large book could (and probably should) be devoted to this remarkable monument of biographical mendacity, more than a decade of research abetted by correspondence with Mrs. Brodie's defenders has failed to discredit a single observation made in our 1946 review. [22]

Nibley later made the following comment regarding the staying power of not only *No Man Knows My History*, but also of many other older and equally flawed antagonistic works:

> When friends and enemies protest that the charges against Joseph Smith [and the Book of Mormon] are brought by witnesses so obviously prejudiced and unprincipled that only a[n] . . . idiot would make an issue of their accusations, it is the writer's painful duty to point out that those accusations are to this day the soul and substance of a large and flourishing school of [adversarial] literature, most of it going under the banner of serious scholarship. [23]

A New Day for Book of Mormon Scholarship

John W. Welch, the first person to find chiasmus in the Book of Mormon (see Chapter 15), speaking in August 2017 at the 50th anniversary commemorating his discovery, noted how little was known in a scholarly sense about the book in 1967, and how much progress has been made since that time. This growth can be measured not only in the quantity and quality of research and publication by Latter-day Saint scholars, but also in the work of non-Latter-day Saint scholars who have found the Book of Mormon to be an authentic ancient text worthy of examination.

Regarding the increased attention the Book of Mormon has received from non-Latter-day Saint scholars in recent years, Stephen O. Smoot's review of John Christopher Thomas's *A Pentecostal Reads the Book of Mormon: A Literary and Theological Introduction* provides a good illustration of the kind of focus on the book (Eduard Meyer's precedent not withstanding) that "is entirely welcomed by the Latter-day Saints, especially when such attention comes from a place of fairness and open-mindedness." Smoot praises the volume as an "example of how non-Latter-day Saint academics can fruitfully engage the Book of Mormon" and as

> a good faith attempt to open an ecumenical conversation on the religious traditions of Pentecostals and Latter-day Saints. It is free from the acrimony, spitefulness, and dishonesty that can often be seen in the shabby literature of Christian [antagonists]. For this Thomas is to be immediately commended. Unlike many of his predecessors who have provided commentary on [the restored gospel], Thomas performs actual scholarship, including a close and fair reading of the Book of Mormon. It is refreshing to have a non-[Latter-day Saint] engage the Book of Mormon in such a manner and an encouraging sign that the academic discourse surrounding the Nephite record is improving. [24]

An incident recounted by Latter-day Saint scholar John A. Tvedtness, though anecdotal, is significant:

> A little-known critic of the . . . Church wrote a series of inflammatory letters designed to elicit negative comments about the Book of Abraham from prominent Near Eastern scholars. In his response, William F. Albright of Johns Hopkins University expressed doubts that Joseph Smith could have learned Egyptian from any early nineteenth century sources. Explaining that he was a Protestant and hence not a believer in the Book of Mormon, he observed, "It is all the more surprising that there are two Egyptian names, Paanch [Paanchi] and Pahor(an) which appear in the Book of Mormon in close connection with a reference to the original language being 'Reformed Egyptian.'" Puzzled at the existence of such names in a book published by Joseph Smith in 1830, Albright vaguely suggested that the young Latter-day Saint leader was some kind of 'religious genius' and defended the honesty of Joseph Smith and the good name of the Church of Jesus Christ of Latter-day Saints.[25]

Margaret Barker, a Methodist preacher and Bible scholar, has devoted her life to research about ancient Judaism and Christianity. Barker's approach to biblical studies is known as *Temple Theology*. Her writings resonate with Latter-day Saint scholars and with many Church members in her approach to the temple as the center of ancient religious life. On the occasion of the publication of one of Barker's books *(Temple Themes in Christian Worship)*, John W. Welch spoke of her work:

> I am optimistic that Margaret's insights will become widely acceptable, precisely because they make such good sense of the world that Jesus knew and thereby breathe life into our worship of him. Jesus's world

Manti Utah Temple

was a world in which temples were pervasive, dominant, identity-forming and community-shaping institutions. We haven't understood well enough that temples were of the essence in all ancient religions. . . . In historical Jesus studies, more attention now needs to be given to Jesus and the Temple, for it dominated every landscape in Jerusalem in Jesus's day. Whenever we see Jesus in Jerusalem, we see him in or in the vicinity of the Temple. Too rarely have we noticed how many of his teachings, conversations, and actions are reported in a temple setting. By my count, some 12% of the words in all 4 gospels are set in the Temple or its confines. After Margaret's work, everything in the New Testament [and the Book of Mormon] needs to be reconsidered in terms of temple themes.[26]

Additionally, so called "Mormon" studies programs are now providing inspiration and insight for a new generation of rising scholars through a broad array of Book of Mormon and related courses. Outside of the three BYU campuses—Provo, Idaho, and Hawaii—these university sponsored academic programs are found on campuses across the U.S., ranging from Claremont and USC in California, through Eastern universities such as Harvard, Columbia, North Carolina, and Virginia, and the Intermountain West, including Utah State University, Utah Valley University and the University of Wyoming.

A Genetic Engineer Applies His Research Skills

Dr. Mario Ottaviano, a noted Italian researcher in biophysical genetic engineering, is one who undertook an intense months-long examination of the book. As a confirmed atheist and Marxist, Mario would not allow his three children to attend religion classes in their Rome, Italy, school. This led to taunting by schoolmates, which led to tears from his children. Under this pressure, he decided to find a church for his children. Because he was of Jewish descent, the organization could not be anti–Jewish. Mario reviewed all the churches in a catalog produced by the Vatican but found no church that seemed to pass his test of logic—he found them to be basically churches established by men rather than by God.

Dr. Ottaviano discovered a reference to the Book of Mormon and The Church of Jesus Christ of Latter-day Saints in a small book he owned, and he acquired literature about the Church from a professor friend. The things he read made sense to him, influencing him to locate a local Latter-day Saint meeting house, which he and his young son visited the next Sunday. He met the missionaries and arranged for them to teach his daughters who were old enough to join the Church, emphasizing that he and his wife, who likewise was unbelieving, were not interested.

The doctor, feeling the missionaries were not on his intellectual and educational level, initially stayed away from the discussions with the children at his home. He did agree to meet with their mission president, Dwight B. Williams, which did not happen until he attended his two daughters' baptisms. Later, the two had many doctrinal discussions. In the meantime, Dr. Ottaviano began reading the Book of Mormon and became so earnest in his investigation that he quit his job so he could spend full time studying. The family lived on his savings and his wife's salary. For months, he subjected the book to various tests he considered empirical and took detailed notes designed to check the book's internal consistency. The book passed all the tests.

Mario took small sections of the book to learned friends, rabbis, or scientists familiar with ancient texts and asked them what they thought. They assured him the texts were authentic and asked from what ancient source they came. He refused to tell them, fearing they would scoff at him. He finally realized he knew it was the word of God when he was pained to see a sister missionary slam the book down on the table in disgust at his hard-headedness. He was baptized on March 18, 1987. His wife was baptized two months later, followed by their young son when he reached the age of eight. Dr. Ottaviano's examination of the Book of Mormon yielded an unexpected outcome. He concluded it was appropriate that the Church was not listed in the catalog of religions he first studied. He determined the restored gospel was "not a religion in the same sense as those churches founded by men, we are the true faith. As such, the church does not need to be classified with the religions of the world. It stands alone."[27]

The Book Invites Ongoing Scrutiny

Scholar and Church leader B. H. Roberts declared: "The Book of Mormon of necessity must submit to every test, to literary criticism, as well as to every other class of criticism; for our age is above all things critical, and especially critical of sacred literature, and we may not hope that the Book of Mormon will escape closest scrutiny; neither, indeed is it desirable that it should escape."[28] Still, no one, no matter how intense the effort, has successfully proven it a forgery. "Those that wish to contend that [the restored gospel] is merely a rather haphazard pastiche of American Frontier nostrums, a bit of folk magic, and a few half-understood chunks of popular theology . . . face an increasingly difficult task," writes Daniel C. Peterson.[29] The book continues to be examined by scholars, investigators, and critics alike—the sincere, the merely curious, and those attempting to disprove it—and this will doubtless continue until the end of the world.

Chapter 17

Over Time, the Evidence
for the Book Will
Grow Ever Stronger

In the decades following its publication, scientific investigation, historical evidence, and archaeological discovery will support detail after detail of your book's claims.

A little-known episode in the life of the Prophet Joseph Smith reveals his deep concern that people would not believe his account of how he received the gold plates from which he translated the Book of Mormon. With this burden upon him, the Prophet knelt before the Lord in prayer: "O God, what will the world say?" The Lord answered in these words: "Fear not, I will cause the earth to testify of the truth of these things." The fulfilment of this promise began during Joseph's lifetime and continues to the present day. "We see the Lord's promise being fulfilled almost daily. Ongoing scholarly studies of the Book of Mormon continue to reveal the book's consistencies and bear witness of its veracity."[1]

One of the purposes of *The Challenge the Book of Mormon Makes to the World* is to present evidence that the unschooled Joseph Smith could not have produced such an accurate account of the physical world of the Nephites as that found in the Book of Mormon. The book mentions various metals, cement buildings, highways, a weapon of war known as the cimeter, and horses, as well as elephants (in earlier Jaredite times), all of which drew early criticism because 19th century science had not yet discovered these things in ancient America. However, as ongoing archeological work has corroborated the existence of these items, naysayers now have a considerably more difficult challenge to overcome.

Doctrine More Important than Geography

The Church of Jesus Christ of Latter-day Saints has taken no official position on where the events in the Book of Mormon occurred. Nevertheless, there are many theories about the location of Book of Mormon lands. The Lord promised Lehi, his family, and the others who fled Jerusalem with them that they would be led to a "land which is choice above all other lands" (1 Nephi 2:20). However, a precise knowledge of the location of the events in the Book of Mormon is not essential to a testimony of the book. President Gordon B. Hinckley counseled:

> The evidence for the truth, for its validity in a world that is prone to demand evidence, lies not in archaeology or anthropology analysis, though these may be confirmatory. The evidence for its truth and validity lies within the covers of the book itself. The test of the truth lies in reading it. It is a book of God. Reasonable men may sincerely question its origins, but those who have read it prayerfully have come to know by a power beyond their natural senses that it is true, that it contains the word of God, that it outlines saving truths of the everlasting gospel, that it came forth by the "gift and power of God to the convincing of the Jew and Gentile that Jesus is the Christ."[2]

The words of this prophet make it clear that the Lord wants faith to be the foundation of our testimonies of the Book of Mormon. Great truths are found within the book, including the doctrines of salvation, the rewards and consequence of our choices, the appearance of Christ and His teachings to the people in the Americas after His crucifixion and resurrection. Prophecies regarding America's essential role in the unfolding spread of the gospel to the world all testify that the book is a true, miraculous gift from God.

Many Peoples and Languages in Ancient America

Archaeologists, the scientists who recover and study material evidence from past human life and culture by examining the graves, buildings, monuments, tools, pottery, and other remains of ancient civilizations, have studied various locations where it is feasible that the events in the Book of Mormon could have occurred. As the methods and tools of archaeology improved, items have been unearthed from periods before, during, and after Book of Mormon time at various places throughout the Americas. This chapter examines some of the evidences found throughout North, Central and South America.

When Lehi and his group arrived in the New World in approximately 587 BC, it had already been inhabited for thousands of years.[3] Archaeology, linguistics, and related areas of study have established beyond doubt that a variety of peoples inhabited virtually every place in the Western Hemisphere for many centuries—with the possible exception of limited regions that may have been lightly populated for a few generations at certain times. "The presence of almost 1,500 different languages belonging to dozens of major groupings which were found in the Americas when the Europeans arrived can be explained only by supposing that speakers of the ancestral tongues had been in America for thousands of years. The notion that the 'Indians' constituted a single ethnic entity is a totally outdated conclusion which neither scholars nor lay people can justifiably believe nowadays."[4]

"All Manner of Ore"

The Book of Ether, (next to the last book in the Book of Mormon) tells of various metals used by the Jaredites, the earliest Book of Mormon civilization. "And they did work in all manner of ore, and they did make gold, and silver, and iron, and brass, and all manner of metals; and they did dig it out of the earth; wherefore they did cast up mighty heaps of earth to get ore, of gold, and of silver, and of iron, and of copper. And they did work all manner of fine work" (Ether 10:23).

Some believe that people populating the ancient Americas were ignorant savages with no knowledge of metallurgy, weaponry or other advanced items, but archaeological evidence proves otherwise. The ancients had these skills not only in Ether's time but also centuries later when Lehi and his party arrived in the "promised land." Nephi wrote of teaching his "people to work in all manner of wood, and of iron, and of copper, and of brass, and of steel, and of gold, and of silver, and of precious ores, which were in great abundance" (2 Nephi 5:15). Nephi "did take the sword of Laban, and after the manner of it did make many swords" (2 Nephi 5:14).

More than two hundred years later, these metals are again mentioned in the record: "And we ... became exceedingly rich in gold, and in silver, and in precious things, and in fine workmanship of wood, in buildings, and in machinery, and also in iron and copper, and brass and steel, making all manner of tools of every kind to till the ground, and weapons of war—yea, the sharp pointed arrow, and the quiver, and the dart, and the javelin, and all preparations for war" (Jarom 1:8).

The relatively recent discovery of a steel sword near the modern city of Jericho provides evidence that the Jews of Lehi's time were capable of producing steel. The meter-long sword (made of tempered, carburized iron—a primitive form of steel) dates to the late seventh century BC and possibly to the reign of King Josiah, whose reign ended eleven years before Lehi and his family fled Jerusalem.[5] This discovery indicates that Nephi could have known something about steel making even before the family's migration to the New World.

Where are some of the places that metals have been found in the Americas? Archaeological and metallurgical investigations have verified that these metals were present at various locations in the New World, including hundreds of metal artifacts found at dozens of sites throughout Mesoamerica. These discoveries date to at least 100 BC. (As noted previously, the Book of Mormon covers a period from 600 BC to AD 421, excluding the earlier Jaredites.) In addition, works of art—human figures carved on stone or in ceramic—portray what are quite surely metal objects. These artifacts date to as early as 300 BC.[6] Many metallic minerals have also been found in the Eastern United States.

"Significant commercial mining of gold, silver and copper has taken place at the historic San Juan mine in Baja California and at a mining complex called

El Arco." Ancient metal instruments found in the area are on display in the La Paz Museum in Baja California.[7] "Rich ore deposits of the Andes are also legendary. They include the great silver mines of Potosi, Bolivia, the vast copper deposits of northern Chile and southern Peru, and the gold mines of the Incas." The ancient Peruvians were the only people in the New World known to have mined iron ore from which they made swords, although iron is found in most parts of the world.[8]

Use of Cement Confirmed by Modern Discoveries

The Book of Mormon mentions the widespread use of cement to build houses and other structures before the Savior's appearance among the people. For example: "And there being but little timber upon the face of the land, nevertheless the people who went forth became exceedingly expert in the working of cement; therefore they did build houses of cement, in the which they did dwell" (Helaman 3:7).

In 1830, when cement was barely known,[9] Book of Mormon reports of its use were met with skepticism—if not outright scorn by the book's detractors. This attitude continued well into the twentieth century, as a 1929 incident in the life of Heber J. Grant, seventh president of The Church of Jesus Christ of Latter-day Saints, illustrates. President Grant met an educated young man who ridiculed him for believing the Book of Mormon. The man said he could point out two lies in the book, both in regard to the supposed use of cement. First, the man stated that the ancient inhabitants knew nothing about cement; and second, the man claimed there would never be a house found made of cement. If that man were alive today, he would face compelling evidence to the contrary.[10]

Cement has been found at many sites in southern Mexico, Guatemala, and Honduras—dating to at least as early as 150 BC. The presence of expert cement technology in pre–Hispanic locations is a remarkable archaeological fact, and it first appears there at the time when the Book of Mormon says this development occurred,[11] about 45 BC. "One of the most notable examples of its use is found at the temple complex at Teotihuacan, north of present-day Mexico City. The cement floor slabs at this site were remarkably high in structural quality. Although exposed to the elements for nearly two thousand years, ancient structures built with high quality concrete of various composition, at times exceed many present-day building code requirements."[12]

Scholars who have studied the remains of buildings in Baja California suggest that

> Book of Mormon people in that region did not employ the same process for creating cement as we do today, but rather used a "cemented" adobe-like material that is found in many southwest locations of the United States and Mexico, in Biblical lands and throughout the ancient

and modern world. This type of material was often made into varying sizes of bricks that were "cemented" by moistening clay material and then drying them in the sun. Anciently it was the most ubiquitous of all "cemented" building materials. The brick walls of adobe-like structures are often covered with a thin, limestone-based cement material plastered (stuccoed) to the walls. This plaster or stucco material is made with lime and sand mixed with water. . . . These adobe-like buildings use wood for the supportive roof structures that span the outer walls. Thatched materials, such as leafs [sic] from fan palms, provide a water-resistant outer roof covering. These types of "cement" adobe buildings are found in many parts of Baja California today because of its Mediterranean climate and semiarid environment and the ready availability of limestone and gypsum, clay materials, and timber and fan-palm thatching materials for roofs.[13]

Mesa Verde National Park, Colorado, is where proponents believe those fleeing conflicts in the Baja California area possibly fled and built the "cement" (brick) dwellings that still remain there today.[14]

Evidences of Highways and Wheels

As mentioned in Chapter 14, horses and wheels were used in Book of Mormon times. In Alma 18:9, we read: "Now the king had commanded his servants . . . that they should prepare his horses and chariots, and conduct him forth to the land of Nephi." In recent decades, archaeologists have discovered not only many small wheeled toys, which are evidence for knowledge of the wheel, but on the shores of Lake Titicaca, located between Bolivia and Peru, they discovered four ancient giant wheels nine feet in diameter with a tread sixteen inches wide.[15]

The use of the wheel during Book of Mormon times suggests there would be roads or highways of some kind. In 3 Nephi, we find this description: "And there were many highways cast up, and many roads made, which led from city to city, and from land to land, and from place to place" (3 Nephi 6:8). More than twelve hundred kilometers of carefully prepared ancient *sacbes*, or lime-surfaced highways, have been identified in the Maya area by Mexican scholars and have been found in many other locations throughout South and Central America.[16]

Extensive pre–Spanish roads in Baja California are still visible from space by means of satellite photography. The Book of Mormon says the roads were "cast up." "The process of 'casting up' a road or highway consisted of clearing the ground of an existing path or trail of obstacles such as stones, rocks and vegetation and then moving the larger rocks and stones to the side of the path to clear the way and visually demarcate a preexisting route." The prophet Isaiah explains the "casting up" process in the making of highways when he states: "prepare ye the way of the people, cast up, cast up the highway; gather out the stones" (Isaiah 62:10.) The description of "cast up" highways in the Book of Mormon account matches the cast-up roads in Baja.[17]

Even though no direct evidence of any utilitarian wheeled vehicle for common use has been found anywhere in the Americas, it is not "surprising when we learn that no fragment of a chariot has ever been uncovered in the Holy Land, despite the fact that thousands of them are reported by the Bible to have been used."[18] "If the wheels in general use at that time were wooden, which is most likely, we would not expect to find evidence of them today because of the poor preservation factor caused by the high humidity of Mesoamerican lowlands."[19] The same reasoning applies to the humid climates of the Eastern United States or at other humid locations in the Americas.

Horse Skeletons Support Jaredite and Nephite Accounts

Horse remains have been found at various locations in the Americas. A 2013 excavation by archaeologists in Carlsbad, California, unearthed skeletons of two horses and a donkey that may have died fifty years before the Spanish began their conquest of California. The remains lay within a few feet of one another and showed no signs of having been shod, an indication that the horses were not brought by the Spanish who fitted their horses with iron shoes. This was a significant find because native North American horses were thought to have become extinct more than ten thousand years ago and then been reintroduced by the Spanish.[20]

A 1957 excavation at Mayapan in Yucatan, Mexico, provides corroboration of horses among the Jaredites. "In southwest Yucatan, horse remains were found in three caves associated with potsherds and other artifacts, and with no sign of fossilization, showing that these horses did not live earlier than the Jaredites, the first Book of Mormon civilization. Excavations in 1978, at Loltun Cave in the Maya lowlands, turned up more horse remains."[21] In 1977, radiocarbon dating of strata in twenty-nine Yucatan caves placed horse remains from around 1800 BC,[22] which is well within the period of the Jaredite civilization. Petrified horse hoofs have been discovered in Baja California, providing evidence that they also existed earlier in that location.[23] The horse is mentioned in Ether 9:19, along with other animals common to the Jaredite civilization.

Perhaps the Spaniards did not find horses upon their arrival in the Americas because "researchers have determined that the ancient horse was eaten by natives of South America. In fact, horse meat is still eaten in Mexico today. Additionally, historians have noted that in times of war and famine, the horse was used primarily as a source of food rather than a means of transportation." So the disappearance of the horse could well be due to food shortages. The Book of Mormon records that Gadianton robbers attacked the Nephites, making it necessary for the Nephites to flee. They took with them their provisions "and horses and cattle, and flocks of every kind that they might subsist for the space of seven years" (3 Nephi 4:4). "It is, therefore, reasonable to assume that, as a result of Lamanite rustling and the Nephites' need to sustain their people, the horse became extinct."[24]

"Even if remains had not been found of any horses, it would not prove they had not existed there at one time. The horse was the basis of the wealth and military power of the Huns of central Asia (fourth and fifth centuries AD). It is of interest that not a single usable horse bone has been found in the territory of the whole empire of the Huns . . . and they must have possessed hundreds of thousands of horses."[25]

Providentially Elephants Found Only in the Book of Ether

Elephants are mentioned in the book of Ether (Ether 9:19), which is the history of the Jaredites who arrived in the Americas about 2200 BC, well before Lehi arrived in the New World. *The Scientific Monthly* reports that early Americans hunted the elephant. Even though they have been extinct for some three thousand years, the elephant would have existed during early years of the Jaredite civilization.[26]

Archaeologist Hyatt Verrill described a figure from Coclé, Panama:

The most astonishing of the idols is one bearing a figure which is so strikingly and obviously elephantine that it cannot be explained away by any of the ordinary theories. . . . Not only does this figure show a trunk, but in addition it has the big leaf-like ears and the forward-bending knees peculiar to the elephants. Moreover, it shows a load or burden strapped upon its back.[27]

Dr. Hugh Nibley also commented on the existence of the elephant in ancient America:

Archaeology has proved that the American Indian hunted and killed elephants. It is also strongly indicated that these elephants have been extinct for several thousand years. This means that the traditions of the Indians recalling these animals have retained their historical validity for great stretches of time. . . . Probably the minimum is three thousand years. . . . This suits very well with the Book of Mormon account, and in that case the Indian legends must go back to Jaredite times.[28]

Carvings that may represent elephants have also been found in such locales as Gallo Canyon, New Mexico; Glen Canyon, Colorado; Flora Vista, New Mexico; Cuernavaca, Mexico; and Cali, Columbia.[29] The La Brea tar pits in the urban heart of Los Angeles, California include the skeletal remains of elephants, lions, and horses on the list of animals found there.[30]

The Cimeter, a Weapon of War

Cimeters, mentioned several times in the Book of Mormon, are designated as a weapon of war. Mosiah 9:16 reads: "And it came to pass that I did arm them with bows, and with arrows, with swords, and with *cimeters*, and with clubs, and with slings, and with all manner of weapons which we could invent, and I and my people did go forth against the Lamanites to battle" (emphasis added).

Critics have long claimed that the cimeter was unknown before the rise of Islam and that references to this weapon in the Book of Mormon are anachronistic; however, "We now know that scimitars of various forms were known in the Ancient Near East as early as 2,000 BC. They are subsequently portrayed in martial art from Mesopotamia and Egypt. Rare archaeological specimens of this weapon have also been found. The cutting edge was usually on the convex side, however some were double-edged." It is more commonly spelled "scimitar," and *Webster's Third International Dictionary*, 1993, describes it as a sword "having a curved blade with the edge on the convex side" or "something resembling a scimitar (as in sharpness or shape), especially a long-handled billhook."[31] The Book of Mormon is vindicated yet again.

Earthquakes and Destruction at the Time of Christ's Crucifixion

Nephite prophecies foretold signs that would appear at the time of the Savior's crucifixion. These prophecies told of cataclysmic destructions followed by three days of intense darkness, as described in 1 Nephi 19:10–12. To the skeptic, accounts of the massive devastation chronicled in 3 Nephi 8 and 9 may seem improbable, but history agrees with the Book of Mormon record.

Daniel C. Peterson provides this insight:

> The [3 Nephi] account mentions the simultaneous occurrence of earthquake, fire, strong winds, extensive flooding, the complete burial of cities, and thick darkness. The description of the great destruction given in 3 Nephi 8 finds remarkable parallels with what modern seismology and volcanology show about cataclysmic geological events and with historical reports of such catastrophes. Yet Joseph Smith never saw a volcano and never experienced a significant earthquake, nor is it likely he had read any substantial literature on the subject. An examination of the characteristics of known natural disasters in historical times reveals that the Book of Mormon in no way exaggerates.[32]

The Book of Mormon records cities being sunk "into the depths of the sea" (3 Nephi 8:9) or "buried up in the depths of the earth" (3 Nephi 9:6). This happened when an earthquake hit Jamaica on June 7, 1692. The city of Port Royal sank into the ocean, and within minutes, much of the city and its inhabitants lay under fifty feet of water. In the year 1772, the Papandayang area of Java was devastated by a series of earthquakes that caused a mountain to split, creating a large depression six miles wide and fifteen miles long into which an entire town of two thousand people disappeared.[33] "The findings of archaeology point to such an occurrence as the Book of Mormon describes. Cities have been located beneath lava flows or buried beneath lakes. Ruins have been found in the tops of mountains. In the valleys north of Mexico City, great cities and temples have been found buried beneath some twelve feet of volcanic ash. The beds of old cement highways show indications of terrific earth disturbances after their completion."[34]

In the year 2000, two Guatemalans, both experienced in underwater archaeology, discovered a submerged site just off the south coast of Lake Atitlan. The divers concluded that the submergence of the city beneath the water had been comparatively sudden, as they could find little damage to the structures, which would have been evident had the process been lengthy. Immediately after the great catastrophes that accompanied the crucifixion of Christ, the Lord's voice from the heavens told the Nephites that "the [Lamanite] city of Jerusalem and the inhabitants thereof" had been covered by water, an event that took place within a matter of hours[35] (see 3 Nephi 9:7).

Scientists who study the history of the atmosphere, as it is preserved in polar ice, provide further evidence of great destruction that took place immediately before the Savior's visit to ancient America. "Fallout material from major volcanic eruptions, in the form of ash or sulfuric acid particles, are often trapped in the ice sheets covering Greenland and Antarctica." Published studies of ice-core research reveal a likely eruption in the [AD 30-40] time period, which correlates with the great destruction described in the Book of Mormon. Ice-core research helps confirm other climate changes, and these records have been correlated to known volcanic eruptions in Mesoamerica.[36]

Native American traditions clearly point to a catastrophic destructive event on the North American continent. The historian Bancroft writes of a Toltec tradition: "The sun and the moon were eclipsed, the earth shook, and the rocks were rent asunder, and many other things and signs happening. This was in the year Ce Cali, which chronology being reduced to our system, proved to be the same date when Christ, our lord suffered—33 AD." The historian Prescott also records many Indian traditions describing a great catastrophe and dates it to about the time of the death of Christ.[37]

DNA and the Book of Mormon

In 2003, Thomas W. Murphy and Simon Southerton advanced the idea that because the Book of Mormon is the history of Israelite families who came to the unpopulated Americas and eventually populated the entire land, this would make them the forefathers of all the American Indians and that DNA should confirm this fact. They concluded that because the DNA of the American

Samuel the Lamanite

Indians tested thus far possess genetic signatures closely resembling modern-day Asians—not Israelites—the Book of Mormon, and all that goes with it, is therefore false.

A couple of things the writers overlooked are as follows: 1) It is common knowledge among scientists and most members of The Church of Jesus Christ of Latter-day Saints that the Americas had been inhabited for thousands of years before Lehi's and Mulek's groups arrived, and 2) Lehi and others, whose history is partially contained in the Book of Mormon, most likely resided in a limited geographical area of a few hundred miles, not the whole western hemisphere of North and South America; and they no doubt intermarried with preexisting populations. If Murphy and Southerton were aware of this information, they ignored it.

These two critics did no studies themselves regarding genetic research to test their claim, nor were they getting their information from a study designed by scientists studying human population genetics. Their proposal would not pass the muster of peer review by scientists in this field, because they ignored the real complexity of the problem. It is unlikely that anyone could recover the genetic signature of a small migrating family from twenty-six hundred years ago. Further, there is no reason to assume that Native American ancestors must be *exclusively* Israelite.[38] A study was done in 2003 on 131,060 Icelanders, the majority of whom had ancestors living only 150 years ago. Their known ancestors could not be detected based on DNA tests, even though genealogical records showed that these people lived and were real ancestors.[39]

No one knows what a "Lehite" Israelite gene would have looked like, so we don't know what to look for. And it is likely that the Middle Eastern DNA of Lehi's day looked completely different from the "Israelite" DNA available today. Population genetics demonstrate that the DNA signature of small

133

populations—which the Book of Mormon peoples were—can and usually does disappear when infused into larger populations.[40]

Numerous books and articles have been written on this complex subject. One major problem is that DNA is passed down only through the mother. In the Book of Mormon's situation, the origin of the two mothers, Sariah, Lehi's wife, and Ishmael's wife, are unknown. The consensus seems to be that it is impossible, at this time, after hundreds of years, to trace their precise origin using DNA.

What seems clear is that the DNA of Book of Mormon peoples likely represented only a tiny fraction of all DNA in ancient America. Finding and clearly identifying Lehite DNA today may be asking more of the science of population genetics than it is capable of providing.[41]

The Grolier Codex

Facts revealed by new discoveries are often difficult to accept when they disrupt conventional wisdom. The case of the Grolier Codex provides some parallels to how the Book of Mormon is treated by some specialists. In 1971, "unauthorized archaeologists," that is to say "looters," in southern Mexico found what seemed to be an ancient Mesoamerican codex (manuscript), eventually named the "Grolier Codex." Because Mesoamerican scholars initially gave the document very little scrutiny before classifying it as a fake, it took many years before it was shown to be authentic. Those who rejected the Grolier Codex as a hoax made the same mistakes commonly made by people who reject the Book of Mormon out of hand: 1) the unconventional origin prejudiced them; 2) they did not examine it closely; 3) they closed their minds to other options; 4) on eventual examination, they chose to pick on little details rather than look at the entire document; and 5) when all else failed, they turned to name calling, which is easier than serious investigation.[42]

Sincere investigators of the Book of Mormon will discover that a testimony of its truthfulness comes through a witness of the Holy Ghost rather than by external evidences, as helpful as those might be. "Those who rely exclusively on scholarship," writes Elder Dallin H. Oaks, "reject revelation and fulfill Nephi's prophecy that in the last days men 'shall teach with their learning, and deny the Holy Ghost, which giveth utterance' (2 Nephi 28:4). . . . They ignore or gloss over the incredible complexity of the Book of Mormon record. Those who rely on scholarship, *faith and revelation* are willing to look at the entire spectrum of issues, content as well as vocabulary, revelation as well as excavation"[43] (emphasis added).

Chapter 18

The Book Will Be the Primary Instrument of the Gathering of Modern Israel

Your book must eventually be published to every nation, kindred, tongue, and people as the authentic word of God and, with the Bible, another witness for the Lord Jesus Christ. It will be God's primary instrument of the gathering of modern Israel scattered throughout the world.

In the summer of 1830, Parley P. Pratt, a farmer and itinerate preacher, was led by the spirit to sell his farm in Ohio and travel to western New York. Along the way he was introduced to a Baptist deacon who told him about a newly published book of scripture and lent him his copy. Parley writes of first reading the Book of Mormon, an experience that forever changed his life:

> I opened it with eagerness and read its title page. I then read the testimony of several witnesses in relation to the manner of its being found and translated. After this I commenced its contents by course. I read all day, eating was a burden, I had no desire for food; sleep was a burden when the night came, for I preferred reading to sleep.

> As I read, the spirit of the Lord was upon me, and I knew and comprehended that the book was true, as plainly and manifestly as a man comprehends and knows that he exists. My joy was now full, as it were, and I rejoiced sufficiently to more than pay me for all the sorrows, sacrifices and toils of my life.[1]

Convinced of the truth of the book, Parley soon received the ordinances of baptism and confirmation, and in 1835 was ordained one of the original apostles of The Church of Jesus Christ of Latter-day Saints. His extraordinary life includes experiences such as a memorable reunion with the Prophet Joseph Smith in the city of Philadelphia in 1839. By the providence of God, a large church was made available for the Prophet to preach, and a congregation of 3,000 mainly non-Latter-day Saints turned out for the meeting. Sidney Rigdon, an early church leader and gifted orator, spoke first, citing only the Bible in an attempt to establish common ground with the people, but to little effect. When

Rigdon finished, the Prophet spoke. Elder Pratt provides a brief account of the consequential occasion:

> Brother Joseph arose like a lion about to roar; and being full of the Holy Ghost, spoke in great power, bearing testimony of the visions he had seen, the ministering of angels which he had enjoyed; and how he had found the plates of the Book of Mormon, and translated them by the gift and power of God. He commenced by saying: 'If nobody else [has] the courage to testify of so glorious a message from Heaven, and of the finding of so glorious a record, [I feel] to do it in justice to the people, and leave the event with God.' The entire congregation was astounded; electrified, as it were, and overwhelmed with the sense of the truth and power by which he spoke, and the wonders which he related. A lasting impression was made; [and] many souls were gathered into the fold.[2]

An Improbable Prophecy

Among Joseph Smith's earliest revelatory experiences were those of the evening of the 21st and the early hours of the 22nd of September 1823, when he was visited four times by an angel who identified himself as Moroni, the last prophet-historian of the Book of Mormon, now a resurrected being. Along

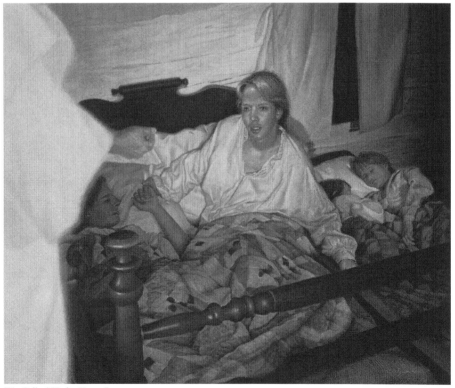

"He Called Me by Name"

with many vital instructions communicated to the obscure seventeen-year-old farm boy was a prophecy that must have seemed impossible. Joseph was informed that "his name should be had for good and evil among all nations, kindreds, and tongues, or that it should be both good and evil spoken of among all people" (see Chapter 2 and Joseph Smith—History 1:33).

By what means might such an implausible promise be fulfilled? The answer is found in the ever-growing number of translations and global distribution of the Book of Mormon, and the sharing and teaching of the book by Latter-day Saint missionaries and other Church members, as well as its availability through bookstores and various electronic media. This dissemination is linked to the purposes of God in prophecies found in both the Bible and the Book of Mormon, especially those concerning the ancient scattering and modern worldwide gathering of the Twelve Tribes of Israel.

In this regard, the Bible can fairly be called "the book of the scattering" because it chronicles Israel's long history of rebellion against God which lead to major diasporas over a nearly 800-year period from about 721 BC to AD 70. Conversely, the Book of Mormon can accurately be called "the book of the gathering," since it is the primary instrument, along with the witness of the Holy Ghost, of personal conversion to the restored gospel of Jesus Christ, and the gathering of latter-day Israel—past, present, and future—both spiritually and temporally. The ongoing fulfillment of Moroni's prophecy is a powerful witness of both the truth of the Book of Mormon as authentic scripture, and of the divine, prophetic calling of its translator.

The Mission of the Book of Mormon

Like the Bible, the Book of Mormon is among a small group of religious writings—texts such as the Quran, the Torah, the Vedas, the Upanishads, the Bhagavad Gita, and the Buddhist Sutras—that have immeasurably blessed the peoples of the world. As the prophet Alma declared, "For behold, the Lord doth grant unto all nations, of their own nation and tongue, to teach his word, yea, in wisdom, all that he seeth fit that they should have" (Alma 29:8). The Book of Mormon is akin to these other scriptures in that it is of ancient origin, but unlike them it was revealed and translated in modern times "by the gift and power of God." Its singular message and mission to the world restores knowledge of the Lamb of God and His Gospel lost from the Bible over many centuries.

Early in the Book of Mormon narrative, Nephi is shown a vision of the future in which "many plain and precious things [would be] taken out of the [Bible], which were plain unto the understanding of the children of men, according to the plainness which is in the Lamb of God—because of these things which are taken away out of the gospel of the Lamb, an exceedingly great many do stumble, yea, insomuch that Satan hath great power over them" (1 Nephi

13:29). By virtue of the widely held belief among many who have not carefully read the Book of Mormon that God speaks only through the Bible, the Book of Mormon's relationship with the Bible is often misunderstood. With the Bible's divine origin and historicity under persistent attack, rather than competitor or critic, the Book of Mormon, as Dr. Robert J. Matthews has written,

> is a companion to the Bible, it is its defender and champion, and it will be the means of convincing many people that the Bible is true. The Bible available in our day is not as complete nor as doctrinally accurate as it was when written by the ancient prophets and apostles, and the loss of material is both substantial and extensive. . . . These missing parts are restored in the Book of Mormon.[3]

The 2001 edition of the *World Christian Encyclopedia* lists 33,830 denominations that claim to be Christian. This reality alone speaks to the need for clarification of the countless ways the Bible is being interpreted and the resulting disagreements among churches. God is not a God of confusion. He cannot be the originator of conflicting teachings and beliefs (see Ephesians 4:14). The Book of Mormon clarifies many things in the Bible which have been a source of controversy among churchgoers and clergy alike for centuries.

Richard D. Rust, a retired Latter-day Saint professor from the University of North Carolina, tells of a presentation he made to forty-five divinity students that illustrates the important role the Book of Mormon plays in restoring lost Bible scripture. Rust asked the students "to assume that the lost ten tribes had received God's word by way of prophets and . . . that the ten tribes had now returned with scriptures." He then asked what fundamental questions of mankind they thought would be addressed in those scriptures.

The students proposed seven questions, all of which Rust answered from the Book of Mormon: 1) What is God like? (3 Nephi 11); 2) What evidence is there of the existence of God? (Alma 30, especially verse 44); 3) What is the purpose of life? (2 Nephi 2; Mosiah 2–3); 4) Why is there suffering and evil in the world? (2 Nephi 2:11; Alma 20:29); 5) What is the relationship of man to God? (Mosiah 2–3); 6) What happens after death? (Alma 40–42, especially 40:11–14); and 7) What are the proofs of a true prophet? (Jacob 4, especially verse 6).[4]

The Scattering of Israel

At an October 2016 gathering of Jewish and Latter-day Saint leaders commemorating the 175th Anniversary of Apostle Orson Hyde's historic journey to dedicate the land of Israel for the return of the Jews, Elder Jeffrey R. Holland said (speaking to the Jews present): "You know better than I the promises made to Abraham, Isaac, and Jacob and posterity which did not, it turned out, preclude the scattering and dispersion of that posterity, sifted 'like as corn is sifted in a sieve,' as the prophet Amos described it, fulfilling what Moses had recorded in the Torah: 'And the Lord shall scatter you among the nations, and ye shall be left few in number among the heathen, whither the Lord shall lead you.'"[5]

Dr. Victor Ludlow, who holds a PhD in New Eastern and Judaic Studies from Brandeis University, outlines Israel's four major diasporas and why the scattered tribes are referred to as lost:

> Because of many generations of wickedness, the nation of Israel was broken up into four main parts: 1) the "lost" ten tribes, some of whom disseminated throughout the Middle East and others of whom fled from the Assyrian yoke after their deportation from Israel in 721 BC; 2) the Book of Mormon exiles (Nephites, Lamanites, and the people of Zarahemla or the so-called Mulekites), who fled Jerusalem around 600 BC (and whose descendants are now usually called Lamanites); 3) the house of Judah (the Jews), which was scattered by the Babylonians (586 BC) and the Romans (AD 70); 4) and other scattered remnants of Israelites (particularly the house of Ephraim) who mixed in among the Gentiles over the course of many centuries.
>
> Except for the Jews, the great majority of the descendants of these ancient Israelite groups lost their distinctive identity. They became "lost" as they mixed in among the nations of the earth or forgot their religious heritage. With the passage of time, they forgot their origins in Samaria and Judea as they blended in among other religions and cultures. But they were not hidden to the Lord.[6]

The Gathering of Israel

Since scattering and gathering are major themes of the Book of Mormon, it is fitting that the masterful Allegory of the Tame and Wild Olive Trees in Jacob 5 appears within its covers (see Chapter 15). The Allegory, authored by the previously unknown prophet Zenos, is a 77-verse prophetic portrayal of the Lord's centuries-long labor to preserve and gather habitually backsliding Israel. The text reveals that even the patience of God can be tried as he repeats several times a lament in the form of a question: "And it came to pass that the Lord of the vineyard wept, and said unto the servant: What could I have done more for my vineyard" (Jacob 5:41)? The Lord's labor, assisted by his servants, involves the periodic transplanting of some of the olive trees' branches (various tribes) throughout the world (the scattering). The Book of Mormon itself begins with one such transplanting as Lehi and his group flee the imminent destruction of Jerusalem for the New World. The Lord then orchestrates the harvest involving gospel conversion and restoration to the covenant lands of inheritance (the gathering) in the latter days. Professor Ludlow comments on the dual nature of the Allegory:

> Zenos provides a profound prophetic overview of essential elements about the scattering and gathering of Israel. Although the scattering and gathering are literal, historical, physical events, they also reflect a more important dimension of a spiritual scattering, and in the latter days their gathering as seen in the mission of The Church of Jesus Christ of Latter-day Saints. . . . The inseparable relationship between the concept of gathering and the spiritual mission of spreading the gospel, nurturing members in the Church, and maintaining family ties is beautifully illustrated in the allegory. [7]

A Book for the World

To appreciate the global influence of the Book of Mormon as an instrument of conversion and gathering, it is useful to review some numbers. When the one hundred millionth copy was published in February 2000, it was heralded as the third most-published book in the world. The Book of Mormon is not sold for profit. An average of 4.5 million physical copies of the book are distributed annually.

On this subject, Elder D. Todd Christofferson of the Council of the Twelve, while speaking of the Book of Mormon's lasting legacy at the Library of Congress in December 2016, referred to the miracle of "what began with 5,000 copies in a small print shop in Palmyra, New York, in 1830 has resulted in millions of copies available in multiple languages around the globe." Elder Christofferson then provided a brief publishing, translation, and recognitions update:

> As of today, over 176 million copies of the Book of Mormon have been printed since [the first edition was published]. To date, the Book of Mormon has been translated into 110 languages—89 full translations, with selections of the book in another 21 languages. The first non-English translation was published in 1851 in Danish. Other major translations include Spanish, French, German, Italian, Portuguese, Japanese, and Russian. However, the array of translations is evidence of the Church's growing international presence and includes languages as diverse as Amharic, Kekchi, Mongolian, Quichua, Swahili, Tok Pisin, Igbo, Pangasinan, and Yapese. . . . In 2013 the Book of Mormon was added to the Library of Congress's list of "Books That Shaped America." Most recently [it] has been listed fourth on the Library of Congress's "America Reads" list of most influential books in American history.[8] [In October 2017 the Church announced plans to also translate the complete Book of Mormon into Burmese, Efik, Georgian, Navajo, Pohnpeian, Sesotho and Tshiluba.]

Not for the Casual Reader

John F. Heidenreich, a divinity school graduate and minister at the time he first read the Book of Mormon, describes the way his study of the book affected his life: "It was like seeing the thundering Niagara Falls for the first time. It is a book one cannot read casually. Its claims are too enormous to be ignored." In his hunger to know the truth, Heidenreich read his new-found treasure five times over a period of seven months while making a comparative study with the Bible. "This was the most fruitful labor of my life," he observes. "My most startling discovery about the Book of Mormon was the light it threw on the Bible. I later came to realize God planned it that way."

Heidenreich's intensive study led him to see how the book fulfills the prophecy of Ezekiel 37:16-17 that the stick of Judah (the Bible) and the stick of Joseph (the Book of Mormon) should be joined together to "become one in thine hand" as a tool in the latter day gathering of scattered Israel (see "two sticks" in Chapter 21). The argument some make against the Book of Mormon—since we have a Bible we do not need another witness for Christ—Heidenreich found as illogical as claiming that since we have the Gospel of Matthew we do not need the other three gospels to tell essentially the same story. "If you love Jesus Christ you will love the Book of Mormon because it bears witness of Him. The Book of Mormon is permeated with the Spirit of the Lord, and whoever reads it with that same Spirit will know it is true."[9]

To Sweep the Earth as with a Flood

Moses, the great prophet of the Exodus who restored the keys of the gathering of Israel to the Prophet Joseph Smith (D&C 110:11), recorded Jehovah's words regarding the means by which He would spread truth and righteousness throughout the earth in the last days:

> And righteousness will I send down out of heaven [the angel Moroni]; and truth will I send forth out of the earth [the golden plates], to bear testimony of mine Only Begotten; his resurrection from the dead; yea, and also the resurrection of all men; and righteousness and truth will I cause to sweep the earth as with a flood, to gather out mine elect from the four quarters of the earth, unto a place which I shall prepare, an Holy City, that my people may gird up their loins, and be looking forth for the time of my coming; for there shall be my tabernacle, and it shall be called Zion, a New Jerusalem. (Moses 7:62, intertextual with Psalms 85:11)

President Ezra Taft Benson was a powerful advocate for the Book of Mormon, which he identified as "the instrument that God designed to 'sweep the earth as with a flood, to gather out [His] elect'" (Moses 7:62). He further declared that the time is long overdue for a massive flooding of the earth with the Book of Mormon. . . . In this age of the electronic media and the mass distribution of the printed word, God will hold us accountable if we do not now move the Book of Mormon in a monumental way.

We have the Book of Mormon, we have the members, we have the missionaries, we have the resources, and the world has the need. The time is now! . . . We hardly fathom the power of the Book of Mormon, nor the divine role it must play, nor the extent to which it must be moved.

"Few men on earth," said Elder Bruce R. McConkie, "either in or out of the Church, have caught the vision of what the Book of Mormon is all about. Few are they among men who know the part it has played and will yet play in preparing the way for the coming of Him of whom it is a new witness. . . . The Book of Mormon shall so affect men that the whole earth and all its peoples will have been influenced and governed by it. . . . There is no greater issue ever to confront mankind in modern times than this: Is the Book of Mormon the mind and will and voice of God to all men?" We testify that it is.

The Book Must Maintain "an Uncanny Consistency That Is Never Caught in a Slip or Contradiction"

Your book must not contain any absurd, impossible, or contradictory statements, and its many story lines and historical threads must remain untangled down through the centuries.

Evan Hunter, author of more than eighty books, writes, "I learned a long time ago if there's any one thing in a book that sounds a false note the reader will disbelieve all of the book. So the research on any book I'm doing . . . is impeccable. I can't be false on any one point. And if I ever do make a mistake, boy do I hear about it."[1]

Critics of the Book of Mormon, who scrutinize the text with ill intent, keep fancying they have found that absurd, impossible, or contradictory statement that would disprove it. When we consider the length of the book, if Joseph Smith had created it out of thin air, surely it would have been debunked by now. At times, some readers have believed they have found flaws—only to have time and research prove them wrong. Following are a few examples.

Time of the Crucifixion

One of the errors early critics believed they found in the Book of Mormon is the passage that specifies the time of the crucifixion. Third Nephi 10:9 says it was "in the morning" when the Savior was crucified, whereas the Bible tells us that the crucifixion ended around the ninth hour (Luke 23:44), which would be 3:00 p.m.

Some have seized upon this as a discrepancy; however, they

Crucifixion of Christ

fail to take into consideration the different time zones involved. Critics would have had a point had the Book of Mormon recorded the event as happening in the afternoon, and readers eventually would have recognized the time-zone differential. It is unlikely that Joseph Smith, with his limited education, would have recognized the reason for this time difference when he was translating the Book of Mormon.

Alma a Male Name

The male name *Alma* in the Book of Mormon has been questioned by some who claimed it is a woman's name of Latin derivation rather than Hebrew. However, while excavating Judean caves in 1960–1961, Israeli scholar Yigael Yadin found a land deed from the early second century AD that furnishes strong support for the masculine *Alma*. The deed bore the names of four people who had leased property there, one of whom was "Alma, son of Yehudah." This discovery demonstrates that the name Alma is an authentic ancient Semitic masculine personal name and that its use in the Book of Mormon is correct.[2]

Plausible Population Growth

Seemingly unrealistic large population sizes, cited in the Book of Mormon, have been criticized by some who view such numbers as unreasonable. The Book of Mormon deals only with the history of three groups who migrated to the New World—not any other groups already living there. Book of Mormon scholar John L. Sorenson writes that "it is inescapable that there were substantial (non–Book of Mormon) populations in the 'promised land' . . . throughout the period of the Nephite record, and probably in the Jaredite era, also."[3]

One indication of this is found in the book of Jacob, which reports that "there came a man among the people of Nephi whose name was Sherem" (Jacob 7:1). He told Jacob, "I have sought much opportunity that I might speak unto you, for I have heard . . . that thou goest about much, preaching that which ye call the gospel, or the doctrine of Christ" (Jacob 7:6). Where did Sherem come from, why had he not met Jacob before, and where did Jacob go to preach? There were no doubt other groups near the city of Nephi besides Lehi's descendants.[4]

The Book of Mormon states that all those who followed the prophet Nephi—and his set of ideals—joined together and were called Nephites. Others, who were often wicked, were called Lamanites. At an early point in their history, the Nephites found it necessary to separate themselves from the Lamanites. Nephi gives details of all those who chose to follow him, listing family members and Zoram and his family. He then adds, "And all those who would go with me were those who believed in the warnings and the revelations of God" (2 Nephi 5:6). This account suggests there were likely others already living in the lands of the Book of Mormon besides those who arrived with Lehi and his family.

A model for reconstructing ancient population figures was developed at Cambridge University in England. Applying the Cambridge model to the Book of Mormon and using conservative numbers from the text reveal that Book of Mormon population numbers are on the high end of the spectrum but are within a realistic range.[5] In spite of the sparse data regarding population sizes, "some plausible demographic inferences can be made, and the picture of Nephite population history that emerges is a realistic one."[6] Further, if the assumption is used that the Nephites and Lamanites absorbed other populations, the numbers cease to be at all problematic.[7]

The Beheading of Shiz

Another incident, which critics initially thought to be an obvious error, is found in the book of Ether. The Jaredites had been fighting a long and gory battle, and all had been killed except the two leaders, Coriantumr and Shiz. Using his last ounce of strength, Coriantumr beheaded Shiz. "After he had smitten off the head of Shiz, . . . Shiz raised up on his hands and fell; and after that he had struggled for breath, he died" (Ether 15:31).

Detractors found this account to be absurd. However, Dr. M. Gary Hadfield, a doctor and professor of pathology, provides a plausible explanation: "Shiz's death struggle illustrates the classic reflex posture that occurs in both humans and animals when the upper brain stem is disconnected from the brain. The extensor muscles of the arms and legs contract, and this reflect action could cause Shiz to raise up on his hands." In Coriantumr's weakened condition, he most likely did not completely sever Shiz's head from his body. Moreover, in both Hebrew and Greek, words translated as "smote off" mean "to hammer" or "to strike down"—but not generally to smite off. In Judges 5:26, a similar account is described: "With the hammer she smote Sisera, she smote off his head." [8]

The Book Does Not Contradict Itself

As for the books internal consistency we recommend the conclusion of Dr. Hugh Nibley, who for many years intensely studied the Book of Mormon: "Only one who attempts to make a full outline of Book of Mormon history can begin to appreciate its immense complexity; and never once does the author get lost . . . and never once does he contradict himself." Nibley continues, "Throughout the book we get the impression that it really is what its authors claim it to be, a highly condensed account from much fuller records. We can imagine our young rustic [Joseph Smith] getting off to this flying start, but can we imagine him keeping up the pace for ten pages? For over 500 pages the story never drags, the author never hesitates or wanders, he is never at a loss. What is really amazing is that *he never contradicts himself*."[9]

The Book of Mormon neither contradicts itself nor ever loses track of events or people. In the early pages of the book, Mosiah 8, we learn that the people of Limhi found twenty-four engraved plates they could not read. Ammon, who contacted this people in their highland home, tells them he knows of a man who could translate the records through a gift of God known as interpreters (Urim and Thummim). These records are not forgotten by the writers; and 324 pages later, the translation from the plates appears as the book of Ether, the next-to-the-last book in the Book of Mormon.[10]

Another incident, found in Mosiah 17:7, 13–19, tells of the prophet Abinadi suffering death by fire at the behest of the wicked priests of King Noah. Before dying, Abinadi prophesies that these priests' descendants would become afflicted with all manner of disease, be smitten, driven, and scattered, and finally be killed. Ninety pages later, in Alma 25:4, 9–12, we learn of their fate, which was precisely as Abinadi had prophesied. Such absolute consistency would be impossible if the Book of Mormon had been a work of fiction, when we consider the short time Joseph had to translate the book, and the scribes who testified that the prophet did not use notes or any written material to help him keep track of people, places, and events.

The Book of Mormon contains a self-consistent Nephite chronology throughout the thousand-year history of the Nephites. The book "records that the Nephites reckoned their time with days, weeks, months, and years, but it does not include enough information to reconstruct their calendar." Lehi and his family were certainly familiar with the calendar used in ancient Israel, they may have been familiar with those used in ancient Egypt, and they were certainly influenced by the different peoples they lived among in the Americas.[11]

Scholar John P. Pratt writes that a probable Nephite calendar would have had twelve months with thirty days in each month. The calendar would have had five "end" days between the first and last months, and it would likely be "based on the Egyptian civil year, which would have been well-known to Lehi." Research has established that important speeches were given on what are believed to be holy days. For instance, King Benjamin's great discourse (Mosiah 2–5) was likely given at the Hebrew Feast of Tabernacles.[12] No dates found in the Book of Mormon contradict any of the hundreds of other dates, an impossible task for an author to keep straight without an outline.

What is the chance of any person, let alone the marginally literate Joseph Smith, keeping such a detailed text consistent? "How could any author keep all the historical, geographical, chronological, personal, textual, literary, doctrinal, legal, political, and military details, strands, plots, and subplots concurrently in mind in order to dictate the Book of Mormon one time through without notes or a rough draft?" asks law professor John W. Welch.[13] And, over time new discoveries consistently corroborate the Book of Mormon account.

Chapter 20

Your Account of the Book's Origin Will Become the Only Plausible Explanation

Many theories as to your book's origin must arise, and after the historical and literary evidence becomes available, each of these theories will eventually fail. You must claim that your ability to produce your book came "by the gift and power of God," and this claim will continue to grow in strength until it becomes the only plausible explanation.

"I have no real problem with what your Book of Mormon contains," confessed a Baptist minister to Brigham Young University Professor Brent L. Top. "In fact, I really like its teachings and its testimony of Christ. My problem is with how you say it came about. All that talk about angels, visions, gold plates, etc.—that is the problem."[1]

The Heavens Are Open

If there were no angels, gold plates, or divine origin, and if the heavens no longer reveal scripture, as some maintain, Elder Hugh B. Brown asks, why this would be? Is it that He, the Lord, cannot speak, that He has lost His power to speak? Is it that He doesn't love us anymore and is not interested in our affairs? Or have we made such rapid strides in education and science that we don't need Him anymore?[2] Of course, these questions are absurd. He does speak He spoke to Joseph Smith and called him to bring forth more of His word and restore His church.

The Old and New Testaments were authored by Old World prophets as they were inspired by God. In like manner, the Book of Mormon was written by inspired prophets in the New World whose words on metal plates were translated by Joseph Smith. Author Darl Anderson declares that "it would be utterly impossible for an unlearned youth, or any other person, to produce a book that could so powerfully impact the lives of so many millions of people as the Book of Mormon has done, without divine help."[3]

For those unwilling to accept a heavenly source or believe that God is "the same yesterday, and today and forever" (Hebrews 13:8), Elder B. H. Roberts notes that "the origin of the book was a direct challenge to the teachings of modern Christendom that revelation had ceased; that the awful voice of prophecy would no more be heard; that the volume of scripture was completed and forever closed, and that the Bible was the only volume of scripture. Hence Christendom must find some other explanation for this book than that given by Joseph Smith."[4]

Many Contradictory Theories

Skeptics of the book's origin have advanced numerous theories to explain the Book of Mormon.[5] "These theories range from Joseph Smith writing it as a conscious fraud; conspiring with Sidney Rigdon or others; perhaps there was help from the devil; or, more recent, that even though it is fiction, Joseph wrote it under some sort of religious inspiration."[6] One writer even theorized that "Joseph Smith was visited by spacemen!"[7] Further, while grasping at straws, some naysayers maintain that the Book of Mormon can be explained on various psychological grounds—Joseph Smith was "an epileptic," "a paranoid," or had "a disassociated personality"—even though those who knew him never noticed any such problems. Or the Book of Mormon "can be explained by the environment and knowledge common to the area in which it was produced."[8] However, no one has produced as much as one similar book.

Graduate students participating in a Duke University seminar studying Jewish and Christian writings, after learning pertinent (and impressive) facts about the Book of Mormon, concluded that Joseph Smith might have been a reincarnated Jewish scribe.[9] "Of all the arguments thrown at the Book of Mormon . . . one completely overshadows all the rest. . . . The book is a fraud because its existence is attributed to *divine revelation*"[10] (emphasis added).

David Marks was an early nonbeliever who dismissed the book after its publication in 1830. Upon hearing how the book came forth, he was convinced it was a hoax. Marks writes, "I wished to read it, but could not, in good conscience, purchase a copy, lest I should support a deception." He claimed he read half of it and then wrote, "The style is so insipid, and the work so filled with manifest imposture, that I could feel no interest in a further perusal." Yet this biased, poorly researched conclusion has been used and quoted by generations of Book of Mormon critics as the ultimate in "scholarly objectivity."[11]

Marks was followed in 1831 by Minister Alexander Campbell who was angered because he lost many of his Campbellite followers when they joined the Latter-day Saints.[12] Campbell writes, "There never was a book more evidently written by one set of fingers. . . . I cannot doubt for a single moment but that he [Joseph] is the sole author and proprietor of it."[13] This theory was short-lived when it became obvious that the poorly educated Joseph could not have written such a masterful book.

Next came caustic writers such as E. D. Howe. Howe, a newspaperman in Ohio, was the editor of the first adversarial book, *Mormonism Unvailed* [sic] in 1834. Howe collaborated with apostate Philastus Hurlbut, who was twice excommunicated from the Church for immorality. Howe's book included the Spaulding theory, which maintained that Joseph based the Book of Mormon on a romantic novel authored by Solomon Spaulding, a former clergyman.[14] That theory fell apart in 1884 when President James H. Fairchild of Oberlin College in Ohio and a Mr. Rice discovered the Spaulding manuscript among a collection of old papers. They compared the manuscript with the Book of Mormon, after which President Fairchild published an article in the *New York Observer*: "The theory of the origin of the Book of Mormon in the traditional manuscript of Solomon Spaulding will probably have to be relinquished. . . . Mr. Rice, myself and others compared it with the Book of Mormon and could detect no resemblance between the two."[15]

Oliver Cowdery answered the critics proposing these theories: "I wrote with my own pen the entire Book of Mormon, save a few pages, as it fell from the lips of the Prophet as he translated it by the gift and power of God, by means of the Urim and Thummim, or as it is called by that book, 'Holy Interpreters.' . . . That book is true. Sidney Ridgon did not write it. Mr. Spaulding did not write it. I wrote it myself as it fell from the lips of the Prophet."[16]

Origen Bacheler's *Mormonism Exposed,* published in 1838, concluded that the book "has no merit even as a forgery." Fawn M. Brodie's 1945 book, *No Man Knows My History*, argued that Joseph's religious career began fraudulently and that he gradually came to believe his own lies.[17] Walter Martin, professional antagonist, and author of *Kingdom of the Cults*, in which he labeled The Church of Jesus Christ of Latter-day Saints a cult, maintained for twenty-five years that Solomon Spaulding was the true source of the Book of Mormon.[18] Sandra and Jerald Tanner, who made their living opposing the Church, maintained the Book of Mormon was lifted from the writings of Ethan Smith, another minister in Joseph Smith's time. Ethan Smith wrote *View of the Hebrews*, from which they say Joseph borrowed.[19] However, "there is not *one single thing* in common between *View of the Hebrews* and the Book of Mormon that is not also found in the Bible," writes Hugh Nibley.[20] After making a close study of *View of the Hebrews*, John W. Welch reported that the differences between the two books far outweigh the similarities.[21] Nevertheless, as recently as 2006, adversarial writers who clearly have not read the Book of Mormon are still touting and raising this unfounded and discredited claim.[22]

Many who try to explain the origin of the Book of Mormon and The Church of Jesus Christ of Latter-day Saints, make money selling publications or films. For some, it has been, or still is, their fulltime vocations. "The makers, promoters, and distributors of such scandalous misrepresentation are possessed of a

Pres. Gordon B. Hinckley at Pulpit with a Book of Mormon

spirit—but it is not the spirit of fairness, not the spirit of charity, not the spirit of truth," writes historian David Britton.[23]

Seldom do leaders of The Church of Jesus Christ of Latter-day Saints respond to critics' attempts to disprove the Book of Mormon and the account of the Church's origin. Why waste time and money on such things when efforts can instead be put into teaching and doing good in the world? As biblical Nehemiah says, "I am doing a great work, so that I cannot come down: why should the work cease, whilst I leave it, and come down to you?" (Nehemiah 6:3). Individuals and scholars in the Church, however, do frequently respond and point out the fallacies in critics' accusations. Antagonists, for the most part ignore truthful answers knowing their sensationalist fabrications will continue to generate profitable sales.

A Simple Explanation

"If the Book of Mormon did not come from revelation or inspiration, it must have come from the devil" is one of the arguments that critics of the Book of Mormon make. The Reverend Carl Pedersen, a retired professor of literature who also spent many years as a minister, subscribed to this line of reasoning. Upon finally deciding to read the book, he came to the following conclusion:

> No ignorant man could have produced this book. . . . I decided that he was an absolutely evil and positively brilliant genius. . . . It must have been the devil who helped him. Then one day, when I had gotten further into the book, it occurred to me that I had not read a single word which would lead a man into sin or to lose his faith in Christ. In fact, it was the most Christ-loving book I ever had read, and if true, the greatest proof of Christ's divinity the world had ever received. I decided that the simplest and most believable explanation for the book was that it came exactly as Joseph Smith said it did.[24]

What Believers Say about the Book

What do *believers* say about the book? Church leader Robert K. Dellenbach says, "I have had the glorious experience of quietly examining several pages of Joseph's original manuscript of the Book of Mormon, which is safely protected in the Church archives. I was overwhelmed at the purity of the transcription which had only a very few, insignificant corrections, such as a misspelled word.

Joseph's original manuscript is so perfect it could only have come from one source—divine revelation."[25]

When the Book of Mormon was first published in 1830, stylometry (word-print analysis, as discussed in Chapter 9) had not yet been developed. Stylometry has since shown that it would be humanly impossible for one man to have written the Book of Mormon. Nor could anyone in the 1820s write a lengthy book that describes ancient Near Eastern society so accurately. Nor could Joseph have known the vast amount of information regarding the geographical features, two hundred or more, of their lands, cultural features of their populations, or their language and beliefs contained within the Book of Mormon.[26]

Though critics still attempt to manufacture an author, the variety of theories purporting to explain the book are not compatible with one another, and each is deeply flawed. "As these flaws become more widely understood and as the evidence of the book's ancient character continues to mount, it becomes less and less reasonable to maintain that the book is a modern invention. And that leaves Joseph's account as the leading alternative."[27]

A Convert's Discovery

Shortly after Richard I. Winword, joined the Church at age twenty-five, he was given a book, *Who Really Wrote the Book of Mormon,* by a well-meaning friend. The contents of the book disturbed him, and Richard wondered if he had been deceived about the reality of the Restoration. This caused him to do extensive research into the vast sinkhole of anti-Latter-day Saint literature. Winword soon discovered the book his friend had given him was filled with errors and half-truths. The authors openly lied about historical facts. They used scriptures as Satan would, ignoring or distorting the true meaning. Quotes and references were made to sources that appeared, on the surface, to be valid, but upon closer examination proved to be spurious and reprehensible. The book was cover-to-cover lies, pure and simple.

Through his research, Winword discovered that in this adversarial literature, movies, lectures, TV or radio talk shows, there is a thread of continuity that runs through their expressions: *They lie.* Sometimes they openly lie, misquoting or fabricating statistics. Other times they slant their material in such a way that good appears as bad and bad as good in direct fulfillment of Isaiah 5:20. Out of this research grew a book, *Take Heed That Ye Be Not Deceived— A Revealing Look at Anti–Mormon Literature, Its Authors and Their Motives.* Winword shared his book at no cost for several years, in sharp contrast to the typically high prices charged by antagonistic authors for their falsehoods.[28]

A Gracious Apology

Fortunately, there are some members of other churches who recognize these false accusations and writings as un–Christian attacks. In the foreword to *The New Mormon Challenge,* a prominent leader of an evangelical seminary, Richard J. Mouw, writes that he is "ashamed of our record in relating to the Latter-day Saints community." He admits that by propagating "distorted accounts of what [they] believe . . . and bearing false witness against our [Latter-day Saint] neighbors, we evangelicals have often sinned not just against [them] but against the God who calls us to be truth tellers."[29]

Evangelical ministers Carl Mosser and Paul Owen made an extensive study of Latter-day Saint beliefs and scholarship. After surveying twenty evangelical books criticizing the restored gospel, Mosser and Owen found that *none* (their emphasis) interact with the writings of Latter-day Saint scholars. "Many of the authors promote criticisms that have long been refuted, some are sensationalistic while others are simply ridiculous." They note that this attitude "is a stain upon the authors' integrity and causes one to wonder about their credibility."[30]

The Bible teaches that the Lord "hates" six things. One of these is "A false witness that speaketh lies, and he that soweth discord among brethren" (see Proverbs 6:16–19). There seem to be those who are either unfamiliar with these scriptures or simply ignore them. We should consider the suffering and wars that could have been avoided if people lived by the Church's eleventh article of faith affirmation to let all men "worship how, where, or what they may." "We recognize the good that every other church in the world does," said Church President Gordon B. Hinckley. "We have no quarrel with other churches. . . . We simply say to people not of our faith, 'You bring with you all the truth that you have, and let us see if we can add to it.' That is the mission and message of this church."[31]

Critics and their theories would do well to take the advice of Gamaliel when the Sanhedrin wanted to slay the Apostles: "Let them alone: for if this . . . work be of men, it will come to nought: but if it be of God ye cannot overthrow it; lest haply ye be found even to fight against God" (Acts 5:38–39). Nephi put it even more plainly in the Book of Mormon: "It [the Book of Mormon] speaketh harshly against sin, according to the plainness of the truth; wherefore no man will be angry at the words which I have written save he shall be of the spirit of the devil" (2 Nephi 33:5).

Ongoing Attempts to Disprove the Book

It is clear why there is such a concentrated effort to disprove the Book of Mormon: if it can be discredited and proven to be false, then everything connected to it also falls. But if Joseph Smith was telling the truth about how he received the gold plates from the angel Moroni and translated them into the Book of Mormon, then it follows that he was indeed a prophet sent to usher in the dispensation of the fullness of times, restoring the Church as it was in Christ's time. If this is true, then where does it leave other churches? This is a conflict that is not taken lightly—and that some Evangelicals say they "cannot afford to lose."[32]

If the Lord commanded His prophets to keep a religious record of their people, knowing that, because of iniquity, these inhabitants would disappear from the earth, would He not make plans to safely preserve those records? Would He take a chance on someone randomly finding them? And if they *were* found, no one would be able to read the reformed Egyptian characters on the metal records, nor would they have any comprehension of their spiritual value. The discovery could possibly make the finder very famous, perhaps even wealthy, and the records would undoubtedly end up in a museum. Losing great spiritual truths accumulated over centuries was not the Lord's plan. He had the last prophet, Moroni, deposit the plates in a New York hillside and then arranged to have the Smith family move to the vicinity so the young Joseph could be shown their location, be divinely tutored for four years, and then retrieve them. Joseph, through the Urim and Thummin and the gift and power of God, would then translate them into the Book of Mormon.

Joseph Smith wrote of a prediction his grandfather made regarding one of his descendants: "My grandfather, Asael Smith, long ago predicted that there would be a prophet raised up in his family, and my grandmother was fully satisfied that it was fulfilled in me. My grandfather, Asael died in East Stockholm, New York, after having received the Book of Mormon, and read it nearly through; he declared that I was the very prophet that he had long known would come in his family."[33]

Theories Come and Go

Numerous theories about the Book of Mormon's origin have come and gone since its publication. These conjectures contradict and weaken each other. They disagree on important facts, and all deny the possibility of divine aid in the otherwise inexplicable existence of the book. In his October 2009 general conference talk, Elder Jeffrey R. Holland of the Quorum of the Twelve Apostles summed up the situation:

> For 179 [as of 2009] years this book has been examined and attacked, denied and deconstructed, targeted and torn apart like perhaps no other book in modern religious history—perhaps like no other book in *any* religious history. And still it stands. Failed theories about its origins have been born and parroted and have died—from Ethan Smith to Solomon Spaulding to deranged paranoid to cunning genius. None of these frankly pathetic answers for this book has ever withstood examination because there *is* no other answer than the one Joseph gave as its young unlearned translator. In this I stand with my own great grandfather who said simply enough, 'No wicked man could write such a book as this, and

no good man would write it, unless it were true and he was commanded of God to do so.'[34]

President Gordon B. Hinckley adds his witness: "Joseph Smith couldn't have written the Book of Mormon. These people who wear out their lives trying to find some other cause for the coming forth of the Book of Mormon are doing just that—wearing out their lives. This is the word of God restored in this dispensation so that in the mouths of two or more witnesses the truth and validity of the divine Sonship of the Lord might be established. This is true."[35]

Chapter 21

The Book Must Fulfill
Bible Prophecy
Like No Other

Your book must fulfill many Bible prophecies about the manner in which it will come forth, to whom it will be delivered, and its purposes and accomplishments.

Some people claim there can be no new scripture in these modern times, and they quote the Bible as proof, (see Chapter 20). Does the Bible actually say there is to be no more scripture? Book of Mormon prophets knew this question would arise and warned against it: "Wo be unto him that shall say: We have received the word of God, and we need no more of the word of God, for we have enough!" (2 Nephi 28:29).

God Speaks through Modern Scripture

Soon after the Book of Mormon was published, ministers of other denominations began warning their followers about the dangers of reading the book. Their congregations were told there would be no more scripture, and they quoted Revelation 22:18–19, the last book and chapter in the Bible, which warns against adding to or taking away from "the things which are written in this book." They were also told, and are still being told, that the Bible is complete and no more scriptures would be forthcoming or needed (see Chapter 18).

Typical of many who reject the Book of Mormon, evangelist John Stott maintains that "in Christ, and in the biblical witness to Christ, God's revelation is complete; to add any words of our own to his finished work is derogatory to Christ."[1] The Book of Mormon contains neither our words nor Joseph Smith's, but the words of ancient New World prophets—just as the Bible contains the words of ancient Old World prophets.

According to Bible scholars, this passage in Revelation was written between AD 64 and AD 96, when the books of the New Testament, as we now have them, had not yet been compiled. John, who wrote the book of Revelation, also wrote the Gospel of John at Ephesus at a much later date than the book of Revelation.[2] Did he go against his own warning? Why would he warn against adding to a compiled book that did not yet exist? John was clearly referring only to his book of Revelation. A similar warning is given in the Old Testament book of Deuteronomy: "Ye shall not add unto the word . . . neither shall ye diminish ought from it" (Deuteronomy 4:2). If we interpret those words, as some fundamentalists understand the verses above in Revelation 22, we would be required to ignore every book in the Bible except the first five. The Book of Mormon is a positive indication that God intended other scriptures in addition to the Bible to bless His children.

Besides the prophecy in Isaiah 29 regarding the words of a sealed book that are to be delivered to "one that is learned" who, in turn, proclaimed he could not read it, "for it is sealed" (see Chapter 16), what other Bible prophecies does the Book of Mormon fulfill?

A Sealed Book

Prior to meeting Joseph Smith, Martin Harris was instructed by the Lord in 1818 not to join any church until the words of Isaiah were fulfilled. The relevant verses are these: "And the vision of all is become unto you as the words of a book that is sealed, which men deliver to one that is learned, saying, read this, I pray thee; and he saith, I cannot for it is sealed: And the book is delivered to him that is not learned, saying, Read this, I pray thee; and he saith, I am not learned" (Isaiah 29:11–12). Sometime later, it was revealed to Harris that the Lord had a work for him to do (see Doctrine and Covenants 5). Several manifestations convinced Martin Harris that Joseph Smith was a prophet and that Martin should assist Joseph in bringing forth the Book of Mormon.

Within a few months of receiving the plates, Joseph made a transcription of some of the characters, and, by means of the Urim and Thummim[3] translated them. In February 1828, according to his mother's history, Martin Harris left Harmony and took "the characters to the East . . . and on his way . . . [called] on all who were professed linguists to give them an opportunity of showing their talents in giving a translation of the characters."[4]

Of the several men to whom Harris showed the characters, most notable was Professor Charles Anthon of Columbia College, New York City, a leading classical scholar of the day. After viewing the characters and their translation, he willingly gave Mr. Harris a certificate on which he called the samples "short-hand Egyptian." Anthon pronounced the characters authentic and their translation "correct, more so than any he had seen translated from the Egyptian." Harris "then showed him those that were not yet translated, and he said they were Egyptian, Chaldaic, Assyriac and Arabic; and he said they were true characters" (see Joseph Smith—History 1:64).

The professor then asked Harris whence the characters originated and was told they were transcribed on gold plates and had been received from an angel of God. Anthon then asked to see the certificate, tore it up, said there was no such thing as ministering of angels, and said he would translate the plates if they were brought to him. Martin told him that part of the plates were sealed and that he was forbidden to bring them. As noted above, Anthon, in direct fulfillment of the prophecy in Isaiah 29, replied, "I cannot read a sealed book."

Professor Anthon recognized the characters as "short-hand Egyptian," and Mormon called them "reformed Egyptian" (Mormon 9:32). Neither Anthon nor any other person in 1828 could have read them—unless inspired by God—because no American possessed the necessary skills.[5] Unlike Martin Harris, Professor Anthon was not aware that his words fulfilled an Old Testament prophecy by Isaiah about the Book of Mormon. Harris then left Professor Anthon and visited Dr. Samuel Mitchell, "who sanctioned what Professor Anthon had said respecting both the characters and the translation[6] (Joseph Smith—History 1:65).

Martin Harris returned from New York City to Harmony, Pennsylvania, with the utmost confidence in Joseph's translation and gave an enthusiastic report of his experience to his friends and others. He would later mortgage (and lose part of) his farm to finance the publication of the Book of Mormon. In 1834, Professor Anthon denied Martin Harris's account of their visit. However, Martin could not have coined the precise phrase "short-hand Egyptian," a term known only to scholars, including Anthon. Further, he would not have financed the printing of the Book of Mormon had the visit gone as Anthon later characterized it.[7]

Sealed Portion of Plates Reserved for a Later Time

Joseph Smith had been instructed by the angel Moroni that he was not to translate the sealed two-thirds of the plates. The Book of Mormon explains the reason for this restriction:

> And behold the book shall be sealed; and in the book shall be a revelation from God, from the beginning of the world to the ending thereof. Wherefore, because of the things which are sealed up, the things which are sealed shall not be delivered in the day of the wickedness and abominations of the people. Wherefore the book shall be kept from them . . . until I shall see fit in my own wisdom to reveal all things unto the children of men. (2 Nephi 27:7–8, 22)

At some later date, when the sealed portion is revealed, its words "shall be read upon the house tops; and they shall be read by the power of Christ; and all things shall be revealed unto the children of men which ever have been among the children of men, and will be even unto the end of the earth (2 Nephi 27:11). Until that day arrives, the faith of members and investigators of the restored Church of Jesus Christ of Latter-day Saints will be tested to see if they accept or reject the marvelous, but lesser words of the unsealed, currently available portion of the Book of Mormon.

Two Books to Become "One in Thine Hand"

Another important prophecy comes from Ezekiel who foretold a union between two records:

The word of the Lord came again unto me, saying . . . take thee one stick, and write upon it, For Judah [the Bible and the Jews], and for the children of Israel his companions: then take another stick, and write upon it, for Joseph [Lehi was a descendant of Joseph through Manasseh]; hence, the Book of Mormon], the stick of Ephraim, and for all the house of Israel his companions. And join them, one to another into one stick; and they shall become one in thine hand. (Ezekiel 37:15–17)

What are these *sticks*? The Hebrew word *etz* was translated as *stick* in the King James version; however, the general meaning is *wood*.[8] The Greeks and Romans filled writing boards with wax and then wrote on their surfaces. In 1953, an archaeologist discovered a set of sixteen hinged wax writing boards in Assyria that looked strikingly like Greek and Roman writing boards. Ezekiel most likely was referring to these wax writing boards.[5]

The New English Bible translates Ezekiel 37:15–19 as follows:

These were the words of the Lord to me: Man, take one leaf of a wooden tablet and write on it, "Judah and his associates of Israel." Then take another leaf and write on it, "Joseph, the leaf of Ephraim and all of his associates of Israel." Now bring the two together to form one tablet; then they will be a folding tablet in your hand. These are the words of the Lord God: I am taking the leaf of Joseph, which belongs to Ephraim and his associate tribes of Israel, and joining it to the leaf of Judah. Thus I shall make them one tablet.

Two other known examples of wooden tablets written in the Assyrian language have survived. Ancient Jewish writers used wax tablets regularly, but because they were made of perishable organic material, few have survived. Scholars accept the Hebrew word *estim* as "wax writing boards" because the boards were joined together and because tablets are referred to in several places in the Bible.[9]

So why were they translated as "sticks" in the King James Version of the Bible? The word *etz* appears approximately three hundred times in the Hebrew text, but the King James scholars translated it as *stick* only fourteen times. Seven of those times are in Ezekiel 37. Usually, they translated *etz* as either tree (162 times) or *wood* (103 times). It is surprising, then, to discover that the translators of the Septuagint (knowing Hebrew) did not use *wood* in that Ezekiel chapter 37. Instead, they use rod (rabdos). This is the *only* instance in the whole Greek Bible where *etz* is translated as *rabdos* (rod).[10]

Why did they do this? Scholars have hypothesized that the translator was influenced by the story in Numbers 17:2–3, where the Lord required each tribal leader to write his own name upon his staff (*rabdos*) and leave it in the tabernacle overnight. The tribal name connection is obvious. And there is that prophecy at the end of Ezekiel 37 concerning the reuniting of the kingdoms. The one flaw in this explanation is that the word translated as *rod* in Numbers is not *etz* but is *matteh,* a perfectly good Hebrew word that literally means *staff.* So if that's what Ezekiel really meant, why didn't he also use *matteh*?[11]

Both translations are unique, "and since they differ, they cannot both be correct—though, of course both may be wrong."[12] And because they both changed the meaning of the original Hebrew word, that seems to be the logical conclusion. It seems quite plain from reading Ezekiel 37:15–19 that the record of *Judah,* the Holy Bible, would remain with the Jewish people, that the record of *Joseph,* the Book of Mormon, would be joined unto it, and that the two would become one. As noted in chapter 18, the Lord taught the Nephites, "Know ye not that the testimony of two nations is a witness unto you that I am God, that I remember one nation like unto another? . . . And when the two nations shall run together the testimony of the two nations shall run together also" (2 Nephi 29:8). The testimonies of the Book of Mormon and the Bible together constitute the two testimonies mentioned by Christ.

The prophets in the Book of Mormon were commanded to keep records. It was prophesied that their records would "*grow together*" with the records written by "*the loins of Judah*" (2 Nephi 3:12; emphasis added). The Bible and the Book of Mormon have now been joined together to "become one in thine hand" (Ezekiel 37:17).

Out of the Dust

Isaiah foresaw the coming forth of the record of Joseph as the voice of one who has a "familiar spirit" whispering out of the "dust" (Isaiah 29:4). In Psalm 85:11, we read, "Truth shall spring out of the earth; and righteousness shall look down from heaven." The only way people can speak "*out of the earth*" or "*out of the dust*" after they have passed from this earth is by the written word, and this is precisely what the ancient American prophets did through the Book of Mormon.[13] The Lord promised Joseph of Egypt that his descendants would keep records that "shall be as if the fruit of thy loins had cried unto them from the dust. And they shall cry from the dust; yea, even repentance unto their brethren, even after many generations have gone by them" (2 Nephi 3:19–20).

Mormon, who condensed the Nephite history, also wrote about the record coming out of the dust. "And blessed be he that shall bring this thing to light; for it shall be brought out of darkness unto light, according to the word of God; yea it shall be brought *out of the earth,* and it shall shine forth out of darkness, and come unto the knowledge of the people; and it shall be done by the power of God" (Mormon 8:16). He continues, "And no one need say they shall not come, for surely they shall, for the Lord hath spoken it; for *out of the earth* shall they come by the hand of the Lord and none can stay it; and it shall come in a day when it shall be said that miracles are done away; and it shall come even as if one should speak from the dead" (Mormon 8:26).

Moroni's farewell words warn, "For the time speedily cometh that ye shall know that I lie not, for ye shall see me at the bar of God; and the Lord God will say unto you: Did I not declare my words unto you, which were written by this man, like as one crying from the dead, yea, even as one speaking out of the dust?" (Moroni 10:27). The Nephites were destroyed as a nation, yet their record was preserved so it could come forth as the Book of Mormon. The golden plates containing the Nephites' history were buried in the ground for centuries before they were delivered to the Prophet Joseph Smith—as prophesied by Isaiah.

The Savior's Other Sheep

"Other Sheep"

There is another prophecy in the Bible that is fulfilled by the Book of Mormon. In John 10:16, the Savior refers to other people He would visit: "Other sheep I have, which are not of this fold: them also I must bring, and they shall hear my voice; and there shall be one fold, and one shepherd." The Jews in the Old World did not comprehend His meaning because of their "stiffneckedness and unbelief," and "they mistakenly assumed that the 'other sheep' to which Jesus referred were the Gentiles."[14]

Bible scholars have long wondered who these "other sheep" might be. The Book of Mormon solves this mystery. After Jesus was crucified and resurrected, He visited these "other sheep"—the Nephites. He taught them, chose twelve disciples, and organized His Church, as He had among the Jews. An account of His visit is given in some detail in 3 Nephi 11–28.

The Savior informed the Nephites that they were the other sheep He spoke of in Jerusalem: "And verily I say unto you, that *ye are they* of whom I said: Other sheep I have which are not of this fold; them also I must bring, and they shall hear my voice; and there shall be one fold and one shepherd" (3 Nephi 15:21; emphasis added). And their record in the Book of Mormon has brought many into His fold.

A Fruitful Bough

Judah and Joseph were the fathers of two of the twelve tribes of Israel. Their father, Israel, gave blessings to his sons and their posterity; the greater blessing was given to Joseph (Genesis 49:26).[15] Israel prophesied concerning his young son: "Joseph is a fruitful bough, even a fruitful bough by a well; whose branches run over the wall" (Genesis 49:22). Latter-day Saints believe the ocean was the wall over which Joseph's branches were to run "unto the utmost bound of the everlasting hills" and that he would be "separate from his brethren" (Genesis 49:26).

This blessing is similar to that given by Moses when he blessed the children of Israel before he left the earth. Moses spoke of the "ancient mountains" and the "lasting hills" (Deuteronomy 33:13–17). When the descendants of Joseph (Lehi and family) were led to the Americas about 600 BC, it is plausible that "the land to which they were led was in the western part of South, Central and North America, in the Rocky Mountains, which accurately answers Moses' description."[16]

Joseph's blessing indicated that his posterity would be great. The fulfillment of this promise is not found in the Bible because it is the record of the descendants of Judah. Wouldn't it be logical to assume that a record would be kept to document the fulfillment of the many promises given to Joseph and his seed?[17] The Book of Mormon is that record of the House of Joseph.

To Whom It Would Be Delivered

The angel Moroni delivered the plates to Joseph Smith from which the Book of Mormon was translated, and later Christ's gospel and Church were restored to the earth. Revelation 14:6 foretells this event: "And I saw another angel fly in the midst of heaven, having the everlasting gospel to preach unto them that dwell on the earth, and to every nation and kindred, and tongue, and people." This is why a statue of the angel Moroni trumpeting the restoration of the gospel is on the spires of most of the temples of The Church of Jesus Christ of Latter-day Saints throughout the world.

The book, or plates, was not to be delivered to some famous, prosperous, divinity-school-trained minister at a large and prestigious cathedral but to an unschooled, teachable youth. "And the book is delivered to him that is not learned, saying, Read this, I pray thee; and he saith, I am not learned" (Isaiah 29:12).

It should not be surprising that Joseph of Egypt, whose posterity was foreordained to take the gospel to all nations, would prophesy of his namesake who would become the great Prophet of the Restoration.

Thus saith the Lord God of my father unto me [Joseph, son of Jacob],
A choice seer will I raise up out of the fruit of thy loins . . . and that

seer will I bless, and they that seek to destroy him shall be confounded; for this promise I give unto you; for I will remember you from generation to generation, and his name shall be called Joseph, and it shall be after the name of his father; and he shall be like unto you; for the thing which the Lord shall bring forth by his hand shall bring my people unto salvation." (Joseph Smith Translation, Genesis 50:27, 33)

It's worth noting that Joseph Smith was not the firstborn in his family—the son that is usually named after the father. He was the third son, after his older brothers Alvin and Hyrum.

Dr. Joseph Klaussner, professor of Hebrew and Jewish history, wrote a book in which he "pointed out that one of the most ancient and respected traditions among the Jewish scholars is the prophecy that a 'Joseph' should be raised up in the latter days for the specific purpose of preparing the way for the coming of the Messiah." He cited sources to show that not only is this future Joseph mentioned in the Talmud and other Jewish classics, but Christian scholars have also taken note of this tradition. "According to Jewish scholars, this future Joseph was to be killed....

This Joseph of the latter days would be a descendant of Joseph who was sold into Egypt and would come through the line of Ephraim."[18] Joseph Smith's lineage is through Ephraim.

The prophecy further said that this latter-day Joseph's mission would commence about the time Elijah would appear to fulfill the promise that he would return before the second coming of the Lord made in Malachi 4:5–6, which was fulfilled when he appeared to Joseph Smith and Oliver Cowdery in the Kirtland Temple on April 3, 1836 (See Chapter 10). "The thing which puzzled Dr. Klausner most was why this tradition of a latter-day Joseph should be so thoroughly established among Jewish schol-

Elijah appearing in Kirkland temple to Joseph Smith and Oliver Cowdery

ars when there was no reference to it in the Hebrew Scriptures." It was originally in Genesis as quoted above, but it had been removed and was restored in the Joseph Smith Translation of the Bible. Dr. Klaussner adds that "the Samaritans are even more zealous than the Jews in keeping alive the tradition of the latter-day Joseph. Some of them claim to be of the tribe of Joseph and therefore this prophecy is extremely important to them."[19]

The Book of Mormon, in a prophecy by Joseph of Egypt, tells of this modern Joseph—a latter-day Moses who would be raised up in the latter days:

> Behold that seer will the Lord bless; and they that seek to destroy him shall be confounded; for this promise, which I have obtained of the Lord, of the fruit of my loins, shall be fulfilled, Behold, I am sure of the fulfilling of this promise; And his name shall be called after me; and it shall be after the name of his father, And he shall be like unto me; for the thing, which the Lord shall bring forth by his hand, by the power of the Lord shall bring my people unto salvation.[20] (2 Nephi 3:14–15)

The Dead Sea Scrolls contain "numerous references to a future prophet named 'Asaph' who will restore the priesthood, commence the great gathering, and be a forerunner to the Messiah in the last days. He will face great opposition and be killed by lawless men. Asaph is translated into English as 'Joseph.' The scrolls . . . contain many references to 'Messiah-ben-Joseph' who is to precede 'Messiah-ben-David' in the last days. 'Messiah' means 'anointed one' and 'ben' means 'son of.' The scrolls mention that Messiah-ben-Joseph will restore true temple worship and bring to pass the restoration of the ten tribes."[21]

Purposes of the Book

Isaiah foretold latter-day conditions in which the people would "draw near to me [the Lord] with their mouth . . . but have removed their heart far from me . . . and [are] taught by the precept of men: Therefore, behold, I will proceed to do a marvelous work among this people" (Isaiah 29:13–14). The Book of Mormon plays a central role in this marvelous work, as it brings light and joy with increased knowledge of Christ: "And in that day shall the deaf hear the words of the book, and the eyes of the blind shall see out of obscurity, and out of darkness. The meek also shall increase their joy in the Lord, and the poor among men shall rejoice in the Holy One of Israel" (Isaiah 29:18–19).

The Book of Mormon title page, which was inscribed on the plates by one of the last prophet-authors of the book, defines the purpose of the record: "To show unto the remnant of the House of Israel what great things the Lord has done for their fathers; and that they might know the covenants of the Lord, that they are not cast out forever—and also to the convincing of the Jew and Gentile that Jesus is the Christ, the Eternal God, manifesting Himself unto all nations."

Thus the Book of Mormon was written for us today. Further, as noted earlier in chapter 18, it is to be a witness for the truthfulness of the Bible—to establish its authenticity and its credibility by bringing other witnesses than those of the Eastern World to testify, clarify, and restore many great truths that have been lost in whole, or in part, from the sacred pages of the Bible. And it shows that revelation has not ceased.

The prophet Mormon taught that the remnants of the Lamanites should lay hold upon the gospel of Christ, which shall be set before you, not only in this record [the Book of Mormon] but also in the record which shall come unto the Gentiles from the Jews [the Bible], which record shall come from the Gentiles unto you. For behold, this [the Book of Mormon] is written for the intent that ye may believe that [the Bible]; and if ye believe that [the Bible] ye will believe this [the Book of Mormon] also. (Mormon 7:8–9)

The Book of Mormon strengthens the Bible. In the book of Helaman alone, there are four separate areas of study where Helaman restores or verifies the biblical text: (1) biblical personages and incidents; (2) Bible prophets; (3) Bible prophecies; and (4) New Testament principles that were originally taught in the Old Testament.[22]

Dozens of references are found throughout the Book of Mormon that teach virtually the same gospel truths and refer to incidents that took place in the Bible. Many of these teachings were brought with Lehi and his followers from Jerusalem on the Brass Plates of Laban, and many were revealed to Book of Mormon prophets through the years. In addition, Christ visited and taught them personally after His crucifixion and resurrection.

The Book of Mormon is "God's servant in preparing both Israel and the Gentiles to remember and enter into covenants that will prepare them to be a part of the great gathering of the latter days that will prepare them for the return of the Savior."[23] The book has brought millions unto a fuller knowledge of Christ, and it should be embraced with open arms by all who profess a love for Him.

Accomplishments of the Book

If anyone contemplates the purposes of the Book of Mormon, it is apparent that its purposes have been, and are being fulfilled through its significant accomplishments. One of its greatest accomplishments was the important part it played in the restoration of the gospel of Jesus Christ and in the reestablishment of His church on the earth in the latter days.

A falling away from the truth is prophesied in the Bible, along with the need for a restoration. This universal apostasy began in the days of the ancient apostles themselves (2 Peter 2:1–2). Paul recorded that the Second Coming would not occur "except there come a falling away first" (2 Thessalonians 2:1–12; see verse 3). In Matthew 21:43, Jesus says, "Therefore say I unto you, The Kingdom of God shall be taken from you, and given to a nation, bringing forth the fruits thereof."

There are those who believe the apostasy never happened, and they cite Matthew 16:18 as their proof: "And I [Jesus] say unto thee, that thou art Peter, and upon this rock I will build my church, and the gates of hell shall not prevail against it." Some believe this verse means that "Peter" is the rock upon which Christ's church is built, but if we read the preceding verse 17, it's clear Jesus is saying it was revelation from the Father that testified He is the Christ. Then, verse 18 uses a play on the word "Peter," which in Greek is *petros*, or small rock (Christ being the stone of Israel). Thus, "upon this rock I will build my church" means the rock of revelation.

Paul warned of the "perilous times" that should come "in the last days"—times when men would have "a form of godliness" but would deny "the power thereof;" times when men would be "ever learning, and never able to come to the knowledge of the truth (2 Timothy 3:1–7); and times in which they would be turned "from the truth . . . unto fables" (2 Timothy 4:1–4). He foretold they would "depart "from the faith . . . speaking lies in hypocrisy; having their conscience seared with a hot iron; forbidding to marry; and commanding to abstain from meats" (1 Timothy 4:1–3). Amos prophesied, "Behold, the days come, saith the Lord God, that I will send a famine in the land, not a famine of bread, nor a thirst for water, but of hearing the words of the Lord; And they shall wander from sea to sea, and from the north even to the east, they shall run to and fro to seek the word of the Lord, and shall not find it" (Amos 8:11–12). The Lord foretold the perplexities, calamities, and apostate wickedness of these dark days (Matthew 24; Mark 13; Luke 21).[24] (see also Isaiah 24:4–5; 2 Timothy 4:3–4; and Acts 20:28–30.)

The actions through the years of many who call themselves Christians indicate they have fallen away from Christ's teachings. Would He recognize the doctrines and condone the rituals performed in many Christian churches today?

Gospel interpretations were decreed by those strong enough to suppress differing opinions. As presented in Chapter 10, the selected council called by the Emperor Constantine made decisions that were binding on others—whether they believed in the resolutions or not. The Christians who had been persecuted now joined with the Roman Empire and became the oppressors. The followers of Arius believed the Father and the Son to be two different personages, the Son being inferior to the Father. To suppress this opposition to the Nicene Creed [and its trinitarian Godhead], the Roman Emperor Theodosius had thirty thousand Arian Christians killed during a single night in an amphitheater. Following Theodosius, Charlemagne decided the Saxons did not become Christians quickly enough, so he invited forty-five hundred noble sons of the Saxons to a meeting and had all of them killed.

The Inquisition by the Roman Catholic Church in the Middle Ages persecuted and killed many for holding beliefs contrary to Catholic orthodoxy. William Tyndale, who translated and published the New Testament in English, was hunted, imprisoned, and finally strangled and his body burned at the stake because of his translation and "apostate" beliefs. The Protestant Reformation was answered with the arrest and imprisonment of untold numbers of "heretics," who, after a brief appearance before the Court of the Inquisition, were summarily condemned and cruelly executed. Thirteen thousand Huguenots, who were members of the Reformed Church, were killed in one night, including men, women, and children, by the reigning Catholic government. Nearly all the Anabaptists in Germany were killed.

The "Christian" crusaders' slaughter in Jerusalem was so complete that by their second day, no Jew (man, woman, or child) was still alive. And the Maya, Aztecs, and Incas suffered a similar fate under the motto of "the Holy Cross in true faith towards victory" by their "Christian" invaders. In other words, "Christianity has a long history of intolerance toward those holding different opinions."[25]

Thomas Jefferson believed that creeds "have been the bane and ruin of the Christian church, its own fatal invention, which, through so many ages, made of Christendom a slaughterhouse, and at this day divides it into castes of inextinguishable hatred to one another."[26]

Apostasy and Restoration Foretold

It seems apparent there was an apostasy and the need for a restoration, when the true love of Christ, with peace on earth and goodwill toward men, will be taught and practiced. The Book of Mormon foretells an apostasy and restoration, stating that the book would come forth in a day of apostasy: "Yea, it shall come in a day when the power of God shall be denied, and churches become defiled and be lifted up in the pride of their hearts; yea, even in a day when leaders of churches and teachers shall rise in the pride of their hearts" (Mormon 8:28). "There shall be many who will say, Do this, or do that, and it mattereth not, for the Lord will uphold such at the last day, But wo unto such, for they are in the gall of bitterness and in the bonds of iniquity. And it shall come in a day when there shall be churches built up that shall say: Come unto me, and for your money you shall be forgiven of your sins" (Mormon 8:31–32).

The Restoration is mentioned several times in the Book of Mormon: "And the Lord will set his hand again the second time to restore the people from their lost and fallen state. . . . He shall bring forth his words unto them . . . and they shall be given them for the purpose of convincing them of the true Messiah" (2 Nephi 25:17–18).

Proclamations by Joseph Smith and The Church of Jesus Christ of Latter-day Saints announcing a restoration of the true gospel of Jesus Christ have brought suspicion, resentment, misgivings, envy, and fear to some leaders of traditional Christian churches. The early members of the Church of Jesus Christ of Latter-day Saints suffered many of the same persecutions as the courageous souls throughout the history of Christianity. Latter-day Saint members have a deep respect and love for those who suffered so much to make the Bible available to the common man, and the great reformers, who they believe, were raised up by God for special missions. Martin Luther and John Calvin recognized that practices and doctrines had been changed or lost. They tried to reform the churches to which they belonged. Their Reformation efforts did not, however, effect a restoration. Some degree of religious freedom and tolerance was necessary for Christ's true church to be restored.

The coming forth of the Book of Mormon is tangible evidence (exhibit A) that a restoration has taken place. It is the clearest confirmation that the gospel has been restored to the earth in these latter days! We need not depend on Joseph Smith's, or any other person's, word; here is tangible evidence that God cares about us and has again spoken to man. With this restoration came the authority to act in His name and the restitution of all the covenants and blessings of His primitive church, along with prophets and apostles.

Christian Reformers Looked for a Restoration

Roger Williams opposed the Church of England and left it. He joined the Puritans, came to America, and eventually founded the Baptist Church, from which he later withdrew. He declared himself to be a "seeker," accepting the fundamental beliefs of Christianity but not a particular church or creed. He maintained, "There is no regularly constituted church on earth, nor any person qualified to administer any church ordinances; nor can there be until new apostles are sent by the Great Head of the Church for whose coming I am seeking."[27]

Thomas Jefferson expressed similar dissatisfaction:

The religion builders have so distorted and deformed the doctrines of Jesus, so muffled them in mysticisms, fancies and falsehoods, have caricatured them into forms so inconceivable, as to shock reasonable thinkers. . . . Happy in the prospect of a restoration of primitive Christianity, I must leave to younger persons to encounter and lop off the false branches which have been engrafted into it by the mythologists of the middle and modern ages.[28]

Millions have rejoiced with the coming forth of the Book of Mormon, which has corrected false doctrines and helped usher in the sought-after restoration of Christ's original Church.

Chapter 22

The Divinity of the Book Will Be Confirmed by the Visitation of an Angel to Three Witnesses

An angel from heaven must appear in broad daylight, with the golden plates in hand, and bear testimony to three honest, respected citizens of your community that your book is the word of God. These witnesses' testimonies must be put to the test when each of them becomes estranged from you. The witnesses must remain true to their testimonies of this event—without profit or gain and at times under great personal sacrifice—until the end of their lives. Eight other reliable witnesses must also testify that they saw and hefted the plates.

When Joseph Smith received the golden plates from the angel Moroni, he was initially instructed to show them to no one. His family was permitted to feel the plates only through a fabric covering. Even during the translation process, the scribes were not allowed to view the plates.

Witnesses to Testify of Gold Plates

During the translation, the text revealed to the young prophet that "three witnesses shall behold it [the plates] by the power of God, besides him to whom the book shall be delivered; and they shall testify to the truth of the book and the things therein. And there is none other which shall view it, save it be a few according to the will of God, to bear testimony of his word unto the children of men for the Lord God hath said that the words of the faithful should speak as it were from the dead" (2 Nephi 27:12–13). The three witnesses are also mentioned in Ether 5:3–4.

Bible verses tell us that "in the mouth of two or three witnesses shall every word be established" (see 2 Corinthians 13:1 and Deuteronomy 19:15). Would the world accept the testimony of Joseph Smith alone regarding the angel, the plates, and his role as translator? Most likely not.

Joseph Smith inquired of the Lord to learn who the witnesses should be and subsequently informed Oliver Cowdery, Martin Harris, and David Whitmer that if they would humble themselves, they would have the privilege of seeing the ancient record with the responsibility of testifying to the world what they knew to be true. All three had assisted in one way or another with the work, and each had a strong desire to see the plates.

Soon thereafter, the four men retired to the woods near the Whitmer home in southern New York and knelt in prayer.[1] Each of the men took a turn praying fervently for the desired manifestation. After their second failure, Martin Harris proposed that he withdraw from the group, feeling that his presence was the cause of their problem.

The Angel Moroni Shows the Three Witness the Plates

After Harris's departure, the group again knelt in prayer. In Joseph's words, "We had not been many minutes engaged in prayer, when we presently beheld a light above us in the air and an angel stood before us."[2] The angel "held the plates which we had been praying for," continued Joseph. "He turned over the leaves one by one, so that we could see them, and discern the engravings thereon distinctly. . . . Immediately afterwards, we heard a voice from out of the bright light above us saying, 'These plates have been revealed by the power of God, and they have been translated by the power of God. The translation of them which you have seen is correct, and I command you to bear record of what you now see and hear.'"[3]

Angel with witnesses

Joseph subsequently went to Martin Harris, who was earnestly engaged in prayer. He joined him in his appeal, and ultimately they obtained the same manifestation that was shown earlier to the other two witnesses. In the midst of this experience, Martin cried out, "'Tis enough; mine eyes have beheld; mine eyes have beheld," and he then rejoiced at what he had seen.[4]

The Testimony of the Three Witnesses

Joseph's mother, Lucy, describes the feelings of the Three Witnesses after their sacred experience:

Martin Harris [then] came in: He seemed almost overcome with joy, and testified boldly to what he had both seen and heard. And so did David and Oliver, adding that no tongue could express the joy of their hearts, and the greatness of the things which they had both seen and heard. Martin said, 'I have now seen an angel from heaven. . . . I have received for myself a witness that words cannot express, that no tongue can describe, and I bless God in the sincerity of my soul that he has condescended to make me . . . a witness of the greatness of his work and designs in behalf [of] the children of men.'[5]

Their resulting written testimony of this momentous event is found in all editions of the Book of Mormon. Their testimony reads as follows:

Be it known unto all nations, kindreds, tongues, and people, unto whom this work shall come: That we, through the grace of God the Father, and our Lord Jesus Christ, have seen the plates which contain this record, which is a record of the people of Nephi, and also of the Lamanites, their brethren, and also of the people of Jared, who came from the tower of which hath been spoken. And we also know that they have been translated by the gift and power of God, for his voice hath declared it unto us; wherefore we know of a surety that the work is true. And we also testify that we have seen the engravings which are upon the plates; and they have been shown unto us by the power of God, and not of man. And we declare with words of soberness, that an angel of God came down from heaven, and he brought and laid before our eyes, that we beheld and saw the plates, and the engravings thereon; and we know that it is by the grace of God the Father, and our Lord Jesus Christ, that we beheld and bear record that these things are true. And it is marvelous in our eyes. Nevertheless, the voice of the Lord commanded us that we should bear record of it; wherefore, to be obedient unto the commandments of God, we bear testimony of these things. And we know that if we are faithful in Christ, we shall rid our garments of the blood of all men, and be found spotless before the judgment-seat of Christ, and shall dwell with him eternally in the heavens. And the honor be to the Father, and to the Son, and to the Holy Ghost, which is one God. Amen.

Oliver Cowdery
David Whitmer
Martin Harris

The Testimony of the Eight Witnesses

Within a few days, eight more men were given the privilege of seeing and handling the plates. This group included Joseph's father and two brothers, Hyrum and Samuel, and four of the Whitmer brothers, along with Hiram Page, a brother-in-law to the Whitmers. Joseph showed them the plates, and they were given the liberty of leafing through the unsealed portion and examining the engravings.[6] Their testimony appears in all editions of the Book of Mormon, following The Testimony of Three Witnesses:

> Be it known unto all nations, kindreds, tongues, and people, unto whom this work shall come: That Joseph Smith, Jun. the translator of this work, has shown unto us the plates of which hath been spoken, which have the appearance of gold; and as many of the leaves as the said Smith has translated we did handle with our hands; and we also saw the engravings thereon, all of which has the appearance of ancient work, and of curious workmanship. And this we bear record with words of soberness, that the said Smith has shown unto us, for we have seen and hefted, and know of a surety that the said Smith has got the plates of which we have spoken. And we give our names unto the world, to witness unto the world that which we have seen. And we lie not, God bearing witness of it.

Joseph's mother provides this detail: "After these witnesses returned to the house, the angel again made his appearance to Joseph, at which time Joseph delivered up the plates into the angel's hands."[7]

The Estrangement of the Three Witnesses

In the years of trials and persecutions that followed, all of the Three Witnesses and three of the Eight Witnesses were either excommunicated from the Church or left with feelings of bitterness toward it or its leaders. Cutting off the membership of those who failed to conform to the high gospel standards the Lord had set took great courage on Joseph's part. It preserved the Church from corruption but multiplied his own personal problems. However, none of the witnesses ever denied at any time their testimony regarding their experience of seeing and handling the plates—or seeing an angel in the case of the Three Witnesses.[8] This would not have been the case had Joseph been trying to deceive or perpetuate a fraud. One or more of them would certainly have taken the opportunity to expose him. Thomas B. Marsh, President of the Quorum of the Twelve in 1838, later questioned Oliver Cowdery and David Whitmer about their testimonies found in the Book of Mormon. Although both were then filled with personal resentment toward Joseph Smith and the Church, each reaffirmed his witness of the divine origin of the Book of Mormon.[9]

After having seen such a glorious event, how could any of these men permit himself to leave the Church? The answer could be in part that the Three Witnesses had problems with egotism. "Because they had seen for themselves with regard to the Book of Mormon, most of the witnesses considered their judgment equal to Joseph Smith's on all other matters."[10] Their alienation makes them even more credible as witnesses because no collusion or conspiracy could have withstood the years of separation from the Church and from each other.[11] Two of the Three Witnesses later asked to be readmitted into the Church.

What were the backgrounds and character of these "Three Witnesses?"

Oliver Cowdery

Oliver Cowdery, a school teacher, was boarding with Joseph Smith's parents when they eventually trusted him enough to tell him Joseph's story. Joseph Smith Sr. and Lucy advised Oliver to pray for a personal testimony. "[The] Lord appeared unto . . . Oliver Cowdery and shewed unto him the plates in a vision and also the truth of the work." As Oliver told Lucy, "I have made it a subject of prayer, and I firmly believe that it is the will of the Lord that I should go [and] help Joseph with the translation."[12]

Oliver acted as scribe for most of the translation of the Book of Mormon and labored as a missionary. During the first year after the organization of the Church, he and three other companions walked three hundred miles from upstate New York to Kirtland, Ohio, where they baptized 130 converts in less than a month. They walked another six hundred miles to Independence, Missouri, the last three hundred at times in snow up to their knees in the bitter cold and preached in newly settled country. Oliver did not exaggerate when he later referred to the many "fatigues and privations which have fallen to my lot to endure, for the gospel's sake."[13]

Eight years later, a clash of wills and various other problems emerged, leading to Oliver's separation from the Church. He had been close to Joseph and had passed through numerous trials and persecutions with him. Personally, Oliver "was generally recognized by [Latter-day Saints and non-Latter-day Saints] alike as an astute and highly intelligent individual, and [the rest of] his mature life was spent in the vocation and avocation of law and politics." He was regularly before the public as an active Democratic Party worker, a coeditor of the *Walworth County Democrat,* a public speaker, and an occasional candidate for civic office. He served as a member of the Board of School Examiners of Seneca County, tested candidates for admission to the bar, was elected as one of three township trustees, and was nominated as a state assemblyman. A close associate in Tiffin, Ohio, writes, "His honesty, integrity, and industry were worthy the imitation of all, whilst his unquestioned legal abilities reflected credit as well upon himself as upon the profession of which he was a member."[14]

Oliver Cowdery's wife said of him, "He always without one doubt . . . affirmed the divinity and truth of the Book of Mormon."[15] This confidence stood the test of persecution, poverty, loss of status, failing health, and the tragic deaths of five of his six children.

Joseph wrote to Oliver in 1843 inviting him to return to the Church. Oliver waited another four years before swallowing his pride and traveling to

Kanesville, Iowa, with Phineas Young (his brother-in-law, who was a brother of Brigham Young) in 1848 to ask for baptism. Oliver, along with his wife and daughter, traveled from their home in Wisconsin to Kanesville, arriving during a local conference on October 21, 1848. Orson Hyde was conducting the meeting and, upon spotting Oliver, left the stand and went to him, embraced him, took his arm, and escorted him to the platform. He was invited to speak to the congregation of nearly two thousand. He bore his testimony as one of the Three Witnesses and testified of the truthfulness of the Book of Mormon. He later met with the high council. "I wish to come humbly and be one in your midst," he declared. "I wish to become a member of the church again."[16] He was rebaptized by Orson Hyde on November 12. He planned on going west the next year, but lack of means and deteriorating health prevented that from happening. He died on March 3, 1850, in Missouri.

> A few months before his death, Oliver received a visit from Jacob Gates, an old [Latter-day Saint] acquaintance. . . . After conversing about troubled times in early church history, Gates asked Cowdery about his testimony printed in the Book of Mormon. He wanted to know if the testimony was based on a dream, the imagination of his mind, an illusion, or a myth. Jacob wanted the truth. As the account goes, Oliver Cowdery got up from his resting place, retrieved a first edition Book of Mormon, and read solemnly the testimony. Turning to face Gates, he said, "Jacob, I want you to remember what I say to you. I am a dying man, and what would it profit me to tell you a lie? I know that this Book of Mormon was translated by the gift and power of God. My eyes saw, my ears heard, and my understanding was touched, and I know that whereof I testified is true. It was no dream, no vain imagination of the mind—it was real."[17]

Oliver rejoined the Church "at a time when there was nothing of earthly value to gain in joining a homeless people on their way to the barren valleys of the Rocky Mountains."[18]

David Whitmer

David Whitmer met Joseph Smith after David's family received an enthusiastic letter from Oliver Cowdery testifying that the work he was doing with the prophet was divine. Persecution had begun to intensify in Harmony, and at Joseph's request, Oliver wrote to the Whitmer Family asking if he and the Smiths might stay with them in Fayette. David's father invited them to reside on his farm as long as they wished. David and Joseph, only one year apart in age, became good friends.

David suffered persecutions for his convictions. In 1833, he and other Church leaders were taken from their homes by members of a mob of about five hundred armed men. They were told to say farewell to their families because they would never see them again. They were taken to the public square at Independence, Missouri, where they were stripped, tarred and feathered, and verbally abused. The commanding officer then called twelve of his men, ordered them to cock their guns and point them at the prisoners' breasts, and be ready to fire when he gave the order. The officer then threatened the captives with instant death unless they denied the Book of Mormon and confessed it to be a fraud. David Whitmer lifted up his hands and bore witness that the Book of Mormon was the word of God. Surprisingly, the mob then let them go.[19] He later said, "The testimony I bore the mob made them tremble before me."[20] But, Whitmer's trials continued. "When mobs terrorized the Missouri settlement, burning homes and brutally whipping men, it was David who vigorously organized the resistance."[21]

David was appointed President of the Church for the members in the Missouri area. In 1838, he was "excommunicated on charges of usurping too much authority, writing letters of dissension to apostates, and breaking the Word of Wisdom."[22] Historians say "he resisted change and was jealous of the power and suspected influence of Sidney Rigdon." Whitmer felt Rigdon had Joseph's deep affection and exercised undue influence over him.[23]

Whitmer stayed in Richmond, Missouri, for fifty years where he was a distinguished and respected member of the community, serving as mayor. He was the most interviewed of all the Book of Mormon witnesses, because he lived longer than the others. At his death, it was said of him "that no man ever lived here who had among our people more friends and fewer enemies. Honest, conscientious and upright in all his dealings, just in his estimate of men, and open, manly and frank in his treatment of all, he made lasting friends who loved him to the end."[24]

"I have been visited by thousands of people," David said in an interview, "believers and unbelievers, men and ladies of all degrees, sometimes as many as 15 in one day, and have never failed in my testimony. And they will know some day that my testimony is true. . . . I heard the voice of the Angel just as stated in said Book and the engravings on the plates were shown to us, and we were commanded to bear record of them; and if they are not true, then there is no truth, and if there is no truth there is no God; if there is no God then there is no existence. But there is a God, and I know it."[25]

Two encyclopedias reported that David denied his testimony, prompting him to publish a pamphlet addressed "To All Believers in Christ." In it, he stated, "I will say once more to all mankind, that I have never at any time denied that testimony or any part thereof. I also testify to the world, that neither Oliver Cowdery or Martin Harris ever at any time denied their testimony." Whitmer maintained that none of the Eight Witnesses ever denied their testimonies.[26]

On the evening of his death, January 22, 1888, he called his family and some friends to his bedside. He then addressed them in these words: "Now you must all be faithful in Christ. I want to say to you all, the Bible and the record of the Nephites [Book of Mormon] is true, so you can say that you have heard me bear my testimony on my death-bed. All be faithful in Christ, and your reward will be according to your works. . . . My trust is in Christ forever, worlds without end. Amen."[27]

Martin Harris

Martin Harris, a prominent businessman in Palmyra who played an important role in the bringing forth of the Book of Mormon, financed its publication. "He was appointed to the first High Council of the Church, but his main contribution was in his missionary service and private conversations. He and his brother Emer baptized a hundred converts in a few weeks, and he was imprisoned for his forthrightness in proclaiming the restored gospel."[28]

Martin endured other trials. The great respect he had enjoyed in his community changed to scorn, and he suffered estrangement and finally separation from his wife and children.[29] A year after his wife died, in 1836, he moved to Kirtland, Ohio, and married Caroline Young, a niece of Brigham Young. In 1856, Caroline and their four children emigrated to Utah. Martin, now seventy-three years of age, remained in Kirtland. He told a census taker in 1860 that he was a "Mormon preacher," and later he told a visitor, "I never did leave the Church, the Church left me." (Meaning that the Church moved to the West while Martin stayed in Kirtland.) He demonstrated his loyalty to the Church while acting as a self-appointed guide-caretaker of the deserted Kirtland Temple, which he loved.[30]

Harris felt resentment against Church leaders because he was never given a major Church office after he had sacrificed so much. He later said that he "lost confidence in Joseph Smith" and that "his mind became darkened." He was excommunicated three weeks after he was released from the high council in Kirtland, Ohio, in 1837.[31] He stayed in Kirtland when the Saints left in 1838.

On one occasion, he was given wine by old acquaintances to get him "tipsy." His companions then carefully asked, "Now Martin, do you really believe that you did see an angel, when you were awake?" They were delighted when he replied, "No, I do not believe it." But they were not so happy when he continued, "Gentlemen, what I have said is true, from the fact that my belief is swallowed up in knowledge; for I want to say to you that as the Lord lives I do know that I stood with the Prophet Joseph Smith in the presence of the angel, and it was in the brightness of day."[32]

Harris was universally respected in his community for his industry and integrity. He was described by his contemporaries as "an industrious, hard-working farmer, shrewd in his business calculations, frugal in his habits . . . strictly upright in his business dealings."[33]

He applied for baptism and was rebaptized into the Church on November 7, 1842, and again in Salt Lake City in 1870 when he finally decided to join the Saints and his family there. He died at Clarkston, Utah, on July 10, 1875, at the age of ninety-three. On the afternoon of his death, he was bolstered up in his bed where, with the Book of Mormon in his hand, he bore his last testimony to those who were present.[34]

Martin Harris—The Man Who Knew Musical Pageant

An outdoor musical pageant, *The Man Who Knew*, which depicts Martin's life, is presented every two years in Clarkston. Tens of thousands have seen this production since it opened in 1983.

Belief in Angels Now Common

When Joseph Smith and the Three Witnesses declared they had seen and conversed with and been shown the plates by an angel, they were largely rejected by their 1829 society. People like them were laughed at or looked upon as either crackpots or liars. But these days it seems that a belief in angels is generally accepted, and judging from the number of books written about angels, belief in them seems almost commonplace.[35] In fact, a Harris interactive poll in 2005 found that 68 percent of Americans now believe in angels.[36]

While Elder Jeffrey Holland was working on his doctorate at Yale University, he requested a favor of the senior reference librarian who had helped him do research for his dissertation. He asked her to find how many books in that nine-million-volume library "claim to have been delivered by an angel." Giving him a peculiar look, she told him she didn't know of any such books. He asked her to run a check because he really would like to know for some religious writing he was doing.

For several days, he heard nothing. Then one day, all smiles, she said, "I have a book for you. I found one book which, it is claimed, was delivered by an angel. But it's one from your people," and she held up a paperback copy of the Book of Mormon. "I'm told you can get them for a dollar. My word," she continued, "an angel's book for a dollar. You would think angels would charge more, but then again, where would they spend it?"[37]

In reality, a price cannot be placed on the Book of Mormon. It is "a treasured testament. There is no other book quite like it," proclaimed Elder Russell M. Nelson. "Can you find any other book delivered by an angel? Can you think of any other book prepared for people to read centuries later? Its writers did not write it for readers of their day. No royalties accrued to its authors from sales to contemporary consumers. In fact, its authors paid dearly for their privilege of authorship, as did its translator."[38]

The Necessity of Witnesses

Joseph Smith not only was visited by and conversed with angels, but unlike others who claimed similar experiences, he introduced angels to his associates, who provided written testimony of the event. "It is as important to believe the witnesses of the Book of Mormon," writes former Brigham Young University Professor Richard L. Anderson, "as it is to believe the testimony of Peter and Paul that they had seen the resurrected Christ. In 1 Corinthians 15:15, Paul said people could set aside the Apostles' testimonies and essentially call the witnesses liars, but God's chosen witnesses were not liars. They were honest men telling the truth." Anderson spent many years studying the lives and testimonies of the eleven witnesses of the Book of Mormon. He first encountered the concept of witnesses in law school where he learned that in legal documents, two or three witnesses are needed to attest to a signature and all history is reconstructed by witnesses. Anderson writes, "I have been in every county where the witnesses lived, read the newspapers of their time, and seen the court records, and I know they were honest men with a divine mission."[39]

These eleven honest witnesses, testifying of the divinity of the Book of Mormon, played a great part in the restoration of the gospel of Jesus Christ to the earth.

Chapter 23

The Honest in Heart
Will Be Drawn
to Your Book

Millions of the honest in heart—both renowned and ordinary—must accept your book and its teachings, many making significant sacrifices, even to the point of laying down their lives, rather than denying their testimonies of it.

Among the millions of members of The Church of Jesus Christ of Latter-day Saints are those born to Latter-day Saint families, who gain their own testimonies, and then lead lives as faithful members. Others gain an interest in the restored gospel when a friend invites them to a church social or Sunday meeting, or they obtain information about the Church through the internet, news articles, etc., which lights the flame of testimony. Missionaries knock on the doors of thousands of others who listen, study, pray and are baptized. New members often express the feeling that they have finally found that for which they have been searching. "It's like coming home"—"It just makes sense"— are frequent remarks.

Members of the Church have become presidents of major universities, scientists, statesmen, diplomats, engineers, educators, attorneys, doctors, acclaimed writers, artists, sculptors, presidents of large corporations, professional athletes, military officers, governors, mayors, entertainers, insurance and real estate executives, political leaders, and more.

"Today, as in the day Joseph Smith lived, many would die rather than relinquish the religion he established."[1] Following are a few of these thousands of people, famous and obscure, who would, and some who did, lay down their lives for their faith:

Joseph F. Smith, son of Hyrum Smith, (Joseph Smith's brother) was only fifteen when he was called to serve as a missionary in the Hawaiian Islands. After serving for nearly four years, he traveled with a small wagon train company through California on his way back home to Utah. They had made camp for the night when a group of drunken men rode into the camp, cursing and swearing and threatening to kill any Latter-day Saints that came in their path. When some of Joseph F. Smith's group heard them coming, they fled into the brush, out of sight, waiting for the band to pass. Joseph F. was a little distance from the camp gathering wood as the men rode up. When he first saw them, his first instinct was to do as the others had done. But then the thought came to him, "Why should I run from these fellows?" and he boldly walked up to the campfire.

One of the men, pointing his pistols at the young man and cursing, declared that it was his duty to exterminate every Latter-day Saint he met. He then demanded in a loud, angry voice, "Are you a Mormon?"

Without a moment of hesitation and looking the man in the eye, Joseph F. boldly answered, "Yes, siree, dyed in the wool; true blue, through and through."

The bold answer, given without any sign of fear, completely disarmed the man. He grasped the missionary by the hand and said, "Well you are the [blankedy blankest] pleasantest man I ever met! Shake, young fellow. I am glad to see a man that stands up for his convictions."

Joseph F. said in later years that he fully expected to be shot, but he could take no other course, even though it seemed death would be the result. The group thanked the Lord for their safe deliverance.[2] In 1901, Joseph F. Smith became the eighth president of the Church and served for seventeen years until his death at age eighty.

Joseph Standing, who was serving as a missionary in Whitfield County Georgia in 1879, wrote to Governor Colquitt asking for protection for the Church missionaries serving there who had been subject to mob violence and for the safety of members of the Church whose homes were being broken into by lawless bands. The governor's reply was that he would look into the matter. So far as is known, that was the last those Saints heard and the governor did nothing.

Rudger Clawson and Joseph Standing

The missionaries' success had generated much adversarial literature by sectarian churches in the area. Elder Standing and his companion, Elder Rudger Clawson, were enroute to a conference in Rome, Georgia, when they encountered a mob of twelve men who took them into the woods and shot and killed Elder Standing, eventually putting twenty bullets into his head and neck. Thinking that Elder Clawson would attempt to escape, someone yelled, "Shoot that man!" He quickly turned, facing the mob whose guns were all aimed at him, and folding his arms, said,

"Shoot!" His coolness seemed to disarm the mob, and they lowered their guns.

Although the names of all twelve men were known, only three were arrested and brought to trial, yet all were acquitted. Elder Clawson, who later became a Member of the Quorum of the Twelve in the Church, was sent back to Varnell Station to testify at the trial, which he described as a farce.

Elder Clawson accompanied Elder Standing's body to Salt Lake City for burial. Thousands attended the funeral which was held in the Salt Lake Tabernacle. Part of the inscription on his tombstone reads: "Our brother rests beneath his native sod, His murderers are in the hands of God. Weep, weep for them, not him, whose silent dust here waits the resurrection of the just."[3]

Joseph Standing headstone and monument in Salt Lake City

William Berry, John Gibbs, Martin Condor, and James Hudson were all slain by members of a mob in Cane Creek, Tennessee, in 1884. As missionaries, Elder Gibbs and Elder William Jones had been sent by their mission president, B. H. Roberts, to visit towns throughout Tennessee to help correct the false impressions and outright lies being spread about the Church. They joined two other missionaries, Elders William Berry and Henry Thompson, at Cane Creek.

Their enemies had already burned down their little church, and services were being held in the James Condor home. On a Sunday morning, when church services were about to begin, approximately twenty masked men came out of the woods and grabbed Mr. Condor, who then shouted to his son, Martin, and stepson, James Hudson, to run into the house to protect the missionaries, the obvious target of the mob. In the ensuing skirmish, two of the four missionaries, along with Martin Condor and James Hudson, were killed, and Mrs. Condor was critically wounded. The leader of the mob, David Hinson, a minister who saw the restored Church as a threat to his own flock, was also killed. The Condors obtained wooden coffins and buried the dead in their yard. The mob set up guards, vowing not to let any Latter-day Saint come to take away the missionaries' bodies.

President Roberts was determined to get the elders' bodies home to their families but was told he would be going to his death if he should try. However, he heard a voice say, "You will go to secure those bodies and all will be well with you, but you must go."

Disguising himself as a stable worker, he obtained a wagon, metal caskets, and, along with two young men, drove to Cane Creek. They were able to ride in, dig up the bodies, and return without incident.

Another missionary, Elder Willis Robinson, accompanied the bodies back to Utah.[4] Elder Gibbs had previously told President Roberts that he was "willing to lay down my life for the truth's sake and for the testimony of Jesus."[5]

James S. Brown was called in the fall of 1849 to serve as a missionary to the Polynesian Islands. As a lone missionary on the island of Raivavae, French Polynesia, he was threatened with death many times. Once, a hot fire was prepared to burn him to death, and he was carried to the beach to be burned.

Elder Brown recalled, "The Spirit of the Lord rested mightily upon me," and with great power, he defied them to carry out their plans, saying, "In the name of Israel's God, I defy ten of your best men, yea, the host of you, for I serve that God who delivered Daniel from the den of lions, and the three Hebrew children from the fiery furnace." A fight started between the executioners and the judge's counselors, and Elder Brown and his companions were able to slip away unharmed.

He later learned the rest of the story from one of the old counselors. The man recounted how a brilliant light or pillar of fire came down close over the missionary's head. The would-be executioners took it as a sign that his God would burn them if they harmed him. He said the young warriors did not see the light and were determined to burn the missionary. The older men tried to stop them, and thus a fight ensued.

Elder Brown continued his missionary work on the island unmolested.[6]

Brigham Young, "was perhaps the greatest colonizer that the world has ever known." wrote Dr. Frederick L. Paxson, former chair of the history department at UC Berkeley. "After founding Salt Lake City, Brigham Young sent settlers in every direction from that center, resulting in the colonization of an expansive desert country."[7] His colonization parties laid out agricultural villages in some 350 locations in Utah and parts of Idaho, Wyoming, Nevada, Arizona, Colorado, and Canada.[8]

Before joining the Church, Brigham spent many months making sure that what he was studying was the truth. Shortly after his baptism, he spoke of his feelings toward the restored gospel he had embraced, "Nothing would satisfy me but to cry abroad in the world, what the Lord was doing in the latter days." Although he would be driven from five homes because of his testimony, he spent the rest of his life declaring what he knew to be true.[9] "Commenting on his conversion, Brigham testified, 'When I saw a man without eloquence, or talent for public speaking, who could only say, 'I know, by the power of the Holy Ghost, that the Book of Mormon is true, that Joseph Smith is a Prophet of the Lord,' the Holy Ghost proceeding from that individual illuminated my understanding . . . and I knew for myself that the testimony of the man was true."[10]

Brigham was president of The Church of Jesus Christ of Latter-day Saints from 1847 until his death in 1877. Brigham Young University, one of the largest privately-owned universities in the United States, honors his name. Unfortunately, regardless of being a great man and leader, he is more often remembered in the world for having plural wives, a practice he entered into with much reluctance.[11] Brigham's last words in mortality were of his earthly mentor, "Joseph! Joseph! Joseph!" According to his daughter Zina, the divine look on his face seemed to indicate that he was communicating with his beloved friend.[12] A statue of Brigham Young, one of Utah's most revered citizens, stands in the nation's capital in Washington, DC.[13]

B. H. Roberts immigrated to America from England at the age of nine. Roberts not having the privilege of schooling, was illiterate, a situation very distressful to him, leaving him wondering if the time would "ever come when books and papers will speak to me? Will I ever read books?" To this query, a quiet voice spoke within him, "Aye, and you'll write them too."[18]

That promise proved to be true. He became the valedictorian of the University of Deseret in Utah, "a journalist-editor, plus an orator, U.S. Army chaplain, and mission president over the Southern States and Eastern States Missions. Before his death at age seventy-six, he had written more than a thousand articles, printed sermons, pamphlets, and tracts, as well as thirty books."[19] Included among his many writings is a six-volume *Comprehensive History of the Church of Jesus Christ of Latter-day Saints* and a three-volume *New Witness for God*, evidence of his dedication as a student of the Book of Mormon.

Roberts was prominent in the Enabling Convention that led to Utah's statehood and was elected to Congress in 1898. His election caused much opposition and heated hearings were held to determine if he should be seated as a polygamist, having married three wives. Some of the national press was sympathetic. The Texas legislature thought Roberts should complain about the immorality of those who judged him. C. W. Elliot, President of Harvard, and Susan B. Anthony, famed woman suffrage advocate, both voiced their support for Roberts to be seated. Elliot said, "He was absolutely right in continuing to maintain his wives and their children," and Anthony agreed. "He was elected by the voters from his State and the Constitution does not give Congress the power to throw him out." Nevertheless, he was not seated.[20]

In his sixties, through much perseverance, Roberts became the first member of the Church to serve as a chaplain in the U.S. Armed Forces. However, he was shunned by the chaplains of other denominations. Their resentment became very apparent in France when a worship service was held on Thanksgiving Day in 1918 to show gratitude for the signing of the Armistice and the end of the war.

While the other chaplains sat on the grandstand, Elder Roberts was given a rear seat and was not asked to participate on the program. Thus it was with great surprise that he heard announced, "Elder B. H. Roberts, the [Latter-day Saint] Chaplain, will give the Thanksgiving Psalm." Roberts, though familiar with the Psalms, had never heard of the "*Thanksgiving* Psalm," but he arose to go to the podium, not knowing what he would say when he arrived. He later testified that during that long walk to the podium, a clear voice said to him, "The 100th Psalm." He opened his Bible and read the 100th Psalm, which is the Thanksgiving Psalm. The late BYU Professor Truman Madsen, who wrote of this account, continues: "Returning to his seat, Roberts noticed that his fellow chaplains were not looking at him but at the floor. He concluded that this public invitation had been an attempt to embarrass him and the Church. Back at his tent he knelt in prayer, thanking the Lord for coming to his aid in this moment of need."[21]

The Sale Manu Family was called to serve as missionaries on a neighboring island in Samoa to establish a branch of the Church. Their success did not sit well with a minister on the island, and the family was physically attacked. The mother and children were knocked to the ground, and Sale was pushed up against a tree and a machete held to his throat by the minister who accused him of stealing his "sheep." Sale was threatened that he and all his family would be killed if they did not deny their faith. They refused. The harassment continued, and they received a note from the village high chief saying, "Leave the village or die." Through prayer, they decided they would stay and die if necessary.

On Christmas Eve, their gardens were destroyed, and the village high chief said they must be gone by morning or they would be burned alive. On Christmas morning, they dressed in their best and awaited their fate. Their house and cookhouse were set on fire, from which they escaped. A huge bonfire was built, and the high chief gave the family one last chance. Sale Manu told them he was there because [The Church of Jesus Christ of Latter-day Saints] is the true church of God, and he and his family were ready to die. Sale asked them, "What are you waiting for?" The chief, unable to follow through, said he now knew Sale was a man of God, adding, "I cannot do this great thing."

The villagers left one at a time, and the bonfire burned out. That evening, the police arrested the high chief, the minister, and some forty others. In court, the judge told Sale he could choose the punishment of his persecutors, but there would be religious freedom on the island. Sale forgave them and was told by the judge he could preach anywhere on the island. Within a couple of months, all but a handful of the nine hundred villagers had joined the Church, and later a large chapel was built on the site of the huge bonfire.

"Today, all of Samoa is covered by stakes (comparable to a diocese, several congregations constitute each stake). It was the first country in the world [in 1974] to be entirely organized into stakes of Zion."[22] As of 2016, there were 77,353 members living in 145 wards. One of every three persons in Samoa is a member of the Church.

Ezra Taft Benson, who in 1985 became the thirteenth President of The Church of Jesus Christ of Latter-day Saints, served as U.S. Secretary of Agriculture under President Dwight D. Eisenhower from about 1953–1961. He was featured on the cover of numerous magazines. Books have been written about him, and he authored many books, several of which were about the Constitution, which he loved and regarded as a sacred document.[23] President Benson was one of America's greatest advocates for freedom. Among the books he authored are *The Proper Role of Government, A Witness and a Warning,* and *God, Family and Country.*

Serving as Secretary of Agriculture enabled him to meet world leaders in over forty nations. On a trip to Russia, Secretary Benson literally took the newsmen traveling with him to church. They attended the large Central Baptist Church service in Moscow where he was asked to speak. He told the congregation that he brought greetings from the millions of church people in America and around the world. "Our Heavenly Father is not far away," he told the packed church. "He can be very close to us. I know that God lives. He is our Father. Jesus Christ, the Redeemer of the world, watches over this earth. He will direct all things. Be unafraid, keep His commandments, love one another, pray for peace and all will be well." His words left scarcely a dry eye in the church. Even the few young people were weeping openly. The congregation broke into singing "God Be with You Till We Meet Again," waving their handkerchiefs and reaching out to shake Secretary Benson's and the newsmen's hands as they left. It was a church service that the reluctant United States press attendees would not soon forget. The services had such a profound effect upon all, that one newsman, a former marine, ranked it with the sight of the American flag rising over the old American compound in Tientsin, China, at the end of World War II.[24]

Benson was elected to the American Patriot's Hall of Fame in 1965[25] and was awarded fourteen honorary degrees from universities throughout the country. Paul Harvey wrote of him, "Ezra Benson is a rare man in politics, thoroughly sincere, uncompromising, and above all, a good man." Edward R. Murrow invited the Benson Family to be on his *Person to Person* TV show, where they presented a Latter-day Saint family home evening. Several million viewers watched, and the program received more fan mail than any other in the history of the program.[26]

Ezra Taft Benson was ordained a Member of the Quorum of the Twelve in 1943.[27] After World War II, the Church sent him to Europe with food and supplies to help feed and clothe the suffering Church members. Through miracles he was able to get into places inaccessible to others. An inspiring book, *On Wings of Faith*, was written about this incredibly successful experience.

The Book of Mormon was President Benson's first scriptural love. Wherever he went, he bore testimony of the book and gave copies to world dignitaries.[28] As a fearless advocate of the book, he encouraged all to feast within its covers and testified of great blessings to those who took his advice. "I promise you that . . . if you will daily sup from its pages and abide by its precepts, God will pour out . . . a blessing hitherto unknown."[29]

Julia Mavimbela had been a convert to the Church for only nine years when she was elected vice president of the National Council of Women for South Africa, the first black woman to be so honored. She was chosen unanimously by white members of the council in Johannesburg on November 4, 1991. Being a pioneer for women and her people was not new to Julia. In the late 1930s, she obtained an education available to few black women at that time and became one of the first black female school principals in the Transvaal Province of South Africa.

Julia married a successful businessman, John Mavimbela, and left her teaching career to join him in his grocery business. In 1955, he was tragically killed in an auto accident, leaving her to raise their five children and run the business. To add to her burdens, the apartheid laws came into effect, and the family were forced to move from their large house to a small dwelling on a rocky patch of ground in Soweto. The Mavimbelas had experimented successfully with organic gardening, and using this knowledge, she turned her small rocky yard into a flourishing garden and went about the whole area teaching others how to work the soil. All were mobilized to transform their neglected ground into productive gardens, some no bigger than doorways. She stressed forgiveness: "Let us dig the soil of bitterness, throw in a seed, show love, and what fruits it can give." These projects helped extinguish the anti-apartheid uprisings in Soweto. But Julia did not stop there. For more than twenty years, she traveled to rural villages and large cities teaching organic gardening. She also taught nutrition classes, was knowledgeable about herbs, and wrote about herbal remedies.

As a fluent speaker of seven languages, Julia was particularly concerned about the high levels of illiteracy among her countrymen, and for many years she was involved in literacy programs. She negotiated with national and community leaders to protect the rights of young people and women. She started a women's club and a youth group and became president of the Transvaal Region of the National Council of African Women. She was a co-founding member and co-national president of Women for Peace, an organization of all races with a membership of more than fifteen thousand women.[30] Brigham Young

University awarded her a Presidential Citation, presented by University President Rex E. Lee during 1995 graduation exercises in Provo, Utah.[31]

No honor meant more to her, she said, than her first meeting with Latter-day Saint missionaries in 1981. She received a copy of the Book of Mormon and was baptized two months later. She served as president of the women's Relief Society organization in the Church in her locality and brought many of her friends and family into the Church.[32] She died in July of 2000 at the age of eighty-two.[33]

Dale Murphy's law is "nice guys finish first," wrote Steve Wulf in *Sports Illustrated*. "He's proven that you don't have to drink beer, spit tobacco, laugh at dirty jokes or curse at the umpires to be a winner in baseball," added *Saturday Evening Post's* Jack Hayes.[34] Murphy was introduced to the Church through a baseball teammate, Barry Bonnell, who he noticed was usually reading his Book of Mormon on their trips, Murphy started asking him questions, and their discussions led to his baptism at the age of nineteen.

The baseball great was named National League MVP in 1982 and 1983, was a seven-time All-Star player, winner of the Gold Glove award five times in a row, honored with the 1988 Roberto Clemente award for humanitarianism, and *Sports Illustrated's* 1987 Sportsman of the Year.[35] "Money and fame never motivated Dale Murphy," his friend Jim Engebretsen said of him. "He knew what was really important. He knows the Lord. He loves people."[36] Chuck Tanner, manager of the Atlanta Braves, called him "Mr. Perfect. . . . God puts somebody down here like Murphy only every 50 years . . . I'm not talking just about baseball, either. I'm talking about him as a person. In my opinion, there is no finer fellow on earth."[37]

"One reason people liked Dale so much is his firmness in never compromising his beliefs. Yet he doesn't push his beliefs on anyone," said his friend Curtis Patton, executive news editor for the *Atlanta Journal and Constitution*. "When he objects to something he goes about it subtly." For example, a beer company that helped sponsor the Atlanta Braves placed their logo above the locker of all the players, thus getting free advertising during locker-room interviews. Not wanting to promote beer, Dale took a piece of paper and wrote a soft drink name on it and taped it over the beer sign.

"This life is about proving our faith to our Heavenly Father," says Dale. "There would be so many fewer problems in society if people just lived the Ten Commandments. . . . Living the principles of the gospel is the only secure plan we have to be safe. We're here to be happy." He finds happiness being with his wife Nancy, enjoying their eight children, and giving service to others.[38] Dale served as president of the Church's Massachusetts Boston Mission.

Kresimir Cosic, from Yugoslavia, was a 6' 11" star basketball player for Brigham Young University in the early 1970s. His great skill, entertaining style of play, contagious smile, and on- court antics made him not only a great favorite of BYU fans, it earned him a place on five All-American teams. Cosic was elected to the National Collegiate Basketball Hall of Fame, the first non-American player to earn this honor. When his college eligibility ended, he turned down a lucrative offer to play in the NBA and a $200,000 contract in Italy[39] to return to Yugoslavia where as a player and coach he helped his national team win an Olympic gold medal, two silvers, and a bronze.[40] With these achievements, "Kres" was hailed as a national hero, known and loved by all.[41]

Like many others from the Eastern Bloc during this period, he said he was an atheist, and, like them, he had smoked and drunk, but his third year at BYU he decided he wanted to learn about the restored Church. "I had things I wanted to know," he said. He studied the Book of Mormon and was highly impressed with it. "You just read the book and want to get baptized–and that's it," he continued. "It's certainly the best book I have ever read. There's no question about that. It applies to today's people . . . because it speaks about the way it is now. . . . There are many things in it [prophecies] that are coming true now."[42]

Christina Nibley was the girlfriend of Cosic's roommate—Cosic eventually accepted an invitation to be taught by her father, BYU professor, Hugh Nibley. When he returned to BYU in the fall of his junior year he went to Dr. Nibley and requested baptism. When asked, "Why?" He said he could think of a hundred reasons why not and only one why, "Because it is true." He later said that when he came to realize how much time he had wasted in coming to understand the sacred and important principles, his desire to know more became unquenchable.[43]

With a strong desire to help establish his new-found religion in his native country, Cosic did not hide his conversion. Kres arranged to have two films produced of BYU basketball games for half time shows, with Church videos inserted in them, and personally narrated both films. During this same period he served as the Church's presiding elder in the country. Even though his religion was an irritant to Communist leaders, his popularity and talent as a basketball player kept him safe from punishment.[44]

Two objectives were high on the young Church leader's list of priorities: First, translate the Book of Mormon into the Serbo-Croatian language. To accomplish this, Cosic hired a Catholic priest, who was laid up from an accident, to do the work. Members and missionaries helped with the editing, which took nearly five years. The new translation was published in 1979.[45] The second objective was to obtain legal recognition for the Church in Yugoslavia which was accomplished with Kres' help in late 1985. The Church's first meeting house was dedicated in November 1985 by Thomas S. Monson. Kres invited government officials and members of the press to the dedicatory services.[46]

Cosic's marriage in 1981 to Ljerka Kobasic was the social event of the year. Surprising to the press, no liquor was served to the guests, unheard of at a wedding in Yugoslavia, but that was understandable to those who knew the substance of Cosic beliefs.[47]

After the dissolution of Yugoslavia in 1991 the newly independent country of Croatia appointed him their ambassador to the United States.[48]

Kresimir was a frequent speaker and committed missionary for the church and served as a district president in Yugoslavia. Unfortunately, while serving as ambassador to the U.S. he died of cancer in 1995 at age forty-six, leaving his wife, Ljerka, and three children. "Ten thousand people paid their respects when he was interred among other heroes in the national cemetery in Zagreb."[49]

In May 2005 a major public square was named after him in the city of Zabreb, Croatia. "Kresimir Cosic Square" is located adjacent to Croatia's main sports arena, to honor him for his national and international contributions.[50] In March 2006 his #11 BYU basketball jersey was retired during a special half time ceremony at the Marriott Center in Provo, Utah and attended by his wife and daughters, one of whom was attending his beloved BYU.

Kim Ho Jik was the first Korean national to be baptized into the Church. Earlier, he had earned university degrees in Korea and Japan, and these enabled him to rise to positions of influence in his country. He was president of a women's university and then became director of an agricultural experimentation station. Wanting more education regarding agriculture and nutrition, he was happy when South Korean president, Syngman Rhee, gave him the opportunity to go to America to study and find more efficient ways to feed their malnourished people. It was at Cornell University where he met and became friends with another graduate student, Oliver Wayman, who happened to be a member of the Church. Kim, noticing his clean-living habits, asked him about his church. He was given *The Articles of Faith,* a book that he read and accepted as true, and, soon after he was given a copy of the Book of Mormon. He deemed this book to be the word of God, more complete and easier to understand than the Bible.

Already a Christian, but not satisfied and looking for more, Kim had been attending various churches in his quest. He started studying with Latter-day Saint missionaries, and when he was taught about the Word of Wisdom, the Lord's law of health, tears flowed down his cheeks. It was what he had been looking for to improve the diet of his countrymen.

The Spirit bore witness to him that the Book of Mormon was true, and he decided he wanted to be baptized. He chose the Susquehanna River where Joseph Smith and Oliver Cowdery had been baptized. As he came up out of the water, a voice said to him, "Feed my sheep, feed my sheep." After receiving his doctoral degree, he returned to his war-torn country and started "feeding His sheep." He met with U.S. servicemen for worship services and requested them, some of whom had served as missionaries, to teach his family. He invited interested Koreans to his home for weekly cottage meetings, and the Church began to grow.

Meanwhile, he was appointed to positions of prestige, including Vice-Minister of Education for South Korea. It was through this position that he was able to get the Church incorporated in Korea, which some considered a miracle. He gained permission for Church of Jesus Christ of Latter-day Saints missionaries to enter South Korea. The first ones arrived in 1956. He was the unofficial patriarchal figure and spiritual leader for all the Korean Saints, who once, speaking to a group of Church members, declared, "I wouldn't care if I had to give up my life, or my money, or my title, as long as I could be with my Savior."

Brother Jik was not ashamed of the gospel of Jesus Christ. Once when asked by the Korean Broadcasting System to lecture on a topic in biology during a nationwide broadcast, he spent the entire time talking about the Church. "It was just like he was talking in his Sunday School class," said Park Jae Am, a supervisor working for the Presiding Bishopric.

In 1956, he resigned his national post to devote more time and energy to the Church, serving as a branch and district president, and translating Church literature into Korean, while still serving his country when asked. In August 1959, while representing South Korea at a United Nations Food and Agriculture Organization meeting in India, he fell ill during the meetings, and less than a month after returning home died of a stroke. Brother Jik's eight years of service to the Church was of great consequence to its establishment in Korea[51] and prepared the way for the conversion of tens of thousands of Koreans. By 2016 there were more than 87,000 members in South Korea with four missions. A temple was built and dedicated in Seoul in 1985.[52]

Gertrude Specht. Elder Scott Anderson was serving as a missionary in Munich, Germany, in the late 1960s when he and his companion knocked on the door of Dr. Gertrude Specht. She said she had seen them walking around the neighborhood and was excited to meet them. After inviting them in and sitting down at her desk, she pointed to three PhD diplomas hanging over her head covering such topics as philosophy and European history, with a specialty in Christianity. She then pointed to a row of books explaining she had authored all of them. She explained that she was a theology professor at the University of Munich, had been lecturing for forty-one years, and loved to talk about religion. She then asked, "What would you like to discuss?" They said they'd like to tell her about the Book of Mormon. She confessed, "I don't know anything about the Book of Mormon." When they left about half an hour later, they had given her a copy of the book and she invited them to return. In a few weeks, she received confirmation that the book and the Church were true, and she decided to be baptized.

At her baptism, she said, "I don't think you members know what you have. After those years of studying philosophy, I picked up the Doctrine and Covenants and read a few little verses that answered some of the greatest questions of Aristotle and Socrates! When I read those verses, I wept for four hours." Then she said again, "I don't think you know what you have. Don't you understand the world is in a famine? Don't you know we are starving for what you have? I am like a starving person being led to a feast, and over these eight and a half weeks I have been able to feast in a way I have never known possible."

Shortly after Sister Specht's baptism, two other missionaries knocked on the door of a Catholic seminary in Regensburg where 125 young men were studying to become priests. Both elders being fairly new, were relieved when they were told the seminary students didn't have time to talk to them just then. They were then told, "Would you come back next Tuesday and spend two hours addressing all 125 of us and answer questions about your church?"

The excited—and startled—missionaries informed their mission president of the appointment, and their concerns about it. He suggested they ask Sister Specht to help them. She was thrilled to do so. Dr. Specht told the elders to express their testimonies about the Church and then turn the meeting over to her. She talked to the seminarians about historical apostasy, citing every date and fact. Then she explained how teachings had been changed after the apostasy. She looked directly at the students and said, "In 1820 a boy walked into a grove of trees. He had been in a famine just like I had been. He knelt to pray. . . . He saw God the Father and His Son. I know that is hard for you to believe that they could be two separate beings, but I know they are." She then shared scriptures backing up her belief.

During the last twenty minutes of her talk, she put the truth back in place, point by point, principle by principle, concluding with, "I have been in a famine as talked about in Amos. You know that because last year I was here teaching you." It was then the missionaries realized that she had been the prospective priests' theology professor. "I told you that I was still in a famine. I have been led to a feast. I invite you to come." She finished with her testimony of the truthfulness of what she had told them, and sat down.

The missionaries couldn't comprehend what happened next. They said, "These 125 sincere, wonderful men stood and for the next seven minutes, gave her a standing ovation." The elders were in tears and noticed tears in the eyes of others. They asked the students why they were applauding after her message. They said, "To hear someone so unashamed of the truth, to hear someone teaching with such power, to hear someone who finally has conviction."

President Joseph Fielding Smith gave Dr. Specht a permanent missionary assignment. She was able to open many doors and helped many people gain testimonies of the gospel. Because of her efforts, many favorable articles about the Church were published in German newspapers. She spent the rest of her life working with those she called the "blessed" folk. She especially loved working with the missionaries, several of whom raised money for a trip so she could come to Salt Lake City and the Brigham Young University campus in Provo, Utah. Dr. Specht was thrilled to visit the headquarters of the Church and its university. She often said, "The truth can set you free" and "Who can doubt?" Gertrude Specht's life and the lives of many others were changed forever.[53]

Ahmad S. Corbitt grew up in Philadelphia where his parents were involved with the Nation of Islam. He joined the Church at age eighteen, along with other members of his family after missionaries knocked on their door in New Jersey. He served as a missionary for the Church in Puerto Rico, became a lawyer, then joined a New York public relations firm where he became a spokesman for the Salt Lake City Winter Olympics. Corbitt joined the church just two years after the priesthood was extended to all worthy males. As an African American, he said, "It was clear to me that the Church was moving forward and I was willing to judge it by its fruits." He said he was struck with a "deep sense of the Church's righteousness and goodness." He was determined that "I would die as an old man as a Latter-day Saint." Corbitt has served as president of the Cherry Hill, New Jersey Stake[54] and as the Church's public relations spokesman in New York.[55] In 2014, he was called as President of the Dominican Republic Santo Domingo East Mission.[56]

Joseph William "Billy" Johnson of West Africa is not well known for great worldly accomplishments, but his humble service to others has affected the lives of scores of people. Johnson was given a copy of the Book of Mormon and other Church literature in 1964 by Dr. A. F. Mensah, in Accra, Ghana. He read the literature and became convinced it was true. He began to receive "wonderful manifestations that I was to do the work of the Lord." One morning early in 1964, a voice from heaven spoke to him saying, "If you will take up my word as I will command you, I will bless you and bless your land." With tears and trembling, Johnson told the Lord he would do whatever He would command him.

He started going from house to house and town to town teaching the things he had learned. Persecution commenced, and pamphlets were written against his group, but the number of believers grew. In 1969, he left Accra to establish the Church in his hometown of Cape Coast. Persecutions followed, but he established many small churches in that area.

As the years passed and no missionaries came from his newfound church, his group became discouraged; nevertheless, they carried on valiantly and gained more followers. Other churches taunted him saying that the Salt Lake City church would never recognize them, for at that time blacks could not receive the priesthood. The other churches offered to pay him to join with them. Undaunted, he continued on.[57]

"Reverend" Johnson became renowned as a man of great faith who possessed healing powers. He experienced manifestations that strengthened the group. His deceased brother once appearing to him in a dream saying, "Dear Brother, don't give up. This is the only true church in the world and also here in the spirit world. I am being taught the gospel here and I know it is true. Don't give up!" Johnson's brother said he wanted to be baptized, knowing it could be done by proxy for him in a Latter-day Saint temple.

Three months before President Spencer W. Kimball announced the revelation granting the priesthood to "all worthy males" throughout the world, Reverend Johnson felt impressed to tell a congregation that within four months, Salt Lake City would recognize the Church in Ghana and send representatives to help them.

On July 9, 1978, he heard the wondrous news late one night on BBC radio, which he hadn't listened to in months. After fourteen years of struggle and prayer, he could scarcely believe his ears. Tears of joy flowed from his eyes.[58] When two missionary couples arrived, they were amazed to find that Reverend Johnson had established ten congregations in the area, all of which had adopted the title Church of Jesus Christ of Latter-day Saints. All were waiting for baptism.[59] After interviews to make sure they understood the gospel, eighty-nine were baptized the first day. The missionaries worked into the night.

Johnson, who was earning his livelihood from his followers' donations understood the church has no paid ministry. He made arrangements with his brother for a new profession and continued volunteering service to the Church.[60] Prayers were answered when the Accra, Ghana Temple was built and dedicated on January 11, 2004, twenty-five years after missionaries first arrived there. By 2017, there were 78,065 members in Ghana in 305 wards.[61]

Chapter 24

It Will Contain a Promise Not Found in Any Other Book

You must include within your book this promise: "And when ye shall receive these things, I would exhort you that ye would ask God, the Eternal Father, in the name of Christ, if these things are not true; and if ye shall ask with a sincere heart, with real intent, having faith in Christ, he will manifest the truth of it unto you, by the power of the Holy Ghost."

This remarkable promise to those seeking a witness of the truthfulness of the Book of Mormon is found in Moroni 10:4, the last book in the text. Verse 3 is also significant: "Behold, I would exhort you that when ye shall read these things, if it be wisdom in God that ye should read them, that ye would remember how merciful the Lord hath been unto the children of men, from the creation of Adam even down until the time that ye shall receive these things, and ponder it in your hearts."

How to Receive an Answer

"We first need to meditate and realize how merciful the Lord has been to us," says Elder Gene R. Cook, "and as we count our blessings, our hearts should turn to the Lord in love and gratitude. We are then "more humble, more willing and ready to receive the information we are seeking with an open mind."[1]

Faith in Christ prepares us to receive the personal revelation promised in verse 4: "He will manifest the truth of it unto you, by the power of the Holy Ghost." Faith in Christ means we accept the reality of God's existence and that through the power of the Holy Ghost, He can answer our prayers and manifest the truth to us.[2] A sincere seeker of truth who has *read and pondered* the words of the Book of Mormon, has paid a price in time and effort and can then confidently ask God in prayer for a personal revelation about the book's truthfulness.

The Lord may not respond immediately or exactly how and when we expect, but our compliance with these conditions qualifies us to receive an answer. In verse 5, we are taught that "by the power of the Holy Ghost ye may

193

know the truth of all things."[3] Legions have received a definitive answer to this most important question.

Knowing the power of faith and prayer, some preachers warn their followers against praying with Latter-day Saints. One minister gives three standards, which, if followed, he says "assures that [his parishioners] will not be caught in the [Latter-day Saint] net:" (1) Don't pray about the message, as you could be deceived; (2) Don't trust your feelings, as they can be deceptive, and (3) Don't trust your mind because "our minds are reprobate."[4] "Don't pray. Don't trust. Don't think." Is this the true Gospel of Jesus Christ? Does the minister imply that we should never pray about anything because we could be deceived? Isn't faith trust? Should we not use our God-given intellect? The Bible and Book of Mormon teach us to pray always—Luke 21:36, 2 Nephi 32:9; and be believing—John 20:27, Mosiah 4:9-10; and learn wisdom—Proverbs 1:5, Alma 32:12.

Faith in Bible Prepares for Book of Mormon Testimony

Latter-day Saint author Darl Anderson believes people who have faith in the Bible can also gain faith in the Book of Mormon:

> There are many who do not believe the Bible to be the word of God. This is not so much because of the contents of the book, but because of the attitude of people and their unwillingness to take the necessary steps to gain the feeling for themselves that it is true. It seems that anyone who believes the Bible can come to believe the Book of Mormon if they have the same attitude and take the same steps that led them to believe the Bible. They can receive that same peaceful, satisfying assurance.[5]

Although mounting evidences may help an individual gain an intellectual conviction, Elder Hugh B. Brown, who served as a member of the Church's First Presidency, testified that it is "Only by the whisperings of the Holy Spirit [that] one can come to know of the things of God." And through these whisperings about the truthfulness of the Book of Mormon, "I say I know that Joseph Smith is a prophet of God. I thank God for that knowledge. I pray that you may in humility ask him whether it be true, and I promise you that he will respond and that you will know from the warmth in your heart that . . . it is God's eternal truth."[6]

Referring to the Book of Mormon, Elder B. H. Roberts wrote that "its truth shall be attested to individuals by the operations of the Holy Spirit upon the human mind. . . . This must ever be the chief source of evidence for the truth of the Book of Mormon. All other evidence is secondary to this, the primary and infallible. No arrangement of evidence, however skillfully ordered; no argument, however adroitly made, can ever take its place, for this witness of the Holy Spirit to the soul of man for the truth of the Nephite volume of scripture, is God's evidence to the truth."[7]

Interior of The Conference Center of The Church of Jesus Christ of Latter-day Saints, Salt Lake City, Utah

The Introduction to the 2013 Latter-day Saint edition of the Book of Mormon offers this invitation:

> We invite all men [and women] everywhere to read the Book of Mormon, to ponder in their hearts the message it contains, and then to ask God, the Eternal Father, in the name of Christ if the book is true. Those who pursue this course and ask in faith will gain a testimony of its truth and divinity by the power of the Holy Ghost.
>
> Those who gain this divine witness from the Holy Spirit will also come to know by the same power that Jesus Christ is the Savior of the world, that Joseph Smith is His revelator and prophet in these last days, and that The Church of Jesus Christ of Latter-day Saints is the Lord's kingdom once again established on the earth—preparatory to the Second Coming of the Messiah.[8]

A Book for the Honest in Heart

This promise is so powerful that Satan has fought and continues to fight against the Book of Mormon. He does not want people to come to this knowledge of the truthfulness of the Book of Mormon because then they would also know that Jesus is the Christ, that Joseph Smith is the Prophet of the Restoration, and that the Lord has again established His Church upon the earth preparatory to Christ's second coming.

Enemies go to great lengths to cast doubts upon the book, "for if it can be discredited," writes President Ezra Taft Benson, "the Prophet Joseph Smith goes with it. So does our claim to priesthood keys, and revelation, and the restored Church. But in like manner, if the Book of Mormon be true—and millions have now testified that they have the witness of the Spirit that it is indeed true—then one must accept the claims of the Restoration and all that accompanies it."[9] This conclusion may be uncomfortable to some, but it is a great source of joy and peace to many others.

This is why members of The Church of Jesus Christ of Latter-day Saints endeavor to place a copy of the Book of Mormon in the hands of all who seek truth. Elder Jay E. Jensen explains that members encourage people to read the Book of Mormon because "there are doctrines taught in the Book of Mormon that can be seen with a greater view than in the Bible, such as the law of mercy and justice, the doctrines of the fall, agency, and the redemption of Christ, the reality of Satan and how he operates among peoples and nations, the principles of faith, hope, and charity, the purpose and necessity of baptism and the redemption of little children and the doctrine of the resurrection."[10] These are eternal truths for everyone!

Chapter 25

Those Who Ask God Will Testify That They Know the Book Is True

Millions who accept your book will testify that they know it is true because when they put its promise to the test its divinity is revealed to them by the power of the Holy Ghost.

Soon after Joseph Smith and Oliver Cowdery received priesthood authority from angelic ministrants Peter, James, and John, it was made known to Joseph that The Church of Jesus Christ was to be organized once again upon the earth. Consequently, on April 6, 1830, a date revealed to him by the Lord, the Prophet and approximately sixty others gathered in the home of Peter Whitmer, Sr. to witness this monumental event. Per New York statute, six men participated in the formal organizational proceedings: Joseph Smith Jr., Oliver Cowdery, Hyrum Smith, Peter Whitmer Jr., Samuel H. Smith, and David Whitmer.[1]

The Church is organized

The Savior Named the Church

On April 26, 1838, the Lord revealed the formal name by which His church was to be called: "For thus shall my church be called in the last days, even "The Church of Jesus Christ of Latter-day Saints" (Doctrine and Covenants 115:4).[2] "Latter-day Saints" was included in the name to differentiate present-day members from those during Christ's earthly ministry and the apostolic era who were also called "Saints." In the Book of Mormon, the disciples asked Jesus, "Lord, we will that thou wouldst tell us the name whereby we shall call this church." Jesus referred them to the scriptures and then declared: "And how be it my church save it be called in my name? For if a church be called . . . in the name of a man then it be the church of a man; but if it be called in my name then it is my church, if it so be that they are built upon my gospel" (3 Nephi 27:3, 8).

From this small beginning, the Church has grown into a worldwide organization with members numbering in the millions. Joseph prophesied to early priesthood holders, "You know no more concerning the destinies of this church and kingdom than a babe upon its mother's lap. You don't comprehend it. . . . This church will fill North and South America—it will fill the world."[3]

This prophecy is being fulfilled. During the 1990s, the National Council of Churches named The Church of Jesus Christ of Latter-day Saints the fastest-growing mainstream church in the United States.[4] In 2006, the Church was listed as the second fastest-growing religion.[5] The year 2000 was a watershed. In that year there were more non-English-speaking members than English speaking.[6] In 2015, the Church numbered over 15 million with more than half living outside the United States and Canada, and was organized in more than 160 nations. Large numbers are found in Mexico and Brazil. It can no longer be called a purely American church, but it is at present the fourth-largest Christian denomination in the United States.[7]

A New World Faith

Some say the restored Church, is poised to become the first new global faith since Islam emerged from Arabia in the seventh century.[8] In 1984, non–Latter-day Saint sociologist Dr. Rodney Stark of the University of Washington shocked the scholarly world by characterizing its future growth as "the rise of a new world faith." Stark projected its membership to be sixty million by the year 2080. In follow-up predictions in 1995 he found that membership exceeded his estimates by almost a million people.[9] The Church completes construction of several new chapels each week and has done so for many years.[10] Church President Gordon B. Hinckley attributed the growth of the Church to the fact that "people are looking for a solid anchor in a world of shifting values. They want something they can hold to as the world about them increasingly appears to be in disarray."[11]

Church Office Building, Salt Lake City, Utah

Hundreds of thousands have prayed, as Moroni 10:4 admonishes, and received testimonies by the power of the Holy Ghost that the Book of Mormon is true and that it was translated by the gift and power of God just as Joseph Smith said it did. Among those who put Moroni's promise to the test, and received assurance that the record is true, are members of every major religion, including ministers and priests from many churches. At times clergymen leave their churches and their livelihood and are baptized into The Church of Jesus Christ of Latter-day Saints after having a witness of its truthfulness revealed to them by the Holy Ghost. Following are testimonies of some of the many lay members and ministers who converted from both Christian and non-Christian churches when they embraced the truthfulness of the Book of Mormon and the restoration of the gospel.

The Green and Young Families

Shortly after the Church was organized, Joseph called his brother Samuel as a missionary, to travel to Livonia, New York and preach the gospel, and if possible, sell copies of the Book of Mormon. On his second day, Samuel stopped at the home of John P. Green, a Methodist preacher. Green was not interested in the book but said he would take a subscription paper and if he found anyone interested he would let Samuel know. Samuel later returned to the Greens' home. John Green was not there, and, according to Mrs. Green, had not found anyone interested in the book. Samuel advised her to ask God for a witness of its truthfulness. After much discussion, she persuaded her husband to read the book and to ask God for a witness, as Samuel had suggested. The truth of it was made known to them as the Lord promised, and the Greens were baptized shortly thereafter.

The Greens shared the book with other members of Mrs. Green's family, including her brother Phineas Young, who later gave it to his brother, Brigham Young.[12] After Brigham's conversion, he contacted his brother Joseph, who was in Canada preaching the Methodist faith. Initially, fifteen members of the Young family, including the parents, John and Hannah Young, became convinced of the truth of the book and were baptized into The Church of Jesus

Christ of Latter-day Saints. Thousands of their descendants have since become faithful members.[13]

Joseph Giacalone

Joseph Giacalone's wife was a member of the Church, and through her, he learned to love the people in the Church. He adopted their way of life—so much so that many of his close friends thought he was a member. Finally, after 35 years, Joseph decided to be baptized, but he knew he didn't really believe the gospel; he would be doing it just to please his wife, his sweetheart and best friend. Then one night his wife again asked him to read the Book of Mormon and pray about it, and if he didn't accept the gospel, she promised she would never mention it again. He knew how much the Church meant to her and that it was a great sacrifice for her to make such a promise, so he agreed.

Joseph started reading a few chapters in the Book of Mormon each day at lunch, and each evening he went home with questions. He finally finished his reading, closed the book, closed his eyes, and prayed. Nothing happened. Nothing. As he drove home that evening, he decided to look at it analytically. "This book is either completely true or completely false. It can't be anything in between," he reasoned. "Then came a beautiful, memorable experience, and a feeling settling like peaceful wings on my heart and mind: I could not believe that an uneducated farm boy wrote an epic book, this complex and incredible, that blended perfectly with all existing scripture and history. Even if he could, why would he want to? It ultimately cost him his life. If it wasn't a hoax, then it was entirely true. And if the Book of Mormon was true, then everything he said and wrote was true. The thoughts and feelings went to the core of my being." Joseph was baptized shortly thereafter. As he emerged from the water, he saw tears running down his children's cheeks and "saw in the eyes of my wife a fulfillment of a dream. And I realized how blessed I was."[14]

Isaac Swartzberg

Isaac Swartzberg was raised in Transvaal, South Africa, in a formal Jewish family. He became an attorney. In the 1950s, he married a Jewish girl, regularly went to synagogue, and tried to maintain a kosher Jewish home. Although he knew there was a God, he felt something was missing in his life. The marriage later ended in divorce.

He later met, dated, and fell much in love with a young woman, Edwina, whom he learned was a member of The Church of Jesus Christ of Latter-day Saints. Although he was not initially concerned, this caused many problems with his family. Isaac decided he and Edwina should investigate each other's religion for six months, and then the problem would be solved—they would be Jews. However, while reading Psalm 22 (see verses 13–19), he came to realize that David was describing the crucifixion in all its terrible grandeur, and he suddenly knew that Jesus was the Messiah. With this new knowledge, his whole life changed. He started to read the Book of Mormon in earnest, realizing it was *in fact* written "to the convincing of the Jew and Gentile that Jesus is the Christ."

As Isaac read, he prayed, and the Holy Ghost revealed to him the truth of the restoration and its keystone book. When he told Edwina about his conversion and desire to be baptized, she was most pleasantly surprised and they were soon married. Isaac summed his decision in these words: "In my entire life, I have never found such satisfaction and purpose as I now have."[15]

Gabriel Kelphala Sesay

Gabriel Kelphala Sesay, of Sierra Leonean nationality, was born to Muslim parents and associated mostly with Muslims as a child. But by the time Gabriel was fifteen, she started investigating Christianity and eventually began worshiping with a Pentecostal group. In 1989, she came in contact with missionaries from The Church of Jesus Christ of Latter-day Saints who were visiting the college she was attending. She began meeting with the missionaries but was skeptical about the Prophet Joseph Smith and the Book of Mormon. The missionaries gave her a copy of the Book of Mormon and challenged her to read it and pray about it. She took their challenge, and over the next few days, as she read and prayed, the Holy Ghost bore witness to her "that the Book of Mormon is indeed another testament of Jesus Christ."

Later that month, she was baptized and began to experience great changes in her life. She feels she is now a true Christian. "When I have a problem . . . I read the Book of Mormon and pray, and often I see a way to solve that problem. When I have difficulties with my family, my friends, or my educational career, I feel better when I read through the book. . . . I don't know how to express my appreciation for the coming forth of the Book of Mormon," she says. "Through it, I know that God lives, that Jesus is the very Christ, and that Joseph Smith was a prophet of God and a powerful witness of Jesus Christ."[16]

Ronald Palmer

Ronald Palmer, as a young married man, attended his wife's church to please her, but he didn't feel comfortable there. He wanted to serve God, knowing that the only permanent thing in life is one's relationship with the Lord, so he decided to get involved in his Southern Baptist Church. He joined the choir, taught Sunday school, worked as a deacon, and then tried his hand at preaching. The congregation voted to make him their minister, but he continued his air-conditioning business.

In time, Ronald became curious about the beliefs of other churches. He couldn't understand how Christian ministers could be inspired and yet all teach conflicting doctrines. He reasoned that Christ would not teach conflicting beliefs. He discussed religion in depth with ministers of several churches, feeling that perhaps the Lord wanted him to collect as much truth as possible and start his own church. Deep down he knew that it would only be another church, and he needed to be sure the complete truth couldn't be found in any existing church. Although he had been taught that Latter-day Saints weren't Christians, he was so thirsty for knowledge that he obtained a copy of the Book of Mormon by calling the home of a local Latter-day Saint bishop, whose wife gave him a used copy of the book on condition that he would read it. He agreed, and he kept his word. While reading, he wanted to know specifically what the Church taught, so missionaries arranged to meet with him.

The concept of latter-day apostles and prophets attracted his interest. It seemed logical that the Lord would speak directly to us again. The missionaries challenged him to put Moroni 10:4 to the test. His prayers were being answered that the Book of Mormon and Church were true, but his wife, who had been very opposed to his interest in the Church, said, "When we pray, I get one answer and you get another." Two weeks later, she announced that while praying, she had received an affirmative answer. "I know nothing about [this] Church except that it is true, and I'm ready to be baptized," she told her surprised husband. He was baptized the next Saturday. His wife and two sons took the missionary lessons, Ronald received priesthood authority, and he baptized them the following Saturday.

Ronald's parents, now very upset, apologized to all the relatives on his behalf. To get him to leave them alone, they agreed to read the Book of Mormon. Within four months, they had their own testimony of the book, asked for baptism, and were teaching other family members. Within a year, thirteen more family members were baptized, and Palmer says he will be forever grateful to the bishop's wife for committing him to read the Book of Mormon.[17]

Norman Carlisle

Norman Carlisle bought a copy of the Book of Mormon for fifty cents from a classmate while attending classes at a seminary for future ministers of the Church of Christ. He didn't read it, but he became curious and started reading adversarial literature. Upon graduation from the seminary, he was assigned as minister to the Eastland, Texas, Church of Christ. After several months, he had proved himself and was told he would be ordained to the ministry. The church elders signed a certificate, shook his hand, and he was "ordained." He enjoyed being a minister, life was good, and he was not looking for anything else.

The arrival of Latter-day Saint missionaries in Eastland changed that. They were knocking on doors where he was the minister and he had to do something about it. At first it was just curiosity on his part, wanting to talk to them to find out what they believed and how they would answer some of the arguments he had read in the adversarial literature. He went to the library and checked out *A Marvelous Work and a Wonder*,[18] which explains Latter-day Saint beliefs. Carlisle read it through and couldn't find anything wrong with the doctrine. Now he was even more curious.

One morning he was reading 1 Corinthians 13:8–12, which he had previously understood to mean that revelations were to cease. Upon further study, he realized that revelations were not to cease and that God would continue to speak through prophets, and "yet in the eternal state we will see God face to face." This insight prompted him to call the missionaries. Carlisle recalled the Latter-day Saints claim to have a living prophet on the earth, and he wanted to learn more. He met with the missionaries the next morning and enjoyed their discussion, so he arranged to meet with them again. After the second lesson, he read about thirty pages in the Book of Mormon and sincerely prayed about it. "Right then I knew it was true," he said, "but I didn't know what in the world to do about it—or with it."

Carlisle began studying more intensely than before, and things started falling into place. A few months earlier, he had researched and preached a sermon on the Trinity in which he concluded there had to be three separate personages in the Godhead and God must have a physical body like His Son's. When the missionaries taught that concept, Carlisle was very receptive. He concluded that no other church taught these truths, so he wrote a letter of resignation to the leaders of his congregation, explaining that after much study and prayer, he knew that Joseph Smith was a prophet and he could no longer preach in the Church of Christ.

The missionaries were stunned and thrilled with his decision. In a community of just three thousand people, the whole town was buzzing with the news of his conversion. He found that The Church of Jesus Christ of Latter-day Saints is modeled after Christ's original church and asked others to compare their church with the model in the scriptures. Norman Carlisle believes they will see that theirs is not the New Testament church.[19]

Don Vincenzo di Francesca

Don Vincenzo di Francesca was a young Italian Protestant minister from Sicily studying and serving in New York City when, on a cold February morning in 1910, he happened upon a book lying on top of a barrel of ashes. It looked like a religious book, but the cover and frontispiece were torn away. He took the book home and read the testimony of the witnesses, which gave him "confidence that it was a true book." Francesca read and reread in the book, convinced it was a fifth gospel of the Redeemer. After extensive reading, he locked his door and knelt and prayed as Moroni 10:4 counsels. He then experienced something powerful within his soul: "I felt my body become cold as the wind from the sea. Then my heart began to palpitate, and a feeling of gladness, as of finding something precious and extraordinary, bore consolation to my soul and left me with a joy that human language cannot find words to describe. I had received the assurance that God had answered my prayer and that the book was of greatest benefit to me and to all who would listen to its words."[20]

Francesca began using information from the book in his sermons. He became the most popular speaker among his colleagues, causing much envy and discord. His fellow ministers denounced him, and twice he was taken before the Committee of Censure for disciplinary action. He was told he must burn the book. Vincenzo answered that he could neither deny the words of the book nor burn it because in doing so, he was sure he would offend God. In addition, he informed them that he had prayed about the book and knew positively that it was true and that he was looking forward to the day when he would learn of the faith from which it came and join with them.

His refusal to burn the book resulted in his being stripped of his position as a pastor of the church, along with every right and privilege he had enjoyed in his Methodist Church. He later returned to Italy, and while looking through a French dictionary, saw the word "Mormon." He learned that a church had been founded in 1830, and he was able to make contact with Church headquarters in Salt Lake City. They sent him information and books, making it possible for him to learn the origin of the torn book—thirty years after he found his copy. His great desire was to be baptized, but because of wars and missed connections, it was not until January of 1951 that his baptism was performed, after more than a forty-year wait.[21]

To those who inquired about his long wait, he replied, "You can see that I have toiled hard to find the salvation, the kingdom of God which was spoken of in the remainder of the pages of the book without a title page or cover." Vincenzo di Francesca died November 18, 1966, strong in his long-sought faith.[22]

Piera Bellavita Schorr

Piera Schorr decided to become a nun at age seventeen. She trained to be a teacher, then was asked to work in the office of the Vatican. Here she worked with three popes and met people from all over the world. One, a bishop from the United States, asked the Vatican if they would like to send some nuns to North Carolina to do missionary work. She and two other sisters from the same convent went and stayed for five years. She loved America and didn't want to return to Italy, but she respected her vow of obedience.

After returning to Italy, she met two Latter-day Saint missionaries on a streetcar one night who struck up a conversation with her when they noticed she was studying English. After learning they were missionaries, she asked them what they believed. They told her they believed in the Book of Mormon. She had never heard of it, but she gave them her address and asked them to bring one to her if they had time. Two weeks later, they delivered a copy to the convent, and she said she would read it and see if she could find anything that disagreed with her beliefs.

Schorr found it was all about Christ. She became so excited about it that she asked her priest why they didn't use it in the Catholic Church, for it was such a good book. She talked to other priests and nuns, but no one knew anything about the Latter-day Saints, so she decided if she wanted to learn more she would have to study by herself.

The missionaries brought her a copy of *A Marvelous Work and a Wonder*, and she became excited about that book, also. To the chagrin of some priests, she told them the Latter-day Saints had captured the Bible better than they had. The missionaries stopped by occasionally with other reading material, including a copy of *No More Strangers*, which included the story of Sister Eileen Davies, a former Catholic nun from England who had served in the Vatican for six of her thirty-one-year vocation as a nun before she joined The Church of Jesus Christ of Latter-day Saints. Piera thought maybe she could do that too, because she believed what she was learning and there were things she questioned about her church. But she wanted to be sure what the Lord wanted her to do, so she fasted and prayed for three days before getting her answer. "I didn't know it before, but now I knew it," she proclaimed.

She realized that her new knowledge meant giving up everything, especially her security, and no place to go. The missionaries put her in touch with Eileen Davies who came from England, picked her up, and with a few miracles along the way helped her emigrate to America. She was able to get a job and even marry a member of her new church. Her family initially was very upset with her decision, but, happily, they eventually accepted her, along with her husband. "I love the Book of Mormon. I know it is another witness of Christ," she says. She and her husband have sent out seventy-five hundred copies to help "flood the world with this precious book."[23]

Anneke Margreet je deGroot Marshall

Anneke Margreet je deGroot Marshall of Holland traveled to the United States at age sixteen as an exchange student. She had no religion, nor did her friends. She was warned about those "religious freaks," as her boyfriend called the Latter-day Saints. She found her host family warm and loving and she enjoyed participating in their family home evenings and going to church with them. She started asking many questions, reading the Book of Mormon, and attending early morning seminary with one of her American sisters. After reading Moroni 10:4, she decided that she would find out for herself if the Book of Mormon was true. She asked, but nothing happened. Nothing happened even after several attempts.

This went on for several days until one night she suddenly realized the Lord wanted to make sure she was willing to make the sacrifices that would be required of her when she returned to her native country where 90 percent of the people have no religion in their homes. Her humble prayer following this knowledge was answered. "Immediately, I had a feeling of joy go through me! I remember being a little afraid to make these enormous commitments, but now it was as though there were arms around me to make me feel very safe. My fear disappeared and a great peace filled my soul so no doubtful thoughts were in my head anymore. My whole being realized that Joseph Smith is a prophet, that the Church is true, that Jesus Christ lives!"

She returned to Holland but wasn't able to be baptized without permission from her parents, who thought she would surely lose interest. It took nearly two hours for Anneke to get to church on Sundays, but she attended regularly. Convinced of her sincerity after a year, in 1978 her parents finally gave her permission, even paying her airfare to California so her American "father" could baptize her. She later attended Brigham Young University where she renewed a friendship with one of the missionaries who had taught her in Holland, and they were later married in the Swiss Temple. "More blessings" she says, "have come into my life from that one decision to be baptized than I could ever have dreamed."[24]

Scott J. Giaimo

Dr. Scott Giaimo, MD, grew up with a Catholic father and Lutheran mother but felt personally distanced from God. He stopped attending church for ten years, going only at Christmas to please his mother. As a small child, he had questions about religion that were never adequately answered. He wondered how unbaptized infants get into heaven—or do they sin at all? Who really are the "chosen" people? Aren't we all God's children, and doesn't He want all of us back? He said no one would touch that question. And what about the New Jerusalem? Will it be built up from the ashes of the old city? What does the book of Revelation mean about Christ's Second Coming and the Millennium? These were some of his questions awaiting answers.

Dr. Giaimo was twenty-eight years old when Latter-day Saint sister missionaries moved next door to him in Commerce, Georgia, a situation he believed was not coincidence. After meeting them and starting to take their missionary lessons, he attended his first Latter-day Saint church service. He describes his reaction in these words:

> I almost hit the floor with amazement. It was everything I thought church should be and never knew existed. The answer to all my questions was common knowledge and matter-of-fact. . . . I had never heard God's Plan of Salvation in its entirety. . . . Finally God is my Father and

I His child. It's like being five years old and lost in the mall and in a panic, then all of a sudden your parents come around the corner, and now you're home, or at least found. The comfort and joy that swells up inside you is beyond any words I could write.

Once I began to read the Book of Mormon, and prayed about if for a couple of days, a wonderful thing happened. After finally just honestly asking God, "Is it true?!" the Holy Ghost grabbed both my adrenal glands and gave them a squeeze, or at least that's what it felt like. At that point I knew the Book of Mormon was God's word, and I knew the Church to be true.

Dr. Giaimo was so convinced of its truthfulness that he received the remaining lessons from the missionaries in a little over a week's time and was baptized soon afterward.[25]

Helio da Rocha Camargo

There are various ways seekers receive their answer to Moroni's promise. It is not always immediate—nor dramatic. Brazilian Helio da Rocha Camargo loved reading and studying theological questions so much that, although married and with a family, he decided to change the course of his life and enrolled in a college of theology. A year later, he was assigned as a Methodist minister in Sao Paulo, Brazil, while still receiving his seminary training. However, he and two other students withdrew from the seminary after realizing they could find no justification for infant baptism.

Being inclined to a religious life, he began studying a variety of other churches, eliminating them one by one as his potential spiritual home. Eventually, he paid more and more attention to the doctrines of The Church of Jesus Christ of Latter-day Saints and verified critical points in his Greek and Hebrew Bibles as well as in his Portuguese Bible. He read books for and against the Church, but kept an open mind and maintained a sincere desire for truth. The truth gradually came and grew more obvious, so Helio began paying tithing and living the other standards of the Church while doing his research. In due time, he received his answer as promised by Christ, "If any man will do his will, he shall know of the doctrine, whether it be of God, or whether I speak of myself" (John 7:17)—but not in the manner he had expected.

As he studied the Book of Mormon and weighed all he was learning, he was praying for an answer. "I had waited anxiously for a swift streak of lightning," he said, "but I now realized that I had already been walking in the fullness of light for a long time. The knowledge of the truth had not come to me suddenly; it had come gradually in such a gentle and natural way that I had not perceived that it had already been shining upon me for so long." He was baptized, and his wife was baptized shortly afterward. Camargo served as a bishop, stake president, mission president, and head of the translation department for the Church in Brazil.[26] In 1985 he was called to the First Quorum of the Seventy, the first General Authority from Brazil. (See chapter 10 for more of his story.) He died at age 91 in 2017.

Janae P. Miller

Janae Miller of Salt Lake City was a lifelong member of the Church. She had read Moroni's promise dozens of times in Moroni 10:3-5, but she decided the promise was only for investigators newly studying the gospel. It wasn't until her early morning seminary teacher challenged each of her students to put the promise to the test that Janae decided, "Well, why not?"

Janae was almost fourteen years old and had not yet read the entire book, but she began reading in earnest. Her older brother had received a call to serve a mission and was studying intensely to prepare for his missionary work. As she was helping him with his lessons one day, she stopped abruptly and asked him if he knew the gospel was true. When he answered, "I do," she wanted to know, "How?"

He told her he had read the complete Book of Mormon and then got down on his knees and asked. He said, "God answered my prayer. I can't explain it, but my heart was touched and my mind was opened, and I just knew without the tiniest sliver of doubt." Janae was determined to get her answer, even though she hadn't read the entire Book. Each night, she asked the same questions: "Heavenly Father is the Book of Mormon true? Did you really appear to Joseph Smith in the grove of trees? Is our church really true?" But no answer came.

One night she abruptly ended her prayer and climbed into bed, angry and in tears. After calming down, she got on her knees again, apologized, and said she would try to be patient. She then asked the same questions again. After a pause, a voice from within asked, "What do you think?"

"Well," she stuttered, "ah, well, of course I believe these things are true. They've just always made so much sense to me that I've never doubted."

"Then why do you ask?"

The message left her speechless. It hadn't occurred to her that her simple acceptance of those truths was sufficient and that she had been asking for an unnecessary revelation. She concluded that revelation from the Lord is reserved for those who need it and that her trusting faith in the scriptures was sufficient.[27]

J. Carlos Martin Clari

Carlos was raised in a good Catholic family in Spain, baptized as a baby and lived the faith. "Little by little" he laments. "I strayed from the correct path and finally removed God from my life." He felt things were good—he had a family, money and friends and believed he didn't need anything else in his life. "Satan convinced me that I was powerful, I had everything," but all that changed between 2006 and 2012. During this time he lost both parents, his business failed, and he was evicted from his house. The worst loss was the abandonment of family and friends. He felt completely alone without direction or purpose in his life. One desperate sleepless night he contemplated suicide. As he lay there thinking he remembered a phrase from a Catholic priest 38 years earlier, "Only God has power over life and death. He is the only one who can give life and take it away." He suddenly realized that God didn't want him dead, but he also realized he didn't want him to continue living in hopelessness. He got out of bed, knelt, and asked for forgiveness and for God to show him the way to change his life.

The next day, while working at home, he felt a whispering that urged him to walk his dog at a nearby park. He ignored it, but the impression came back two more times so he put a leash on his dog and took him to the park. This is where he met two Latter-day Saint missionaries. He knew it was not a coincidence, but an answer to his prayer. The missionaries told him they had a message for him from Jesus Christ if he was willing to accept it. He was, and gave them his address. On their first visit they invited him to read the Book of Mormon and to pray about it and ask Heavenly Father if it was true. He read several chapters and felt an inner sensation of peace and goodness.

Still skeptical about receiving an answer as to the book's truthfulness, he went to bed without praying. But he could not sleep, and eventually he got out of bed, knelt down and asked Heavenly Father if the book was true. A still small voice told him to, "Get up, get the book, open it to Moroni, Chapter 10, and read verses 4 and 5." After reading the two verses he said, "My soul was filled with joy, all my doubts and skepticism vanished as if by magic." He understood that the Book of Mormon was a divine gift from God containing revealed words to His prophets in the Americas, and he realized that Joseph Smith was a prophet chosen by God to restore His Church and usher in a new dispensation. He was baptized, and now studies the scriptures daily."[28]

Alan C. Ashton

Alan C. Ashton, co-founder of the one-time software giant WordPerfect, graduated from high school in Salt Lake City and was later accepted into the 23rd National Guard Army Band. During his six months of basic training he carried a pocket-sized copy of the Book of Mormon with him. The soldiers were given a ten-minute break each hour during which he read the Book of Mormon. After a few weeks he had finished reading the book.

Ashton was then determined to put Moroni's challenge to the test. One night he climbed down from his bunk and went into an adjoining classroom in their barracks where he could be alone. He knelt in prayer. "I asked God directly if the Book of Mormon was true. I had felt good about the teachings and precepts contained therein as I read it," he recounts, "but I desired a greater witness. As I asked, a feeling of warmth and certitude came over me that I could not deny. . . I felt a definite peace, warmth, a prickling sensation and the assurance of the Spirit confirming the truth of the Book of Mormon." This confirmed to him that Joseph Smith was a prophet, and the gospel of Jesus Christ was the way to eternal salvation and happiness. Knowledge that the Lord had restored His true church to the earth became a reality for Ashton that night.

When serving a mission in Germany, Ashton felt that same warm comforting spirit many times, especially as he knelt with others who were seeking that same confirming spirit. He later received a strong spiritual prompting to start WordPerfect, and after unexpected setbacks an opportunity presented itself that allowed the word-processing program to succeed, becoming a world-wide success. Ashton served as President and CEO of the famous company, which was later sold. He and his wife, Karen, parents of eleven children, founded Thanksgiving Point, a recreational and educational facility in Lehi, Utah.[29] He had previously taught at Brigham Young University, having a PhD degree. He has served on many important civic boards. Church callings include President of the Canada Toronto West Mission and President of the Provo Utah Temple.

Leo P. Talbot

In 1961, for no apparent reason, Leo P. Talbot introduced himself to a pair of Latter-day Saint missionaries in a bowling alley and invited them home for dinner. He wanted to know why they were in Australia. After several discussions with them and after attending a Church meeting and participating in a few other Church activities, he realized that the gospel meant involvement—and he didn't want any. He broke off his association with them and was "not at home" when they called. However, one elder's fervent testimony of the truthfulness of the gospel never left him.

Talbot had refused a copy of the Book of Mormon from them, but he found one in his letter box. He tried to ignore some influence he felt beckoning him to pick up the book. He ended up tossing it in his closet and piling clothes on top of it to get the book out of his mind.

Four years later, realizing his life lacked purpose, he looked for something comforting to read and finally dug out the Book of Mormon. The book had bookmarks inserted in it asking questions. One read: "How can you know this book is God's word? Moroni 10:4–5." He read the text and was impressed. He continued to read as the days went by. One day, while sitting outside in the sunshine reading about procrastination in Alma 34:31–35, he realized that that was precisely what he had been doing and decided then and there he would pray. He clenched the book firmly in his hand, looked up into the heavens, and cried, "Dear God, is it true?" He recalls, "Immediately I felt a deep burning within my bosom, and a sweet feeling pervaded the atmosphere. And then I heard a still, small voice which simply said, 'It's true.'" Ten days later, he was baptized. Talbot realized he would be eternally grateful to the two faithful, persistent missionaries who left a copy of the Book of Mormon in his letter box.[30]

These holy experiences have taken place countless times, in thousands of places throughout the world—all sincere seekers receive the same testimony: the Book of Mormon is true; it is the word of God.

Chapter 26

More Than a Million Volunteers Will Take Your Book to the World

Hundreds of thousands of volunteers must be so committed to your book that they willingly give eighteen to twenty-four months or more of their lives to take its message to the world. They will not only pay their own way, but upon returning consistently testify that their missionary service was one of the most rewarding experiences of their lives.

During the Savior's earthly ministry, He foretold one of the major events that will occur before His Second Coming: "And this gospel of the kingdom shall be preached in all the world for a witness unto all nations; and then shall the end come" (Matthew 24:14). The Lord's last admonition to His Apostles before His ascension into heaven was: "Go ye therefore, and teach all nations, baptizing them in the name of the Father, and of the Son, and of the Holy Ghost" (Matthew 28:19).

The Gospel unto Every Nation

It necessarily follows that the true Church must fulfill the Lord's great command to take the gospel to the world: "Any church that does not assume [this] obligation to take the message of salvation to those of every kindred, every tongue, every nation, and every people, has no claim to represent the God of Heaven," declares Joseph F. McConkie, author and former Brigham Young University religion professor.[1]

In an early 1831 revelation given through Joseph Smith, the Lord commanded His authorized latter-day servants to go forth preaching His gospel in modern times: "Behold, verily I say unto you, I give unto you this first commandment, that ye shall go forth in my name. . . . And ye shall go forth in the power of my Spirit, preaching my gospel, two by two, . . . lifting up your voices as with the sound of a trump, declaring my word like unto angels of God. And ye shall go forth baptizing with water saying: Repent ye, repent ye, for the kingdom of heaven is at hand" (Doctrine and Covenants 42:4, 6–7). Christ's disciples went forth as missionaries in New Testament times as He "sent them two by two before his face into every city and place" (Luke 10:1).

Later in 1831, the Savior repeated the need for the gospel to go to all the world before He comes again: "And this gospel shall be preached unto every nation, and kindred, and tongue, and people" (Doctrine and Covenants 133:37). Joseph Smith began that work by calling his younger brother Samuel as the first missionary. Samuel's mission was not easy. "After walking 25 miles and being rejected at four homes and thrown out by an irate innkeeper that evening, he spent his first night sleeping under an apple tree."[2] Samuel's proselytizing efforts were not in vain, however. His missionary work in western New York eventually led to the conversion of Brigham Young, among others.[3]

During the Kirtland, Missouri, and Nauvoo periods, hundreds of missionaries were called to preach the gospel in various places around the world. These missionaries included Members of the Quorum of the Twelve, who were called to serve in England. One member of the Twelve, Orson Hyde, was called to Jerusalem to dedicate Palestine for the return of the Jews and other tribes of Israel. "At the time of Elder Hyde's visit and dedication . . . there were comparatively few Jews at Jerusalem. . . . [An] 1876 British Consul Report shows . . . fifteen to twenty thousand Jews in Judea. But twenty years later . . . the number of Jews was sixty to seventy thousand."[4]

Other missionaries were sent to places throughout the United States, Eastern Canada, and the Pacific islands. Several members of the Twelve accepted calls when they were seriously ill with ague.[5] Some, including Brigham Young and Heber C. Kimball, needed to be carried or helped into a wagon to begin their journey. These missionary sacrifices brought thousands of converts into the Church.[6]

Early Converts Migrate to America

Because of missionary activity between 1837 and 1890, about ninety thousand Saints emigrated to America on more than five hundred ocean voyages, mostly from the British Isles and Scandinavia. Their journeys were hard and lives were lost, but they also witnessed many miracles. During raging storms, the winds were rebuked, and angry seas were calmed through the power of the priesthood. Many captains of different ships liked to have members of the Church of Jesus Christ of Latter-day Saints as passengers because there seemed to be some supreme power watching over the Saints. The captains noticed the high degree of morality, order, and cleanliness the Saints exhibited, in contrast with that of many other passengers. Latter-day Saint emigrants converted many other passengers and ships' personnel. For example, fifty converts were baptized on one voyage and forty-eight on another, including the captain, his two mates and eighteen sailors.[7]

"Missionary work has been a hallmark of the Church since its earliest days. Joseph Smith, setting the standard and example of missionary service, traveled thousands of miles in perhaps as few as 14 months, oftentimes preaching to hundreds in a congregation, teaching with such power and authority that many requested baptism on the spot."[8] The Prophet received revelations that charged all who receive the gospel with the duty "to warn [their] neighbor. Therefore, they are left without excuse, and their sins are upon their own heads" (Doctrine and Covenants 88:81–82). Because of this directive, Latter-day Saints often lovingly share their faith with their neighbors, friends, and families. Membership in the Church is such a powerful source of happiness that many members naturally want to share.

Missionaries have gone forth, first by tens, then by hundreds, and eventually by tens of thousands. Because of the thousands who joined the Church in England and emigrated to America, some of the clergy were upset. "An attempt on the part of ministers and rectors in the south of England to get a bill through Parliament, prohibiting the Latter-day Saints from preaching in the British dominions, failed. Their petition stated that one Latter-day Saint missionary had baptized fifteen hundred persons, mostly members of the English Church, in a period of seven months. This doubtless referred to Wilford Woodruff and is hardly an exaggeration."[9]

Wilford Woodruff Finds the Gospel

Wilford Woodruff was raised in Connecticut in the area where an aged man by the name of Robert Mason, known as Old Prophet Mason, lived. Mason believed it was necessary to have prophets, apostles, visions, and revelations in the church of Christ, as in ancient days, and that the Lord would raise up such a church in the last days. In 1830, Mason told Wilford Woodruff of a vision he had in 1800 in which the Lord made known to him that His church was to be restored to the earth again in all its fullness. His last words to Woodruff were that he, Woodruff, would "be a conspicuous actor in that kingdom," but that he, Mason, would never be privileged to be a part of it in this life.[10] In 1833, the twenty-six-year-old Woodruff heard an elder of The Church of Jesus Christ of Latter-day Saints preach at a schoolhouse near his home in New York State. The Spirit bore witness to him that what he heard was true, and he was baptized the next day. Thus began the fulfillment of Robert Mason's prophecy.

As this young convert thrust himself into the work of his newfound faith, he grew to become one of the Church's greatest missionaries. "In 1837, he converted almost the entire population of the Fox Islands, off the coast of Maine."[11] At the age of thirty-two, Woodruff was ordained an apostle and was soon called on a mission to England where he taught and baptized a six-hundred-member congregation. These converts included twenty-five ministers who had left the Methodist Church. This group, calling themselves the United Brethren, had prayed earnestly for light and knowledge to guide them to the true gospel. Among the hundreds of others Elder Woodruff and his companions baptized were some two hundred ministers of various denominations. "The power of God rested upon us and upon the mission," he reported.[12] Elder Woodruff later served as fourth president of the Church from April 7, 1889 until his passing on September 2, 1898.

Since those early days, hundreds of thousands of young men, young women, and retired couples, with copies of the Book of Mormon in hand, have answered the call to serve as missionaries. The 500,000th missionary was called in 1991,[13] and by June 2007, one million had served. As of 2016, there were more than seventy-four thousand missionaries ministering in more than four hundred missions throughout the world, and an additional thirty thousand service missionaries serving closer to home.[14] And like the earliest missionaries, they are not paid for their service.

Regarding the great latter-day gathering, Joseph Smith declared: "The Standard of Truth has been erected; no unhallowed hand can stop the work from progressing; persecutions may rage, mobs may combine, armies may assemble, calumny may defame, but the truth of God will go forth boldly, nobly, and independent, till it has penetrated every continent, visited every clime, swept every country, and sounded in every ear, till the purposes of God shall be accomplished, and the Great Jehovah shall say the work is done."

How Missionaries Are Called and Financed

How does one become a missionary, and what is life like for those accepting the call to serve and share the Book of Mormon? Occasionally, news reports state that it is mandatory for all young men in the Church to serve missions, but such stories are inaccurate. Young men are counseled that it is their sacred duty to serve the Lord, and thus they are encouraged to serve. Elder Boyd K. Packer explained, "We are not obedient because we are blind, we are obedient because we can see."[15] Compulsion is contrary to the gospel, and forced service would not produce faithful servants.

When young men approach eighteen years of age or young women nineteen, their bishops will usually invite them into his office to discuss the possibility of a mission call. A young man, or a young woman, may also initiate the meeting with his or her bishop to discuss potential service. The bishop interviews the candidate for personal worthiness as well as physical, mental, and emotional readiness for missionary service. If found worthy and otherwise fit, she or he will then need to pass a medical exam and take care of any needed dental work. After filling out forms and having an interview with the stake president, the prospective missionary's application is submitted to the Church Missionary Department in Salt Lake City. If the applicant is approved, he or she will receive a missionary call (assignment) signed by the President of the Church. Receiving a mission call is a much anticipated event and is now received electronically after decades of being delivered by mail.

Missionaries are not paid for their service, nor do they choose where they will serve, which could be in any one of the 421 missions in 145 nations across the world.[16] (The church does pay for the air fare and other transportation costs of the missionary.) Missionaries will learn to speak any of the 164 languages spoken by the people of their assigned field of labor. They put their academic and vocational plans on hold and often make other sacrifices, such as giving up sports and scholastic scholarships, in order to serve. Because they serve without pay, many young people start saving for their missions at a very young age.

A donation to the International Missionary Fund arrived at Church headquarters in Salt Lake from the family of a young man who died in an accident two days before his mission call arrived in the mail. Greg had saved money for his mission since he was a young child. A letter accompanying the donation stated the family felt the money had been dedicated to do the Lord's work, and their feelings were that Greg "wants it used for this purpose." The letter ended, "We are grateful for our blessings. May the Lord's work continue to spread in the world." The letter was signed "Greg's mother." Enclosed was a check for nearly $9,000.[17]

Mission presidents, who serve for three years, likewise receive their calls from Church headquarters in Salt Lake City. President. Gordon B. Hinckley, fifteenth prophet in succession from Joseph Smith, describes how the Church gets men to leave their vocations and homes to serve the Church in faraway places. "We simply ask them, and we know what their answer will be." He attributes it to "this powerful conviction that says the Church is true. It is God's holy work. . . . The strength of this cause and kingdom is not found in its temporal assets, impressive as they may be. It all comes of the gift of faith, bestowed by the Almighty upon His children who doubt not and fear not, but go forward."[18]

Missionary Training Centers

One of the first requirements of missionary service, with its attendant rewards, is to prepare at one of the missionary training centers (MTCs). The largest MTC is located in Provo, Utah, with others in other countries throughout the world, including Brazil, Colombia, England, Ghana, Guatemala, Mexico, New Zealand, Peru, Philippines, and South Africa. At MTCs, missionaries study Church doctrine, primarily from the Bible and the Book of Mormon. They learn how to teach in the language of the area in which they will serve, if it is not their native tongue. Most important, missionaries learn how to teach the gospel by the Spirit. They learn that it is the Spirit that brings people to

The Missionary Training Center in Provo, Utah, including the two new large buildings, top right.

Christ—worthy dedicated servants are merely instruments in the Lord's hand to help people learn to study and pray. In this way, the honest in heart can come to know for themselves that the Savior's true church has been restored to the earth once more. Missionaries learn to become ambassadors of the Lord Jesus Christ.

A July 2011 article in *The Christian Post* asserts that "almost all [Latter-day Saints] who have excelled in business and public life have been trained at an MTC. . . . [They] form less than two percent of America's population, but many of their members have gone on to become among the most distinguished and recognizable faces in American business and civic life, thanks to an MTC."[19] The MTC does help prepare missionaries, but it's the experiences after leaving the MTC—working with and teaching people—that provide the most useful training for their success later in life.

Most missionaries stay at the MTC for two to six weeks. Fifty-one languages are taught at the Provo MTC, which will accommodate approximately four thousand missionaries at any given time. Several hundred missionaries usually enter or depart each week. Those learning a new language are typically taught by former missionaries who served in the country to which the new missionary has been called. Many languages are also taught through state-of-the-art computer programs. Those learning new languages find the Lord often quickens their minds through the gifts of the Spirit. Miracles are common. Missionaries frequently remark they learned more in the few weeks at the MTC than they did in four years of high school language classes.[20]

Sacrifice Brings Blessings

During their period of service (two years for young men and eighteen months for young women), missionaries do not date, go to movies, watch TV, or listen to radios. They normally call their families only twice during each year on Christmas and Mother's Day. They are encouraged to email or write to their parents or families weekly. Their time is spent studying, teaching, and contacting people. One day a week, "preparation day," is set aside for shopping, cleaning, laundry, sports activities, relaxation, and letter writing. Missionaries plan on several hours of community service each week. They are expected to rise by 6:30 a.m. and, after showers, breakfast, scripture, and possibly language study, be out the door at 10:00 a.m. They usually do not return until 9:30 p.m. and are to be in bed by 10:30 p.m. Obviously, missionary work is not for the undisciplined.

Missionaries serve under the close supervision of a mission president. He, along with his wife, watch over and lead the missionaries, serving in that capacity for three years. Mission presidents take leave from their regular professions—unless they are retired. They do not receive a salary but are furnished living accommodations and expenses. Some have children with them. Serving a mission with their parents can be a valuable experience for young people, but it is still a sacrifice for the children to leave their schools and friends for such an extended period of time.

Mission boundaries could be a state (Oklahoma, for instance), part of a state (California has seventeen missions), part of a country (Brazil has twenty-seven missions), or an entire small country (Costa Rica, for example). Missionaries usually meet with their mission president every six weeks for a personal interview and for training conferences where they receive spiritual guidance and instructions. Missionaries are expected to write reports and letters weekly to their mission president to keep him informed of their labors. Missionaries serving as district and zone leaders supervise other missionaries in between meetings with the mission president.

Missionary service may require great changes in the lives of the missionaries. Many leave a car at home and walk, ride bikes, or use public transportation during their missionary tenure. The Church maintains a vehicle fleet in some areas. In some missions, missionaries sleep in hammocks or on the floor and perhaps do their laundry in a bucket or via some other primitive method. They may shower by pouring a bucket of water over their heads. Missionaries must be dedicated as they might face rejection, often with doors slammed in their faces, verbal abuse, water sprayed from hoses, people spitting on them, dogs set on them, and robbers stealing from them. This uncharitable treatment is usually the result of misinformation about the Church, which fosters misunderstanding. Once people understand the missionaries' purpose and their message, they are usually welcomed and loved as a result of all the good they do for others.

"After President of the Church, Gordon B. Hinckley [the late fifteenth President of the Church] appeared on the TV show *60 Minutes,* a [non-Latter-day Saint] viewer sent this note to CBS: 'I enjoyed your . . . segment Easter Sunday. . . . These people do provide an anchor in a sea of ever-changing values. Fifty thousand [1996] chaste missionaries in 150 countries probably do more good for society then all the government social programs put together.'"[21]

Opposition to the Work

Sometimes, well-meaning friends give adversarial pamphlets and books to those the missionaries are teaching as soon as these friends realize they are studying with the missionaries. Renee Olson was one of those actively oppos-ing any missionary efforts among those she and others of her Florida Baptist Church found were meeting with Latter-day Saint missionaries. She completed training classes at her church on "What the [Latter-day Saints] Believe" and received an affidavit showing she was a certified Latter-day Saint basher. Renee

Missionaries in Bacolod Philippines Mission going to a teaching apointment

really thought she was doing a good thing trying to "save those nice people from going to Hell," but, when she listened to her Latter-day Saint neighbors and learned what they *actually* believed, she accepted it and was baptized into the Church after a move to Atlanta, Georgia. Her comments then were, "The Baptists don't have a clue about what we [members of The Church of Jesus Christ of Latter-day Saints] believe."[22]

Happiness Found in Service

Even with aggressive opposition and rigorous schedules, most missionaries, upon their return home, will say their missions were the happiest and most fulfilling times of their lives up to that point. The vast majority do not look upon missionary service as a sacrifice. Because of the spirituality and love for others they gained from the experience, many consider their mission the best two years (or eighteen months) of their life, but also the best two years *for* their life.

David Neeleman – Besides gaining stronger testimonies about Christ and the restoration, how else are missions the best years *for* their lives? David Neeleman, founder and former CEO of JetBlue Airways, who served as a missionary in Brazil, says his mission "saved him." He struggled in school and later found he had ADD, attention deficit disorder. He said his mission was the first time in his life that he ever felt like he had a talent of some kind. It "gave me this opportunity to serve and really appreciate people for their contribution." He said he learned to treat everyone the same, it obliterated class distinction, and, as a result, there are no first-class sections on JetBlue planes.[23] He earned $200,000 annually but donated his entire salary to a catastrophic fund set up for JetBlue workers who fell on hard times—an act that is virtually unheard of in a world where chief executives often make enormous salaries.[24]

Kevin Rollins – Strict missionary rules stuck with Kevin Rollins, former CEO of Dell computers, who served in Alberta, Canada. Getting up at 5:30 a.m. as a missionary became a lifelong habit. "A mission teaches you to get up, get going, and do things," he is quoted as saying. He acknowledges that much of his business attitudes of hard work and never giving up are mission-based.[25]

Kim B. Clark – Former Dean of Harvard Business School, Clark served his mission in Germany where he served as the mission financial secretary. Although he had completed one year at Harvard, he had no experience with finances. His mission president, Orville Gunther, had been a bank CEO and not only cared about the quality of their mission teaching but also about the way finances were handled. Clark says he learned a lot about organization, finance, budgeting, and accounting, and he applied those lessons in his management style at the Harvard Business School. "My mission for the Church was a very important influence in how I think about organizations."[26] Clark later served as president of BYU Idaho and was sustained as a General Authority Seventy of

The Church of Jesus Christ of Latter-day Saints on April 4, 2015. Additionally, he served as Church Commissioner of Education.

Clayton Christensen – Harvard Professor Clayton Christensen, was twice named world's top management guru by Thinkers 50.[27] He has consulted with companies like Intel, Eli Lilly, Dell, Kodak, and others. Having served his mission in Korea, he feels missionary work is "the hardest sales job known to mankind. . . . You go out there with a deep devotion and you are convinced that your product is the best product in the world." In the process, you get knocked down and rejected and have to figure out how to keep your self-esteem and motivation as you face opposition. The challenges are so great that "then you come into the business world and it's duck soup compared to that. . . . Missions cause you to be a better leader."[28]

Senior Missionaries – Missionary schedules for "senior missionaries" (married couples or older women) are less rigorous than for young people. Senior missionaries serve in a variety of settings. They can have TVs and radios and can call their families as often as they wish. Like their younger colleagues, they pay their own living expenses, put in many long hours of service, are much appreciated wherever they serve, and love being missionaries. Besides being proselytizing missionaries, they may serve in a variety of other capacities, such as health, humanitarian, office staff, genealogical, agricultural/landscaping, education (particularly religious instruction), temple workers, temple visitor centers, employment centers, or at a church historical site. They usually serve for eighteen months, but they can serve for six months, one year, or even two years or more. Many love doing missionary work so deeply that they volunteer for several missions. Some senior couples have served missions in six or more different locations around the world.

Missionaries Love the People

Younger missionaries often find the biggest challenge of a mission is learning all they need to know to teach others gospel principles of the restored Church, even though most have completed four years of seminary training during their high school years (see Chapter 27). The easiest part, many say, is loving the people.

Andy Gray, a promising quarterback at the U.S. Air Force Academy when he left to spend two years in South Africa, had more on his mind than throwing a football when he returned. "I never felt on the football field what I felt over there," he reported when he returned to the Academy following his mission. "I was there to help people understand how a life can be blessed through the grace and the love of Jesus Christ."[29]

Elder H. Wells Meeks and his companion were knocking on doors in a small town in Iowa when a door on which Elder Meeks knocked was opened by a woman who said, "Come on in; I've been waiting for you." The lady then explained that as a student of the Bible, she had for many years searched for a church with apostles and prophets, one that taught the gospel in its entirety. Having looked into many churches without satisfaction, she began earnestly praying to the Lord to know if His church were on the earth and, if so, would He guide her to it. During the night, she received a vision that the Lord's messenger would come to her door, and she saw Elder Meeks in the vision. The missionaries were invited to return that evening and found two rooms filled with neighbors the woman had invited to come hear about a church that was the same as the one Christ had organized in his day. To the missionaries' great joy, nearly everyone who attended that evening was eventually baptized.[30]

The Book of Mormon Musical versus What Real Missionaries Do

The Book of Mormon musical, staged on Broadway and in cities across the U.S. and other countries, has put a spotlight on the Book of Mormon and the Church's missionaries, but it hardly portrays them in their true character. It is said the creators spent seven years writing and producing the show which depicts the missionaries as serving in Africa where they are described as coming from "some kind of a surreal world of self-deception and illusion." However, there is a wide gap between the way the elders are portrayed and their actual character and service. What were real missionaries for the The Church of Jesus Christ of Latter-day Saints doing in Africa during that period?

In 2017, Michael Otterson, former managing director of public affairs for the Church, highlights some of the service that missionaries and their families would have likely been involved in, financially or in person in Africa. During those seven years, more than four million Africans in 17 countries have gained access to clean drinking water through Latter-day Saint humanitarian efforts; more than 34,000 physically handicapped African children now have wheelchairs through the same organization; millions of African children have been vaccinated against killer diseases like measles; more than 126,000 have had their sight restored or improved through partnership with African eye-care professionals, with the Church providing training, equipment and supplies; another 52,000 health-care professionals have been trained to help newborns who otherwise may not have survived. The Church has helped treat AIDS victims in African countries and has responded to multiple disasters, such as the flooding in Niger where the Church provided clothing, quilts and hygiene items to 20,000 people in six inundated regions of the country.

Otterson concludes with these comments:

What of those thousands of remarkable and selfless [real Latter-day Saint] missionaries who opted to pay their own expenses during the past seven years to serve in Africa while their peers were focused on careers or getting on with life? They have returned home bringing with them a connection with the African people that will last a lifetime. Many will keep up their Swahili language or their Igbo dialect. They will keep in their bedrooms the flags of the nations where they served. They will look up every time they hear Africa mentioned on the evening news. Their associations with the people whose lives they touched will become lifetime friendships. And in a hundred ways they will become unofficial ambassadors for the nations they served.[31]

Following are a few activities real Latter-day Saint missionaries initiated, programs to help their brothers and sisters whom they had served:

Tim Evans. Missionaries' love for their missions and for those they bring into the gospel fold knows no bounds. Many stay in contact with their converts for the rest of their lives, and some return to their mission field for humanitarian reasons. That is what Tim Evans did after he became a dentist practicing in Oakley, Utah. He heard of the death of little four-year-old Hilda because she had to drink tainted water. He had known her family as a missionary in Peru. He and other former Peruvian missionaries returned and helped dig wells that provided safe water for Hilda's community. They have continued with additional water projects, schools, and health and hygiene training. Tim founded CHOICE Humanitarian, and other effective International Organizations.

Nate Shipp and Benjie Becker of Salt Lake City and Bountiful, Utah, respectively, reached out to orphan children in Ukraine. Shipp had worked with them as a missionary and witnessed their great needs. Since the year 2000, their organization, Project Reach Out, has been sending supplies, such as bedding, clothing, diapers, medicine, appliances, and food to eleven orphanages.[32]

Peter Reichman of Provo, Utah, was aware of the hardships endured by the people he served among in the Philippines, so he organized a support group called "Vaccines for the Philippines." With the help of local government officials, they have sponsored free medical clinics, trained recipients in the use of first-aid kits, distributed over a thousand doses of rabies vaccine, and more. As Dr. Tim Evans, who went to Peru said, "These people you work with become your family, become a part of you, like your own brothers and sisters. You want to give back, to respond to the needs of the people because of their love and kindness to you."[33]

Mitt Romney, former missionary to France, governor of Massachusetts, and twice a U.S. presidential candidate, tells of the effects that serving a mission had on his five sons:

They grew up in an affluent household, and by age nineteen . . . their lives were centered on themselves; education, clothes, music, and girls. Each was asked to serve a mission. They would live in very humble circumstances, eat only two meals a day to save money, and walk or ride a bike in sun, rain, or cold. And most difficult of all, they would be treated worse than a door-to-door salesman. . . . Incredibly, each of our sons has said that his mission was the most formative period of his life. It was a time to learn something about humility. Our sons beseeched God, in behalf of others, and learned that He was always there. They worked harder than they had ever worked before. And they tasted the sweet fruits of service at a time when their lives could have otherwise been directed toward solely selfish pursuits. At that critical juncture in time, when young people may turn entirely inward, the Church asked them to serve their fellowman. . . . And that has made all the difference.[34]

Mark M. Trunnell. Upon finishing his mission, Mark Trunnell reflected on what his mission meant to him as he returned home after serving for two years in Rome, Italy:

It occurred to me that I had been blessed with a heightened capacity to love. . . . The beauty of these people was etched in my heart. . . . The Savior had blessed me with a love for these people that I didn't know was possible. . . . In a simple and profound way, they had become a part of me. . . . In giving two years of my life, I had gained so much more, I had learned to love. I had learned that it was possible to see people through the eyes of the Spirit—to overlook faults and appreciate strengths. I had gleaned powerful lessons for my own life.[35]

Missionaries *do* love and care for those they teach and serve. Two missionaries had been teaching a young single mother of two, and one day found her in a very depressed state of mind. Through her tears, they learned that the water to her apartment had been shut off for several days, leaving her and her children with no laundry or bathroom facilities. She was working two jobs and had given a trusted person money to pay the water bill expense. Instead, that person had pocketed the money and disappeared. The missionaries were deeply concerned. They decided that if they combined their monthly expense allotment and rode their bikes rather than drive their car, they could pay the water bill. As a result of their sacrifice, they ran out of food with a week to go before their next allotment, but on Sunday, they were invited to dinner and afterward given three bags full of groceries. No one but the Lord knew of their situation, and they felt He had heard their prayers.[36]

Richard Blodgett. Just how great is the love that missionaries feel for their converts? Elder Richard Blodgett was among the twelve missionaries in his area who were fortunate monthly dinner guests of the Kerbs Family of Wuppertal, Germany. The couple was elderly, and Mr. Kerbs was blind. Elder Blodgett curiously asked why they went to so much trouble and expense for the missionaries.

Mr. Kerbs offered to tell them a story. All the missionaries had been sent home from Germany when World War II broke out. Some returned as soldiers. This was the case of one[37] young American who found himself patrolling the same streets he had walked on a short time earlier as a missionary. He was now a corporal in the United States Army. A group of German citizens were rounded up for looting, an understandable act when people are starving. Suddenly the corporal, without thinking, ran and threw his arms around an aging gentleman in the group. His sergeant was furious and accused him of insubordination. The corporal tried to explain about being a missionary there before the war. He had taught the man the gospel—a good man and the only person he had baptized!

The corporal was already a thorn in the sergeant's side—a boy who neither drank, smoked, nor caroused. The old man was caught looting, and early the next morning he was to be shot and the corporal would do the shooting! When he told his sergeant he could not do that, the sergeant said he would either shoot the man or be standing beside him. He chose to die with his German brother. Then Mr. Kerbs finished his story. "That [German] man was my father."[38]

Missionaries Are Protected

Alma Sonne grew up in Logan, Utah, where he had a friend named Fred. Fred was not active in the Church, but when it came time for Alma to serve a mission, he talked Fred into preparing to serve a mission as well. Both were called to England. At the end of their mission in April 1912, Alma was responsible for arranging their trip home, along with some other missionaries. He booked them on the *Titanic*. For some reason, his friend, Fred, couldn't make it in time to sail, so Alma canceled all their bookings. They were all looking forward to sailing on the new luxury liner that was making its maiden voyage, and they were very disappointed. After learning that the *Titanic* had sunk, Alma said to Fred, "You saved my life," to which Fred replied, "No, by getting me on this mission you saved mine."[39]

Missionaries on the whole are relatively safe compared to their contemporaries who are not serving missions. Some research has shown them to be ten times safer. Only one-tenth of one percent lose their lives through accidents, illnesses, or other causes. It appears that the safest place in the world for a young person to be is on a full-time mission.[40] Missionaries do receive impressive protection from the Lord.

Brandon Miller. Elder Brandon J. Miller, while serving as a missionary in the Philippines, was bitten by a Philippine cobra, the deadliest snake in that country. He and his companion were able to make it to their bishop's home where, while losing consciousness, he requested and was given a blessing by the two priesthood holders. He began to come to his senses during the prayer, and his vomiting stopped with the final words of the blessing. A doctor was called, and as he drove them to the hospital, he was asked if he shouldn't speed up. The doctor replied, "Why? He should already be dead. He is a lucky young man." Elder Miller knew his life was spared by a loving God of miracles. He suffered no lasting effects. Then he remembered the promise given in the Book of Mormon about protection given to the Lord's faithful: "Yea, even the fiery furnace could not harm them, neither wild beasts nor poisonous serpents, because of the power of his word" (Mormon 8:24).[41]

Craig Bernard and Jeremy Bushnell. These two missionaries serving in Scotland, Elder Craig Bernard from the state of Washington, and Elder Jeremy Bushnell, from Utah, were attacked by a group of young men in Glenburn in October 2001. The attackers punched and kicked them before stabbing the young men in the back. Both survived. The missionaries said, "We love Scotland and the people of Scotland and won't let this incident detract from our previous wonderful experiences."[42]

Travis Tuttle and Andrew Propst. In March 1998, Elders Travis Tuttle of Gilbert, Arizona, and Andrew Propst of Lebanon, Oregon, were serving as missionaries in Saratov, Russia, when they were kidnapped and held hostage. A $300,000 ransom was demanded. Worldwide prayers in their behalf were answered when after five days, the two were released unharmed. No ransom was paid. The Church will never pay a ransom for missionaries; otherwise, no missionary would ever be safe from such a fate. The kidnappers were apprehended and prosecuted.[43]

Shaun Rosemann. Missionaries love sharing their message of Christ. "The reward is when you see a change in a person. You see a light turn on and you know they found the love of God and Jesus Christ" said, Elder Shaun Rosemann while serving as a missionary in Mongolia.[44] Missionaries use no strong-arm tactics but only gentle persuasion when teaching people. They ask people to read the Book of Mormon, pray about what they have been taught, and then listen to the voice of the Spirit to discover its truth.

The Temple Square Mission

Visitors who tour Temple Square in Salt Lake City will likely see some of the two hundred sister missionaries from over forty countries who are serving there. They speak more than thirty languages. Some are college graduates and they gladly conduct tours of Temple Square. Millions have taken these informative tours at Utah's most popular tourist attraction which accommodates more than five million visitors each year. About twenty senior-married couples also serve in this unique Temple Square Mission,[45] which is the smallest geographic mission in the Church.

Joseph V. Hamilton from Lexington, Kentucky was stationed in Salt Lake City while serving in the U.S. Military. He was unaware that such a place as

Temple Square even existed when he and some other servicemen just happened upon it one Sunday morning. They went on a tour. Hamilton read a pamphlet and was impressed with what he learned. Soon afterwards, he was deployed to India where he coincidentally bunked next to a Latter-day Saint serviceman whom he pestered with questions. Joseph read the Book of Mormon and other Church literature. Although he was the son of a Pentecostal minister, Hamilton was baptized into the Church when he returned to the United States. He served a mission, married, became a dentist, and was instrumental in the conversion of his four brothers and two sisters to the Church.[46]

All Are Welcome to Latter-day Saint Services

All are welcome to attend worship services of The Church of Jesus Christ of Latter-day Saints. The nearest building can be found on the internet through the "Meetinghouse Locator" on the Church's website. Searches are done by city or postal code. The address and meeting times for the Church unit will be displayed, and maps with directions to the meetinghouse can be viewed or printed. Visitors will find themselves most welcome and will probably be pleased to find that no collection plates are passed.

In the early days of the Church, and until recent years, missionary work has typically been done by knocking on doors to introduce people to the restored gospel, or by making contact on the street. In March 2018 the Church instigated an initiative for missionary contacting called Global Online Teaching. Although this method had already been part of missionary work for a few years it had not been widely known nor implemented Churchwide. In 2017 there were 21.1 million visitors to this missionary website, located at 20 visitor's centers and historic sites, such as the Hill Cumorah, New York, and around the globe. Or, at the North Visitors Center at Temple square in Salt Lake City, where 22 sets of sister missionaries are online at any given time preaching and teaching the gospel. Daily about 600 missionaries are teaching the gospel online around the world, speaking more than 40 languages. During 2017 they had 349,670 chats, 91,250 phone calls and 299,665 information requests, and taught more than 140,000 people through their worldwide conferences. The missionaries try to teach the first two lessons then refer them to their local missionaries, but sometimes they are with the investigator through all the lessons. With the time zones being worldwide, the global outreach is 24/7.[47]

Regarding missionary work, LeGrand Richards a Member of the Quorum of the Twelve, wrote:

No other church except the church that Jesus established in the meridian of time, has ever undertaken such a responsibility of missionary work, carrying the gospel of Jesus Christ to "every nation, kindred, tongue, and people" as has the Church of Jesus Christ of Latter-day

Saints. The missionaries of this church are going . . . from door to door, city to city, and nation to nation, in carrying out the instructions of the Lord as received from him through the restoration of the gospel. They have been doing this ever since the organization of the Church. They will continue to do so until the head of the Church of Jesus Christ, shall come in the clouds of heaven to claim his kingdom.[48]

Tens of thousands of young people, senior members, and mission presidents and their families have given valuable years of their lives to share their beloved Book of Mormon with unselfish love for others and love for Christ.

Non-Latter-day Saints are invited to request copies of the Book of Mormon from the missionaries. The missionaries will likely have books to share, or will know how to get one. The book has been the key element in missionary work since its publication. It will speak for itself, but investigators must read it to hear its voice. It is the most powerful tool missionaries could possibly possess—the ultimate keystone to conversion.[49]

Chapter 27

Believers in the Book Will Become Powerful Examples of Christian Living

Your book must not only help raise the standards of millions of people, but do it in such a way that they become power-ful examples of Christian living whose faith and works are known and respected throughout the world.

Henry A. Wallace, 33rd vice president of the United States was well acquainted with the Book of Mormon. He wrote, "Of all the American books of the nineteenth century, it seems probable that the Book of Mormon was the most powerful. It reached perhaps only one percent of the United States, but it affected this one percent so powerfully and lastingly that all the people of the United States have been affected."[1] A Rochester newspaper agreed: "It was not the book itself, but the wonderful influence it had on America that counted."[2]

In 1970, Robert B. Downs authored *25 Books That Changed America*. The Book of Mormon ranked near the top. He wrote: "Throughout history . . . the Church's most powerful and effective weapon has been the Book of Mormon. Other religious movements in America have come and gone and today are largely forgotten—mere footnotes in social history. The possession of their own scriptures, the reading of which has persuaded many prospective converts, has proved to be the Mormons' greatest missionary tract, giving permanence and stability to their religion, and providing them with a faith by which to live."[3]

Thirty-three years later, Barnes and Noble's *Book Magazine* published *20 Books That Changed America*. Only four of the books on Downs's 1970 list survived. The Book of Mormon was among them. The introduction to *20 Books* reads: "In honor of America's 227th birthday, we set out to find the twenty novels and nonfiction titles that have had the greatest impact on the history of the country: the ones that led to concrete, definable changes in the way Americans live their lives. . . . Here, then . . . are the books that forever changed the nation." *20 Books* says this about the Book of Mormon: "The book given to Joseph Smith by the angel Moroni launched the country's biggest homegrown religion. . . . The book provides the theological underpinnings for one of the world's most vibrant religions."[4] A survey by the Library of Congress asking readers what book had most influenced their lives finds the Book of Mormon to be among the top ten books selected for many years.[5]

Without the Book of Mormon, The Church of Jesus Christ of Latter-day Saints could not have become the powerful force for good in the world that it has. The book, and the doctrines that fill its pages, needed to be published before the Church was organized to provide a strong foundation for the new religion to build upon. Latter-day Saint's firm belief in the Book of Mormon, its origin, and its Christian teachings gives Church members the desire to live gospel standards, to serve others, and to make large sacrifices of time and talent to serve in the Church. Following are some of the teachings, programs, and activities that the Church sponsors or is involved in that have helped raise the standards of millions.

The Family Is Central to God's Plan

The Church and its members are among the greatest advocates of the family in the world today. "The theology of the Church centers on the family, and the programs of the Church are designed to support and strengthen the family," writes best-selling author Richard Eyre. "The Church has enabled our children to be somewhat protected from the world without being removed from it." The Eyre children attended and served as student-body officers and leaders in colleges like Harvard, Wellesley, Columbia, and Boston University while still maintaining high personal priorities and perspectives. "This simply would not be possible without the Church," he adds.[6]

In an October 2005 interview with *Newsweek* magazine, then Church President Gordon B. Hinckley was asked how the Church, with its strict code of living, still attracts so many converts. His reply: "We live in a world of shifting values. The family is falling apart. Parents [are] failing in what they ought to do. . . . They find in this church something that expects something of people, that has standards and holds to those standards and speaks of requirements and definitions and so on. And they find here a rock that is solid and strong and true and isn't wavering with every gust of wind."[7]

The Book of Mormon is a major part of the doctrinal foundation of those standards that provide protection from societal storms assaulting families everywhere. Latter-day Saints set aside one evening a week to teach the gospel and family values, play games together, sing, discuss family duties and goals, eat treats, and participate in other fun and wholesome activities. This weekly family night was initiated by the Church decades ago to strengthen families. The Church has published manuals to provide families lesson materials and ideas for activities. Latter-day Saints believe that families are meant to be together forever in the afterlife, and weekly family home evenings help them work toward that goal.[8]

Each year, American Mothers, Inc., a nondenominational organization that honors mothers who promote spiritual and moral strength in families, chooses a National Mother of the Year and a Young Mother of the Year from among state winners. Latter-day Saint mothers are consistently chosen for this honor from several states, and many Latter-day Saint mothers have, within a year, been selected as national winners in both categories.[9]

More than thirty years ago, the Church embarked on a public service campaign known as "Homefront." The brief messages in this campaign were designed to teach positive values and encourage parents to have a greater degree of involvement in the lives of their children. The messages became so well recognized that many people began to think of The Church of Jesus Christ of Latter-day Saints in terms of what it does to strengthen the family. These popular spots were shown, or aired, on thousands of TV and radio stations throughout the world in a dozen languages, reaching an audience of millions. One listener wrote, "Who would have believed that after so many years my first fan letter would be to a T.V. commercial! Whenever I am privileged to see one of your delightful messages I am moved to go to my daughter and give her a hug, or to go into the kitchen to prepare a special dinner." Potent Homefront messages have encouraged and uplifted parents and helped families throughout the world.[10]

Not only does the Church believe in strong families, its members have the largest families in the United States according to the Pew Forum on Religious and Public Life. Nine percent of Latter-day Saint households have four or more children, compared with three percent nationally. The Church also has the highest percentage of adults who are married,[11] and Utah's new moms are the least likely to be teens or unmarried.[12]

Some groups criticize those having large families, but large families (or at least families large enough to provide some population growth) are essential to the national survival of every country on earth. At the World Congress of Families IV, held in Poland in 2007, the world's "birth dearth"—declining fertility rates that are threatening a "demographic winter—" was a major topic of discussion. In nearly every corner of the world, replacement fertility levels have dropped significantly below the 2.1 children-per-woman average needed to sustain nations. This trend presents serious problems for families and the future of the world. Nearly seventy nations, representing more than half the world's population, have fertility rate levels below replacement levels. There are not enough people being born in those countries to support their economies and to provide for their aging populations.[13]

Latter-day Saints Know and Live Their Religion

Utah, where more than 60 percent of residents are members of The Church of Jesus Christ of Latter-day Saints, is known as a good place to live. Utahans show they care about their communities and their neighbors. The state leads the nation in the rate of adults who volunteer, and has for ten straight years—46 percent of adults in Utah volunteer, according to a 2015 study.[14] In 2011, a Corporation for National and Community Service's "Volunteering in America" report revealed Utah adults volunteered, on average, 89.2 hours each. "They build houses for the poor, man hospital waiting rooms, teach literacy and step up in countless other ways, as well."[15]

Utah and Salt Lake City are growing in numbers. The *Economist* noted that "the thing that guarantees that Salt Lake City will continue to grow is precisely what built it in the first place: The Church of Jesus Christ of Latter-day Saints." Rodney Stark, a professor of sociology at the University of Washington, says, "In many ways, Utah is an enormously sophisticated population." Among other things, he noted the state's highly educated labor force, its burgeoning high-tech industry, and its pool of missionaries with thier foreign-language skills and cultural experience.[16]

A column that appeared as commentary in the *Los Angeles Times* provides an unambiguous picture of Latter-day Saint beliefs:

[The Church has] what is probably the strictest set of beliefs and practices of any major religion. They don't back off one inch about the divinity of Christ as the literal son of God. The resurrection is an absolute. Life after death is an absolute. The Atonement is an absolute. No tobacco or alcohol, tithe the full ten percent. [Latter-day Saints] stick with their principles. Yet they are experiencing explosive growth. . . . Growth in religion and in political parties comes from clarifying the principles, not from diluting them.[17]

"Research has shown again and again, that a defined moral beacon is part of what attracts many people to the church," writes sociologist Rodney Stark.[18]

How does that moral beacon work for young members of the Church? When research was conducted by the National Study of Youth and Religion in March 2005, it was data about teenage members of the Church that impressed the researchers. They found that Latter-day Saint teens know about their faith, believe it, and act accordingly. Similarly, a four-year study on teenagers and religion conducted by the University of North Carolina found that though the majority of American teenagers demonstrate a vague knowledge of beliefs and loose commitment to their faiths, it was not so with Latter-day Saint youth. By almost any measure, they stood above the crowd: "It is [Latter-day Saint] teen-agers who are sociologically faring the best." They were found best at avoiding risky behaviors, doing well in school, and having a positive attitude about the future.[19]

If Latter-day Saint teenagers know and live their beliefs, it stands to reason that their parents do, too. In 2010, the Pew Research Center conducted a U.S. Religious Knowledge Survey and found that Latter-day Saints eighteen and older know more about the Bible and Christianity than does any other Christian group in America. Latter-day Saint adults scored highest as the most frequent readers of religious materials at 51 percent, whereas white evangelicals followed at 30 percent.[20] The Glenmary Research Center found Utah to be the most religious state in the nation,[21] and Gallup found Provo-Orem, Utah, to be the most religious metro area in the United States, with 77 percent of its residents classified as "very religious."[22]

The example of the Latter-day Saint children in David J. Marianno Jr.'s first-grade class in Fairfield, California, spurred his conversion to the Church. After four years of observing their behavior, he reports, "What they did at school made them stand out among my other students. . . . They unselfishly helped and taught other students regardless of their ability, race, or perceived popularity. They befriended just about everyone, including the teachers, and particularly those children who had difficulty making and keeping friends. They were always happy, diligent in their work, and extremely well-behaved. And they were all so full of love for [everyone]. . . . But most impressive was that they did all of these things so naturally. To them it was no big deal. To me it was much more."[23]

How do the leaders of the Church fare? There are those who believe that power corrupts. Former Senator Robert F. Bennett of Utah relates the attempt of a major newspaper, *The Arizona Republic*, to "expose" the Church, following the time-honored maxim to "follow the money" by compiling a complete financial profile of the Church. "The reporters chased down every lead, probed every file, interviewed every source they could to find out how much the Church was worth and how its leaders used that financial power. When they were done, the paper reported that there were no instances of corruption—not one. No one in the Church had used his position to enrich himself."[24]

Members of the Church under the Communist regime in East Germany learned that living the principles of the gospel earned them respect and trust. At first, everything they did was watched, including attendance by the secret police at their meetings, and everything they printed had to be approved.[25] But they lived by the twelfth Article of Faith of the Church which states, "We believe in being subject to kings, presidents, rulers, and magistrates, in obeying, honoring and sustaining the law."

The faithful members continually asked permission to leave the country to go to the temple in Switzerland and were repeatedly turned down. They were astonished when the Communist leaders suggested they build their own temple in Germany, a blessing they never dreamed possible! The State Secretary for Religious Affairs for the German Democratic Republic said, "We know you. . . . We've observed you and your people for twenty years. We know you are what you profess to be: honest men and women."[26]

President Gordon B. Hinckley, speaking to a national gathering of religion writers, said, "No one believes more literally in the redemption wrought by the Lord Jesus Christ. No one believes more fundamentally that He was the son of God, that He died for the sins of mankind, that He rose from the grave, and that He is the living resurrected Son of the living Father. All of our doctrine, all of our religious practice, stems from that one basic doctrinal position."[27]

Living the principles of the Church noticeably changes lives. Recording superstar Gladys Knight joined the Church in 1997, some ten years after her son and daughter and their families had become members. When she was asked what led her to inquire into the Church and its beliefs, she replied, "I just watched them and their families. I watched them change. And what I saw was so remarkable that I finally decided I had better find out for myself if what they had found was true." Gladys Knight later married William McDowell, who also joined the Church, of which he remarked, "Today, I know without a doubt in my mind that this is one of the greatest gifts my wife brought to me."[28]

An Educated People

In an early revelation to the Prophet Joseph Smith, the Lord admonished the people of the Church to "seek ye diligently and teach one another words of wisdom; yea, seek ye out of the best books words of wisdom; seek learning, even by study and also by faith" (Doctrine and Covenants 88:118). Joseph Smith taught that knowledge is essential to the eternal progression of mankind: "It is impossible for a man [or woman] to be saved in ignorance"; "A man is saved no faster than he gets knowledge"; and "The Glory of God is intelligence." Schools were among the first structures built during the short stay of the Latter-day Saints in Missouri and after their arrival in the Salt Lake Valley.

The Church's Quorum of Twelve Apostles in 2017 included three with law degrees, two cardiovascular surgeons, an airline pilot/executive, seven with MBA and PhD degrees from Harvard, Yale, Purdue, Duke, BYU and Stanford, and three former university presidents. They were all prominent men in their fields prior to their call to be Church leaders.

In contrast to the experience of most churches in the United States, the more education members of The Church of Jesus Christ of Latter-day Saints receive, the greater is their religious activity.[29] According to a Pew report, 84% of the members of the Church with a college degree say religion is very important in their lives and attend church services regularly. The report lists the national average for college graduates among most other religions at 55 percent, which is lower than those with some college, or those with a high school degree.[30]

The Church's emphasis on both spiritual and secular learning has, for example, produced a large number of Latter-day Saint scientists: "For 80 years every study has shown that, in relation to population, Utah was number one in spawning scientists."[31] Latter-day Saint scientists have either conceived or been involved in the invention of television, stereophonic sound, psychoacoustics (the theory of hearing), psychopharmacology (including drugs to suppress epilepsy), synthesis of diamonds, high octane gasoline, synthetic textiles, artificial kidneys, artificial heart and lungs to keep a patient's body functioning during heart surgery, artificial ears through cochlear implants, laser surgery, amniocentesis (health of fetuses), Thymidine Kinase 1 (the Tk1 test to detect cancer at early stages), artificial kidneys, the discovery of enzymes that fuel energy production within the cell (winning a Nobel Prize), and pioneering in word processing. Latter-day Saints invented the transistor radio, the odometer, the electric traffic light, the electric guitar, digital sound recording (CDs, DVDs etc.),[32] and many other innovations. From chemistry to computers, the lives of millions have been affected by and benefited from their discoveries and inventions.

Perhaps because of the Church's emphasis on education, a 2005 Census Bureau report showed that Utah exceeds national averages in its educated populace. An estimated 91 percent of the population twenty-five and above have earned a high school diploma.[33] An October 2007 analysis found that Utah is the only state in the country that does not have a "dropout factory" where fewer than 60 percent of students make it to their senior year.[34] Utah young women were the most likely to graduate, and a study by the National Woman's Law Center revealed that Utah's female dropout rate is the lowest in the nation.[35]

Brigham Young University

Brigham Young University, located in Provo, Utah, is owned and operated by The Church of Jesus Christ of Latter-day Saints. It is one of the largest church-sponsored universities in America, with over thirty thousand students. BYU's stated mission is "to assist individuals in their quest for perfection and eternal life." With this goal in mind, its leaders consider the university to be at heart a religious institution, where religious and secular education are interwoven in a way that encourages the highest standards in both areas. This integration of the secular and religious aspects of a university goes back to Brigham Young himself, who gave the school's first principal, Karl G. Maeser, this charge: "I want you to remember that you ought not to teach even the alphabet or the multiplication tables without the Spirit of God."[36] Following this counsel, more than 150 congregations totaling about twenty-four thousand students meet on the BYU campus each Sunday, making it one of the busiest and largest centers of worship in the world (other students attend congregations at off-campus locations).

In 2011, for the second year in a row, BYU was rated first as America's most popular university by *US News and World Report*. This means that a higher percentage of those who apply and are accepted, ultimately enroll in that school, ranking the school ahead of runners-up Harvard and Stanford.[37] BYU athletic teams are popular and have a national fan base. Wherever they play, they can usually plan on a sizable crowd of fans rooting for them.

BYU students come from all fifty states and 120 foreign nations. Upon finishing their studies, students are among the most-sought-after graduates in business, law, languages, music, and other disciplines.[38] This is not surprising when we consider the quality of education available to them at the university. The *Princeton Review* ranked BYU the best value for college in 2007,[39] and its library is consistently ranked in the nation's top ten. Based in part on the school's emphasis on undergraduate research, BYU was ranked No. 10 nationally in 2008–2009 for the number of students who go on to earn PhDs, No.1 nationally for students who go on to dental school, No. 6 nationally for students who go on to law school, and No. 10 nationally for students who go on to medical school. In 2009, the university's Marriott School of Management was ranked No. 5 by *Business Week* for its undergraduate programs. Among regional schools, the MBA program was ranked No. 1 by *The Wall Street Journal* for 2007. For 2009, the university's School of Accountancy was ranked No. 3 for its undergraduate program by *U.S. News & World Report*. BYU has outstanding music programs, including possibly the world's largest men's chorus; hundreds audition every year to join the more than 180 member choir.

In 2015, five BYU graduates made the list of the worlds' fifty best business management thinkers. On the list was Clayton Christensen, who ranked No. 1 for the years 2011 and 2013. The 2015 list included Dave Ulrich, Liz Wiseman, Hal Gregersen, and Whitney Johnson. That was the fourth year for Dave Ullrich who says BYU can't take all the credit. He noted what he called the Church's focus on leadership and leadership development. With no paid clergy in the Church, girls and boys begin to serve in leadership positions when they turn twelve. He further says, "I don't think the world understands how great missions are for learning gospel and theology, of course, but also social learning, organizational learning, personal management learning. An eighteen-month or two-year mission is like five years working at one of the world's best consulting firms." Ullrich concludes, "For me, BYU was life-changing. It put words on my experiences and [I] discovered the principles I'd learned earlier were my principles."[40]

BYU is regularly in the top ten of U.S. colleges in the "quality of life" category. This is in large measure because the students sign an honor code stating they won't have premarital sex, use foul language, drink alcohol, use tobacco, or drink coffee or tea. They are also committed to dress modestly. Students do not have to be members of the Church to attend BYU, but they must agree to live up to the school's standards. Twenty-Fifteen marked the eighteenth straight year in which *The Princeton Review* found BYU the top stone-cold sober university in the country.[41] As a result of these standards, in January 2016, *Business Insider* named BYU the safest college campus in America.[42]

BYU students have worked on projects with far-reaching benefits. The children of Ghana lacked both play equipment and light by which to study when

retired engineer Ben Markham, who had served as a Latter-day Saint missionary in that country, challenged BYU engineering students to find a solution. Under the direction of engineering Professor Charles Harrel, the students worked for more than a year designing a prototype merry-go-round that will charge batteries for desk lamps as children push and play on the machine, which was built with materials available

A team of BYU technology students installs an innovative power-generating merry-go-round in a schoolyard in Essam, Ghana

in Ghana. Now an ever-increasing number of children in that country (and later expanded to other countries) have merry-go-rounds to play on, as well as light at their desks and in their homes because the students can take their lanterns home at the end of every school day.[43]

Another group of BYU students recognized that in developing countries many amputees lacked the thousands of dollars needed for expensive carbon-fiber prosthetic limbs. After months of testing, they discovered that PVC pipe can be melted and molded into limbs that are both firm and flexible for about $25 per limb. The students have traveled at their own expense to countries such as El Salvador, Guatemala, and Tonga where they have built legs as a nonprofit venture. When asked why they do it, the students replied that helping improve the lives of people in need is just something they love doing.[44]

A team of BYU engineering professors and students have developed an artificial spinal disc replacement that treats chronic low-back pain. "This device has the potential to alleviate the pain and restore the natural motion of the spine—something current procedures can't replicate," they say. It is as functional as a healthy disc would be. International sales began in 2013[45]

Knowing that 3.6 million people die every year from scarce or contaminated water, in 2011 another team of six BYU students took on the problem of developing a drill for affected African villages. The engineering students worked on more than a hundred concepts before developing a simple hand-cranked drill that can bore 250 feet into the ground to find water. Using human power, they have drilled wells in three days that are now providing clean water. Following footpaths if necessary, the "Village Drill" can be taken into areas, where big, expensive drilling rigs cannot reach. No other drills use human power. It is estimated that each drill will create jobs for ten or more families.[46] By 2017 the drill had been taken to 25 countries by WHOlives.org where 55 Village Drills are now used. More than 1,200 boreholes now provide clean water to hundreds of thousands of appreciative people, many of whose lives have no doubt been saved by having clean water.[47]

The BYU Motion Picture Studio has produced hundreds of titles for multiple purposes and audiences during its fifty-plus years at the school, winning awards and distributing millions of copies of their uplifting productions.[48] In 2011, BYU's students in the animation program won eleven College Television Awards (student Emmys) and four Student Academy Awards. Ed Catmull, president of animation for both Pixar and Disney remarks, "Over the years, Pixar has worked with a lot of different universities around the country and hired people. . . . We found that BYU had risen to the top. It's the perception, not just at Pixar but also at the other studios, that something pretty remarkable is happening here." Major animation studios are drawn to BYU students not only for their specialized skills and collaborative experience but also for their high moral standards. They have been encouraged to bring their faith and beliefs with them to Hollywood where many have been employed.[49] The BYU Center for Animation was established in 2010.

Among BYU's other achievements, the Marriott School of Management was named first in the nation by 4,400 corporate recruiters. High marks were given for the students' leadership potential, maturity, competitive drive, integrity, and international experience, which has resulted from their missionary work for the Church.[50] The Marriott School of Management's MBA program has the fastest return on investment of any school. The average salary of a BYU MBA five years after graduation is $108,000, compared to $47,000 before graduates entered the program.[51]

Three-fourths of the BYU student body speak at least one foreign language, in large part because they have served as Latter-day Saint missionaries throughout the world.[52] After the 9/11 terrorist attacks in 2001, the U.S. Department of Education recognized that too few Americans had a working knowledge of Arabic, Hebrew, Persian, and Turkish, except at BYU, so the department created the first National Middle East Language Resource Center at the university.[53]

BYU is one of three world centers for Dead Sea Scrolls research. Four members of the international scrolls research team are on the BYU faculty.[54]

Other institutions of higher learning the Church operates include BYU–Hawaii, in Oahu; BYU–Idaho, in Rexburg, Idaho; the BYU Jerusalem Center for Near Eastern Studies, in Jerusalem; the Church's Business College in Salt Lake City; and the new BYU Pathway, with headquarters in Salt Lake City (discussed below).

BYU–Hawaii sponsors the Polynesian Cultural Center which is Hawaii's number-one paid tourist attraction. When construction started in 1962, many were skeptical of the idea, but Church President David O. McKay prophesied that millions would come. True to his prediction, the PCC has been Hawaii's most popular attraction with 750,000 to one million people visiting the center each year. By 2010, it had welcomed 35 million visitors.[55]

How has the center helped raise the standards of many people? Seventy percent of the twelve hundred people working at the PCC are BYU–Hawaii students. Seventy percent of the revenue from the center, more than $175 million per year, goes to the university to help pay for the education of the students, who come from seventy different countries. The center has directly helped thousands of students from Polynesian backgrounds earn degrees. Many of these students otherwise would not have been able to go to college. After their schooling, they return by the hundreds to their home areas in Asia and the South Pacific to help educate others and keep alive their diverse cultures. Most significantly, they increase their earning power and thereby influence the lives of millions.[56] One such student is Albert Mailo from Samoa who worked at the center, received his education from BYU–Hawaii, finished with a law degree from BYU–Provo, and returned to Samoa where he became American Samoa's attorney general.[57]

The Church, with its strong emphasis on education, was concerned about other young members in third world countries who did not have the resources to pay for an education. Thus, a program titled the Perpetual Education Fund was established in 2001 to help young men and women get a good education and become self-reliant, especially after serving a mission for the Church. The program is funded through contributions of Church members and friends. It is a revolving resource in which money is loaned to an individual to help pay for advanced education or training. When a student has graduated and is working, he or she then pays back the loan to the fund at a low interest rate. The PEF currently helps participants between the ages of 18 and 30 in 55 countries and has assisted more than 55,000 students, according to John J. Carmack the first head of the program.[58]

In February 2017 the First Presidency of the Church announced the creation of a new additional global higher education organization called BYU-Pathway

Worldwide. Three pilot programs had been created in 2009 under BYU-Idaho Pathway, and grew to 497 sites in 50 countries with 37,000 enrolled. By 2017, some 57,000 students had been served. The new program, which began operating May 1, 2017, with headquarters in Salt Lake City, Utah, will expand to many more thousands of US and foreign students. The program is unique in that it combines online education with religious education in local institutes and meetinghouses. The first president of BYU-Pathway Worldwide, Clark G. Gilbert, left a teaching position at Harvard University to work at BYU-Idaho, where he later became president of the university. Gilbert led the team that created Pathway and was responsible for all online certificate and degree programs. The classes it offers will be accredited through the existing Church Education System. Countless more students will be blessed through this new program.[59]

The Word of Wisdom

Members of The Church of Jesus Christ of Latter-day Saints are well known for their health practices. The Church's law of health, known as the Word of Wisdom, is a revelation given to Joseph Smith on February 27, 1833. It promises spiritual and physical blessings to those who live its principles.[60] The Word of Wisdom prohibits the consumption of alcoholic beverages, hot drinks (understood to mean coffee and tea), and the use of tobacco. The Word of Wisdom promotes the use of grains, herbs, vegetables and fruits and directs that meat and fowl should be eaten sparingly. The Word of Wisdom, though not part of the Book of Mormon, rather is found in the Doctrine and Covenants (Section 89), one of the four standard works of the Church. It is a basic lifestyle tenet for Latter-day Saint believers in the Book of Mormon.

The revelation gives a promise from the Lord to those who follow His law of health: "They shall receive health in their navel and marrow to their bones; and shall find wisdom and great treasures of knowledge, even hidden treasures; and shall run and not be weary, and shall walk and not faint" (Doctrine and Covenants 89:18–20). *Health Digest* called the Word of Wisdom "the greatest experiment in correct eating and correct living ever conducted."[61] It contains inspired guidance for good health practices that were unknown to the medical or scientific world at the time. Without revelation from God, Joseph Smith could not have known of the negative consequences that would afflict people who used substances the Lord warned against. Neither could he have known of the great health benefits that result from obedience to this law's positive suggestions. The revelation was many decades ahead of science, and the millions of people who have adhered to it have reaped the rewards of good health and a longer life, along with added wisdom and spiritual knowledge.

A twenty-five-year study of nearly ten thousand practicing Latter-day Saint men and women found that they live longer and have healthier lives than the general population if they follow this strict Church of Jesus Christ of Latter-day Saints health code. The study, conducted by non–Latter-day Saint UCLA professors, found that members of the Church experienced dramatic benefits, such as lower death rates from cancer (21 percent fewer), less cardiovascular disease (30 to 50 percent less than average), less diabetes (50 percent less), and less kidney disease (51 percent less than average). The researchers found an increase in longevity 9.8 years longer for men, and 8 years longer for women. The probability of early death is 56 percent less for Latter-day Saint men and 43 percent less for Latter-day Saint women, compared with their counterparts.[62]

The Tabernacle Choir at Temple Square

The Tabernacle Choir at Temple Square is one of the best known and most beloved musical organizations in the world. Millions of visitors have attended its free weekly rehearsals and broadcasts in the famed Tabernacle on Temple Square or in the nearby Conference Center in Salt Lake City. Tens of millions more have listened or watched via radio, television, and the internet. The 360-member all-volunteer choir has sung throughout the United States and in many countries of the world. It has released nearly two hundred musical albums, earning five Gold Records, two Platinums, and a Grammy Award. The choir has been featured in many television productions, and sang for three and a half billion people in the opening ceremonies of the 2002 Winter Olympics held in Salt Lake City.[63] In February 2015, the choir was inducted into the American Classical Music Hall of Fame for "140 years of dedication to the choral arts and for its significant presence in the world of classical music."[64] They have sung at seven U.S. presidential inauguration ceremonies. When they sang for Ronald Reagan's inauguration, he dubbed them "America's Choir."

In May 2006, when the choir presented its four thousandth broadcast, Craig Jessop, conductor of the choir at the time, reported: "I get letters from all over this nation from people who are in prison, people who are shut up in a nursing home facility, or homebound, who say this is their church, this is their religious service, this is their devotional for the week, Music and the Spoken Word." Lloyd Newell, the voice for the choir, says the purpose of the program "is to give people just a few minutes of inspiration, lift their spirits, steady their hearts a little bit, give them some hope."[65] The choir celebrated its one hundredth year recording anniversary in 2010. It has been making musical recordings longer than any other group in modern history except the Vienna Boys Choir.[66]

Famous British singer Sting was visibly touched after performing with the choir at the 2002 Olympics. He spoke to choir members: "You make me very proud to be a member of the human race and one of God's children. I didn't know people were capable of producing such beauty. I've been really touched by the beauty of the singing. I don't know why, but I've never felt anything like this before."[67]

Church Programs for All Ages

There is a place for everyone to learn, serve, and grow in The Church of Jesus Christ of Latter-day Saints. For example, for many years the Church had a close partnership with the Boy Scouts of America, a program that involved most young men. The Scouting program was scaled back in 2017, and will be replaced by the Church's own program after 2019. Young Latter-day Saints are encouraged to attend Church-sponsored seminary classes, which are held each day during their high school years (ages fourteen to eighteen). In some areas, youth are able to attend these classes during their regular school hours on released time, but most other students participate in classes held for an hour beginning at 6:00 or 7:00 a.m. before regular school classes begin.

Students study the Old Testament, New Testament, Church history, and the Book of Mormon, each for one year. For students in remote places where there are few members and no seminary, they may do a home study course. They are given the same materials and outlines that students study in organized classes. Graduation ceremonies are held annually for those who complete four years of seminary, or a certificate is presented to home study students in a Church meeting.

The Church provides religion classes for college-age students at Institute of Religion buildings near many colleges and universities throughout the United States and in dozens of other countries. Along with classes, the Institute is a center of social activity—firesides, service projects, parties, and dances, etc.—becoming a "home away from home" for its students. Hundreds of thousands of students are enrolled in these seminary and institute classes throughout the world.[68]

Most Latter-day Saint youth twelve through eighteen years of age, attend a weeknight character-building activity called Mutual. Dances are often held monthly on Friday or Saturday evenings. Young people in the Church are discouraged from dating before the age of sixteen; however, those fourteen and fifteen years old may attend the dances.

The many activities available to the youth of the Church give them confidence to stand up for their beliefs. When Latter-day Saint Kristen Tanner of El Centro, California, was crowned National Miss Junior Teen in December 2003 at Orlando, Florida, she earned an outstanding score in her interview with the judges. "I talked a lot about how I stand up for what I believe in." She explains that people "don't need to try to fit in with the crowd by doing things such as dressing a certain way or drinking alcohol."[69]

In addition to Sunday sacrament meeting services, where members of all ages worship together and partake of the sacrament, there are classes for all ages, starting with the Primary organization (eighteen months to twelve years of age); the Young Men's and Young Women's organizations (ages twelve to eighteen); and Gospel Doctrine classes for adults. Women attend a Relief Society class for adult females. Men and boys, age-twelve and older, attend priesthood classes, where they are instructed on gospel principles and their opportunity and duty to serve others.

The Church offers highly effective courses that are not part of Sabbath services. Members develop skills to improve their education, get a better job, better manage their personal finances, or start and grow a business. The Church teaches that spiritual and temporal lives are vitally linked, both important for our happiness in this life and our eternal life in the world to come.

The women's Relief Society was organized in 1842 by the Prophet Joseph Smith. Today, it is the oldest and largest women's organization in the world. In addition to meeting each Sunday, members meet during an evening as needed for special projects or presentations. Through the Ministering program introduced in 2018, each adult female member is visited monthly by an assigned pair of sisters who address any needs that may benefit the household. One example of Relief Society service, among thousands, is inspiring: If parents of children who die in a hospital in El Salvador cannot provide a suitable coffin for their deceased child, they are denied custody of their youngster's body and are unable to bury it as they would choose. As a result of this coffin law, many poor parents take their seriously ill children from the hospital, who might have recovered, fearing they might die there. As a result, many do die. A stake president in El Salvador, Dr. Angel Duarte, also a concerned physician, contacted Church Humanitarian Services, and his stake was provided with enough wood and materials for the members to build three hundred coffins. The Relief Society sisters from several wards were heavily involved in the project, and they felt many children's lives have probably been saved through their loving labors.[70]

The women of the Church have been in the forefront of women's rights, and in 1870, they were the first women in the nation to vote in a municipal election. However, before the U.S. Congress would grant Utah full territorial status, the territorial legislature was forced to rescind women's right to vote. The women persisted and regained this privilege in 1895, many years before the nation as a whole followed suit. Latter-day Saint women worked closely with Susan B. Anthony and other leaders of the National Women's suffrage movement.[71]

Worldwide Humanitarian Service

"A man filled with the love of God is not content with blessing his family alone," proclaimed Joseph Smith, "but ranges through the whole world, anxious to bless the whole human race." "Smith would be proud of his flock today," wrote a reporter in the *Vancouver Sun* after visiting the Church's humanitarian operations in Salt Lake City. "When it comes to compassion and helping others, the Latter-day Saints take a backseat to no one."[72]

Following Christ's admonition to care for the poor and needy, the Church has established an extensive worldwide humanitarian program. Giving aid is never conditional. The only question asked is, "Do you suffer?" The Church believes that "when a disaster occurs, the time for preparation is past." As a result, through Latter-day Saint Charities and other resources, the Church is able to respond rapidly to emergencies or disasters virtually anywhere in the world, whether it be a flood, blizzard, tornado, hurricane, wildfire, tidal wave, earthquake, power outage, refugee crisis, famine, or drought.

Food, clothing, bedding, tents, medical supplies, and other items are sent out from the Bishop's Central Storehouse in Salt Lake City, which functions in tandem with the Latter-day Saint Humanitarian Center.[73] The Deseret Industries Sort Center, nearby, which covers 153,400 square feet, about the size of 2.6 football fields, has been the hub of the Church's humanitarian efforts worldwide since 1991. Millions of pounds of clothing and shoes are sorted here each year, along with thousands of pieces of medical equipment and tons of textbooks and other supplies. They are processed and shipped to areas of need throughout the world.[74]

A new 570,391 square foot Bishops Central Storehouse was dedicated in Salt Lake City on January 26, 2012. The new facility has the capacity to store 65,000 pallets of food and supplies and includes 63,000 square feet of freezer and cooler space. A fleet of forty-three semi-trucks and 98 trailers log about 3.5 million miles per year delivering goods to some 110 Church storehouses across the United States and Canada.

The storehouse is organized so supplies can go out to those in need at a moment's notice. When the storehouse received the call that an earthquake had struck Haiti, trucks were on their way within minutes. An hour later, television reporters showed up to tape the procedure—the loading of the trucks and so forth—but they were told they were too late. "Sorry, the trucks are an hour down the road" (to the airport). When Hurricane Katrina struck the southern United States in 2005, fully loaded semi-trucks were dispatched from Texas to South Carolina. When the storm hit South Carolina, supplies were on site within twenty-four hours. Four hundred and fifty semi-trucks with food, water, and other needed items were sent to the disaster zone from the Salt Lake Bishop's Central Storehouse in the weeks following the emergency.[75]

Throughout the world the Church maintains 143 storehouses, 102 home storage centers, 54 production centers, and 23 processing centers. "Since 1985, the Church has given more than $1.3 billion in aid and goods in 178 different

Inside the Bishops' Storehouse

countries and territories—from earthquake relief to tsunami relief. The Church has given 63,377 tons of food, 14, 345 tons of medical supplies, 93,196 tons of clothing, and 11.1 million hygiene, newborn, and school kits. The vast majority of the aid given goes to people who are not members of The Church of Jesus Christ of Latter-day Saints."[76]

In 2014 alone, "[Latter-day Saint] Charities responded to 132 disasters . . . in 60 nations of the world, including a major typhoon in the Philippines, a destructive cyclone in the Kingdom of Tonga, the Ebola outbreak in West Africa and extensive refugee assistance for Syria and Iraq . . . in addition to providing wheelchairs [57,800] in 48 countries, maternal and newborn care in 42 countries, clean water and sanitation projects in 26 countries, gardening projects in 17 countries and medical immunization in nine countries."[77] These are all ongoing projects for the Church.

The welfare program of the Church has been cited as a model for other welfare programs. Members who receive welfare assistance from the Church become independent on average in about one hundred days. Federal welfare recipients, on the other hand, typically remain on the dole for more than ten years. "The explicit aim of [Latter-day Saint] welfare is to wean people from it. That it succeeds is its greatest achievement," writes the Heritage Foundation in its *Journal Policy Review*. The article cites several reasons for its success: The Latter-day Saint recipients work for what they receive; local members visit homes to determine problems so they can be corrected before they become critical; the program is administered by local bishops, unpaid clergy who are often professionals, wise in worldly matters and able to speak from experience; and the bishop tailors the benefits to the needs of the family and helps them get back on their feet.[78]

In 1998 the Church initiated an organization that is now called *Helping Hands*, a name under which members of The Church of Jesus Christ of Latter-day Saints perform volunteer community service. The name and its logo are on yellow t-shirts and vests worn by the church members while providing various services. This might entail responding to catastrophes such as Hurricane Harvey in Texas, or Hurricane Irma in the Florida Keys in 2018 where approximately 10,000 Helping Hands responded to help victims at both disasters. Or they might be supplying building materials along with carpentry training for those left homeless in Queensland, Australia, or San Juan, Puerto Rico after Hurricane Maria, or an earthquake in Mexico, or fires in California. But, responding to major catastrophes is just one facet of the hundreds of projects undertaken by Helping Hands around the world. They could be found helping at an orphanage in Peru, painting a primary school in South Africa, or cleaning up parks, etc., which is done annually in cities all over New Zealand and in other location throughout the world. Their cheerful service has been welcomed and appreciated by thousands worldwide.

Another program sponsored by the Church is *JustServe.org:* A free service "that uses the power of the internet to connect willing volunteers with needy individuals." There is no cost or obligation to the organizations or the volunteers that use this service. Through the internet connection groups can specify their needs and get the help they need, connecting with others who have a desire to serve. North Carolina state government, for instance, posts a Just Serve link on its volunteerism website. Church leaders have been working to build and expand the website since 2011. In 2018, there were 355,111 registered volunteers, 11,455 current projects, and more than 54,000 projects since they started. They have also begun training specialists in the United Kingdom, Australia, Mexico and Puerto Rico.[79]

In 1983, Tom Shell, a national correspondent with ABC News, was in Salt Lake City reporting on massive flooding caused by melting snow. Shell was amazed as he witnessed the organization and service rendered by thousands of residents. "I've covered dozens of disasters in my life," he says, "but I have never seen unity and brotherhood like this." He was not only moved by the actions of the thousands of flood victims but also by those who weren't affected by the floods. "It's scary," he says. "I've seen one man make one phone call, and in less than one hour 200 residents are building a wall of sandbags around a house to save it. It really is amazing. . . . I've never witnessed this kind of concern for others," he adds. "It's powerful; it really is."[80]

Members of the world's largest food aid organization, the United Nations

World Food Program, visited the Church's Humanitarian Center and Welfare Square and thanked the Church for its commitment to helping "people who are poor and hungry and at risk and vulnerable." James Morris, executive director of the program, toured the centers and said the thing he will remember most about his time in Salt Lake City is the many people "living out day after day, their faith and commitment. It is one thing to talk about your beliefs and spiritual commitments, but this is a place that realizes it, actualizes it, and lives it day in and day out. You see volunteers of all ages here doing good things to help people all over the world who desperately need it."[81]

The Church Recognized as an Influence for Good

In 1892, the renowned Russian author, statesman, and philosopher, Count Leo Tolstoy, after visiting America, observed that Latter-day Saints "teach the people not only of heaven and its attendant glories, but how to live so that their social and economic relations with each other are placed on a sound basis. If the people follow the teachings of this Church, nothing can stop their progress—it will be limitless. . . . If [it] is able to endure unmodified until it reaches the third and fourth generation, it is destined to become the greatest power the world has ever known."[82] By 2017, the Church was already in its eighth or ninth generation. President Gordon B. Hinckley explained that "our objective is to make bad men good and good men better."[83] The Church does this by bringing people to Christ.

When Russian President Nikita Khrushchev visited Washington, DC, with his family in 1959, he spent considerable time with Ezra Taft Benson, the U.S. Secretary of Agriculture and a leader in the Church. Benson's son Reed, who was able to travel with the Khrushchev family, outlined Latter-day Saint doctrine and told them about the Book of Mormon. Back in Russia, Khrushchev's son-in-law was later heard to say that America as a whole did not impress him very much and that the only thing that touched him deeply was the Latter-day Saints and their philosophy of life.[84] The Book of Mormon is a big part of this positive philosophy, with its laudatory influence on so many.

In 1987, U.S. President Ronald Reagan wrote the following for the 150th anniversary of the Church in the British Isles: "[Latter-day Saint] contribution to American life is beyond measuring, and the contribution of the British Isles and Ireland to the . . . Church is also immense. They are the contributions of love and joy, of faith and family; of work and community. They are a dedication to the values that are the heart of free nations—and good ones—and they are a faith in the promise of tomorrow."[85]

The Book of Mormon has affected the lives of people throughout the world. Robert Remini wrote that Joseph Smith was "arguably the most important religious reformer and innovator in American history. . . . He was a man of little formal education, yet he possessed a striking intellectual power. He produced a vast religious output that has influenced for the good many millions of people. From the beginning, [the restored gospel] instilled into the lives of its adherents . . . a sense of self-worth, belonging, meaning and direction, as well as a spirit of collective responsibility of community welfare and hopefulness."[86]

Members of The Church of Jesus Christ of Latter-day Saints do not believe they have a corner on achievement or goodness. They know there are millions of wonderful, good, caring people in the world who accomplish great things while serving others. Latter-day Saints, however, are thankful for the abundant blessings that have come into their lives through the Book of Mormon and the Church.

The Church's 13th Article of Faith, which members strive to emulate, reads: "We believe in being honest, true, chaste, benevolent, virtuous and in doing good to all men; indeed we may say that we follow the admonition of Paul—We believe all things, we hope all things, we have endured many things, and hope to be able to endure all things. If there is anything virtuous, lovely, or of good report or praiseworthy, we seek after these things."

Fifty years ago, U.S. President John F. Kennedy, speaking in the Salt Lake Tabernacle, said, "Let us remember that the [Latter-day Saints] of a century ago were a persecuted and prosecuted minority, harried from place to place, the victims of violence and occasionally murder, while today, in the short space of 100 years, their faith and works are known and respected the world around, and their voices heard in the highest councils of this country."[87]

Chapter 28

Adherents of Your Book Will Suffer Severe Persecution

For fourteen years following the publication of your book, you must witness the persecution of your family, friends, and tens of thousands of other believers. They will suffer extreme hardship, often in freezing conditions, as they are driven from their homes, mobbed, starved, and some killed because they believe your book is the word of God.

Scores of books have been written about the persecutions suffered by the Latter-day Saints during the early years of the Church. Following is a brief account of some of the unlawful and inhumane actions perpetrated against them and the hardships they endured. Joseph Smith and his family suffered enormously and witnessed persecutions of others.

Persecution of the Smith Family

From the time Joseph Smith first gave an account of his vision in the Sacred Grove, persecutors were relentless. The Smith family built a comfortable two-story home on their large farm in Palmyra, New York. Joseph Smith Sr. had one final payment to make to obtain the deed, and arrangements had been made to pay it. However, a group of dishonorable men went to the agent holding the deed and fabricated a story in which they claimed that the Smiths had cut down maple trees, burned rails, trashed the place, and then run off. Without checking the facts, the agent sold the Smith farm to these fraudsters for the amount of the last payment and handed over to them the deed to the property. When the agent learned the truth, he did all he could to return the property to the Smith family—to no avail.

The new owners bragged about their ill-gotten gain: "We've got the land, sir, and we have got the deed, so just let Smith help himself. Oh, no matter about Smith. He has gold plates, gold money; he's rich. He don't want anything." An agreement was eventually reached requiring the Smiths to pay $1,000, for which the men promised they would relinquish the deed. The Smiths worked diligently to raise the money, which was finally paid by the son of a friend, who happened to be the high sheriff. The deed was given to him. The Smiths never were able to secure it. The deed owner allowed them to rent the farm for a year if Samuel, their fourth son, would work for him for six months.[1]

The persecutions persisted. Joseph's father owed a debt of $14 to a man who had purposely bought the note against the debt in an attempt to pressure the senior Smith to deny his testimony of the Book of Mormon. The man demanded immediate payment. Joseph Smith Sr. had only $6, which he gave to the man, saying the rest would be paid later. The man informed him he must either pay the full amount immediately or go to jail. Joseph's mother, Lucy, offered her gold beads, which would have satisfied the debt, but the man refused to settle. However, as he made wild gestures toward the fireplace, the man promised to forgive the debt if they would burn all their copies of the Book of Mormon.

When the family would not agree to the man's demands, Joseph Sr. was taken to jail. He was ill and had not eaten that day. The constable had Smith sit in the waiting wagon in the hot sun, faint and sick, while he went inside the Smith home and ate the food Lucy had prepared for her husband. During the trip to jail the officer employed every means possible to get their prisoner to renounce the Book of Mormon—with the promise that if he would do so, the note would be forgiven, the money paid would be returned, and he would not be disgraced and imprisoned. Their offers were met with silence.[2]

Upon arrival at the jail, Joseph, Sr. was cast into a dungeon with a murderer. Over the next four days, he was fed only one bowl of weak broth. His son Samuel arrived with some food and made arrangements for his father to be let out into the jail yard. Father Smith was able to work in the prison's cooper shop, making enough money to pay the rest of the debt. While there he converted two men to the restored gospel during his month-long imprisonment. He later recalled, "I shuddered when I first heard these heavy doors creaking upon their hinges; but then I thought to myself, I was not the first man who had been imprisoned for the truth's sake; and when I should meet Paul in the paradise of God, I could tell him that I, too, had been in bonds for the gospel which he had preached. And this has been my only consolation."[3]

Early in the fall of 1829, three men arrived at the Smith home and used every conceivable trick they knew to get Lucy to show them the manuscript of the Book of Mormon, which they planned to grab and throw into the burning fireplace. Lucy refused to show them the manuscript, and the men told her not to testify of the Book of Mormon and other things she knew to be true. "If you do believe those things, you [should] never proclaim anything about them." Mother Smith's courageous reply was, "Deacon Beckwith, even if you should stick my body full of faggots and burn me at the stake, I would declare, as long as God should give me breath, that Joseph has that record, and that I know it to be true."[4]

Strong opposition to the preaching of the gospel commenced in the New York area shortly after the Church was organized. Ridicule, vandalism of members' property, and other actions designed to disrupt the growth of the Church were common occurrences. On January 2, 1831, Joseph received a revelation from the Lord commanding that the Saints as a body move to Ohio to escape the power of their enemies in New York (see Doctrine and Covenants 38:31–32).

The Move to Ohio

Obedient to the Lord's command, most of the New York Saints prepared to leave for Ohio, though it meant great sacrifices and suffering because the people were required to leave behind farms, homes, livelihoods, and friends. Some were disowned by their families. The Prophet's mother, Lucy, was asked to take charge of the exodus of the Fayette Branch. Arriving in Buffalo for the boat trip, they found the harbor on Lake Erie clogged with an ice field and the ship unable to leave. Lucy called upon the members to exercise their faith through prayer, which they did. Immediately, there was a loud noise "like bursting thunder," and the ice parted, forming a narrow passage through which the boat was able to move. Shortly after the boat passed through the opening, the ice closed again. By the middle of May, nearly all of the New York members had gathered to Kirtland.[5]

On June 1, 1833, a revelation to Joseph Smith instructed the Saints to build a temple in Kirtland. The building was shown in a vision to Joseph and his counselors, Sidney Rigdon and Frederick G. Williams, who then communicated construction details to the craftsmen.[6] This was a brave undertaking because

Kirtland Temple, first Latter-day Saint Temple

Kirtland Temple today

the Church treasury was empty. Persecution and apostasy threatened the temple's completion, yet the edifice, costing $60,000, an enormous sum for the time, was finished in less than three years and dedicated in 1836.[7] "The building of this structure by a few hundred persons, who, during the period between 1832 and 1836, contributed voluntarily of their money, material, or labor, the women knitting and spinning and making garments for the men who worked on the temple, was regarded with wonder throughout all northern Ohio."[8] This temple, fortunately, still stands today but is not owned by the Church.

Two Centers of Gathering

Between 1831 and 1838, new converts to the Church were congregating in two main locations: Kirtland, Ohio, and Independence, Jackson County, Missouri. In July of 1831, Joseph and other leaders of the Church visited Missouri, traveling the one thousand miles from Kirtland. Here the Prophet received a revelation that Jackson County was "Zion" and was to be the gathering place for the Saints.

During this period, missionaries were called and sent out by the Prophet to preach the restored gospel. They had substantial success in bringing converts into the Church, especially in England. Many of these new members emigrated to the United States and then to one of the two gathering places in either Ohio or Missouri. The Church's rapid growth created serious problems between the Saints and their neighbors. The newly arrived Latter-day Saints in Missouri were different from the established settlers around Independence. The new settlers were often accustomed to fine homes with extensive acreage and were typically more educated than their new neighbors who had few domestic comforts and little education. Missourians generally believed in slavery, and therefore were suspicious of Northerners. They feared that the Latter-day Saints would vote as a block for candidates and issues contrary to their wishes.[9]

Based on teachings found in the Book of Mormon, Latter-day Saints believe that Native Americans are partly descendants of the Lamanites and therefore took a special interest in them. Church leaders sent missionaries to them so they could learn about the restored gospel and to teach them of Christ. The people were generally receptive to the message of the restored gospel, and when news of their interest reached the frontier settlements in Missouri, it stirred up jealousy and envy among the Indian agents and sectarian missionaries. The Latter-day Saint missionaries were charged with disturbing the peace and soon ordered out of Indian country.[10] To rid the area of Latter-day Saints, one agent reported to the governor of Iowa that the Latter-day Saints and the Indians had entered into a conspiracy to destroy all white settlements on the frontier.[11]

Additionally, the Church's belief that Missouri would become their "Zion" did not set well with the established settlers, and this caused more friction.

Conditioned by previous negative experiences with neighbors in other states, the Saints naturally isolated themselves socially and economically, organizing large cooperative farms and buying and selling mostly among themselves.

The incoming Latter-day Saints were also making converts among the small congregations of Protestant churches in the area, so it is little wonder that the ministers felt threatened and tried to drive the Saints out.[12] The Saints' actions, beliefs, and growth, however, did not merit the horrendous, unconstitutional, and inhuman treatment they suffered from individual people and various state governments.

Early Persecutions in Missouri

The spring of 1832 brought the earliest rumblings in Jackson County, Missouri. Mobs threw rocks through the windows of several Latter-day Saint homes, fired shots into their homes, burned haystacks, and used abusive language against Church members. Within a year, the pastor of the Cumberland Presbyterian Church stirred up more opposition with a publication that declared, "The Mormons are the common enemies of mankind and ought to be destroyed."[13]

Early in July of 1833, a circular known as the Secret Constitution was passed around, collecting names of those willing to help eliminate the "Mormon scourge." A mob of some four hundred men met at the courthouse in Independence and demanded that the Saints cease printing their newspaper, close their stores and shops, not allow additional members into the country, and leave Jackson County. Church leaders would not agree to those unlawful demands.

Enemies of the Church held other mass meetings. People at one of those meetings expressed the fear that the Latter-day Saints "will soon have all the offices in the county in their hands, and that the lives and property of other citizens would be insecure, under the administration of men who are so ignorant and superstitious as to believe that they have been the subjects of miraculous and supernatural cures; hold converse with God and his angels, and possess and exercise the gifts of divination and unknown tongues."[14]

A mob broke into the house of W. W. Phelps where the Church's printing press was located. They wrecked the press, destroyed many valuable documents, threw papers outside, and demolished the building. Two young Phelps boys were buried in the debris, but they survived. Two sisters, Mary Elizabeth and Caroline Rollins, ages twelve and fourteen, gathered some of the scattered papers, which were unbound folios of The Book of Commandments (the first compilation of revelations received by the Prophet Joseph Smith).[15] Pursued by two mobbers, the girls ran "into a large cornfield, laid the papers on the ground, and hid them 'with our persons.' The corn was from five to six feet high, and very thick; they hunted around considerable, and came very near us but did not find us."[16]

The mob then broke into the homes of the Saints, searching for the leading elders. Men, women, and children ran in all directions, fearing for their lives. The attackers caught Bishop Edward Partridge and Charles Allen and dragged them a half mile to the public square, where they were given the choice of denying the Book of Mormon or leaving the county. The hostages would agree to neither. Bishop Partridge was permitted to speak before he was tarred and feathered: "I told them that the Saints had suffered persecution in all ages of the world; that I had done nothing which ought to offend anyone; that if they abused me, they abused an innocent person; that I was willing to suffer for the sake of Christ." Nevertheless, the two were stripped of their clothing. Their bodies were smeared with tar mixed with pearl ash, a flesh-eating acid, and a pillow of feathers was emptied over them. Their meek resignation to the assault touched their tormentors' sympathies, and they let the two victims leave without further abuse. "I was so filled with the Spirit and love of God," recalled Bishop Partridge, "that I had no hatred towards my persecutors or anyone else."[17]

Within a few days of these events, a mob of about five hundred men rushed into Independence, brandishing guns, whips, and clubs as they searched for Church leaders. In the meantime, the mobbers had their slaves lay waste to the Saints' crops. "If they will not go without force," they threatened, "we will whip and kill the men; we will destroy their children, and ravish their women."[18] Leading Latter-day Saint men offered themselves as ransom if the mob would not harm the people—but to no avail. After a few weeks, Church leaders were forced to agree that all Latter-day Saints would leave Jackson County. Because the mob's actions were clearly illegal according to the constitutions of the United States and the state of Missouri, Church leaders appealed to Governor Daniel Dunklin for help. Rather than offering protection or mercy, he advised them to get legal counsel.[19]

The beatings of members and destruction of property continued. The Saints tried to avoid direct conflict, but the continued persecutions resulted in a battle near the Big Blue River, where two members of the mob and one Church member were killed. Another Latter-day Saint, Philo Dibble, was shot in the stomach three times but was miraculously healed after Newel Knight gave him a blessing. "Brother Newel Knight came to see me and sat down on the side of my bed," he recounted. "I felt the Spirit resting upon me at the crown of my head before his hand touched me, and I knew immediately that I was going to be healed. . . . [after the blessing,] I immediately arose and discharged three quarts of blood or more, with some pieces of clothes that had been driven into my body by the bullets. I then dressed myself and went outdoors. . . . From that time not a drop of blood came from me and I never afterwards felt the slightest pain or inconvenience from my wounds, except that I was somewhat weak from the loss of blood."[20]

In his journal, Knight recorded that Dibble had later been "examined by a surgeon of great experience . . . who said he never knew a man to live who was wounded in such a manner." On the day of the attack Knight managed to get past the mob surrounding the house. . . . I looked upon Brother Dibble lying there in extreme agony. . . . [I then] pulled the bed curtains, put [my] hands on his head and prayed secretly, then left to escape the mob. The next day, ten miles distant, [I] was understandably surprised when [I] 'met Brother Dibble making his escape from the county.'"[21]

Saints Disarmed and Driven from Jackson County

Lieutenant-Governor Lilburn Boggs finally interceded, instructing Colonel Thomas Pitcher to disarm both sides. The colonel took the weapons from the Saints, conveying to them the "feeling that they might be able to return to their homes in peace."[22] However, he then immediately delivered their guns to the mob. Now defenseless, the attacks against the Saints intensified, and their homes were burned or otherwise destroyed. In late 1833, Church leaders instructed their people to flee from Jackson County. In November, about twelve hundred men, women, and children crossed the Missouri River north into Clay County and found temporary refuge there, doing what they could to survive a harsh winter.

Newel Knight wrote the following in his journal, *Scraps of Biography*:

In one of the settlements were four families of very old men, infirm and very poor. They seemed to think that they would not be molested and so remained behind, but no sooner did the mob learn of it, than they went to their houses, broke the windows and doors, hurled great stones into their rooms endangering their lives; thus were these poor old men, and their families, driven before the ruthless mob in mid-winter. These men had served in the Revolutionary War, and Brother Jones (one of the four) had been one of General Washington's bodyguards, but this availed them nothing, for they were of the hated people.[23]

The March of Zion's Camp

In February 1834, the Lord revealed to Joseph Smith that he should organize a group of men to march from Kirtland to Missouri to help the Saints regain their property. This expedition, known as "Zion's Camp," consisted of 207 men. The assembled group marched the thousand miles to Missouri in forty-five days.[24] As the camp reached eastern Clay County, a mob of more than three hundred Missourians, intent on their destruction, came out to meet them. The mob began to attack the camp with cannon fire, but the Lord was fighting the battle for the Saints. Clouds quickly began to form overhead, followed by rain, hail, wind, and thunder, and a storm of tremendous strength raged. The plan to "kill Joe Smith and his army" was thwarted.[25]

When it became apparent that Governor Dunklin, who had finally pledged assistance, was not going to keep his promise; and with mobs harassing them, Joseph prayed for instructions from the Lord. The Lord revealed that conditions were not then right for the redemption of Zion. To build Zion, a Zion people was required, and the Saints had much to do to prepare their personal lives. "My people must needs be chastened until they learn obedience, if it must needs be, by the things which they suffer" was the answer from the Lord (Doctrine and Covenants 105:6).

Joseph disbanded Zion's Camp and instructed its members to return home and he also returned to Kirtland. The Missouri Saints settled in Clay County, doing what was necessary to survive a hostile winter by the river and hoping it would be temporary so they could return to Jackson County. Unfortunately, this did not happen, and after two years, in 1836, they were forced to leave Clay County as well.[26]

Apostasy and Persecution in Kirtland

The situation of the Saints in Kirtland, Ohio, during this time was not much better. Many problems were caused by apostasy and persecution. In late 1837, merchants stopped selling grain and other goods to Latter-day Saints, and businessmen would not employ a Latter-day Saint. Many banks across the country failed as the nation suffered a serious recession. In this difficult economic environment, a bank established by Church members collapsed, and some members blamed Joseph Smith for its failure. Organized persecution and violent mob action came from local residents and from bitter former members who had been excommunicated or had apostatized from the Church. The violence escalated to the point that it became unsafe for Church leaders and members to remain in Kirtland. This was especially true for the Prophet, who departed in January of 1838 for Far West, Missouri.[27] The majority of the Saints were forced to abandon Kirtland later that year.

The printing office was set on fire, burning many copies of the Book of Mormon, and an attempt was made to burn the temple.[28] Fires were started in basements, and windows were broken as the Saints' homes were ransacked by mobs and possessions stolen. The Saints were accused of crimes and thefts they had not committed and were hauled into court and convicted. Many simply abandoned their homes and property and fled.

The Prophet's parents and family were among these pitiful refugees. His mother, Lucy Mack Smith, wrote: "Sometimes we lay in our tents, through driving storms; at other times we were traveling on foot through marshes and quagmires. Once in particular, we lay all night exposed to the rain, which fell in torrents. . . . My clothing was perfectly saturated. I wore my clothes in this situation for three days; in consequence of which I took a severe cold, so that when we arrived at the Mississippi River, I was unable to sit up for any length and could not walk without assistance."[29]

Missouri Persecutions Continue

The Saints had a friend in the Missouri state legislature, Alexander W. Doniphan, who helped them establish their own community of Far West in Caldwell County, about sixty miles north of Clay County. Far West was the county seat, with other settlements scattered in outlying areas of Caldwell and Daviess Counties. When the Church members arrived, these lands were wild and uncultivated. Large farms were soon established, improved, and stocked, increasing their value, and soon these were the two wealthiest counties in the state.[30]

It appeared the Saints would finally have peace, but it was not to be. Latter-day Saints continued to arrive, their numbers totaling fifteen thousand by 1838. The continued influx of immigrants alarmed the old settlers. Persecution began again—this time at the polls. A mob formed preventing the Saints from casting their ballots. A bitter fight ensued. Ministers, who were often leaders of the mobs, renewed their charges against the Saints for "healings, signs, visions, etc."[31]

The old settlers knew little about their new neighbors except what they learned from the press and over the pulpit. No official investigation was ever held. The bitterness of some Protestant ministers did much to arouse the prejudices of the majority, and the slaveholders were naturally alarmed.[32] Mobs besieged the outlying communities. De Witt was under siege for nearly three weeks. The people were starving, and some had already died when the Prophet risked his life to slip past the guards into town at night. Since a petition to the governor had gone unheeded, Joseph counseled the Saints to surrender. On October 11, 1838, a sad procession of half-starved men, women, and children filed out of De Witt on their long journey to Far West, leaving most of their earthly possessions behind.[33]

"The fate of De Witt became the fate of all the outlying settlements. From every direction during the following month, refugees filed into the city of Far West. Their lands and homes were occupied by the mobbers or burned to the ground. Crops went unharvested and cattle and hogs were wantonly killed to feed their pursuers."[34] "Many who were sick, worn out, starved, [or] deprived of medical aid, died upon the road."[35]

Immediately after driving the Saints out of De Witt, the mob joined forces with their cronies in Daviess County. Sashiel Woods, a Presbyterian clergyman, called the mob together and told them that if they could drive the Latter-day Saints out, they could get all their land as well as all their money. He told them they had nothing to fear, as he had proof the authorities would not assist the Latter-day Saints.

Joseph Smith agonized over their situation:

Our provisions were entirely exhausted, and we were worn out by continually standing on guard, and watching the movements of our enemies, who, during the time I was there, fired at us a great many times. Some of the brethren perished from starvation. . . . I had the pain of beholding some of my fellow creatures fall victims to the spirit of persecution. . . . They were men, too, who were virtuous and against whom no legal process could for one moment be sustained, but who, in consequence of their love of God, attachment to His cause, and their determination to the faith were thus brought to an untimely grave.[36]

The mobs proceeded to burn houses with only women and children in them, causing them to flee for safety. Women were compelled to carry small children for several miles through snow and then wade across the Grande River. Some of the mob emptied their own homes, which were nothing but log cabins, set fire to them, and then reported to the state authorities that the Latter-day Saints were burning and destroying all before them. Joseph grieved over the predicament of his people. "My feelings were such as I cannot describe when I saw them flock into the village, almost entirely destitute of clothes, and only escaping with their lives."[37]

Lilburn W. Boggs, now the governor, brought in the state militia to keep the peace. However, the situation worsened when the militia kidnapped three Latter-day Saint men, triggering a rescue attempt by their fellow Saints. A fierce battle ensued at Crooked River in which Apostle David W. Patten and two other Church members were killed,[38] along with one militiaman. Several others were wounded on both sides. Rumors and false information about the Latter-day Saints spread rapidly. They were called "abolitionists," to stir up the slaveholders, even though "the Saints had unequivocally declared that they had no intention of interfering with slavery." But they were mostly from the East and none of them owned slaves. As a result, some Missourians seemed incapable of believing the Latter-day Saints' stated intentions.[39] (The Book of Mormon teaches against slavery (Alma: 27:9).)

The Extermination Order

A false and particularly harmful rumor misinformed the governor that the Latter-day Saints had massacred Captain Bogart and all of his company. Governor Boggs issued his infamous "Extermination Order," which was facilitated by these false reports. This executive order, dated October 27, 1838, reads in part: "The Mormons must be treated as enemies, and must be exterminated or driven from the State if necessary, for the public peace—their outrages are beyond all description." A militia officer was appointed to carry out the order.[40]

With a decree from the governor, it was now open season on the Saints. More mobs were formed, and terror intensified. Outlying settlements were the first victims. Three days after the extermination order, a small community of Saints at Haun's Mill in Caldwell County were hit with a surprise attack by some 150 to 200 so-called militia men. "The assailants, in an act of treachery, called for those men who wished to save themselves to run into the blacksmith shop. They then fired into it [through the cracks] until they thought all inside were dead. Others were shot as they tried to make their escape. In all, 17 men and boys were killed and 15 wounded."[41] The houses were looted and women raped.[42] The leaders of the mob boasted they had fired some sixteen hundred shots at a community of barely more than thirty men.[43]

Ten-year-old Sardius Smith was found in the blacksmith shop by a mobber, alive and trembling with fear. The boy was then shot in the head. His murderer bragged afterward, "Nits will make lice, and if he had lived he would have become a Mormon."[44]

After the massacre, Amanda Smith found Sardius and her husband dead in the blacksmith shop. She was overjoyed to find another son, little Alma, age seven, still alive but severely wounded. His hip had been blown away. She pleaded with the Lord for help, whereupon a voice instructed her what to do, and Alma made a full recovery.

Adding to the tragedy at Haun's Mill was the fact that Joseph Smith had advised Jacob Haun, the owner of the mill, to "move in [from your small settlement], by all means if you wish to save your lives." Haun replied that if the settlers left their homes, all of their property would be lost, and the Gentiles would burn their houses and other buildings. Joseph replied, "You had better lose your property than your lives, but there is no danger of losing either if you will do as you are commanded." Haun did not follow the Prophet's warning, and a catastrophe was the result. [45] Worse, he did not tell the settlers at Haun's Mill what Joseph had counseled, or there probably would have been a different outcome.

Church Leaders Imprisoned

With false promises from the militia, Joseph, his brother Hyrum, and other Church leaders were taken prisoners. The following morning, General Lucas dismissed the greater portion of the still-armed militia, who immediately transformed themselves into looting mobs. They ransacked Far West where they destroyed property, beat defenseless men, and raped women.[46] Some of the women were strapped to benches and repeatedly raped, some dying from the effects of this brutality.[47]

After much petitioning of their captors, Joseph and the other leaders were allowed to say goodbye to their families. Joseph wrote the following:

I found my wife and children in tears, who feared we had been shot . . . and that they would see me no more. . . . Who can realize the feelings which I experienced at that time. . . . My partner wept, my children clung to me, until they were thrust from me by the swords of the guards. I felt overwhelmed while I witnessed the scene, and could only recommend them to the care of that God whose kindness had followed me to the present time, and who alone could protect them, and deliver me from the hands of my enemies, and restore me to my family.[48]

A messenger informed Joseph's parents that if they wanted to see their sons alive, they needed to go immediately to the wagon that would leave within minutes for Independence. Joseph Sr. was distraught and so weak that he could not get off his bed. Lucy Smith and one sister were able to make their way through the crowd to the wagon. Joseph and Hyrum were unable to see them, as the wagon was covered with a strong cloth and nailed down so tightly the men could hardly get their hands through. The women were only allowed to shake Hyrum's hand, but Lucy begged Joseph to speak to her, saying, "I cannot bear to go till I hear your voice." "God bless you, mother!" he sobbed out. A cry was raised, and the wagon dashed off.[49]

General John B. Clark, major-general in the militia, addressed the Saints by telling them they must leave the state "and whatever may be your feeling concerning this, or whatever your innocence, it is nothing to me. . . . As for your leaders, do not once think—do not imagine for a moment—do not let it enter your mind that they will be delivered, or that you will see their faces again, for their fate is fixed—their die is cast and their doom is sealed."[50]

General Moses Wilson and his brigade accompanied the prisoners. At their first night's camp, he let them know he was aware from the beginning that the Saints were not the aggressors:

You Mormons were crowded to the last extreme, and compelled to self-defense; and this has been construed into treason, murder and plunder. . . .When we drove you from Jackson County, we burned two hundred and three of your houses; plundered your goods, destroyed your press, type, paper books, office and all. . . . We shot down some of your men, and, if any of you returned the fire, we imprisoned you [and put you] on . . . trial for murder. . . . Let a set of men serve me as your community have been served, and I'll be damn'd if I would not fight till I died.

General Wilson told the men of a plan to protect them from such people as General Clark and his troops "who are so stuffed with lies and prejudice that they would shoot you down in a moment." He added, "We just intend to exhibit you in Independence, let the people look at you, and see what a damn'd set of fine fellows you are." The general seemed proud of his prisoners and of the honor of returning with them to Independence where they would be jailed.[51]

Attorney M. Arthur, not a Church member, wrote to the representatives in the legislature from Clay County, Missouri, regarding the treatment of the Saints by the mobs. "Those demons are now constantly strolling up and down Caldwell county, . . . armed, insulting the women . . . driving off their horses, cattle, hogs, etc., and rifling their homes and farms of everything therein taking beds, bedding, wardrobe, all such things as they see they want, leaving the poor Latter-day Saints in a starving and naked condition."[52] "They went to my house," wrote Joseph, "drove my family out of doors, carried away most of my property."[53]

Emma Smith's Suffering

Emma wrote to Joseph, who still languished in Liberty Jail, describing her dire situation and expressing her loyalty to him:

Emma Smith's winter flight from Missouri with her children

I shall not attempt to write my feelings altogether, for the situation in which you are in, the walls, bars, and bolts . . . and spreading prairies that separate us, and the cruel injustice that first cast you into prison and still holds you there. . . . Was it not for conscious innocence and the direct interposition of divine mercy, I am very sure I never should have been able to have endured the scenes of suffering that I have passed through . . . but I still live and am yet willing to suffer more if it is the will of kind heaven, that I should for your sake. . . . You may be astonished at my bad writing and incoherent manner, but you will pardon all when you reflect how hard it would be for you to write when your hands were stiffened with hard work and your heart convulsed with intense anxiety . . . but I hope there is better days to come to us yet. . . . I am ever yours affectionately. Emma Smith.[54]

Emma was forced to walk 150 miles across Missouri and then cross the frozen Mississippi with her four small children into Quincy, Illinois. She carried two cotton bags full of Joseph's most sacred papers that were hidden under her full skirts.[55] The exposure Joseph's father suffered as he was driven from Missouri in February 1839 brought on consumption, from which he died a little over a year later.[56]

People of Quincy Provide Relief to the Refugees

Hearings were held in Quincy, Illinois, and the citizens voted to extend help and kindness to the homeless Saints.[57] Thus, the people of Quincy aided the refugees in the form of food, housing, and temporary employment. Quincy further adopted a resolution denouncing the Missouri mobs and government officials.[58]

On June 28, 2002, the Tabernacle Choir gave a benefit concert in Quincy to thank the citizens for their kindness extended to more than five thousand suffering Saints when they were fleeing from their Missouri persecutors 163 years earlier. The concert raised $75,000, which was given to the Quincy Area Community Foundation. Plans were made by the Quincy Convention and Visitors Bureau to place a monument at the riverfront where refugees crossed, memorializing the city's role in sheltering persecuted Latter-day Saints in that winter of 1839.[59] A recently established history museum in Quincy features a Latter-day Saint History Room dedicated to telling the story of the fifteen hundred Quincy residents who took in five thousand Latter-day Saints.

Why the Saints Were Driven Out in the Winter

Important documents uncovered during research on The Joseph Smith Papers Project shed new light on the Missouri conflict, especially in Daviess County, and explain why the settlers were not allowed to wait until spring to leave. Not entirely religiously motivated, the mobbers had a baser motive:

greed. Land laws enacted in 1830 were the legal basis for preemption, a process in which individuals could secure the right to purchase public land they had homesteaded and improved. This preemption right gave the Saints time to farm and earn money before having to pay for the land.

November 12, 1838 was announced as the sale date for Daviess County lands, and the notice was published on October 21. Governor Boggs' Extermination Order was issued only six days later. On November 1, the Saints at Far West were forced to surrender to Missouri troops, and John B. Clark commenced the process of systematically arresting key Church leaders. By early November, they had arrested more than fifty Church members who were leaders of the Church and among the most prominent landowners of Daviess County. Judicial hearings were held beginning on November 12, the day the preemption land sales started, and lasted for two weeks. During this time, the most active enemies of the Church purchased nearly eighteen thousand acres of Daviess County land—not just any land but the most valuable improved properties of the Saints.[60] And thus a scheme to steal from the Saints what was lawfully theirs succeeded.

The Saints' "condition was truly pitiable. Thousands lined the shores of the Mississippi on both the Iowa and Illinois sides, living in tents or dugouts, sleeping on the ground and subsisting chiefly on corn. Sickness and disease due to exposure took a heavy toll. Practically all that the people possessed had been left behind. Property, with an estimated value of two million dollars, fell into the hands of their enemies."[61]

In 1900, B. H. Roberts wrote a history of the Missouri persecutions. One purpose of his history was to correct false statements by some critics, as well as Missouri historians, that the Saints were driven from their homes because of some overt acts against the state or national government or because the Church leaders "were determined to be a law unto themselves," disregarding the rights of others. After proving this was not the case, Roberts sets the record straight regarding the state of Missouri and the pitiful expulsion of the Saints:

> I impeach the State of Missouri before the Bar of the Nineteenth Century Civilization; and affirm that in the five years between 1833 and 1838, she permitted and became a party to acts of robbery, violence and blood which are a disgrace to the age and its boasted spirit of progress and toleration. . . . There were committed within her borders and against an unoffending, and law-abiding people, acts of shameful robbery, arson, mob-violence, willful, wanton slaughter of men, women and children; worst of all, rape upon virtuous wives and maidens, and, at the last illegal banishment of some twelve thousand people from the State . . . for which no offender was ever brought to punishment by the state.

Roberts noted that the state gave liberally to defray the expenses of those who committed the crimes but turned a deaf ear to those who were wronged. He expressed his belief that those who applauded such crimes would be held guilty before God, alongside those who shed the blood of the Saints.[62]

Nauvoo "The Beautiful" Settled

The Prophet spent five months in Liberty Jail, a miserably cold dungeon. After he and his companions escaped (arranged with the help of their guards), he made his way to western Illinois, where he was able to purchase some unwanted, swampy, mosquito-infested land on the banks of a bend in the Mississippi River. The location was the site of a small village known as Commerce, consisting of only six dwellings. The Saints drained the land and began gathering in numbers, building homes and buying farms and property. The swamp was transformed into a city. Underbrush became gardens, miserable shelters became splendid houses, penniless people became the most prosperous citizens of the state, and they again began building a temple. Their city, which Joseph named "Nauvoo, the City Beautiful," grew to become one of the largest in Illinois, with a population greater than Chicago's at the time. The Prophet's first home in Nauvoo was a small log house he built on the bank of the river.[63]

Reparations Denied

Church leaders believed they were due restitution from the state of Missouri after the Saints were forced out of Far West, but the Missouri legislature rejected their petitions for an investigation. The Saints then appealed to the United States government. In November 1839, Joseph and Judge Elias Higbee made the trip to Washington and obtained an interview with President Martin Van Buren. Their goal was to get federal intervention in Missouri, but they received little encouragement from the president. They returned in February 1840 for another interview. Van Buren listened reluctantly to their message and simply replied, "Gentlemen, your cause is just, but I can do nothing for you. . . . If I take up for you I shall lose the vote of Missouri." With their petition rejected, the pair returned to Nauvoo with a dim view of Van Buren, shared by many other U.S. citizens. The Prophet expressed his opinion: "May he never be elected again to any office of trust or power, by which he may abuse the innocent and let the guilty go free." Van Buren lost the next election. The Saints acknowledged their final appeal would be to "the Court of Heaven."[64]

Lies and rumors about the Church continued to circulate—even in distant parts of the world. One Englishman who had heard a great deal of the Latter-day Saints decided to investigate the scandalous tales, traveling the long distance from Great Britain to Illinois. After finding lodging in St. Louis, he asked, "What think you of the [Latter-day Saints]?" From all sides the man was bombarded with such accusations as "thieving cheats, blasphemers, devilish men; they deserve to be burned; adultery was not only tolerated, but approved; they plundered everyone they could; and blood and murder was to be found in their skirts"—and other despicable things. The tale grew in horror as the man was told that "traveling strangers would be stripped, thrown into a dungeon underneath the temple, fed only bread and water then left to die like a dog."

With more than a little trepidation, the investigator approached Nauvoo. He describes what he found in these words: "On the highest land in these parts stands the temple, the wonder of the world . . . shops, palaces, and almost all sorts of houses . . . inhabitants busy building manufactories . . . large and beautiful farms . . . abundant crops . . . and all in less than four years; I do not know what other people could accomplish such a feat!"

The man was able to make the acquaintance of the Prophet Joseph, whom he found to be "a cheerful, entertaining, and sociable companion, and he understands something about almost everything in this world. . . . I saw the prophet and his brother Hyrum, standing side by side one day; and I could not but admit that these were two of the handsomest, wisest, and godliest men of the age, and great men of the nineteenth century. . . . I saw only peace, unity, and love, reigning in this young, but happy city."

Regarding the Saints' persecutions in Missouri, he said, "I have not yet found any basis for believing that the [Latter-day Saints] deserved any of it. On the other hand, it is my firm belief that the Missourians did martyr many innocent men, rape and kill defenseless women and destitute children, needlessly and in cold blood! They did all this out of enmity and religious jealousy alone, although under other pretexts, of course."[65]

The Church Expelled from Illinois

The Prophet did not live to see the Saints suffer the many additional trials he had prophesied concerning them; he was murdered, along with his brother Hyrum, on June 27, 1844 (see Chapter 29). Early in September of 1845, mobs commenced burning the homes of the Saints in the outlying settlements of Nauvoo. Joseph had seen the Salt Lake Valley in vision and prophesied in August of 1842 that the Saints would continue to suffer much affliction and would be driven to the Rocky Mountains, where they would make settlements, build cities, and become a mighty people.[66]

Brigham Young was shown the Salt Lake Valley in a vision. He and the others of the Twelve Apostles decided the Church would move west. They advised the Saints to keep things as quiet as possible and to make plans to leave in the spring. But their enemies had other plans, and persecution intensified. Under trying circumstances, the Saints worked day and night to finish and dedicate the temple before leaving.[67] The people built wagons, gathered supplies, and purchased horses and oxen, preparing to leave two months earlier than planned.

Bathsheba Smith, wife of George A. Smith, Joseph's cousin, could not leave her beloved Nauvoo home without a few last-minute tasks. In her journal, she recorded,

My last act in that precious spot was to tidy the rooms, sweep up the floor and set the broom in its accustomed place behind the door. Then with emotions in my heart . . . I gently closed the door and faced an unknown future, faced it with faith in God and with no less assurance of the ultimate establishment of the Gospel in the West and of its true, enduring principles.[68]

An arson fire destroyed the temple's interior in October 1848, and a tornado in May 1850 knocked down one wall and weakened others. The rest of the temple walls were eventually taken down. A century and a half later, the Nauvoo Temple was rebuilt by the Church and dedicated in 2002. The new temple matches the original temple design in exacting detail. The original Nauvoo temple plans were found and followed to the extent possible. Hundreds of thousands of the descendants of those who had lived in Nauvoo, and many others, returned for its open house and dedication.[69]

Nauvoo Illinois Temple

By February 1846, the advance group of about 3,000 were driven out of Nauvoo in weather so cold the Mississippi River froze over. Temperatures as cold as forty-one degrees below zero made it possible for many to drive their wagons across the Mississippi, which greatly facilitated their exodus. These exiled Saints were unlawfully driven from their comfortable homes and farms. Babies were born along the way, and many of all ages died as a result of disease, freezing temperatures, and food shortages. Accounts of their suffering have filled many volumes.[70]

One account comes from Orson Spencer, a graduate from an eastern college who studied for the ministry and became a popular preacher in the Baptist Church. After meeting with a Latter-day Saint elder, he embraced the teachings of the Church. "He and his highly educated wife counted the cost, laid their hearts on the alter and made the sacrifice. How few realize what it involved to become a [Latter-day Saint] in those early days! Home, friends, occupation, popularity, all that makes life pleasant, were gone." His wife was in poor health, prompting Spencer to write to her parents to ask them to take her in until the Saints could find a place to stay. Their answer: "Let her renounce her degrading faith and she can come back, but never until she does." She had her husband read Ruth 1:16–17, "Entreat me not to leave thee. . . . Thy people shall be my people and thy God my God." Her body was buried by the wayside.[71]

The Cost of Discipleship

Colonel Thomas L. Kane, a friend to the Latter-day Saints, was traveling in the vicinity of Nauvoo shortly after the Saints had been driven from its boundaries. He saw

> several hundred . . . bowed and cramped by cold and sunburn. . . . They were, almost all of them, the crippled victims of disease. . . . They could not satisfy the feeble cravings of their sick. They had not bread to quiet the fractious hunger cries of their children. Mothers and babes, daughters and grandparents, all of them alike, were bivouacked in tatters, wanting even covering to comfort those whom the sick shiver of fever was searching to the marrow.[72]

Lucy Mack Smith vowed that she would stand before God to testify against the Saints' persecutors:

> When the small and the great shall appear to answer at His bar for the deeds done in the body . . . the just and the unjust . . . and declare with a voice that shall penetrate the ears of every intelligence . . . in the presence of all these will I declare concerning our persecutors that for eighteen years they hunted us like wild beasts who were thirsting for the blood of their prey; that without any just cause they drove me and my family from our home in New York, Ohio, Missouri [and] Illinois. . . . We appealed to lawyers, judges, governors, and presidents, but they heeded not our cry, their pledges were broken, the laws trampled upon, and the statutes and ordinances of the land were tarnished to gratify murderers, thieves, and robbers. This shall be my testimony in the day of God Almighty, and if it be true, what will Lilburn W. Boggs, Thomas Carlin, Martin Van Buren, and Governor Ford answer me when I shall appear where the prayers of the Saints and the complaints of the widow and orphan come up before a just and righteous judge?[73]

Emma Remains in Nauvoo

The persecution against the Church took its toll on Joseph's immediate and extended family. The Saints' exodus from Nauvoo took place a year and a half after the Prophet's death, when Emma was a forty-one-year-old widow with five children ranging in age from fifteen months to fourteen years (her last was born four months after Joseph's martyrdom). She also cared for her aged mother-in-law, Lucy Mack Smith. Emma did not go west with the Saints. She had little means to provide for her family, she had suffered considerably for many years, and perhaps she did not want to make the trek without Joseph. She said, "I had a home here, I didn't know what lay out there."

Emma remarried three years later and lived to the age of seventy-five. "In her later years she would climb the stairs to her room each evening," writes her great-great-granddaughter Gracia Jones, "sit in her low rocker, and gaze out the window at the western sunset. No one dared approach her because they did not know how to touch the depth of sorrow evidenced by the tears that coursed down her checks." She maintained a lifelong commitment to Joseph as a prophet and to the authenticity of the Book of Mormon, facts that are well documented.[74] Shortly before her death, she declared that she saw the Savior. Her last words were, "Joseph? Yes, yes, I'm coming."[75]

Hyrum's widow, Mary Fielding Smith, went west with the Saints. She had married the widowed Hyrum and become the stepmother to his six children. Together, they had two more children, Joseph F. Smith, who became the sixth president of the Church, and a daughter, Martha. Mary died in Salt Lake City just four years after her arrival in the valley.

Most of the Saints left Nauvoo in the winter of 1846, but about six hundred of the poor and sick remained. The mob again united, led by James W. Singleton and Thomas S. Brockman during an attack on the city of Nauvoo in September of 1846. They drove out the remaining Saints, killing several of them in what became known as the "Battle of Nauvoo." Emma Smith escaped with her family and friends by going north to Fulton City, Iowa. She was able to return soon after the attack.[76]

What the Press Reported

The New York Sun wrote a lengthy editorial condemning the treatment of the Nauvoo Saints. It mentioned books published against them, the murders of Joseph and Hyrum ("the atrocious act shocking the country"), the mobs driving them from their homes with no protection from the state, and the number of persecutors so great that the Saints' only choice was to leave. "Thus 12,000 or 15,000 persons, from a state of comfort and prosperity, were driven from their homes to lie down on the banks of sickly rivers, or to deal as well as they could . . . on the vast prairies of the west."[77]

The article quoted Captain Allen of the U.S. Dragoons, who had five hundred of the Saints in his army and who testified that they "were not only spirited and brave, good and faithful people, but he describes them as wonderfully pure and unexceptionable in their moral conduct, frugal, careful, industrious, and self-denying, and manifesting heroic patience in suffering, worthy of the noblest Christian character." A writer for the *U.S. Gazette* who had traveled and lived among the Saints wrote "that chastity, virtue, and love, together with a spirit of unity, and effort for family happiness, form absolute characteristics of this outcast people, as well as their temperance, orderliness, industry, courage, and steadfast determination in the objects of their desire."

The New York Sun article continued:

There is no parallel to it in the history of our country. . . . A reckless body of people violated all the [Latter-day Saint] property, took possession of their farms, and desecrated their temple; the poor, the sick, and the aged, like the innocent children, were driven half-famished into the woods, and all their safeguards, and their livelihood, were outraged and cut off." The writer insisted that the state of Illinois was bound in honor to restore the victims to their homes, property and rights and that the "governor should issue a proclamation inviting the [Latter-day Saints] to return to their homes, and guarantee them protection against every attack on them."[78]

Those reparations were never made.

The Great Exodus to the Salt Lake Valley

Brigham Young led thousands of poverty-stricken Saints from Nauvoo in the greatest mass exodus in the history of the United States. Approximately seventy thousand Latter-day Saint pioneers, either by wagon train, handcart, or on foot, crossed the plains to the Rocky Mountains in the years that followed—until the coming of the railroad to Utah in 1869.[79] The earliest Saints arrived in the Salt Lake Valley in 1847. Between forty-two hundred and five thousand members of the Church lost their lives in the modern exodus from 1846, when they were driven from Nauvoo, until 1869, when the transcontinental railroad was completed in Utah.[80]

Misconceptions and false rumors about the Church still flourished, even after the Saints were driven west. Leading public officials were eager to extend the railroad to Utah, confident it would bring about the collapse of the Church. Such officials erroneously believed "that Brigham Young was an evil dictator who held his people in captive subjection . . . and [that] the railroad would allow the oppressed Saints a convenient means of fleeing to the freedom of the East." Little did they know that the Saints were enthusiastically working on the railroad to hasten its completion. A trip across the plains in a covered wagon, handcart, or on foot, took three months or more, whereas a train trip would require only three days. The train was both much quicker and less expensive. And instead of fleeing, Saints continued to gather to make the "desert blossom as a rose," as prophesied in Isaiah 35.[81]

Church History Ignored

"Nationally, history books show no concern about the tragedy of the Nauvoo Saints, unlike the other wronged groups in America's past [such as the well-known 'Trail of Tears' when fifteen thousand Indians were forced from their homes in 1830]. But the fact remains that never in the entirety of American history has mob or vigilante action forced a major city's almost entire population to vacate, become homeless, and leave behind a substantial city of streets, houses, gardens, fences, public halls, and commercial buildings built entirely by their own hands."[82]

Even the present city of Nauvoo purposely ignores the city's history. "Other than some elementary field trips, and occasional current events discussions in the upper grades, the [Nauvoo] community's past does not figure heavily in [the] social studies curriculum of the [present-day] Nauvoo." A school board member maintains that to teach the history of Nauvoo would open the door to religion in the schools.[83] With a magnificent House of God back on Nauvoo's Temple Hill, Latter-day Saints are nevertheless returning to the City of Joseph. Nauvoo's best days may still lie ahead.

The Church Moves On

There will, no doubt, always be detractors, critics, and persecutors. The late Latter-day Saint leader and writer Bruce R. McConkie, put these early events in perspective:

The Church is like a great caravan—organized, prepared, following an appointed course, with its captains of tens and captains of hundreds all in place. What does it matter if a few barking dogs snap at the heels of the weary travelers? Or that predators claim those few who fall by the way? The caravan moves on. Is there a ravine to cross, a miry mud hole to pull through, a steep grade to climb? Ahead is the celestial city, the eternal Zion of our God, where all who maintain their position in the caravan shall find food and drink and rest. Thank God that the caravan moves on.[84]

It was only their strong faith and belief that the Lord's true Church had been restored to the earth, that Joseph Smith was God's Prophet of the Restoration, and that the Book of Mormon is true sacred scripture, which enabled the early Saints to suffer the trials they were called to endure. Why did the Lord not intervene in their behalf more often? The answer, no doubt, is that to preserve moral agency, God at times permits the righteous to suffer the consequences of evil acts perpetrated by others. But justice will ultimately prevail. The promised eternal reward at the end will be well worth the difficult journey.

"Hatred and persecution have been the lot of every man that ever lived upon the earth holding the oracles of the Kingdom of Heaven to deliver to the children of men," proclaimed Brigham Young. "Wicked men, Satan, and all the powers of hell and hate are at war with every holy principle that God wished to place in the possession of his children. That is the true reason of the hatred and persecution meted out to us. . . . Now if we would only fall in with the wicked all would be right, and then no person would wish to persecute us."[85] Jesus teaches, "If ye were of the world, the world would love his own; but because ye are not of the world, but I have chosen you out of the world, therefore the world hateth you" (John 15:19). Such is the price of discipleship.

Chapter 29

You Must Die a Martyr to Seal Your Testimony of the Book with Your Own Blood

You must gain no wealth from the publication of your book, but many times lose all that you have. Like many of those who believe your cause, you will submit to vile persecution. And finally, you will voluntarily surrender to your enemies and die a martyr to seal the testimony of your book and mission with your own blood.

"Blessed are ye, when men shall revile you, and persecute you, and shall say all manner of evil against you falsely, for my sake. Rejoice, and be exceeding glad: for great is your reward in heaven: for so persecuted they the prophets which were before you" (Matthew 5:11–12). "If the world hate you, ye know that it hated me before it hated you" (John 15:18). Joseph Smith was both hated and greatly loved.

Latter-day Saint leader Hugh B. Brown states that he could not "understand why Christians who claim to believe in Christ would persecute and put to death a man whose whole purpose was to prove the truth of the things they themselves were teaching, namely, that Jesus is the Christ. I could understand, their persecuting Joseph if he had said, 'I am Christ,' or if he had said, 'There is no Christ,' or if he had said someone else is Christ; then Christians believing in Christ would be justified in opposing him. But what he said was, 'Him whom ye claim to believe in, declare I unto you.' Paraphrasing what Paul said at Athens, 'Whom therefore ye ignorantly worship, him declare I unto you' (Acts 17:23). Joseph Smith in essence said to the Christians of his day, 'You claim to believe in Jesus Christ. I testify that I saw him and I talked with him. He is the Son of God, the Redeemer of the world. Why persecute me for that?'"[1]

Fabricated Charges against the Prophet

"It seems as though the adversary was aware, at a very early period of my life," wrote Joseph, "that I was destined to prove a disturber and an annoyer of his kingdom; else why should the powers of darkness continue against me? Why the opposition and persecution that arose against me, almost in my infancy?"[2]

Threats on the life of Joseph began at the age of fourteen, even before his encounter with heavenly beings. "Being a remarkably quiet, well-disposed child, we did not suspect that anyone had aught against him," wrote his mother, but as he was returning home one evening a rifle was fired across his pathway with the evident intent of killing him. "We never found out the man, nor ever suspected the cause of the act."[3] Clearly, the adversary knew of the great mission in store for the young prophet and had already begun a crusade against him in his youth.

After the Father and Son appeared and communicated with Joseph, others learned of his experience: "I soon found . . . that my telling the story had excited a great deal of prejudice against me among professors of religion, and was the cause of great persecution, which continued to increase; and though I was an obscure boy, only between fourteen and fifteen years of age, and my circumstances in life such as to make a boy of no consequence in the world, yet men of high standing would take notice sufficient to excite the public mind against me, and create a bitter persecution; and this was common among all the sects—all united to persecute me" (Joseph Smith—History 1:22).

Many false charges and arrests were to follow. In 1826, Joseph, now twenty-one, "was tried and acquitted on a fanciful charge of being a 'disorderly person,' and a vagrant in South Bainbridge, New York. New York State Law defined a disorderly person as, among other things, a vagrant or a seeker of 'lost goods.' The first charge was made simply to cause trouble. . . . They were apparently concerned that Joseph might bilk his employer, Josiah Stowell, out of some money. Mr. Stowell's testimony clearly said this was not so and that he trusted Joseph."[4]

This was the first of more than forty times Joseph would be arrested during his life. The charges ranged from treason to murder. Each time he was brought to trial, he was acquitted. One exception to this was a charge brought against him in New York for casting an evil spirit out of Newel Knight. After Joseph was found guilty, the judge observed there was no ordinance against such an act so the Prophet was set free.[5]

Persecution against the Church and its members continued. One particularly bothersome adversary, Grandison Newell, who owned a chair factory in Kirtland, filed as many as thirty civil law suits against the Prophet. The publisher of the *Painesville Telegraph*, E. D. Howe, admitted that the suits were devised to hinder the Church's progress in Ohio.[6] Opposition and persecution followed believers in the Book of Mormon. It was not usually common people who were the leading critics but rather ministers and religious teachers, writes Hugh Nibley: "Blasphemy, alias the Golden Bible!" That in this enlightened age of science and understanding such a fraud should appear! It wasn't on spiritual or religious grounds they protested, they said, but it was an offense to intelligent people. Those were the reasons they gave to their flocks, the religious mobs, that it was a blasphemous work.[7]

Some present-day ministers are also unhappy with The Church of Jesus Christ of Latter-day Saints. "Richard Land, President of the Southern Baptist Convention, has contended that more Baptists leave that faith to join The Church of Jesus Christ of [Latter-day Saints] than any other—by a large factor. . . . That means that many Evangelical pastors will always view the Latter-day Saints with suspicion and hostility, and not just for theological reasons. Their messages to their flocks will reflect that hostility."[8]

Persecutions have been nearly constant. The Church was organized on April 6, 1830, and the first conference was held the next month in Fayette, New York. After the conference, Joseph and others, including Emma, traveled to Colesville, New York, where several converts awaited baptism. A dam was built across a stream for the baptisms planned on the following day, a Saturday. During the night, a mob destroyed the dam. The act was instigated by sectarian priests in the neighborhood who feared losing members to the new church. The dam was repaired, and early Monday morning, thirteen persons were baptized, including Emma Smith, Joseph Knight, and his wife—but not before a mob began to assemble.

To escape the disruptive gang, the group moved to Joseph Knight's home; however, the threats became so violent and alarming it was decided best to move to the house of Newel Knight, Joseph Knight's son. The mob followed, continuing to insult and threaten along the way. A meeting was planned for that evening, but a constable arrived and arrested Joseph Smith on the charge of being a disorderly person and for "setting the country in an uproar by preaching the Book of Mormon."

The constable, having heard rumors about Joseph as a troublemaker, found him to be quite the opposite kind of person. Now determined to protect his prisoner, the officer informed Joseph that a mob was waiting to ambush them. Even though the mob followed the pair, they arrived in South Bainbridge unmolested (see Joseph Smith—History 1:84–89).

Joseph Knight hired two of his neighbors to represent Joseph at this second trial for disorderliness. One of the men, Mr. Reid, described Joseph in a speech he gave in Nauvoo on May 17, 1844: "The first acquaintance I had with Gen. Smith was about the year 1823. He came into my neighborhood, being then about eighteen years of age, and resided there two years; during which time I became intimately acquainted with him. I do know that his character was irreproachable; that he was well known for truth and uprightness; that he moved in the first circles of the community, and he was often spoken of as a young man of intelligence and good morals, and possessing a mind susceptible of the highest intellectual attainments." Reid never joined the Church, but he was always the Prophet's true friend. [9]

The hired neighbors, though not lawyers, were well-versed in the law. The first four witnesses called were examined regarding the "scandalous falsehoods which had been circulated" against Joseph. They bore such favorable testimonies concerning his character that attempts by the prosecutors to substantiate anything against him proved to be futile, and he was acquitted by the court.

Unfortunately, another warrant was served upon him the moment he was cleared, this time for unlawful actions purported to have occurred in Broome County. Joseph, who had not eaten all day, was nevertheless hurried off to Broome County, a distance of fifteen miles, by another constable, who immediately began abusing and insulting him. He was taken to a tavern where the assembled men used every means to ridicule and insult him. They spit upon him, pointed their fingers and taunted him with, "Prophesy, prophesy!" He was eventually given some crusts of bread and water for food.[10]

The trial the following day was much as before—the court could find nothing with which to convict him, even though the prosecution addressed the court with a long and violent harangue against the defendant. Joseph's defense pointed out the attempt to deny their client justice and thanked God "to be engaged in so good a cause as that of defending a man whose character stood so well the test of such a strict investigation." They convinced the court of Joseph's innocence. Joseph later said of his defenders, "They spoke like men inspired of God." Even the constable, who had treated him so badly, apologized and helped him escape the mob, who was determined to seize the Prophet and tar and feather him, if he were acquitted.[11]

After a few days, Joseph, along with Oliver Cowdery, returned to Colesville, arriving at the Knights' home just as another mob began forming. Without so much as stopping to eat, the two left to return home to Fayette, traveling all night with the mob in close pursuit. Only by exerting their utmost effort was the pair able to elude their pursuers. Joseph wrote, "Thus were we persecuted on account of our religious faith—in a country the Constitution of which guarantees to every man the indefeasible right to worship God according to the dictates of his own conscience—and by men, too, who were professors of religion, and who were not backward to maintain the right of religious liberty for themselves, though they could thus wantonly deny it to us."[12]

Birth, Death, Tar and Feathers

Joseph and Emma's first child, a son whom they named Alvin, was born on June 15, 1828, in Harmony, Pennsylvania, but died within a few hours. On April 30, 1831, Emma delivered twins who lived only three hours.[13] John Murdock's wife, Julia, gave birth to twins that same day, but she passed away six hours later. The Murdocks had three other children, so Brother Murdock

Joseph Smith and Sidney Rigdon beaten by a mob

decided to give the twins to Joseph and Emma to raise, wanting them "taught and raised in the faith and principles of salvation." Brother Murdock hoped his act of sacrifice would alleviate some of the pain felt by both families. The twins were named Joseph Murdock Smith and Julia Smith.

The Smiths had been living in Harmony, Pennsylvania, but because of persecution, they moved to the John Johnson farm, thirty miles southeast of Kirtland, Ohio. On March 24, 1832, the twins, less than one year old, were sick with the measles. Emma was especially fatigued from caring for them. Joseph told her to retire and he would care for the sicker child. In the night, Emma suggested he also lie down on the trundle bed, which he did.

Joseph was soon awakened by Emma's screams and instantly found himself being dragged out the door by about a dozen men. He was choked until he passed out, his clothes were torn from him, and one man fell upon him and scratched his body "like a mad cat," swearing at him during the entire ordeal. He was covered with tar and feathers, some of which was forced into his mouth, and the mob attempted to cram a vile of poison into his mouth, chipping a tooth in the process. Sidney Rigdon, likewise tarred and feathered, was knocked unconscious while being dragged by his heels over frozen ground, and was delirious for several days. A tragic consequence of the mob action was the loss of Joseph and Emma's adopted son, Joseph, who caught a severe cold from exposure that night and died four days later.[14]

The leader of this mob was Simonds Ryder, a former member of the Church now an apostate. Joseph's friends spent the night scraping and removing tar and cleaning his body. The next morning was the Sabbath, and despite the events of the previous night, Joseph met and preached to the congregation, which included some members of the mob. In the afternoon, the Prophet baptized three people.[15]

The Failure of the Kirtland Safety Society

During the seven years Joseph and Emma lived in the Kirtland area, they stayed with other families almost half of the time, residing in five different locations. The couple were finally able to build themselves a home, but because of persecution and financial problems, they were prevented from living in it before they were forced to leave Kirtland.[16]

The Saints had finished the temple in Kirtland, at great sacrifice of time and possessions, but dark days lay ahead. Joseph warned the officers of the Kirtland Safety Society, a bank started by Church members, to stop lending money and to collect the unpaid balances due on capital stock. The warning went unheeded, and Joseph withdrew from the Society. In the summer of 1837, hundreds of banks throughout the country failed, including the Kirtland Safety Society, which was forced to close its doors in bankruptcy. Joseph, receiving the brunt of the blame for the bank's failure, was openly confronted in the street and blamed for the Society's financial losses. Many apostatized from the Church, calling Joseph a fallen prophet and he constantly found himself in court on one trumped-up charge after another until it was necessary to leave the city at night, along with Sidney Rigdon, to escape an angry mob. The two waited for their families to join them in Norton Township, Ohio, sixty miles from Kirtland, and continued on to Far West, Missouri, with mobbers in pursuit most of the way. Soon after their arrival, more than sixteen hundred loyal Kirtland Saints joined them in Far West.[17]

Before leaving Kirtland, Joseph appointed Oliver Granger to be his business agent to settle his remaining debts. The Prophet spent considerable effort the rest of his life to repay notes and loans. The fact that he and other founders of the bank repaid the bulk of their debts, even when distanced from Kirtland, testifies of their integrity. Before leaving Kirtland, Joseph told the brethren, "One thing is certain, I shall see you again, let what will happen, for I have a promise of life five years, and they cannot kill me until that time is expired." His martyrdom occurred five and a half years later.[18]

Joseph and Other Church Leaders Taken Prisoner

During the ensuing months, hundreds of converts arrived from various parts of the country and Canada. The Missourians felt threatened by this growing population and made many false charges, while at the same time committing acts of violence against the Saints. The state militia was eventually called out to supposedly keep the peace. At Far West in late October of 1838, Joseph Smith and five other Church leaders, along with several others, were informed by Colonel George M. Hinkle that General Samuel Lucas of the state militia wanted a conference with them. They consented, under the promise that these would be peace talks, but upon reaching the colonel's camp, they found they had been lied to and were immediately taken prisoners.

The prisoners spent the night on the ground in the open air in the midst of a great rainstorm as their guards mocked them with a constant tirade of obscenities and verbal abuse. Parley P. Pratt, who was among the prisoners, writes, "They blasphemed God; mocked Jesus Christ; swore the most dreadful oaths; taunted Brother Joseph and others; demanded miracles . . . then a tumultuous tirade of lewd boastings of having defiled virgins and wives by force, etc., much of which I dare not write."[19]

Joseph wrote: "We petitioned the officers to know why we were thus treated, but they utterly refused to give us any answer, or to converse with us." The next morning, the Prophet confronted General Wilson with these words: "I was not aware of having done anything worthy of such treatment; that I had always been a supporter of the Constitution and of democracy." Wilson replied, "I know it, and that is the reason why I want to kill you, or have you killed."[20] The general knew the mobbers could not win through legal means because Joseph was innocent, so they were determined to take matters into their own hands.

Prisoners Saved by General Doniphan's Courageous Act

During the night, a court-martial was held, consisting of fourteen militia officers, seventeen ministers of different denominations, the circuit judge, and the district attorney—but without the prisoners present. The decision rendered was that the prisoners were to be shot at sunrise in the public square at Far West. This was meant as a warning to the Latter-day Saints. The order was to be carried out by Brigadier General Alexander Doniphan, who refused to comply. He spoke bluntly to General Wilson, "It is cold-blooded murder. I will not obey your order. . . . If you execute these men, I will hold you responsible before an earthly tribunal, so help me God." Fearing the consequences of carrying out the order, General Lucas imprisoned the men in Independence, with plans to take them to Richmond.[21]

A "trial" was held at Richmond for the fifty-six men taken prisoner at Far West "for something they knew not what." Witnesses were called, sworn at the point of bayonet, and told they must testify against the Church if they wished to save themselves. Joseph and his lawyers were asked to supply witnesses for the defense. The forty or fifty men whose names were submitted as potential witnesses for the defense were promptly arrested and put into prison. This happened a second time. The defense was given no opportunity to introduce any of the witnesses, because the men they requested were either imprisoned or run out of the country. One man whose testimony did not please the court was rushed upon with bayonets, and three men with loaded guns pursued him as he fled the court.

Light in the Darkness of Liberty Jail

The mockery of justice continued for several days, with the judge eventually releasing all of the prisoners, "there being no evidence against them." Despite this fact, Joseph, Hyrum, and four others were sent to jail at Liberty, Clay County, to be tried for treason and murder.[23] The charge of treason had to do with the Saints resisting the mob militia, and the charge of murder stemmed from the death of a militiaman during the Battle of Crooked River. Joseph was accused of being an accessory, though he was not present in Missouri at the time of the incident.[24] Despite the lack of evidence against them, the six men were imprisoned, awaiting a trial during the winter and into the spring.[25]

During the coldest months, December through March, Joseph had not even a blanket with which to keep warm. He wrote to Emma, pleading for one, but she replied that William E. McLellin, one of the original Quorum of the Twelve and now a bitter enemy, had stolen all the bedding from their house except one quilt and a blanket, so what could she do?[26]

Another of the trials endured by the brethren during their long months in Liberty Jail was food laced with poison. "The effect it had upon our system," wrote Hyrum, "was that it vomited us almost to death, and then we would lay some two or three days in a torpid, stupid state, not even caring or wishing for life—the poison being administered in too large doses,[causing vomiting] or it would inevitably have proved fatal, had not the power of Jehovah interposed on our behalf to save us from their wicked purpose."[27] As if ingesting poison was not bad enough, for five days the prisoners were served human flesh, which they refused to eat. The guard supposed that his feeding them "Mormon beef" (from murdered Church members) would bring him popularity and notoriety, but he later tried to conceal the deed.

Judge Turnham let Sidney Rigdon leave the jail under cover of darkness but said he dared not let the rest go because the people swore they would kill them if he did.

> He said it was d—-d hard to be confined under such circumstances; for he knew we were innocent men, and he said the people also knew it; and that it was only a persecution and treachery, and the scenes of Jackson County acted over again for fear that we would come too numerous. . . . He said the plan was concocted from the governor down to the lowest judge, and that the Baptist priest, Riley, was riding into town every day to watch the people, stirring up the minds of the people

against us all he could, exciting them and stirring up their religious prejudices against us for fear they would let us go.[28]

As Joseph suffered though the long winter months, the anguish of his soul is measured in his plea to the Lord: "O God, where art thou? . . . How long shall thy hand be stayed, and thine eye, yea thy pure eye, behold from the eternal heavens the wrongs of thy people and of thy servants, and thine ear be penetrated with their cries?" (Doctrine and Covenants 121:1–2).

The Lord answered with these words of comfort: "My son, peace be unto thy soul; thine adversity

Joseph in Liberty Jail

and thine afflictions shall be but a small moment; And then, if thou endure it well, God shall exalt thee on high; thou shalt triumph over all thy foes. Thy friends do stand by thee, and they shall hail thee again with warm hearts and friendly hands" (Doctrine and Covenants 121:7–9).

Joseph was further promised that "The ends of the earth shall inquire after thy name, and fools shall have thee in derision, and hell shall rage against thee." He was counseled that no matter how terrible things might become, with all his perils and travails, "know thou, my son, that all these things shall give thee experience, and shall be for thy good. The Son of man hath descended below them all. Art thou greater then he? . . . Therefore fear not what man can do, for God shall be with you forever and ever" (Doctrine and Covenants 122:1, 7–9).[29]

In a petition to the U.S. Congress for redress for abuses suffered in Missouri, Joseph mentioned their illegal confinement, saying they did not deem it necessary to detail their sufferings while in prison, the horrors of the four long months, in darkness, in want, alone, and during the cold of winter. The Prophet stated it could be better conceived than expressed.[30] Another petition was later sent to the Missouri state legislature, along with a call for a full investigation into their sufferings. The legislature appropriated $2,000 in relief funds for the twelve thousand displaced Saints, whereas $200,000 went to pay their tormentors in the state militia.

Escape Arranged by Missouri Officials

On April 16, 1839, after months of confinement, the prisoners, under the pretense of being transferred to Boone County, Missouri, were allowed to escape, partly to avoid the public embarrassment of bringing them to trial with no evidence to convict them. Samuel Tillery, the jailor at Liberty Jail, told the prisoners that Governor Boggs was heartily ashamed of the whole transaction against the Latter-day Saints and would be glad to set the prisoners free if only "he dared to do it. But, he said, you need not be concerned, for the governor has laid a plan for your release."[31]

With their guards as escorts, the group left Liberty Jail and traveled for some time. They purchased two horses from their guards, who then drank whiskey, told the prisoners they could do as they wished, and went to sleep, except one guard who helped saddle their horses, and allowed them to leave.

A few days later, April 22, 1839, the men were reunited with their families in Quincy, Illinois, where they found them in a state of poverty but in good health. "The Lord had miraculously preserved his Prophet . . . and the Modern-day Israel began to gather once again."[32] Joseph and the Saints then moved to Commerce, Illinois, and founded the city of Nauvoo.

In June 1841, the Prophet was arrested on the false Missouri charges of treason and murder dating from his Liberty Jail imprisonment. The intent was to return him to Missouri for trial; however, the writ for his arrest was dismissed. Joseph said his defense relied in part on the fact "that the indictment in Missouri was obtained by fraud, bribery and duress, all of which I was prepared to prove."[33] In May, he was called into court on charges of perjury and adultery. The prosecution, not being prepared on the perjury charges, delayed the trial until the next term. No more was heard concerning the charge of adultery.[34]

"The Benedict Arnold of Church History"

The Saints in Nauvoo lived in relative peace for three years. Then, as before, dissenters from within and opponents from without combined to create conflict. One man in particular, John C. Bennett, was responsible for much of the persecution that followed. B. H. Roberts has written that Bennett may properly be regarded as the "Benedict Arnold of [Church] history."[35] He had been a physician, a university professor, a military leader, a Methodist minister, and, after joining the Church in Nauvoo, a close associate of Joseph Smith. Bennett was the first mayor of Nauvoo. His intentions, in the beginning, seemed sincere, but "he later fell into transgression and would not repent," becoming a conniving, evil man. Before he was exposed, he had engineered a plot to assassinate the Prophet and take over the Church. It was further learned that he had deserted a wife and family in Ohio.

When Bennett's true character was discovered, he was excommunicated from the Church. He left the city a bitter man and began going from town to town lecturing and printing leaflets against the Church. He published a vile book, *The History of the Saints; or, an Exposée of Joe Smith and Mormonism.* He made false allegations about the practice of polygamy, secret murders, and designs for the overthrow of the United States, with Joseph Smith as emperor and pope of a religious empire.[36] Bennett also alleged that Joseph Smith and Porter Rockwell were responsible for an attempted assassination of former Governor Boggs of Missouri, a charge that resulted in an order by Governor Thomas Carlin of Illinois to arrest the men. This made it necessary for Joseph to go into hiding and for Porter Rockwell to flee the state. Later, under protection from a newly elected governor, Thomas Ford, Joseph went to Springfield in December 1842. The charges were dropped, as there was no evidence to support them. Bennett then revived the old charge of treason against Joseph, and Governor Ford sent out a warrant of extradition for Joseph's return to Missouri for trial. Joseph was arrested, but the Nauvoo municipal court released him on a writ of *habeas corpus.*[37]

Thomas Sharp, the editor of the fiercely adversarial newspaper, *The Warsaw Signal,* also spread much ill-will and incited mob action against the Church. Sharp ran for the state House of Representatives against William Smith, Joseph's brother. William easily won the election which intensified Sharp's antagonism toward the Saints, and he broadened his attack over a ten-county area, insisting on the extermination or expulsion of the Saints. He repeatedly attacked the Church and accused its leaders of every crime imaginable. (Sharp was one of nine eventually indicted for the murders of Joseph and Hyrum Smith.)

A Plot to Kill the Prophet

During this period, Joseph found it necessary to excommunicate several members of the Church—Robert Foster, Francis and Chauncey Higbee, and William and Wilson Law. These men, having decided that Joseph was a fallen prophet, became his bitter enemies. They influenced others to follow them, which intensified the persecutions. They plotted to kill Joseph, but when their plans were uncovered and thwarted, "they discussed how they could get to Joseph Smith, and get him to commit some overt act which would cause the law to come in and get him away from his friends where the enemies could get to him with powder and ball." The apostate group decided that printing a libelous newspaper would fit the bill.[38] Thus, *The Nauvoo Expositor* was conceived.

The first and only edition of *The Nauvoo Expositor* was filled with the darkest accusations imaginable against Joseph Smith and called for his death, as well as the death of other Church leaders. Among other things, the paper accused Joseph of teaching vicious principles, speaking blasphemously of God, and promoting an inquisition. "This paper," wrote a Church member who was living in Nauvoo when it appeared, "put in circulation the most libelous, false, and infamous reports concerning the citizens of Nauvoo, and especially the ladies."[39]

Of the seven men who signed their names to the "Prospectus of the Nauvoo Expositor," only one, Charles Foster, had never been a member of the Church. Five of the other six were known to have committed adultery, including Dr. Robert Foster who had a child with a woman who was not his wife. Many times Joseph labored with these apostates "until I was out of all manner of patience."

The Fateful Decision to Destroy the *Expositor* Press

The Nauvoo City Council, after fourteen hours of deliberation, identified the paper as a public nuisance and issued an order for the city marshal to destroy the press without delay. The council was convinced that if the paper was allowed to continue, it would bring mobs who would "murder our women and children and burn our beautiful city." Joseph's enemies hoped the destruction of the press would lead to his and other leaders' deaths, the repeal of the Nauvoo Charter and the destruction of Nauvoo.[40]

One writer observed that "even though Illinois had experienced twenty similar destructions of printing presses over the previous two decades without such a reaction, the enemies of the Church proclaimed the *Expositor* incident a violation of freedom of the press."[41] Many believed that if the city council had not destroyed the press, the offended community of Nauvoo would have done so as vigilantes. John Taylor wrote, "I do not believe that in any other city in the United States, if the same charges [by a newspaper] had been made against the citizens, it would have been permitted to remain one day."[42]

Quick to take advantage of the situation, a mob set fire to various buildings belonging to themselves, including their own homes, and then alleged they had been driven from their homes by the Mormons under threat of death. They burned their mill and office and declared that Hyrum Smith had offered a reward for the destruction of the *Signal* office and press at Warsaw.[43] Citizen groups in Hancock County called for the removal of the Saints from Illinois. Thomas Sharp's *Warsaw Signal* proclaimed, "War and extermination is inevitable! WE have no time for comment, every man will make his own. Let it be made with POWDER and BALL!!!"[44] Militias were formed in all the surrounding communities as a result of the scandalous, erroneous "news" about the Saints.

Governor Ford sent a letter to Joseph Smith insisting that he and the city council members stand trial in Carthage on the charge of causing a civil disturbance. The governor promised protection, a promise Joseph did not believe he would fulfill.[45] Joseph knew the determination of his enemies to destroy him—he had prophesied that if he and Hyrum were ever taken again, "we should be massacred, or I was not a prophet of God."[46] He wrote to the governor expressing his fears, but the reply from the governor "seemed to show no mercy toward the brothers or other Church members."

To save their lives, Joseph and Hyrum, along with a few other leaders, decided that they should leave the area immediately and go west to a place where the Saints could dwell in peace. Plans were made, and after a tearful farewell to their families, the brothers, along with Willard Richards and Orrin Porter Rockwell, crossed the Mississippi the night of June 22, 1844. The next morning, as they were assembling their provisions, word arrived that a posse had been sent to Nauvoo to arrest them. The posse, upon not finding their intended captives, threatened the citizens with an invasion of troops and destruction of the city if they did not give up their leaders. Joseph and Hyrum believed they had no other choice but to return to Nauvoo and submit to arrest, even though they knew they were guilty of no crimes. As they returned home to their families, Joseph knew it would be his last evening with them.[47]

"Calm as a Summer's Morn"

As Joseph and Hyrum, city council members, and a few other friends[48] left the city for Carthage early in the morning of June 24, 1844, Joseph paused to look back at the temple and the city he loved and remarked, "This is the loveliest place and the best people under the heavens; little do they know the trials that await them." The Prophet told the Saints that if he did not go, the city would be destroyed and he could not think of them going through such suffering again—it was better for him to die. "I am willing to die for them." "My work is finished." He further said, "I am going like a lamb to the slaughter, but I am calm as a summer's morn. . . . If they take my life I shall die an innocent man, and my blood shall cry from the ground for vengeance, and it shall be said of me, 'He was murdered in cold blood!'"[49] Joseph, convinced that they were going to their deaths, tried to dissuade Hyrum from accompanying him—to no avail. The Prophet told Stephen Markham that he wanted "Hyrum to live to avenge my blood, but he is determined not to leave me."[50]

Joseph said he was willing to lay down his life for his brethren to defend the rights of all people. He boldly proclaimed that "If it has been demonstrated that I have been willing to die for a [Latter-day Saint], I am bold to declare before Heaven that I am just as ready to die in defending the rights of a Presbyterian, a Baptist, or a good man of any other denomination; for the same principle which would trample upon the rights of the Latter-day Saints would trample upon the rights of the Roman Catholics, or of any other denomination who may be unpopular and too weak to defend themselves."[51]

Governor Ford knew there were men determined to kill the Prophet, and Joseph's friends in Nauvoo considered it necessary for him to be accompanied by an armed force. Ford told them to bring no arms and again promised he would protect them. Further, he "threatened that if [the Prophet] did not give himself up at that time, that Nauvoo would be destroyed and all the men, women and children that were in it."[52]

As the eighteen men who had writs sworn out against them—Joseph and Hyrum, members of the city council, the marshal, along with the few others—neared Carthage, they were met by a mounted militia who insisted they return with them to Nauvoo and disarm the Nauvoo Legion—by order of Governor Ford.[53] After returning and accomplishing this order, Joseph and the others again bid tearful farewells to their families and arrived back at Carthage at midnight.

The governor took up residence in Carthage to oversee the trial. On Tuesday, June 25, at 8:30 a.m., Ford assembled all the troops and addressed them regarding Joseph and Hyrum. Acting as judge and jury, he declared the Smiths to be dangerous men and guilty of all crimes alleged against them, but the law must have its course. At 9:15 a.m., Ford picked up Joseph and Hyrum from Hamilton's Tavern, where they were staying, and paraded them before the troops, as he had promised he would. The Carthage Greys became unruly, shouting out obscenities and threats at the prisoners, but the governor pacified them and promised they should have "full satisfaction."[54]

Joseph, Hyrum and Others Jailed at Carthage

The men were taken to jail, even though the governor and others knew the law of Illinois prohibited persons from being jailed until the evidence of their guilt had been examined. A false mittimus stating this investigation had taken place was drafted in advance, and thus the prisoners spent a second night in Carthage, lodged in jail where they slept on the floor.

Governor Ford visited the jail the next morning to explain the charges against the prisoners. Joseph stated they were willing to pay for the destroyed press, but they did not want such an "infamous and filthy" paper published in Nauvoo. Regarding the charge of treason, for proclaiming martial law and calling out the Nauvoo Legion, Joseph explained that it was only to protect themselves from mobs and was not an act of rebellion against the government, as charged, and that he, the governor, had, in fact, directed him to do this! The governor replied that he was sorry it had occurred, but he thought it best to let the law take its course. Ford further said he would be going to Nauvoo the next day and promised to take Joseph with him.[55]

Joseph explained to Governor Ford that "upon investigating the matter, we found that our city charter gave us power to remove all nuisances. Furthermore, after consulting Blackstone upon what might be considered a nuisance, it appeared that that distinguished lawyer, who is considered authority, I believe, in all courts, states . . . that a 'libelous and filthy press may be considered a nuisance,' and abated as such. . . . We conceived that we were acting strictly in accordance with law. We made that order in our corporate capacity, and the city marshal carried it out."[56]

Sometime later, several witnesses made sworn affidavits that Governor Ford was complicit in a plot to see that Joseph and Hyrum did not leave Carthage alive. They told of conversations, often in the presence of the governor, which summed up the mob's attitude about how justice should be executed: "If the law will not reach them, powder and ball must."

Joseph and Hyrum were briefly taken from the jail to a court that decreed the men were to be brought for trial the next day, June 27, at 12:00 noon. However, the governor decided to go to Nauvoo the next morning, along with his troops, leaving only fifty men in Nauvoo to supposedly guard the prisoners. The trial was deferred until Saturday, the 29th. The governor did not take Joseph with him, as he had promised.

Neither the prisoners nor their counsel were informed of any of this. Joseph, Hyrum, and seven other men spent a restless night in the jail. These men were John Taylor, Willard Richards, Dan Jones, Stephen Markham, John S. Fuller, Dr. Southwick, and Lorenzo D. Wasson. During the night, Joseph asked Dan Jones if he was afraid to die. Dan said, "Has that time come, think you? Engaged in such a cause I do not think that death would have many terrors." Joseph replied, "You will yet see Wales, and fulfill the mission appointed you before you die." Within a few months, Jones was on his way to Wales, where he filled a successful mission.[57]

Joseph seemed to realize his end was near, but death held no fear. A few months earlier, he had instructed the Twelve Apostles in their duties, saying,

> Brethren, the Lord bids me hasten the work in which we are engaged. . . .
> It may be that my enemies will kill me, and in case they should, and the keys and power which rest on me not be imparted to you, they will be lost from the Earth; but if I can only succeed in placing them upon your heads, then let me fall a victim to murderous hands if God will suffer it, and I can go with all pleasure and satisfaction, knowing that my work is done, and the foundation laid on which the kingdom of God is to be reared.[58]

Joseph asked Dan Jones to go downstairs and inquire of the guard the causes of disturbances that were heard in the night. Frank Worrel, the officer of the guard, bitterly replied, "We have had too much trouble to bring Old Joe here to let him ever escape alive, and unless you want to die with him you had better leave before sundown . . . for neither he nor his brother, nor anyone who will remain with them will see the sun set today."

Joseph next asked Jones to inform the governor of the threats. On his way, he heard one of the troops making a similar threat. Upon informing Governor Ford of the threats, the governor replied, "You are unnecessarily alarmed. . . . The people are not that cruel." The guard would not let Jones re-enter the jail. The governor then prepared to lead the main body of the troops to Nauvoo. Boasts were made by the mobs, within earshot of the governor, that as soon as he was far enough out of town they would rush the jail and "kill Old Joe and Hyrum."

Guards Were among Prophet's Most Bitter Enemies

Before marching to Nauvoo, Governor Ford chose the Carthage Greys, whose conduct had been more hostile toward the prisoners than any other company to "guard" the jail. The Greys were later joined by about seventy-five disbanded and hostile Warsaw troops. Cyrus Wheelock implored the governor to realize that Joseph and Hyrum would not be safe "from the hands of traitors, and midnight assassins who thirst for their blood." The governor assured him they would be protected. Wheelock then visited the jail and was able to slip a six shooter into Joseph's pocket. Joseph had been given a single barrel-pistol by John S. Fullmer, which he then gave to Hyrum. Both brothers voiced their hatred at the use of such things but realized they might need to use them to defend themselves.[59]

At Joseph's request, Stephen Markham left the jail to purchase some medicine for Dr. Willard Richards, who had taken ill. Upon his return, a company of Carthage Greys gathered around him, demanded that he mount his horse, and forced him out of town at the point of a bayonet. Only four men now remained in the jail—Joseph, Hyrum, John Taylor, and Willard Richards—with eight guards on duty. The main body of Carthage Greys was camped on the public square about a quarter mile distant.

At about 5:00 p.m., the jailer, upon hearing of the Markham incident, suggested the prisoners might be safer in a cell. Joseph said they would go in after supper, which they did. Within minutes, a rustling was heard at the outer door of the jail, along with a cry for the prisoners to surrender and a discharge of three or four firearms. Looking from behind a curtain at a window, Dr. Richards observed about a hundred-armed men with blackened faces. The mob "encircled the building, some of them rushed by the guard up the flight of stairs and began the work of death, while others fired in through the open windows."

The Martyrdom

Joseph and Hyrum reached for their guns, and the other two reached for canes. They all sprang against the door, the balls whistled up the stairway, and in an instant one came through the door. Hyrum was hit in the left side of his nose. He fell on his back exclaiming, "I am a dead man!" Three more balls entered his body. When Hyrum fell, Joseph exclaimed, "Oh dear, brother Hyrum!"

John Taylor was hit by four balls, the first one striking his left thigh and causing him to fall across the edge of a windowsill, smashing his watch before falling to the floor. The watch in his vest pocket stopped at 5:16 p.m. The force of the balls knocked him back into the room, preventing him from falling out the window and thus saving his life. Taylor rolled under the bed and was fired upon several more times, a fifth ball hitting him on the left hip.[60] Joseph, reaching around the door casing, fired blindly into the hallway, getting off three shots and striking three men, none fatally.[61]

Seeing there was no safety in the room and possibly thinking he could spare the lives of his brethren, Joseph turned from the door, dropped his pistol on the floor, and sprang to the window. Two balls hit him from the door, and one from the outside entered his right breast. He fell from the second story window exclaiming, "O Lord, my God!"

"Oh, dear brother Hyrum"

Willard Richards wrote of the event, "At this instant the cry was raised, 'He's leaped the window!' and the mob on the stairs and in the entry, ran out." Dr. Richards, although a very large man, miraculously escaped harm, except for a grazed tip of his left ear. This fulfilled a prophecy Joseph had made more than a year earlier "that the time would come that balls would fly around him [Richards] like hail, and he should see his friends fall . . . but that there should not be a hole in his garment." Richards looked out the window to see if there were any signs of life in Joseph. Satisfied that the Prophet was dead, Richards checked and found all of the jail doors unbarred.

Dr. Richards caught John Taylor under his arm and dragged him to the inner jail, expecting the mobs immediate return. He covered Taylor with an old mattress so he would not be detected, saying, "If your wounds are not fatal, I want you to live to tell the story." Some of the mob again rushed up the stairs but they found only Hyrum's body. And then they heard a loud erroneous cry, "The Mormons are coming!" This sent the whole band of murderers fleeing into the woods.[62]

Ford Suspected in Conspiracy

In the meantime, Governor Ford was in Nauvoo giving a most contemptuous and insulting speech to the Saints. He told them they "ought to be praying Saints, not military Saints," and if they misbehaved even a little more, then an already lighted torch would be applied and the city reduced to ashes. He said it pained him to think there was a danger of so many innocent women and children being exterminated.[63]

John Taylor wrote that it was difficult to know for sure, but "it is very certain that things looked more than suspicious against [Governor Ford]," that he was either involved in the plot or at least knew that Joseph and Hyrum had broken no laws; that armed mobs were threatening to exterminate them; that he enrolled the mobs as members of his troops; that he disbanded and disarmed the Nauvoo Legion; that he asked Joseph and the others to come to Carthage unarmed where they were jailed illegally; that he refused to interfere in their behalf; that he left them in jail; that he left the Carthage Greys, their most bitter enemies, to "guard" them; that he was informed of the plans to murder the prisoners; and that when the cannon was fired in Carthage, signifying the deed had been done, he immediately took up his line of march and fled.[64] Another account says the governor assumed enough time had elapsed for the deed to have taken place and then left. Either way, it appears he expected the martyrdom to happen.

A merchant in Warsaw, upon hearing the cannon, jumped on his horse and rode to Quincy, reporting that Joseph and Hyrum were dead, as were all those with them in the jail, and that they had been killed by the guard for attempting to break jail. That was the preplanned fabrication,[65] but all were not dead, and the truth was soon revealed.

Joseph and Hyrum's Bodies Taken to Nauvoo

About midnight, Dr. Richards was able to obtain some help for the seriously wounded John Taylor. The next morning, Richards transported the bodies of Joseph and Hyrum to Nauvoo in wagons covered with brush to keep off the sun. Thousands of mourners lined Mulholland Street in Nauvoo. The following morning, more than ten thousand Church members viewed the bodies of their martyred Prophet and Patriarch.[66] Lucy Smith, the mother of Joseph and Hyrum, wrote of seeing her murdered sons. She "called upon God to strengthen me, but when I entered the room and saw my murdered sons both at once before my eyes and heard the sobs and groans of my family . . . of their wives, children, brothers, and sisters, it was too much; I sank back, crying to the Lord in the agony of my soul, 'My God, my God, why hast thou forsaken this family!' A voice replied, 'I have taken them to myself, that they might have rest.'" Emma, Joseph's wife, was so overcome with grief that it was necessary to carry her back to her room.[67]

Samuel Smith, Joseph and Hyrum's brother, had attempted to go to Carthage to visit them, but when it was discovered he was one of the Smiths, the mob tried to shoot him. He was able to escape but was pursued at top speed for more than two hours. Soon after this, he told his mother, "I have had a dreadful distress in my side ever since I was chased by the mob, and I think I have received some injury which is going to make me sick." He died on July 30, 1844, only thirty-three days after his brothers Hyrum and Joseph were killed.[68]

Statements about the Martyrdom and Trial

Many newspapers got the story right. From the June 29, 1844, issue of the *Lee County Democrat* (Ft. Madison, Iowa) we read: "From all the facts now before us, we regard these homicides as nothing else than murder in cold blood." The *St. Louis Evening Gazette* reported: "We also endorse the whole of the sentiment of the St. Louis Presses, and say that it was *premeditated murder,* and that the offenders ought to be ferreted out and dealt with according to the strict sense of the law."[69]

An official statement regarding the "Martyrdom of the Prophet and the Patriarch" was written by Elder John Taylor. The statement now comprises section 135 of the Doctrine and Covenants. In part, it reads:

Joseph Smith, the Prophet and Seer of the Lord, has done more, save Jesus only, for the salvation of men in this world, than any other man that ever lived in it. In the short space of twenty years, he has brought forth the Book of Mormon, which he translated by the gift and power of God, and has been the means of publishing it on two continents; has sent the fullness of the everlasting gospel, which it contained, to the four quarters of the earth; has brought forth the revelations and commandments which compose this book of Doctrine and Covenants, and many other wise documents and instructions for the benefit of the children of men; gathered many thousands of the Latter-day Saints, founded a great city, and left a fame and name that cannot be slain. He lived great, and he died great in the eyes of God and his people; and like most of the Lord's anointed in ancient times, has sealed his mission and his works with his own blood; and so has his brother Hyrum. In life they were not divided, and in death they were not separated![70]

What justice was served on the murderers? About sixty persons were presented to a grand jury for indictment, but names were struck off until they ended up with only nine. These included Colonel Levi Williams, a Baptist minister; Thomas C. Sharp, editor of the *Warsaw Signal*; Mark Aldrich, captain of a Hancock County militia; Jacob C. Davis, a state senator; and William N. Grover, captain of a company of Warsaw militia.[71]

On the day of the trial, more than a thousand armed men were at the court to keep the Latter-day Saints away. In addition, the jury was chosen from "military followers of the court." The judge fearing his life was in danger, let the armed mob have their way during the court proceedings. John Hay, who wrote an account of the trial in the *Atlantic Monthly,* said, "There was not a man on the jury, in the court, in the county, that did not know the defendants had done murder." "And," he added, "you cannot find . . . an original inhabitant of Hancock County who will not stoutly sustain the [not guilty] verdict."[72]

Although the prosecutor was able to clearly show the defendants' guilt, they were nevertheless acquitted. Frank Worrel, in command of the guard at the time of the massacre, was asked by the prosecuting attorney if the guard had their guns loaded with blank cartridges at the time of the attack on the jail. Worrel refused to answer on the grounds he could not answer without incriminating himself. But the murderers "can rest assured that their case, independent of all earthly tribunals, will be tried by the Supreme Judge of the Universe, who has said, vengeance is mine and I will repay."[73] In November of 1844, Dr. Foster is reported to have said: "I am the most miserable wretch that the sun shines upon. If I could recall eighteen months of my life I would be willing to sacrifice everything I have upon the earth, my wife and child not excepted. . . . I have not seen a moment's peace since [the martyrdom]. I know that [this Church] is true and the thought of meeting [Joseph and Hyrum] at the bar of God is more awful to me than anything else." [74]

The deaths of Joseph and Hyrum Smith brought the number of the Smith Family who died as "martyrs to the cause of Christ" to five, with one more following the next year when William's wife Carolyn Grant Smith died from illness brought on by her exposures in Missouri.[75]

Governor Ford, who was not reelected, turned to writing a history of Illinois for a livelihood. In it he wrote: "The murder of the Smiths, instead of putting an end to . . . the [Latter-day Saints] and dispersing them, as many believed it would, only bound them together closer than ever, gave them new confidence in their faith." Ford added: "Some gifted man like Paul . . . may succeed in breathing a new life into this modern Mahometanism and make the name of the martyred Joseph ring loud and stir the souls of men." Ford lived with a fear that this would happen and his own name would, like the names of Pilate and Herod, be "dragged down to posterity with an immortal name."[76] His fears have rightly been realized.

The Prophet's Candidacy for the U.S. Presidency

At the time of his imprisonment, Joseph was a candidate for the presidency of the United States on an independent party ticket. Stephen Markham, who went to Carthage with Joseph, was told of a meeting held to consider "the best way to stop Joseph Smith's career, as his views on government were widely circulated and took like wildfire. They said if he did not get into the presidential chair this election, he would be sure to be next time; and if Illinois and Missouri would join together and kill him, they would not be brought to justice for it." Governor Ford was in the meeting, as were delegates from every state in the union, except three.[77]

Since the Church and its members had been treated unjustly by both candidates running for president, they decided it was morally impossible for them to support either candidate. It was resolved that if there was to be justice, where the rights and liberties of the people were protected, Joseph Smith should run for president on the independent ticket—of their new National Reform Party.[78]

Three hundred Church members, including the Twelve Apostles, campaigned for Joseph across the nation. "He advocated presidential intervention when states refused to suppress mobs interfering with individual human rights." Joseph's platform included the abolition of slavery with government compensation to slave owners. "He endorsed a judicious tariff whose revenues might foster economic expansion, and a federally owned national bank . . . to pay government expenses; economy in government . . . by trimming the size of Congress; and the annexation of Texas, Oregon, and any liberty-loving people." He advocated prison reforms in which felons would build highways or work on other public works projects, imprisoning only those convicted of capital crimes, but helping reform them by having the penitentiaries become "seminaries of learning." He envisioned an American government led by righteous men.[79] Had he run and won, the course of U.S. history would likely have been changed.

Joseph never thought he would get elected but said, "When I get hold of eastern papers, and see how popular I am; I am afraid myself that I shall be elected; but if I should be, I would not say, 'your cause is just but I can do nothing for you.'"[80] His enemies at Carthage took his candidacy very seriously, seriously enough to plan to eliminate him through murder.

The Prophet's Work Grows

As early as the mid-1830s, Joseph said he would welcome his day of deliverance into the next world, leaving the kingdom in the hands of others. "Oh! I am so tired," he said, "so tired that I often feel to long for my day of rest."[81] From the beginning of his ministry, he knew that he might have to die for his testimony of the Savior and his calling as the prophet of the restoration. In January 1843, he said, "I understand my mission and business. God almighty is my shield, and what can man do if God is my friend. I shall not be sacrificed until my time comes. Then I shall be offered freely."[82]

Although enemies of the Church were convinced The Church of Jesus Christ of Latter-day Saints would come to an end with the deaths of Joseph and Hyrum, they did not understand it was the gospel of Jesus Christ that had been restored and in the words of the Prophet, "no unhallowed hand [would] stop the work from progressing." President Spencer W. Kimball related similar feelings: "'[Their Church] will fail if we kill their prophet,' they said . . . as they murdered Joseph Smith in cold blood. . . . [the Church] was not destroyed by the cruel martyrdom, but here was its vitality. The bullet-torn flesh fertilized the soil; the blood they shed moistened the seed; and the spirits they sent heavenward will testify against them through eternities. The cause persists and grows."[83]

Joseph wrote about his First Vision, the beginning of the gospel restoration in these, the latter days:

It was nevertheless a fact that I had beheld a vision. I have thought since, that I felt much like Paul, when he made his defense before King

Agrippa, and related the account of the vision he had when he saw a light, and heard a voice; but still there were but few who believed him; some said he was dishonest, others said he was mad and he was ridiculed and reviled. But, all this did not destroy the reality of his vision. He had seen a vision, he knew he had, and all the persecution under heaven could not make it otherwise; and though they should persecute him unto death, yet he knew, and would know to his latest breath, that he had both seen a light and heard a voice speaking unto him, and all the world would not make him think or believe otherwise (Joseph Smith—History 1:24).

As it was with Paul, so it was with Joseph. He, too, willingly made the supreme sacrifice rather than offend or disappoint his God. Joseph accomplished the monumental task of bringing forth the Book of Mormon, which has blessed the lives of countless millions, and was the chosen vessel through which the Lord restored His gospel to the earth once more. Praise to the man!

You Must Produce the Book under the Most Trying Conditions in about Seventy-four Days

Start now and write your book, which will cover 2,600 years of ancient history—and do it, not in the peaceful atmosphere of your community, but under the most trying circumstances, which will include constant threats upon your life. Talk a friend into mortgaging his farm to publish the book. Have your manuscript completed and ready for the printer, all in about sixty-five working days.

Making a profit from being a prophet was the furthest thing from the mind of Joseph Smith. He was called to restore the Lord's Church to the earth, and this was why the Lord blessed him with strength. In temporal affairs Joseph and Emma were often homeless and frequently had to rely on the generosity of family and friends for shelter and subsistence. Besides poverty, persecution was their ever-present companion.

By Every Stratagem

Married for only eight months, Joseph and Emma were staying with Joseph's family in Manchester (Palmyra), New York, when the time came to obtain the plates from which he would translate the Book of Mormon. In the early morning hours of September 22, 1827, the couple borrowed a horse and carriage and left on their crucial errand. Emma waited near the foot of the Hill Cumorah while Joseph met with the angel Moroni and received the ancient record.[1] The angel warned Joseph against negligence and told him that if he would do all he could to preserve the gold plates, the precious record would be safe-guarded.[2]

Moroni further warned Joseph that he would need to use all his faculties to keep evil men from taking the plates, and the Prophet soon found this to be true. Of this period, he writes: "Every stratagem that could be invented was resorted to for that purpose."[3] "As soon as the news of the discovery [that he had the plates] was made known, false reports, misrepresentations, and slander flew as on the wings of the wind in every direction; the house was frequently

Bringing the plates off the hill

beset by mobs and evil designing persons. Several times I was shot at, and very narrowly escaped, and every device was made use of to get the plates away from me."[4]

Joseph often moved the plates only minutes before would-be thieves arrived. Once he hid them under the hearthstone of the fireplace in his home and another time in a chest under the wooden floor of the cooper shop on the Smith farm. In this case, he was prompted to move them and hide them under flax in the loft of the shop. That night, a mob tore up the floor, but the plates remained safe.[5]

The mob's ceaseless attempts to obtain the plates and the threats against Joseph's life became so intense that beginning the work of translation was nearly impossible. Joseph wrote, "The persecution became more bitter and severe than before, and multitudes were on the alert continually to get them from me if possible." A flood of falsehoods about Joseph and his family circulated continually. "If I were to relate a thousandth part of them, it would fill up volumes," Joseph said.[6]

John Taylor, who became the fourth President of the Church, believed the reason so many spread fabrications against Joseph was that he introduced principles that struck at the root of the corrupt systems of men. "This necessarily comes in contact with their prepossessions, prejudices, and interests, and as they cannot overturn his principles, they attack his character. And that is one reason why we have so many books written against his character, without touching his principles. . . . But truth . . . is invulnerable. It cannot be destroyed. . . . It will outride all the storms of men."[7]

The Move to Harmony and the Persuasions of Men

Under these circumstances, life became so unsafe that it was necessary for the Prophet and his young family to leave the State of New York. At the invitation of Emma's father, Joseph and Emma moved to Harmony, Pennsylvania, in December of 1827. Martin Harris gave them $50, which enabled them to make the trip.[8] "They left, hiding the record in a barrel of beans in the wagon. Several men detained the travelers, but were unsuccessful in finding the plates."[9] Following a brief stay with the Hales, the couple purchased a small house from Emma's brother, Jesse, along with some farmland bordering the Susquehanna River.[10]

Martin later traveled to Harmony and acted as Joseph's scribe for two months, from April to June, 1828. He transcribed 116 pages, known as the book of Lehi. Martin's wife, Lucy, resented him helping Joseph, with both his time and his money. Because she was suspicious that Joseph was trying to defraud Martin, she wanted proof that Joseph had the plates. On one occasion, she ransacked the Smiths' home in an attempt to find the plates. In addition, she tried to destroy Joseph's reputation by going door to door to her neighbors and spreading rumors, and by filing an unsuccessful lawsuit against him.

Hoping to convince his wife of the truth, Martin pestered Joseph, causing the Prophet to go to the Lord in prayer three times to ask permission for Martin to take the 116 pages and show them to his wife and family. Finally, after the third request, the Lord gave Joseph permission, and Martin took the manuscript, under the most strict and solemn promise that he would show it only to Lucy and a few family members. Shortly thereafter, Emma gave birth to the Smith's first son, Alvin, who died soon after his birth, leaving Emma herself hovering between life and death. Joseph spent two or three weeks at her bedside until she began regaining her health.[11] During this period, Martin had not returned with the manuscript. Emma persuaded Joseph to leave, find Martin, and learn the status of the 116 pages. He left Emma in the care of her mother and traveled to Manchester, about two days' distance by stagecoach.

The Hard Lesson of the 116 Lost Pages

Joseph arrived in Manchester and found Martin in a highly distressed state. Martin informed Joseph that the manuscript was gone, "and I know not where." Fear beset Joseph. He wept and groaned and walked the floor continually, saying, "All is lost! All is lost! What shall I do? . . . I should have been satisfied with the [Lord's] first answer!" Joseph agonized over returning to Emma with such news. "I dare not do it. And how shall I appear before the Lord? Of what rebuke am I not worthy from the angel of the Most High?"[12]

When Joseph returned home, Moroni appeared to the distraught Prophet and took back the plates and the Urim and Thummim. He promised that Joseph could receive them again if he humbled himself and repented. Joseph, being very contrite and prayerful, did obtain them a second time, and was instructed by revelation not to retranslate the 116 lost pages. Wicked men, intending to discredit the Prophet, would alter the words so they did not agree with the retranslation, claiming that Joseph was a fraud. The Lord said, "I will not suffer that they shall destroy my work; yea, I will show unto them that my wisdom is greater than the cunning of the devil" (Doctrine and Covenants 10:43). "It is not the work of God that is frustrated, but the work of men" (Doctrine and Covenants 3:3).

The Lord knew all this would happen, and 1 Nephi 9:5 records that He commanded Nephi to make two sets of records. "Wherefore, the Lord hath commanded me to make these plates for a wise purpose in him, which purpose I know not," wrote Nephi. The larger plates contained a secular history; the smaller ones dealt primarily with sacred things. Earlier, Nephi had written, "But I shall make an account of my proceedings in my days. Behold, I make an abridgment of the record of my father, upon plates which I have made with mine own hands; wherefore, after I have abridged the record of my father [which became the lost 116 pages] then will I make an account of mine own life" (1 Nephi 1:17; see also 1 Nephi 19:3–4).

Oliver Cowdery Arrives and Becomes Scribe

Martin had not kept his promise to show the manuscript to only five individuals, so he was no longer permitted to serve as Joseph Smith's scribe. Emma acted as scribe for a short period, but the Lord had promised Joseph He would send someone to assist him in the translation. Soon thereafter a young schoolteacher, Oliver Cowdery, arrived at the Smith's door. He had heard of Joseph's visions through the Prophet's family and had received a divine confirmation that Joseph was engaged in the work of God. "On the 5th day of April, 1829," wrote Joseph, "Oliver Cowdery came to my house, until which time I had never seen him. He stated to me that having been teaching school in the neighborhood where my father resided, and my father being one of those who sent to the school, he went to board for a season at his house, and while there the family related to him the circumstances of my having received the plates, and accordingly he had come to make inquiries of me" (see Joseph Smith—History 1:66–67).

On Tuesday April 7, 1829 Joseph and Oliver began translating, which was not an easy task in their impoverished circumstances. "Mr. Joseph Knight, Sr., who having heard of the manner in which we were occupying our time," recorded Joseph, "very kindly and considerately brought us a quantity of provisions, in order that we might not be interrupted in the work of translation by the want of such necessaries of life. . . . Several times [he] brought us supplies, a distance of at least thirty miles, which enabled us to continue the work."[13] "Joseph and Oliver had been in great need [and] had recently been looking for employment. If they were forced to work, even temporarily, the translation would be delayed. Therefore, they were deeply grateful for the timely assistance, which they considered a gift from heaven."[14]

There were, nevertheless, many interruptions. They had "been threatened with being mobbed from time to time, and this too, by professors of religion," wrote Joseph. Only the influence of Emma's father kept these enemies away.[15] The persecutions, however, grew to the point that Joseph and Oliver were not safe in Harmony.

Oliver knew David Whitmer, who lived in Fayette Township, New York.[16] Joseph asked him to write to Mr. Whitmer and ask him to "come with his team immediately, in order to convey [them] back to his house, that they might remain with him there until the translation should be completed, as an evil-designing people were seeking to take away Joseph's life in order to prevent the work of God from going forth among the world."[17] Oliver wrote the letter, and later, when David neared the Smith home, Joseph and Oliver walked out to meet him, much to his astonishment, for they had no earthly way of knowing that he was coming, let alone the time of his arrival. This was one of three small miracles David experienced after his decision to come for them.[18]

Some farming duties needed to be done before David could leave—plowing and spreading plaster of paris (used to reduce soil acidity) on the fields. The plowing, which usually took two days, was completed in one day, which the Whitmers took as a miracle. When David went to spread plaster the next morning, he found, much to his surprise, that the work had been done. His sister, who lived near the field, said three men had come the day before and spread the plaster with remarkable skill. She assumed they were men David had hired. The family then realized there had been divine intervention, and David left immediately on his three-day journey to Harmony. Joseph had seen details of David's trip in a vision, which was why he and Oliver met the surprised David as he approached the town.[19]

The three men were soon on their way to the home of Peter Whitmer, David's father, in Fayette. Joseph inquired of the Lord how he should transport the plates, knowing the intense efforts others made to take them from him. He was told to give them to the angel Moroni, who would return them to him in the garden of the Whitmer home. Obedient to these instructions, Joseph received the record as promised, and the translation continued without further interruption until the work was accomplished.[20] Emma followed soon after, and the Whitmers were gracious in providing for them.

Mary Whitmore Is Blessed to See the Plates

The burden of additional house guests was not easy for the Whitmers, however, and David's mother, Mary, although not one to complain, naturally felt overwhelmed. In appreciation for being so faithful and diligent, the angel Moroni met her while she was outside doing chores and showed her the plates. The angel said, "You have been very faithful and diligent in your labors, but you are tired because of the increase of your toil; it is proper therefore that you should receive a witness that your faith may be strengthened." Thereupon he showed her the plates. Mary reported the experience to her family, which also strengthened them as they supported the important work Joseph and Oliver were engaged in.[21]

"Days Never to Be Forgotten"

When Moroni returned the plates to Joseph, he told the Prophet to show them to no one until permission was given by the Lord. The work of translating took place in an upper room of the Whitmer home, in the heat of summer, with Joseph isolated from others except for Oliver Cowdery, who acted as scribe for most of the book. "It was a laborious work for the weather was very warm, and the days were long and they worked from morning till night. Occasionally Emma and one or two of the Whitmers spelled Oliver, but Joseph labored on day after day."[22]

Despite the heat and rigorous schedule, Oliver wrote the following about the "glorious" work of translation:

These were days never to be forgotten—to sit under the sound of a voice dictated by the inspiration of heaven, awakened the utmost gratitude of this bosom! Day after day I continued uninterrupted, to write from his mouth, as he translated with the Urim and Thummim, or, as the Nephites would have said, "Interpreters," the history or record called "The Book of Mormon." (Joseph Smith—History, 1:71).

As soon as the translation was completed, Joseph wrote to his parents, asking them to come as soon as possible. Martin Harris, elated with the news, accompanied Joseph Sr. and Lucy when they left early the next morning. After arriving in Fayette and spending the evening reading the manuscript, Joseph's mother wrote, "We were greatly rejoiced. It then appeared to us, who did not realize the magnitude of the work, as though the greatest difficulty was then surmounted. But with Joseph it was not so, for he knew that a dispensation of the gospel had been committed to him, of which the starting bud had scarcely yet made its appearance."[23]

The next morning the "Three Witnesses" were shown the plates by the angel Moroni (as recounted in Chapter 23). After a few days, the group, including Joseph, Emma, Oliver, and the Whitmers, traveled to Palmyra, and the search began to find a printer for the book. It was during this time that the Eight Witnesses were shown the gold plates by Joseph and were privileged to handle them. After these seminal events, Moroni again appeared to Joseph, and the plates were returned to him,[24] in whose charge they remain "until this day," wrote Joseph in 1838.[25]

Arranging for Publication

Finding a printer for the Book of Mormon was no easy task. Joseph, having acquired a copyright on June 11, 1829, soon approached printers for its publication. Some would not take the job because they did not believe the book's origins. Others demanded an exorbitant price. Arrangements were finally made with twenty-three-year-old Palmyra printer Egbert B. Grandin to print five thousand copies for $3,000, a very large order in those days. As noted earlier, Martin Harris's visit with Professor Anthon had convinced him the book was authentic. Harris came to the rescue when Joseph did not have the money to pay the printer. Martin signed a mortgage agreement on his farm to guarantee payment for the printing.[26]

At one point, Grandin grew nervous and stopped printing because of a threatened boycott. A group of people in Palmyra held a meeting and passed a resolution not to buy the book when it became available for purchase. Joseph quickly returned from Harmony to Palmyra and convinced Grandin to complete the printing. The next year, 151 acres of Martin Harris's farm were sold at public auction to pay Mr. Grandin. Harris's sacrifice made the printing of the Book of Mormon possible.[27] The Palmyra boycott ultimately did little to hinder the book's sales; there was a larger market outside the immediate Palmyra area.

Joseph learned a significant lesson with the loss of the first 116 pages, so he had Oliver make a second copy of the manuscript. As an added precaution, only a few pages were delivered to the printer each day. The original was kept at the Smith home, and the pages in Grandin's shop were picked up each evening. A guard accompanied Oliver to and from the print shop, and the house where the manuscript was kept was under guard day and night.[28] "The original manuscripts contained no punctuation or paragraphing. With the permission of Hyrum Smith, Grandin's typesetter, John H. Gilbert, provided the punctuation and paragraphing." The 1837 edition, published by Parley P. Pratt, and the 1840 edition, revised by the Prophet himself, corrected most of the early printing errors and rectified some of Gilbert's work.[29]

The first edition went on sale March 26, 1830.[30] The Church was organized early the next month, and copies of the Book of Mormon have continued to roll from presses by the thousands, and eventually by the millions, ever since. As of 2017 the Book of Mormon is the sixth most distributed book (175 million copies), and the 9th most translated book (94 full translations) in the world.

Short Time of Translation a Miraculous Singularity

How long did it take to translate the Book of Mormon? Although Joseph received the plates on September 22, 1827, and had them in his possession for nearly two years while he experienced many distractions and interruptions. Serious translating did not begin until Joseph and Emma moved to Harmony and Oliver Cowdery arrived on April 5, 1829. After receiving the plates, the Prophet traveled to Colesville twice, moved twice, participated in the restoration of the Aaronic and Melchizedek Priesthoods, received and recorded thirteen revelations, which are now sections in the Doctrine and Covenants, preached, baptized several people (including his brothers Samuel and Hyrum), acquired the copyright for the Book of Mormon, and began making arrangements for the book's publication.

Joseph and Oliver took time to eat, sleep, and work. Occasionally they worked odd jobs to earn money to buy paper. They also attended to numerous inquirers who visited them, some to find the truth and others to disrupt the work. Among the latter were "several learned priests." "However," wrote Joseph,

the Lord continued to pour out upon us His Holy Spirit, and as often as we had need, He gave us in that moment what to say; so that although unlearned and inexperienced in religious controversies, yet we were able to confound those learned priests of the day; whilst at the same time we were enabled to convince the honest in heart that we had obtained, through the mercy of God, the true and everlasting Gospel of Jesus Christ.[31]

As nearly as researchers can determine, the Book of Mormon was translated in about 74 working days. Accounting for the time spent on other activities, Joseph and Oliver produced an average of nearly 8.5 printed pages per day! "Considering the Book of Mormon's theological depth, historical complexity, consistency, clarity, artistry, accuracy, and profundity, the Prophet Joseph's translation is a phenomenal achievement—even a miraculous feat," observes John W. Welch.[32]

How does the Book of Mormon translation timeframe compare with the translation of the Dead Sea Scrolls? "About 65 members (of the International Team of Translators) are working on the translation of the scrolls into English. It has taken 50 years to translate 40 volumes, about 2,000 pages. This is approximately one page every nine days."[33]

Movie director and Academy Award winner Keith W. Merrill recognizes what an astonishing accomplishment the Book of Mormon is:

I make movies. I write many of the films I make. I have a fertile imagination and a good education. I have a state-of-the-art computer, word-processing software, writer's programs, a thesaurus, a spell checker, a grammar checker, and high-speed access to the internet. I have written films demanding significant research. In one instance I had the assistance of forty Ph.D. historians. I believe that Joseph Smith was a prophet of God because I can substantiate from personal experience the unthinkable difficulty—yes, the impossibility—of composing that elaborately complex document in so little time and yet in perfect form, with primitive instruments, in unfavorable circumstances, and with no education, by any other means than the gift and power of God.[34]

The Prophet's Expanding Influence

Two centuries after his birth, Joseph Smith is finally being recognized as a giant in American religious history. In May 2004, the National Historical Publications and Records Commission, a division of the National Archives, endorsed a project that has been compiling credible information about Joseph Smith that is accessible worldwide on a website launched in 2005. The site, titled "The Joseph Smith Papers," will include more than five thousand documents pertinent to him. Historians will be able to get accurate firsthand information about him—without relying on writers with an agenda, as has all too often been the case in the past. These documents will also be published and available for perusal in libraries or by purchase. Volume 1, *Joseph Smith Journals,* sold more than forty-eight thousand copies in less than a year. Twenty volumes are planned and several are now in print.[35]

William E. Berrett has observed that "the influence of Joseph Smith is indeed being felt in wider and wider circles as the years progress. Today, more than 200 years [213 years in 2018] after his birth, millions revere his memory and testify that he was a Prophet of the living God. These followers represent nearly all the civilized nations of the earth. Perhaps no man, aside from Jesus of Nazareth, can claim disciples from so many lands."[36]

Josiah Quincy, mayor of Boston, visited Joseph Smith shortly before the latter's martyrdom and was so impressed with him that he was prompted to write an account of that visit, in which he declared:

It is by no means improbable that some future textbook, for the use of generations yet unborn, will contain a question something like this: What historical American of the nineteenth century has exerted the most powerful influence upon the destinies of his countrymen? And it is by no means impossible that the answer to that interrogatory may be thus written: *Joseph Smith, the [Latter-day Saint] Prophet.* And the reply, absurd as it doubtless seems to most men now, may be an obvious commonplace to their descendants.[37]

Mayor Quincy's prediction is already coming to pass. The 2015 collector's edition of the *Smithsonian Magazine* highlights "The 100 Most Significant

Americans of All Time." In the category of "Religious Figures," Joseph Smith occupies the top spot in a listing of eleven historically influential personalities. (Brigham Young is ranked third.)[38]

No one, no matter how gifted or educated, could fulfill this last condition to produce a record similar to the Book of Mormon in sixty-five working days. Nor is there any way Joseph Smith could have accomplished it without the Lord. It is His work.

What you do with the information in this book, and its message, could well determine your eternal destiny. Christ's Church has been restored. The authority to perform His earthly ordinances is again upon the earth. Heed Moroni's promise: "And, when ye shall receive these things, I would exhort you that ye would ask God, the Eternal Father, in the name of Christ if these things are not true; and if ye shall ask with a sincere heart, with real intent, having faith in Christ, he will manifest the truth of it unto you, by the power of the Holy Ghost" (Moroni 10:4).

The Savior's saving and binding ordinances are once again available for all who will receive them from the Lord's anointed upon whom Christ has bestowed His authority in these latter days. May your heart and mind be touched that you may be among the millions of grateful recipients.

Statements Regarding the Character of the Prophet Joseph Smith

John Taylor, who was closely associated with Joseph Smith for many years, wrote: "I have traveled with him; I have been with him in private and in public; I have associated with him in councils of all kinds; I have listened hundreds of times to his public teachings. . . . I have been at his house and seen his deportment in his family. I have seen him arraigned before the tribunals of his country, and have seen him honorably acquitted, and delivered from the pernicious breath of slander, and the machinations and falsehoods of wicked and corrupt men. I was with him living, and with him when he died. . . . I have seen him, then, under these various circumstances, and I testify before God, angels, and men, that he was a good, honorable, virtuous man—that his doctrines were good, scriptural and wholesome—that his precepts were such as became a man of God—that his private and public character was unimpeachable—and that he lived and died as a man of God and a gentleman."³⁹

Brigham Young wrote, "I was as well acquainted with him, as any man. . . . I do not think that a man lives upon the earth that knew him any better than I did; and I am bold to say that, Jesus Christ excepted, no better man ever lived or does live upon this earth. I am his witness. He was persecuted for the same reason that any other righteous person has been or is persecuted at the present day."⁴⁰

George Q. Cannon tells what it was like, as a young boy, to see Joseph Smith for the first time: "When [my] eyes fell upon the Prophet, without a word from anyone to point [it] out, [to me] or any reason to separate him from others who stood around, [I] knew him instantly. [I] would have known him among ten thousand. There was that about him, which to [my] eyes, distinguished him from all the men I had ever seen."[41]

Amasa Potter says the following about Joseph: "I became acquainted with the Prophet Joseph Smith and heard him preach many times. . . . I remember once when the prophet preached in the grove west of the temple, a terrible storm came up and large hailstones and rain fell. The people commenced to leave their seats to run for shelter, but Joseph Smith called to them to sit down and let their prayer ascend to the Almighty God that he would stay the winds and storm, and it would be so. The people did as they were told; the storm stopped, the winds abated and all became calm. The Prophet spoke one hour and a half without another drop of rain, and we could see the wind and rain on either side of us falling thick and fast. This was great evidence to all present that Joseph Smith was a man of God, and had power with the elements when needed."[42]

Hugh B. Brown explains why Joseph passes the test as a prophet: "I believe Joseph Smith was a prophet of God because he gave to this world some of the greatest revelations of all time. . . . He foretold many things that have come to pass, things that only God could bring to pass. John, the beloved disciple of Jesus, declared that 'the testimony of Jesus is the spirit of prophecy.' . . . As much as any man who ever lived, the Prophet Joseph had a testimony of Jesus, for, like the apostles of old, saw him and heard him speak, and like them he gave his life for that testimony. I know of no one who has given more convincing evidence of the divine calling of Jesus Christ than did Joseph Smith."[43]

A writer for the *New York Herald* commented after visiting the Prophet in 1842: "Joseph Smith is undoubtedly one of the greatest characters of the age. He indicates as much talent, originality and moral courage as Mahomet, Odin or any of the great spirits that have hitherto produced the revolutions of past ages. . . . While modern philosophy, which believes in nothing but what you can touch, is overspreading the Atlantic States, Joseph Smith is creating a spiritual system, combined also with morals and industry, that may change the destiny of the race. . . . We certainly want some such prophet to start up, take a big hold of the public mind and stop the torrent of materialism that is hurrying the world into infidelity, licentiousness and crime."[44]

Endnotes

Introduction

1. Orson Pratt, in Journal of Discourses, 12:88.
2. Hugh Nibley, Since Cumorah (Salt Lake City: Deseret Book, 1988), 141.
3. Gordon B. Hinckley, In Conference Report, Oct. 1959, p. 118.
4. Ezra Taft Benson, Ensign, May 1987.
5. Neal A. Maxwell, Plain and Precious Things, Salt Lake City: Deseret Book, 1983, 4.
6. Austin Farrer, "Grete Clerk," in Light on C. S. Lewis, comp. Jocelyn Gibb (New York: Harcourt and Brace, 1965), 26.
7. Jeffrey R. Holland, "The Greatness of the Evidence," Chiasmus 50th Anniversary, JSB, Brigham Young University, August 16, 2017
8. Hugh Nibley, Since Cumorah (Salt Lake City: Deseret Book, 1967), 155-156.

Chapter 1

1. Book of Mormon Onomasticon hosted by the Harold B. Lee Library at BYU. See also a series of recent articles by Matthew Bowen in Interpreter: A Journal of Mormon Scripture.
2. John L. Sorenson, "Seasonality of Warfare in the Book of Mormon and in Mesoamerica" in Warfare in the Book of Mormon Salt Lake City and Provo: Deseret Book and FARMS, 1990.
3. Hugh W. Nibley, Collected Works of Hugh Nibley, Vol.7, Ch.6, 137-8.
4. Letter from R.L. and Evelyn Benson, February 23, 2001, to author and husband.
5. Kevin Barney, "Die Boek van Mormon Revisited," https://bycommonconsent.com/2014/06/28/die-boek-van- mormon-revisited/ (accessed June 4, 2016).
6. Danielle B. Wagner, "Baptist Minister 'Embraces and Believes' the Book of Mormon," LDS Living, January 22, 2016.
7. FAIR. Young, My Father's Captivity, Orem, Utah: Al Young Studios, 2009.

Chapter 2

1. It is noteworthy that Joseph's birth, December 23, comes just after the winter solstice, the longest night of the year and the time *when light begins to return to the earth.*
2. See Scot Facer Proctor and Maurine Jensen Proctor, eds., *The Revised and Enhanced History of Joseph Smith by His Mother* (Salt Lake City: Bookcraft, 1996), 83, 84, 91.
3. The family lived in seven locations between Joseph's birth and 1820 when, at fourteen, he received the First Vision. The locations were Sharon, Tunbridge, and South Royalton, Vermont; West Lebanon, New Hampshire; Norwich, Vermont; the village of Palmyra; and Palmyra Township, New York. See "Highlights in the Prophet's Life" *Ensign,* June 1994, 24.
4. Milton V. Backman Jr., "Joseph Smith's Recitals of the First Vision," *Ensign,* January 1985, 9–17.
5. See Donald L. Enders and Daniel C. Peterson, "Can the 1834 Affidavits Attacking the Smith Family Be Trusted?" *Pressing Forward with the Book of Mormon* (Provo, UT: Foundation for Ancient Research and Mormon Studies, 1999), 285–87.
6. Joseph's mother, his brothers Hyrum and Samuel, and his sister Sophronia joined the Presbyterian Church.
7. Joseph's brother, William, reported that a Methodist preacher, a Rev. Mr. George Lane, had preached a sermon on "What Church Shall I Join?" using James 1:5 as his text. Joseph went home and pondered on the verse.
8. B. H. Roberts, *A Comprehensive History of the Church,* 6 vols. (Salt Lake City: Deseret News Press, 1930), 1: xliv–xlv.
9. "Mormonism and the Nature of God/No Man Has Seen God," http://en.fairmormon.org/Mormonism_and_the_nature_of_God/No_man_has_seen_God (accessed May 25, 2016).
10. "Does the Bible Say That No Man Has Seen God?" *Meridian Magazine,* March 13, 2008.
11. Gordon B. Hinckley, "What Are People Asking About Us?" *Ensign,* November 1998, https://www.lds.org/ensign/1998/11/what-are-people-asking-about-us?lang=eng (accessed June 11, 2016).
12. R. Scott Lloyd, "First Vision—Bedrock Theology," *Church News,* January 9, 1993, 14.
13. Elise Soukup, "Solid, Strong, True," *Newsweek,* Gordon B. Hinckley Interview, October 17, 2005.
14. Spencer W. Kimball, *Teachings of the Presidents of the Church—Spencer W. Kimball* (Salt Lake City: The Church of Jesus Christ of Latter-day Saints, 2007), 229.
15. See Proctor and Proctor, *New and Enhanced History of Joseph Smith by His Mother,* 73–77.
16. *Church History in the Fullness of Times,* LDS Church Educational System, Salt Lake City Utah, 1993, 23.
17. Neal A. Maxwell, "How Choice a Seer!" *Ensign,* November 2003, 99.
18. Neal A. Maxwell, "How Choice a Seer!" General Conference Address, October 1983.

19. See John H. Groberg, *In the Eye of the Storm* (Salt Lake City: Bookcraft, 1993), 106–107. In 2002, this book was made into a movie titled *The Other Side of Heaven*. The original book and video of the movie are now available under that new name from Deseret Book Company in Salt Lake City and on Amazon.

20. See Neal A. Maxwell, "Joseph the Seer," in *The Prophet and His Work* (Salt Lake City: Deseret Book, 1998), 41. Elder Maxwell also describes such persons as the "few who seem to prefer old bones to a resplendent banquet." "How Choice a Seer," *Ensign*, November 2003, 99.

21. The Urim and Thummim is mentioned in the Old Testament as follows: Exodus 28:30; Leviticus 8:8; Numbers 27:21; Deuteronomy 33:8; 1 Samuel 28:6; Ezra 2:63; and Nehemiah 7:65. It is a Hebrew term that means "Lights and Perfection, an instrument prepared of God to assist man in obtaining revelation from the Lord and in translating languages" (Bible Dictionary, 787).

22. John A. Tvedtnes, *The Book of Mormon and Other Hidden Books* (Provo, UT: Foundation for Ancient Research and Mormon Studies, 2000), 151.

23. See Donl Peterson, "Moroni, Joseph Smith's Tutor," *Ensign*, January 1920, 22–29.

24. Lucy Mack Smith, *History of Joseph Smith by His Mother, Lucy Mack Smith* (Salt Lake City: Bookcraft, 1958), 82–83; see also Proctor and Proctor, *The Revised and Enhanced History of Joseph Smith by His Mother*, 111–12.

25. Daniel C. Peterson, "Shall We Not Go on in So Great a Cause," in Susan Easton Black, ed., *Expressions of Faith* (Salt Lake City and Provo, UT: Deseret Book and Foundation for Ancient Research and Mormon Studies, 1996), 132.

26. *Teachings of Presidents of the Church—John Taylor* (Salt Lake City: The Church of Jesus Christ of Latter-day Saints, 2001), 82. Original source: *Deseret News: Semi-Weekly*, July 22, 1884, 1.

27. William E. Berrett, *The Restored Church* (Salt Lake City: Deseret Book, 1973), 201.

28. Clyde J. Williams, ed., *The Teachings of Harold B. Lee* (Salt Lake City: Bookcraft, l996), 72.

Chapter 3

1. This experience has been used by *many* critics of The Church of Jesus Christ of Latter-day Saints to discredit Joseph Smith and label him as a "money digger." See *Church History in the Fulness of Times: The History of The Church of Jesus Christ of Latter-day Saints*, 2nd ed. (Salt Lake City: The Church of Jesus Christ of Latter-day Saints, 2003), 43.

2. *Church History in the Fulness of Times*, 42–43.

3. William E. Berrett, *The Restored Church* (Salt Lake City: Deseret Book, 1983), 28.

4. Joseph received the plates on the annual day when Jews throughout the world celebrated the symbolic beginning of Israel's final gathering. See Lenet Hadley Read, *Ensign*, January 2000, 25. See also Book of Mormon Central Knowhy #193.

5. *Church History in the Fulness of Times*, 44.

6. *Church History in the Fulness of Times*, 44–45. See also Joseph Smith—History 1:59.

7. Michael De Groote, "How Gold Were the Golden Plates?" Deseret News, July 7, 2010

8. John W. Welch, ed., "The 'Golden' Plates," in *Reexploring the Book of Mormon* (Salt Lake City and Provo, UT: Deseret Book and the Foundation for Ancient Research and Mormon Studies, 1992), 276.

9. John A. Tvedtnes, *The Book of Mormon and Other Hidden Books: Out of Darkness into Light* (Provo, UT: Foundation for Ancient Research and Mormon Studies, 2000), 151.

10. Franklin S. Harris Jr., "Others Kept Records on Metal Plates, Too," Instructor (October 1957): 318–21; later reprinted in pamphlet "Gold Plates Used Anciently" (Salt Lake City: The Church of Jesus Christ of Latter-day Saints, 1963).

11. See Paul R. Cheesman, Ancient Writing on Metal Plates (Bountiful, UT: Horizon Publishers, 1985). Cheesman's book compiles strong evidence, with photographs, in support of metal plates, stone boxes, and ancient writings

12. Church History in the Fulness of Times, 52-53. A replica of the original home has been built by the Church on the original site.

13. The Hill Cumorah pageant, which has a cast of hundreds and an exceptional sound track for the music and spoken parts, is free to the public, seats 6000 and is held annually during the first part of July. Online sources contain extensive information about the pageant.

Chapter 4

1. See John W. Welch, "Was There a Library in Harmony, Pennsylvania?" in *Pressing Forward with the Book of Mormon* (Provo, UT: Foundation for Ancient Research and Mormon Studies, 1999), 283–84.

2. Robert Paul, "Joseph Smith and the Manchester (New York) Library," BYU Studies, No. 31, 1982.

3. Daniel C. Peterson, "Mounting Evidence for the Book of Mormon," *Ensign*, January 2000, 96.

4. "Other Book of Mormon Witnesses," https://www.fairmormon.org/answers/BookofMormon/ Witnesses/OtherBookofMormonwitnesses, See also Book of Mormon Central Knowhy #7.

5. Eugene England, "Through the Arabian Desert to a Bountiful Land: Could Joseph Smith Have Known the Way?" in Noel B. Reynolds, ed., *Book of Mormon Authorship Revisited* (Salt Lake City: Bookcraft, 1982), 150–53.

6. George Potter and Richard Wellington, *Lehi in the Wilderness: 81 New Documented Evidences That the Book of Mormon Is a True History* (Springville, UT: Cedar Fort, 2003), 171.
7. Potter and Wellington, *Lehi in the Wilderness*, xi.
8. Potter and Wellington, *Lehi in the Wilderness*, 31, 38-39. Also, see George Potter, "Valley of Lemuel," *Journal of Book of Mormon Studies*, vol. 8, no. 1 (1999), 52-63.
9. Hugh B. Nibley, *Lehi in the Desert/The World of the Jaredites/There Were Jaredites*, the Collected Works of Hugh Nibley: vol. 5 (Salt Lake City and Provo, UT: Deseret Book and Foundation for Ancient Research and Mormon Studies, 1988), 78-79.
10. Warren P. Aston, "Newly Found Altars from Nahom," *Journal of Book of Mormon Studies*, vol. 10, no. 2 (2001), 61. See also Book of Mormon Central Knowhy #19.
11. "Book of Mormon Linked to Site in Yemen," *Ensign*, February 2001, 79.
12. S. Kent Brown, "New Light," in Donald W. Perry, Daniel C. Peterson, and John W. Welch, eds., *Echoes and Evidences of the Book of Mormon* (Provo, UT: Foundation for Ancient Research and Mormon Studies, 2002), reprinted in *Journal of Book of Mormon Studies*, vol. 1 (2003), 112.
13. See Warren P. Aston, "The Arabian Bountiful Discovered?" *Journal of Book of Mormon Studies*, vol.7, no. 1 (1998), 5–11.
14. See S. Kent Brown, "Niebuhr Response," http://www.nephiproject.com/this is_a_discussion_of_the_libr. htm (accessed May 27, 2016).
15. See Proctor and Proctor, *The History of Joseph by His Mother*, 73-77.
16. Joseph Smith, *History of the Church of Jesus Christ of Latter-day Saints*, 7 vols. (Salt Lake City: Deseret Book, 1976), 4:42.
17. John L. Sorenson, "The Book of Mormon as a Mesoamerican Record," in Noel B. Reynolds, ed, *Book of Mormon Authorship Revisited* (Salt Lake City, Bookcraft, 1982) 392.

Chapter 5

1. Hugh Nibley, *The Prophetic Book of Mormon* (Salt Lake City: Deseret Book, 1989), 235–36.
2. "Historicity of the Bible," CWHN 1:15-16
3. Nibley, *The Prophetic Book of Mormon*, 254.
4. Here is another example that compares the same verses: The Isaiah scroll and the Book of Mormon both read "and the inhabitants of Samaria" (2 Nephi 19:9), whereas the KJV reads a singular "inhabitant" (Isaiah 9:9). All of Isaiah's writings found in the Bible were also found on the Great Isaiah Scroll of the Dead Sea Scrolls. See Donald W. Parry and Stephen D. Ricks, *The Dead Sea Scrolls: Questions and Responses for Latter-day Saints*, (Provo, UT: Foundation for Ancient Research and Mormon Studies, 2000), 44–45.
5. Grant R. Hardy, "Mormon as Editor," in John L. Sorenson and Melvin Thorne, *Rediscovering the Book of Mormon* (Salt Lake City: Deseret Book, 1991), 15.
6. Robert J. Matthews, "Joseph Smith's Inspired Translation of the Bible," *Ensign*, December 1972, 61–62.
7. Robert J. Matthews, "Plain and Precious Things Restored," *Ensign*, July 1982, 15.
8. Lenel H. Read, "How the Bible Came to Be," *Ensign*, September 1982, 69.
9. Joseph Fielding McConkie, "Why a Book of Mormon?" *The Harvester*, Scotland Edinburgh Mission, March 1992.
10. Joseph Fielding Smith, *Teachings of the Prophet Joseph Smith* (Salt Lake City: Deseret News Press, 1938), 119.
11. Jeffery W. Marsh, *The Joseph Smith Translation: Precious Truths Restored* (American Fork, UT: Covenant Communications, 2002), 19.
12. "Explanatory Introduction," The Doctrine and Covenants of The Church of Jesus Christ of Latter-day Saints (Salt Lake City: The Church of Jesus Christ of Latter-day Saints, 1981). The Doctrine and Covenants also includes several revelations received by Church leaders who led the Church after Joseph Smith's martyrdom. See Arnold K. Garr, Donald Q. Cannon, and Richard O. Cowan, eds., *Encyclopaedia of Latter-day Saint History* (Salt Lake City: Deseret Book, 2000), 300–302.
13. Ezra Taft Benson, "The Gift of Modern Revelation," *Ensign*, October 1986.
14. Gordon B. Hinckley, "The Order and Will of God," *Ensign*, January 1989, 2, 4.
15. "Introductory Note," The Pearl of Great Price (Salt Lake City: The Church of Jesus Christ of Latter-day Saints, 1981).
16. Joseph Smith, *History of the Church of Jesus Christ of Latter-day Saints*, 7 vols. (Salt Lake City: Deseret Book, 1976), 2:236, 349; 4:524.
17. "Early Traditions about Abraham," *Insights*, Foundation for Ancient Research and Mormon Studies, vol. 21 (2001), 6.
18. Michael D. Rhodes, "Book of Abraham," in Garr, Cannon, and Cowan, *Encyclopaedia of Latter-day Saint History*, 114.
19. Dennis K. Brown, *Evidences of the True Church* (Springville, UT: Cedar Fort, 2008), 37.
20. Edwin O. Haroldsen, "Good and Evil Spoken Of," *Ensign*, August 1995, 8.

21. Gerald N. Lund, "Revelation and Reason," in Susan Easton Black, ed. *Expressions of Faith* (Salt Lake City: Deseret Book, 1992), 65.

Chapter 6

1. See Richard Paul Evans, *Why I Believe* (Salt Lake City: Bookcraft, 2002), 140–41.
2. *Last Testimony of Sister Emma*, Saints' Herald 26 (1879) p. 290. Also, Daniel C. Peterson, Mounting Evidence for the Book of Mormon (*Ensign,* January 2000). 20.
3. See B. H. Roberts, *A Comprehensive History of the Church*, 6 vols. (Salt Lake City: Deseret News Press, 1930), 1:130.
4. Roberts, *Comprehensive History of the Church*, 1:131.
5. Royal Skousen, "The Original Book of Mormon Manuscript," in John W. Welch, ed., *Reexploring the Book of Mormon* (Salt Lake City and Provo, UT: Deseret Book and Foundation for Ancient Research and Mormon Studies, 1992), 9–10.
6. Joseph's seer stone was prepared by God, according to the Book of Mormon (Alma 37:23), and like the Nephite interpreters, the seer stone was buried in the earth where Joseph would eventually find It. Michael Hubbard MacKay and Gerrit J. Dirkmaat, *From Darkness unto Light* (Provo, UT and Salt Lake City: Brigham Young University and Deseret Book, 2015), 67.
7. Royal Skousen, "Translating the Book of Mormon," in Noel B. Reynolds, ed., *Book of Mormon Authorship Revisited* (Provo, UT: Foundation for Ancient Research and Mormon Studies, 1997), 63, 67, 76.
8. See "Book of Mormon Symposium Marks Milestone," *Insights*, vol. 21, no. 10 (2001), 1, 4, http://publications.mi.byu.edu/publications/insights/21/10/S00088-21-10.pdf (accessed May 29, 2016).
9. "Scholars Speak at FAIR Conference," *Insights*, vol. 22, no. 8 (2002), 3, http://publications.mi.byu.edu/publications/insights/22/8/22-8%20August%202002.pdf (accessed May 29, 2016).
10. "FARMS Book of Mormon Research Highlighted," *Insights*, vol. 24, no. 5 (2004), 1, http://publications.mi.byu.edu/publications/insights/24/5/S00001-24-5.pdf (accessed May 29, 2016).
11. Alexander L. Baugh, "Joseph Smith: Seer, Translator, Revelator, and Prophet," Brigham Young University Devotional address, June 24, 2014.
12. Donald B. Doty, "Why Is the Book of Mormon the 'Most Correct of Any Book on Earth?'" *Ensign*, August 1988, 28.
13. Robert J. Mathews, "Why Have Changes Been Made in the Printed Edition of the Book of Mormon?" *Ensign*, March 1987, 49.
14. George A. Horton Jr., "Book of Mormon—Transmission from Translator to Printed Text," in *The Book of Mormon: The Keystone Scripture* (Provo, UT: Religious Studies Center, Brigham Young University, 1988).
15. So nit-pickers have gone through the "printer's copy" of the Book of Mormon and compared it with the printed book, counting every added comma, period, and paragraph and labelling them as "changes in the text." Because Oliver Cowdery did not add punctuation as he wrote, these so-called changes, which were made by the typesetter, were naturally ample. These changes were tallied and the results circulated widely by those trying to discredit the book.
16. Title page of 1963 edition of the Book of Mormon.
17. See Carrie A. Moore, "Intro Change in Book of Mormon Spurs Discussion," *Deseret Morning News*, November.r 9, 2007.
18. P. Marion Simms, *The Bible in America* (New York: Wilson-Erickson, 1936), 97. See also Robert J. Matthews, "I Have a Question: Why Have Changes Been Made in the Printed Editions of the Book of Mormon?" https://www.lds.org/ensign/1987/03/i-have-a-question?lang=eng (accessed May 29, 2016). A more recent example of changes, from just one verse in the King James Version of the Bible, is the eleven variations found in 1 Chronicles 4:10 in the New King James Bible, from which the popular *The Prayer of Jabez* book was written. One of the most noticeable changes is "that I may not cause pain" in the NKJV from "that it may not grieve me" in the KJV. (See Bruce Wilkenson, *The Prayer of Jabez* [Sisters, OR: Multnomah Publishing, 2000], 92.) When the fifteen "translators" for the New International Version of the Bible were finished with their revision, more than forty-five thousand changes had been made. (See *The Federalist Patriot*, March 18, 2005.)
19. Royal Skousen, "Changes in the Book of Mormon," *Interpreter: A Journal of Mormon Scripture*, vol. 11 (2014), 173, http://www.mormoninterpreter.com/changes-in-the-book-of-mormon/ (accessed May 29, 2016).
20. Critics still attempt to discredit the Book of Mormon for its corrections, which are comparatively few and do not change any meanings in the message. Also, see Bob Smeitana, "Translators Hope Changes Will Make New Bible More Understandable" (in their new "*Common English Bible*," which also deletes "Begotten" Son), *Deseret News*, July 16, 2011.
21. Title Page, Book of Mormon.
22. Introduction, Book of Mormon
23. Doty, "I Have a Question: Why Is the Book of Mormon the 'Most Correct of Any Book on Earth?'" 28.
24. See Chapter 11 for more details.

Chapter 7

1. Evidence shows that the Americas were populated both before and after Book of Mormon times. "Archaeologists, ethnohistorians, and linguists in recent years have amassed data demonstrating beyond question that for at least four thousand years people, materials, and ideas have moved fluidly between the two American continents. . . . For example, a late Peruvian people like the Incas . . . can be safely assumed to incorporate genes and cultural elements from Book of Mormon peoples." (See John L. Sorenson, "Mesoamericans in Pre–Spanish South America," in John W. Welch, ed., *Reexploring the Book of Mormon* (Salt Lake City: Deseret Book, 1992), 215.

2. See John L. Sorenson, "The Year of the Jaredites," *BYU Today,* September 1968, 18–24. Some Fundamentalist Christians and some scholars of The Church of Jesus Christ of Latter-day Saints have accepted a date of around 2200 BC for the Tower of Babel, but information derived from secular Mesopotamia history indicates the date could be as early as 3100 BC. Sorenson suggests the possibilities could range from perhaps 3250 to 2800 BC and could be off by as much as several centuries on the earlier date.

3. See Chapter 19 for details on the beheading of Shiz by Coriantumr.

4. See David A. Palmer, *In Search of Cumorah* (Bountiful, UT: Horizon Publishers, 1981), 124–45. "In the past few decades archaeologists of the Olmecs have discovered many artifacts and characteristics of culture and civilization which can be seen as parallel to those described in the book of Ether." (See William J. Hamblin, "Jaredite Civilization," in Dennis L. Largey, ed., *Book of Mormon Reference Companion* (Salt Lake City: Deseret Book, 2003), 436.

5. See Michael Coe, *The Maya* (New York: Thames and Hudson, 1962), 90. See also *The Book of Mormon Archaeological Digest,* vol. 1, no. 1 (1998), 12.

6. Mariano Veytia, *Ancient America Rediscovered,* translated from Spanish to English by Rhonda Cunningham (Springville, UT: Bonneville Books, 2000), 40.

7. Marion G. Romney, "Repent or Perish," *Ensign,* April 1975, 3.

8. Robert F. Smith, "New Information about Mulek," in Welch, *Reexploring the Book of Mormon,* 142–43. See also Book of Mormon Central Knowhy #103.

9. John L. Sorenson, "Winds and Currents: A Look at Nephi's Ocean Crossing," in Welch, *Reexploring the Book of Mormon,* 53–55. In 2006, Heyerdahl's grandson and five others built a larger raft, *Tangarora,* and sailed from Peru to Tahiti—also to add to the belief that the South Sea Islands were settled by ancient mariners from South America. See Rick Vecchio, "Kon-Tiki-Style Raft Sails from Peru," *Deseret Morning News,* April 30, 2006, and "French Polynesia: Tangarora Raft Arrives in Tahiti," *Pacific Magazine,* August 2, 2006.

   In 1959, De Vere Baker sailed on his raft *Lehi IV* from the coast of California to Hawaii, making the twenty-eight-hundred-mile trip in sixty-nine days. Baker, a Mormon, wanted to prove the reasonability of Lehi and his band making the trip from Jerusalem to Central America, a distance of nineteen thousand miles, and to show that others later drifted back to settle the islands of the Pacific, a belief maintained by many of the islanders. According to 2 Nephi 10:21, "But great are the promises of the Lord unto them who are upon the isles of the sea; wherefore as it says isles, [and believing they were upon an isle] there must needs be more than this, and they are inhabited also by our brethren." See De Vere Baker, "I Drifted 2,800 Miles on a Raft," *American Weekly,* March 1, 1959, 2.

10. See Doug Mellgren, "Voyage of Kon-Tiki Challenged Theories on Migration," *Press Democrat,* April 19, 2002, 10.

11. See Paul R. Cheesman, "Transatlantic Crossings; A New Look," *Ensign,* January 1975, 50.

12. See John L Sorenson, "Digging into the *Book of Mormon,*" *Ensign,* September 1984, 30.

Chapter 8

1. Daniel C. Peterson, "Book of Mormon Economy and Technology," in Daniel H. Ludlow, ed., *Encyclopaedia of Mormonism,* 4 vols. (New York: Macmillan Publishing Company, 1992), 1:174.

2. See John L. Sorenson, "The New World Promised Land's Economic Base," *Insights,* vol. 23, no. 5 (2003), 5, 7, 8.

3. John W. Welch, "Good and True," in Susan Easton Black, ed., *Expressions of Faith* (Salt Lake City and Provo, UT: Deseret Book and Foundation for Ancient Research and Mormon Studies, 1996), 236–37.

4. John W. Welch, "The Execution of Zemnarihah," in John W. Welch, ed., *Reexploring the Book of Mormon* (Salt Lake City: Deseret Book, 1992), 250–51.

5. Welch, "Good and True," 236.

6. Hugh B. Nibley, *The Prophetic Book of Mormon* (Salt Lake City: Deseret Book, 1998), 224.

7. Nibley, *The Prophetic Book of Mormon,* 216.

8. Hugh Nibley, *The Prophetic Book of Mormon* (Salt Lake City and Provo, UT: Deseret Book and Foundation for Ancient Research and Mormon Studies, 1989), 8:221–22.

9. Richard P. Smith, "The Nephite Monetary System," *Improvement Era,* May, 1954, 316.

Chapter 9

1. Wayne A. Larsen, Alvin C. Rencher, and Tim Layton, "Who Wrote the Book of Mormon? An Analysis of Wordprints," *BYU Studies* vol. 20, no. 3, Spring 1980, 225–51.
2. *Book of Mormon Authorship*, Religious Studies Center, BYU, Larsen, Rencher, and Layton, "Who Wrote the Book of Mormon?" 159.
3. Ibid, 166.
4. Ibid, 163.
5. Ibid, 65.
6. John L. Hilton, "On Verifying Wordprint Studies," in Noel B. Reynolds, ed., *Book of Mormon Authorship Revisited* (Salt Lake City and Provo, UT: Deseret Book and Foundation of Ancient Research and Mormon Studies, 1997), 226.
7. L. La Mar Adams, "I Have a Question," *Ensign*, October 1984, 29. "Literary style in Hebrew is much more accessible to computer analysis than is English."
8. Adams, "I Have a Question," 29.
9. Adams, "I Have a Question," 29.
10. Adams, "I Have a Question," 29.
11. Hilton, "On Verifying Wordprint Studies," 174.
12. Hilton, "On Verifying Wordprint Studies, 226.
13. See Daniel Ludlow, "Research and Perspectives: Recent Studies on the Book of Mormon," *Ensign*, July 1989, 64.

Chapter 10

1. Two places that speak of a universal resurrection are: 2 Nephi 9:22 and Alma 40:4–5, 9–10.
2. Sheri Dew, *No Doubt About It* (Salt Lake City: Deseret Book, 2001), 161.
3. History attests that the prophecies were fulfilled. For a further discussion, see B. H. Roberts, *A Comprehensive History of The Church of Jesus Christ of Latter-day Saints*, 6 vols. (Salt Lake City: Deseret News Press, 1930), 1:293–303.
4. Aaron "was appointed by the Lord to assist Moses in bringing the children of Israel out of Egypt and to be his spokesman" (Exodus 4:10–16, 27–31). . . . On Mount Sinai Moses received directions about the appointment of Aaron and his four sons . . . to a priesthood that is known as the Aaronic Priesthood (Exodus 28:1–4, 29). On the completion of the tabernacle Moses consecrated them to their office (Leviticus 8:9–13)." (See "Aaron," Bible Dictionary, 599.)
5. Roberts, *Comprehensive History of the Church*, 6:183. This incident took place in the woods between Harmony, Pennsylvania, and Colesville, New York, on the banks of the Susquehanna River.
6. As related by President Boyd K. Packer during the missionary farewell sermon for his grandson, Richard Packer, in Kaysville, Utah, July 30, 2000 (based on notes taken by and in the possession of the author).
7. Henry Denzinger, *The Sources of Catholic Dogma*, Roy J. Deferrari, trans. (St. Louis, MO: Herder Book Company, 1957), 45.
8. Their experiences are related in Hartman Rector and Connie Rector, *No More Strangers*, 4 vols. (Salt Lake City: Bookcraft, 1973), 2:101–22. The four volumes of *No More Strangers*, 1971, 1973, 1976, and 1990, contain narratives written by many former ministers and others who have been baptized into The Church of Jesus Christ of Latter-day Saints.
9. "Harvard's First President: 'A Man for All Seasons,'" *Meridian Magazine*, August 7, 2001. Just before he left Cambridge (Harvard), Dunstar said, "I conceived then, and so do still that I spake the truth in the fear of God and dare not deny the same or go from it until the Lord otherwise teaches me."
10. See Frederick W. Babbel, *On Wings of Faith* (Salt Lake City: Bookcraft, 1972), 49.
11. See James E. Talmage, *The Vitality of Mormonism* (Salt Lake City: Deseret Book, 1948), 240.
12. See Daniel C. Peterson and Stephen D. Ricks, "Comparing LDS Beliefs with First-Century Christianity," *Ensign*, March 1988, 8. Members of The Church of Jesus Christ of Latter-day Saints spend many hours and considerable money performing this charitable act for others. The person for whom they are doing these proxy ordinances (baptism, marriage, and so forth) is free to accept or reject the ordinance. It seems only equitable that the person be given the choice regarding these proxy ordinances.
13. See Joseph Fielding Smith, comp., *Teachings of the Prophet Joseph Smith* (Salt Lake City: Deseret News Press, 1949), 253–54.
14. See Joseph Fielding Smith, "The Coming of Elijah," *Ensign*, January 1972, 5.
15. Matthew 22:30 and Mark 12:25 both state, "For in the resurrection they neither marry, nor are given in marriage, but are as the angels of God in heaven." These scriptures are not saying that people do not remain married after they are resurrected; rather, marriage is an ordinance that must take place on earth. Marriages in temples are ordained and recognized by God and are for time and eternity and will remain valid after death.
16. "The Temple Endowment, as administered in modern temples, comprises instruction relating to the significance and sequence of past dispensations, and the importance of the present as the greatest and grandest era in human history. The ordinances of the endowment embody certain obligations on the

part of the individual, such as covenant and promise to observe the law of strict virtue and chastity, to be charitable, benevolent, tolerant and pure; to devote both talent and material means to the spread of truth and the uplifting of the [human] race; to maintain devotion to the cause of truth; and to seek in every way to contribute to the great preparation that the earth may be made ready to receive her King—the Lord Jesus Christ. With the taking of each covenant and the assuming of each obligation a promised blessing is pronounced, contingent upon the faithful observance of the conditions." (James E. Talmage, rev. ed., *The House of the Lord* [Salt Lake City: Deseret Book, 1968], 83–84) Brigham Young said about the endowment: "Your endowment is, to receive all those ordinances in the house of the Lord, which are necessary for you, after you have departed this life, to enable you to walk back to the presence of the Father, passing the angels who stand as sentinels, being enabled to give them the key words, the signs and tokens, pertaining to the holy Priesthood, and gain your eternal exaltation in spite of earth and hell." (John A. Widstoe, ed. *Discourses of Brigham Young* [Salt Lake City: Deseret Book, 1941], 41)

17. G. Homer Durham, comp., *The Discourses of Wilford Woodruff* (Salt Lake City: Bookcraft, 1946), 89–90.

18. See Melvin J. Ballard, *Three Degrees of Glory* (Independence, MO: Zion's Printing, 1922), 21–22. (Melvin J. Ballard, who served as an Apostle in the Church from 1919 to 1939, was Bishop Ballard's son.) See also *Our Heritage: A Brief History of The Church of Jesus Christ of Latter-day Saints* (Salt Lake City: The Church of Jesus Christ of Latter-day Saints, 1996), 99.

19. Personal interview with Lucas by the author.

20. Robert E. Wells, *We Are Christians Because* (Salt Lake City: Deseret Book, 1985), 19.

21. Wells, *We Are Christians Because*, 24.

22. Joseph Fielding Smith, *Answers to Gospel Questions* (Salt Lake City: Deseret Book, 1979), 17–18.

23. See Bruce A. Van Orden, D. Brent Smith, and Everett Smith Jr., eds., *Pioneers in Every Land* (Salt Lake City: Bookcraft, 1997), 216–19.

24. See Richard R. Hopkins, *Biblical Mormonism* (Bountiful, UT: Horizon Publishers, 1994), 11–12.

25. C. S. Lewis, *Mere Christianity* (New York: HarperOne, 1952), 10–11

26. *Britannica World Dictionary*, 1965, 236.

27. Joseph Fielding McConkie, *Here We Stand* (Salt Lake City: Deseret Book, 1995), 182–83.

28. Richard R. Hopkins, *Biblical Mormonism* (Bountiful, UT: Horizon, 1994), 73.

29. Hopkins, *Biblical Mormonism*, 73–74.

30. Bruce R. McConkie, "Our Relationship with the Lord," Devotional Address, Brigham Young University, March 2, 1982.

31. See James Gleick, *Isaac Newton* (New York: Random House, Vintage Books Edition, 2003), 110.

32. *Testimonies* (Renfrew, Scotland: Scottish-Irish Mission, Compiled by Pres. Joseph fielding McConkie, 1960), 2–6.

33. Smith, *Teachings of the Prophet Joseph Smith*, 345.

34. Lewis, *Mere Christianity*, 205–206.

35. In Eliza R. Snow, *Biography and Family Record of Lorenzo Snow: One of the Twelve Apostles of the Church of Jesus Christ of Latter-day Saints* (Salt Lake City: Deseret News Company, 1884), 46; see also "The Grand Destiny of Man," *Deseret Evening News,* July 20, 1901, 22, https://www.lds.org/manual/teachings-of-presidents-of-the-church-lorenzo-snow/chapter-5-the-grand-destiny-of-the-faithful?lang=eng (accessed May 30, 2016). In 1909, the First Presidency of the Church issued a statement regarding the Church's doctrinal position on the creation and evolution: "Man is the child of God, formed in the divine image and endowed with divine attributes, and even as the infant son of an earthly father and mother is capable in due time of becoming a man, so the undeveloped offspring of celestial parentage is capable, by experience through ages and eons, of evolving into a God." (See Joseph F. Smith, John R. Winder, and Anthon H. Lund, "The Origin of Man," *Improvement Era,* November 1909, 81, https://www.lds.org/ensign/2002/02/the-origin-of-man?lang=eng (accessed May 30, 2016).

36. See Jordan Vajda, "'Partakers of the Divine Nature': A Comparative Analysis of Patristic and Mormon Doctrines of Divinization," *FARMS Occasional Papers,* (2002).

37. Donald C. Peterson and Stephen D. Ricks, "Comparing LDS Beliefs with First-Century Christianity," *Ensign,* March 1988, 8.

38. Do miracles still happen, and are prayers still answered? Routinely, members of The Church of Jesus Christ of Latter-day Saints will indeed say that miracles still happen and that prayers are still answered. An example of both is the family of fifteen-year-old Elizabeth Smart who was found alive on March 12, 2003, nine months after being kidnapped from her home in Salt Lake City, Utah. The prayers of millions were answered. Faith must be present for such miracles to occur, either on the part of the recipient, family members or friends, or the ones giving a blessing. Even so, a positive outcome is not automatic, and the answer is not always in the affirmative for the blessing being petitioned. The Lord is always in charge, and He knows the end from the beginning and the appropriate conclusion.

39. See Joseph Smith, *History of the Church of Jesus Christ of Latter-day Saints,* 7 vols. (Salt Lake City: Deseret Book, 1976), 4:3–5 footnote. These events took place on July 22, 1839.

40. See Steve Orton, "Latter-day Miracle among the Zuni," *Meridian Magazine,* March 2, 2007.

41. See "Study: Salt Lake Residents Give Most," Associated Press, *The Press Democrat*, Santa Rosa, CA, April 28, 2002, A2. The study also found that among the top twenty most-giving counties in the country, fourteen were located in Utah and Idaho, which contain "a large percentage of Mormons. In those counties, people gave 19 percent to 27 percent of their discretionary income to charity." (See also "New Englanders among Stingiest in Nation," Associated Press, TheBostonChannel.com, April 28, 2002.)

42. See Morgan Jones, "Recent survey finds that Mormons contribute more financially than other denominations but feel the lest pressure to donate." *Deseret News*, December 27, 2017.

43. The Lord gave a revelation to Joseph Smith in 1838 regarding administration of tithing funds. "The 18 Church leaders designated in the 120th section of the Doctrine and Covenants meet together to administer these sacred funds. Those of us who sit on that council know that this sacred responsibility is done in accordance with the Lord's 'voice unto them.' (See James E. Faust, "Opening the Windows of Heaven," *Ensign*, November 1998, 55.) The faithfulness of the members of the Church in paying their tithing and other donations has made it a wealthy church. However, we must recognize how that revenue is used and be aware of all the blessings it brings to the world.

44. "The Church and Its Financial Independence," Salt Lake City, Utah, July 12, 2012. This was a commentary in response to Bloomberg Businessweek, "Inside the Mormon Empire," July 16, 2012, a misleading article and magazine cover that mocked the Church.

45. See Robert D. Hales, "Tithing: A Test of faith with Eternal Blessings," *Ensign*, November 2002, 26–28.

Chapter 11

1. See Hugh Nibley, *The Prophetic Book of Mormon* (Salt Lake City and Provo, UT: Deseret Book and Foundation for Ancient Research and Mormon Studies, 1989), 228.

2. Nibley, *The Prophetic Book of Mormon*, 126.

3. Nibley, *The Prophetic Book of Mormon*, 236.

4. Daniel C. Peterson, Donald W. Parry, and John W. Welch, eds., *Echoes and Evidences of the Book of Mormon* (Provo, UT: Foundation of Ancient Research and Mormon Studies, 2002), 183. (From Robert Detweiler, "What Is a Sacred Text," *Semeia*, vol. 31 [1985], 213–30.)

5. William E. Berrett, *The Restored Church* (Salt Lake City: Deseret Book, 1973), 48.

6. "Bible" is a term of Greek origin, meaning a collection of writings that contain the records of divine revelation—the work of many prophets and inspired writers acting under the influence of the same Holy Spirit. (See Bible Dictionary, "Bible.") This being the case, the Book of Mormon could qualify as "The Bible of the New World."

7. See Bruce R. McConkie, "Come: Hear the Voice of the Lord," *Ensign*, December 1985, 55.

8. John L. Sorenson, "Digging into the Book of Mormon: Our Changing Understanding of the Book of Mormon and Its Ancient Scripture," *Ensign*, September 1984, 30.

9. See Robert L. Millet, "So Glorious a Record," *Ensign*, December 1992, 9.

10. Millet, "So Glorious a Record," 10.

11. Berrett, *The Restored Church*, 48.

12. Monte S. Nyman and Charles D. Tate Jr., eds., *Third Nephi 9–30: This Is My Gospel* (Provo, UT: Brigham Young University Religious Studies Center, 1993), 19.

13. See Michael B. Parker, "The Book of Mormon and the Fulness of the Gospel," FAIR, June 4, 2003.

14. Joseph Smith, *History of the Church of Jesus Christ of Latter-day Saints*, 7 vols. (Salt Lake City: Deseret Book, 1976), 4:461. "Taken in its entirety, the Prophet's statement refers to the correctness of the book in its religious setting."

Chapter 12

1. William J. Hamblin, "Warfare in the Book of Mormon," *Rediscovering the Book of Mormon* (Salt Lake City: Deseret Book, 1991), 241.

2. Hamblin, "Warfare in the Book of Mormon," 247–48. See Alma 43:23 for an example of the mixing of war and religion.

3. See Neal A. Maxwell, "The Book of Mormon: A Great Answer to 'The Great Question,'" *FARMS reprint*. See also Monte S. Nyman and Charles D. Tate Jr., eds., *The Book of Mormon: First Nephi, the Doctrinal Foundation* (Provo, UT: BYU Religious Studies Center, 1988), 8.

4. Hugh Nibley, *The Prophetic Book of Mormon* (Salt Lake City and Provo, UT: Deseret Book and Foundation for Ancient Research and Mormon Studies, 1998), 365–66.

5. See John W. Welch, *Reexploring the Book of Mormon* (Salt Lake City: Deseret Book, 1992), 32–34. "And other sheep I have, which are not of this fold" (John 10:16), Isaiah 11:11 concerning the "islands of the sea," and other verses that speak of the final conversion of the heathen were favorite scriptures of Columbus. (See Daniel C. Peterson, "Mounting Evidence for the Book of Mormon," *Ensign*, January 2000, 21.)

6. Welch, *Reexploring the Book of Mormon*, 33–34.

7. N. Eldon Tanner, "Pioneers Are Still Needed," *Ensign*, July 1976, 4. (Quoted from a general conference talk by Orson F. Whitney, October 1918.)

8. Bible Dictionary, "Atonement."
9. Spencer J. Condie, "The Fall and Infinite Atonement," *Ensign*, January 1996.
10. David Kupelian, "The Fall and Rise of American Christianity," excerpted from "The Marketing of Evil: How Radicals, Elitists and Pseudo-Experts Sell Us Corruption Disguised as Freedom," *Whistle Blower*, April 2005, 268.
11. C. S. Lewis, *Mere Christianity* (New York: Touchstone, 1996), 131.

Chapter 13
1. See Thomas Hoving, "King of the Confessors," *Reader's Digest*, December 1981, 250.
2. Noel B. Reynolds, "Shedding New Light on Ancient Origins," *Brigham Young Magazine*, Spring 1998, 40.
3. Three of the books Blaine M. Yorgason, Bruce W. Warren, and Harold Brown, *New Evidences of Christ in Ancient America* (Arlington, VA: Stratford Books, 1999); L. Taylor Hansen, *He Walked the Americas* (Amherst, WI: Amherst Press, 1963); and Milton R. Hunter, *Christ in Ancient America* (Salt Lake City: Deseret Book, 1959).
4. Two editions were *Weekly World News*, Lantana, FL, December 28, 1993, and March 20, 2001.
5. L. Taylor Hansen, *He Walked the Americas*, dust jacket.
6. See Yorgason, Warren, and Brown, *New Evidences of Christ in Ancient America*, 148–49.
7. George Potter, *Nephi and the Promised Land: More Evidences that the Book of Mormon Is a True History* (Springville, UT: Cedar Fort, 2009). Potter also documents legends of a bearded white God visiting Peru, Ecuador, Bolivia, and Chile. See also Sean Hoyt, "Viracocha: Christ Amon the Ancient Peruvians?" *BYU Studies* 54:1 (2015).
8. Carly M. Springer, "Tribe Knew Book of Mormon Stories Before Missionaries Arrived," *LDS Living*, April 8, 2015.
9. Mariano Veyta, *Ancient America Rediscovered* (Springville, UT: Bonneville Books, 2000), x–xi.
10. See Jack H. West, *The Trial of the Stick of Joseph* (Sacramento: Rich Publishing Co., 1971), 59.
11. Joseph Allen, "The White God Quetzalcoatl," http://www.nephiproject.com/white_god_quetzalcoatl. htm (accessed June 2, 2016). See also Joseph L. Allen and Blake J. Allen, *Exploring the Lands of the Book of Mormon*, 2nd ed. rev. (American Fork, UT: Covenant Communications, 2011), 309.
12. Allen and Allen, *Exploring the Lands of the Book of Mormon*, 309.
13. Allen and Allen, *Exploring the Lands of the Book of Mormon*, 311.
14. See Andrew C. Skinner, "Serpent Symbols and Salvation," *Journal of Book of Mormon Studies*, vol. 10, no. 2 (2001), 44–55.
15. W. Foerster, *Bemerkungen und Fragen zur Statte der Geburt Jesu*, ZDPV 57 (1934), 1–7.
16. Hugh Nibley, *An Approach to the Book of Mormon: Collected Works of Hugh Nibley* (Salt Lake City, and Provo, UT: Deseret Book and Foundation for Ancient Research and Mormon Studies, 1989), 6:469.
17. Reynolds, "Shedding New Light on Ancient Origins," 40.
18. Daniel C. Peterson, "Mounting Evidence for the Book of Mormon," *Ensign*, January 2000.
19. Noel B. Reynolds, ed., *Book of Mormon Authorship Revisited* "Is the Book of Mormon True? Notes on the Debate," chapter by Daniel Peterson, (Provo, UT: Foundation for Ancient Research and Mormon Studies, 1997), 144–45.
20. Hugh Nibley, "The Book of Mormon: True or False," in *The Prophetic Book of Mormon* (Salt Lake City and Provo, UT: Deseret Book and Foundation for Ancient Research and Mormon Studies, 1989), 233.
21. Noel B. Reynolds, ed., *Book of Mormon Authorship Rediscovered: The Evidence for Ancient Origins*, chapter by John L. Sorenson (Provo, UT: Foundation for Ancient Research and Mormon Studies, 1997), 398.

Chapter 14
1. Lucy Mack Smith, *History of Joseph Smith by His Mother* (Salt Lake City: Bookcraft, 1979), 83.
2. Paved highways existed during the pre–Inca period; one is known to have been four thousand miles long and wide enough for two wagons. It was once believed that wheels were unknown in this early period, but there is reason to believe that they were used to transport the huge stones used in their construction works. (Dewey Farnsworth, *The Americas Before Columbus* [El Paso, TX: Farnsworth Publishing Co., 1947], 94)
3. See John L. Sorenson, "Possible 'Silk' and 'Linen' in the Book of Mormon," in John Welch, ed., *Reexploring the Book of Mormon* (Salt Lake City and Provo, UT: Deseret Book and Foundation for Ancient Research and Mormon Studies, 1992), 162–63.
4. Robert R. Bennett, "Barley and Wheat in the Book of Mormon" (Provo, UT: Neal A. Maxwell Institute, 2000), http://maxwellinstitute.byu.edu/publications/transcripts/?id=126 (accessed June 13, 2016).
5. John L. Sorenson and Robert F. Smith, "Barley in Ancient America," in John W. Welch, ed., *Reexploring the Book of Mormon* (Salt Lake City and Provo, UT: Deseret Book and Foundation for Ancient Research and Mormon Studies, 1992), 130–31.
6. "Barley and Wheat in the Book of Mormon," FARMS Research Report, (August 2000.)

7. Lance Gibson and Garren Benson, "Origin History and Uses of Corn (Zea Mays), Iowa State University, Dept. of Agronomy, Revised January 2002.
8. Lance Gibson and Garren Benson, "Origin, History, and Uses of Corn (Zea Mays)," Iowa State University, Department of Agronomy, Revised January 2002.
9. See Kendall Stiles, "Democratic Government in Ancient America," *Ensign*, April 1992, 62.
10. See Valerie M. Hudson, "Principles of Government," in Dennis Largey, ed., *Book of Mormon Reference Companion* (Salt Lake City: Deseret Book, 2003), 303.
11. Paul H. Hopkinson, "Names in the Book of Mormon," in Dennis Largey, ed., *Book of Mormon Reference Companion* (Salt Lake City: Deseret Book, 2003), 580.
12. Nephi affirmed that he made the record "in the language of my father" (1 Nephi 1:2). This would be the same language the Jews were using to compile their hi story, which later became our Bible. See Arthur G. Pledger, "The 'W' and 'I,'" *Ensign*, September 1976, 25.
13. John A. Widstoe and Franklin S. Harris Jr., *Seven Claims of the Book of Mormon* (Independence, MO: Zion's Printing and Publishing, 1937), 52.
14. See Terryl L. Givens, *By the Hand of Mormon* (Oxford: Oxford University Press, 2002), 140.
15. See Daniel C. Peterson, "Mounting Evidence for the Book of Mormon," *Ensign*, January 2000, 20.
16. See Nibley, *Prophetic Book of Mormon* (Salt Lake City and Provo, UT: Deseret Book and Foundation for Ancient Research and Mormon Studies, 1979), 281.
17. Nibley, *Prophetic Book of Mormon*, 246.
18. See Givens, *By the Hand of Mormon*, 140.
19. See John A. Tvedtnes, "Scholarship in Mormonism and Mormonism in Scholarship," FAIR, 2001 Conference.

Chapter 15

1. Noel B. Reynolds, ed. "*Book of Mormon Authorship Revisited*:" Foundation for Ancient Research and Mormon Studies, chapter by Royal Skousen, "Translating the Book of Mormon,"(1997), 88. Royal Skousen is professor of English at Brigham Young University and since 1988 has served as the editor of the Book of Mormon critical text project.
2. John A. Tvedtnes, "The Hebrew Background of the Book of Mormon," in John L. Sorenson and Melvin J. Thorne, eds., *Rediscovering the Book of Mormon* (Salt Lake City and Provo, UT: Deseret Book and Foundation for Ancient Research and Mormon Studies, 1991), 77–78.
3. See Russell M. Nelson, "A Treasured Testament," *Ensign*, July 1993, 61. Adapted from an address given June 15, 1992, at a seminar for new mission presidents, Missionary Training Center, Provo, Utah.
4. Nelson, "A Treasured Testament," 61.
5. Tvedtnes, "The Hebrew Background of the Book of Mormon," 79–89.
6. Tvedtnes, "The Hebrew Background of the Book of Mormon," 79–89.
7. Hugh B. Nibley, *Prophetic Book of Mormon* (Salt Lake City and Provo, UT: Deseret Book and Foundation for Ancient Research and Mormon Studies, 1989), 227.
8. Tvedtnes, "The Hebrew Background of the Book of Mormon," 32–37.
9. John W. Welch, "Chiasmus in the Book of Mormon," in Noel B. Reynolds, ed., *Book of Mormon Authorship* (Salt Lake City: Bookcraft, 1982), 34, 41– 43, 51.
10. H. Clay Gorton and editors of Ancient American Foundation, "A New Witness for Christ: Chiastic Structures in the Book of Mormon," *Meridian Magazine*, February 27, 2007.
11. See John W. Welch, "Benjamin's Speech: A Classic Ancient Farewell Address," in John L. Sorenson and Melvin J. Thorne, eds., *Reexploring the Book of Mormon* (Salt Lake City and Provo, UT: Deseret Book and Foundation for Ancient Research and Mormon Studies, 1992), 120–21.
12. Richard Dilworth Rust, "Poetry in the Book of Mormon," in Sorenson and Thorne, *Rediscovering the Book of Mormon*, 100, 113.
13. See Donald W. Parry, "Hebrew Literary Patterns in the Book of Mormon," *Ensign*, October 1989, 58–61.
14. You can hear a beautiful song sung as a solo or a trio, on the web inspired from these words. Search on the name of the song: "O That I Were an Angel."
15. See Joseph Fielding Smith, *Answers to Gospel Questions* (Salt Lake City: Deseret Book, 1963), 141–42.
16. See Keith Terry, *Out of Darkness* (American Fork, UT: Covenant Communications, 1995), 114–16.
17. See Gail Call, "Antenantiosis in the Book of Mormon," *Meridian Magazine*, June 4, 2001.
18. See Larry Childs, "Epanalepsis in the Book of Mormon," *Meridian Magazine*, October 16, 2001.

Chapter 16

1. Hugh B. Nibley, *The Prophetic Book of Mormon*, The Collected Works of Hugh Nibley, vol. 8 (Salt Lake City and Provo, UT: Deseret Book and Foundation for Ancient Research and Mormon Studies), 227–28.
2. Hugh B. Nibley, *The Prophetic Book of Mormon*, 227–28.
3. "Good People and Bad People," in *Collected Works of Hugh Nibley*, 7:337-38
4. The Nibley Collection—Eduard Meyer's Comparison of Mohammed & Joseph Smith, Para. 1-2 https://sites.lib.byu.edu/nibley/1900/01/01/eduard-meyers-comparison-of-mohammed-joseph-smith/

5. The Nibley Collection—Eduard Meyer's Comparison of Mohammed & Joseph Smith, Para. 49 https://sites.lib.byu.edu/nibley/1900/01/01/eduard-meyers-comparison-of-mohammed-joseph-smith/
6. Richard H. Cracroft, "Had for Good and Evil—19th-Century Literary Treatments of the Book of Mormon" in *Journal of Book of Mormon Studies, Vol.* 12: No. 2, p.7.
7. Cracroft, "Had for Good and Evil—19th-Century Literary Treatments of the Book of Mormon." 7.
8. Cracroft, "Had for Good and Evil—19th-Century Literary Treatments of the Book of Mormon." 7.
9. Cracroft, "Had for Good and Evil—19th-Century Literary Treatments of the Book of Mormon." 7.
10. Richard L. Bushman, Joseph Smith and the Beginnings of Mormonism. (Urbana, Univ. of Illinois, 1984), 124-25.
11. Richard L. Bushman, Joseph Smith and the Beginnings of Mormonism. (Urbana, Univ. of Illinois, 1984),
12. Terryl L. Givens, By the Hand of Mormon: The American Scripture That Launched a New World Religion (New York: Oxford Univ. Press, 2002), 94.
13. See the Millennial Harbinger, (7 February 1831)
14. Alexander Campbell, *Delusions: An Analysis of the Book of Mormon, with an Examination of Its Internal and External Evidences, and a Refutation of Its Pretence to Divine Authority* (Boston, 1832).
15. Campbell, *Delusions*, 11, 15.
16. Cracroft, "Had for Good and Evil—19th-Century Literary Treatments of the Book of Mormon." 7.
17. *Mormonism Unvailed,* (Painesville, OH, Eber D. Howe, 1834), 289-90.
18. Cracroft, "Had for Good and Evil—19th-Century Literary Treatments of the Book of Mormon." 8.
19. Cracroft, "Had for Good and Evil—19th-Century Literary Treatments of the Book of Mormon." 11-12.
20. Twain, *Roughing It*, 115.
21. Cracroft, "Had for Good and Evil—19th-Century Literary Treatments of the Book of Mormon." 13.
22. Hugh W. Nibley, *No Mam That's Not History, https://publications.mi.byu.edu/fullscreen/?pub=971*
23. Hugh W. Nibley, "Sounding Brass," CWHN 11:581-82
24. Smoot, Stephen O. "Review of John Christopher Thomas, "A Pentecostal Reads the Book of Mormon: A Literary and Theological Introduction." *Interpreter: A Journal of Mormon Scripture* 21 (2016): 291-92.
25. John A. Tvedtness, Scholarship in Mormonism and Mormonism in Scholarship, https://www.fairmormon.org/conference/august-2001/scholarship-in-mormonism-and-mormonism-in-scholarship).
26. John W. Welch, Responses to Margaret Barker, May 2, 2008, http://tandtclark.typepad.com/ttc/2008/05/responses-to-ma.htm)
27. See Don L. Searle, "The Book Convinced Him," *Ensign*, March 1990, 50–52.
28. David A. Palmer, *In Search of Cumorah* (Bountiful, UT: Horizon Publishers, 1992), 220.
29. Daniel C. Peterson, "Editor's Introduction: American Apocrypha?" *FARMS Review of Books on the Book of Mormon*, vol. 1, no. 1 (2001).

Chaper 17

1. Elder LeGrand Richards reported hearing Elder Charles A. Callis, a late Apostle of The Church of Jesus Christ of Latter-day Saints, tell of this incident. See Brent L. Top, "The Remarkable Book That Changes Lives," *Meridian Magazine*, January 6, 2004.
2. Gordon B. Hinckley, "Jesus is the Christ," *Ensign*, November 1984, 52.
3. See John A. Tvedtnes, "More on Recent Archaeological Discoveries," *FARMS Insights*, no. 113, August 1997, 2. A 1997 report that describes evidence for humans living in southern Chile at Monte Verde some 12,500 years ago has caused archaeologists to question the theory that all Amerindians came to the New World across the Bering Strait—as previously thought. Evidence shows ancient farmers lived in Mexico over six thousand years ago. See Paul Recer, "Discovery: Early settlers Farmed in Mexico over 6,000 Years Ago," *The Press Democrat*, May 18, 2001, A10. Archaeologists working in Peru uncovered the ruins of a city more than a thousand years older that any previously reported in the Americas. Radiocarbon analysis dates the city of Caral to between 2627 BC to 2000 BC. See Guy Gugliotta, "4,000-Year-Old City Found in Peru," *The Press Democrat*, April 27, 2001.
4. John L. Sorenson, "When Lehi's Party Arrived in the Land, Did They Find Others There?" *Journal of Book of Mormon Studies*, vol. 1, no. 1 (1992), 8.
5. "Iron Sword from the Time of Jeremiah Discovered Near Jericho," *Ensign*, June 1987, 57.
6. "Challenging Conventional Views of Metal," http://publications.mi.byu.edu/fullscreen/?pub=1121&index=44 (accessed June 3, 2016).
7. Lynn Rosenvall and David Rosenvall, *A New Approach to Book of Mormon Geography* (Provo, UT: Brigham Young University Press, 2013), 368–76.
8. George Potter, "Ten Reasons Why the Book of Mormon Took Place in Peru," Reasons 2 and 3, *Mormon Matters*, September 27, 2009, http://mormonmatters.org/2009/12/03/peruvian-setting-for-the-book-of-mormon/ (accessed June 4, 2016).
9. The most common cement, Portland cement, was patented in 1824 by a British bricklayer, Joseph Aspdin. The first Portland cement in the United States was at Coplay, Pennsylvania, in 1871. *Book Encyclopaedia*, vol. 3, (1975), 256.
10. See David A. Palmer, *In Search of Cumorah* (Bountiful, UT: Horizon, 1992), 121–22.

11. See Matthew G. Wells and John W. Welch, "Concrete Evidence for the Book of Mormon," *FARMS Update*, no. 76, May 1991. See also Matthew G. Wells and John W. Welch, "Concrete Evidence for the Book of Mormon," in John W. Welch, ed., *Reexploring the Book of Mormon* (Salt Lake City and Provo, UT: Deseret Book and Foundation for Ancient Research and Mormon Studies, 1992), 212–13.
12. Wells and Welch, "Concrete Evidence for the Book of Mormon," 212.
13. Rosenvall and Rosenvall, *A New Approach to Book of Mormon Geography*," 238.
14. Rosenvall and Rosenvall, *A New Approach to Book of Mormon Geography*," 235.
15. Jack H. West, *Trial of the Stick of Joseph* (Provo, UT: Brigham Young University, 1954), 68, 84.
16. See John L. Sorenson, *Wheeled Figurines in the Ancient World*, FARMS Preliminary Report (Provo, UT: Foundation or Ancient Research and Mormon Studies, 1983), 14–15.
17. Rosenvall and Rosenvall, *A New Approach to Book of Mormon Geography*, 226–28.
18. See John L. Sorenson, *Images of Ancient America, Visualizing Book of Mormon Life* (Provo, UT: Research Press, Foundation for Ancient Research and Mormon Studies, 1998), 59.
19. Palmer, *In Search of Cumorah*, 122.
20. "Horse Bones That Date 60 Years Prior to the Spaniards," Book of Mormon Archaeological Forum, August 6, 2013.
21. John L. Sorenson, "Once More: The Horse," in John W. Welch, ed., *Reexploring the Book of Mormon* (Salt Lake City: Deseret Book, 1992), 99.
22. "Were Ancient Americans Familiar with Real Horses?" *Journal of Book of Mormon Studies*, vol. 10, no. 1 (2001), 76–77.
23. Rosenvall and Rosenvall, *A New Approach to Book of Mormon Geography*, 355.
24. See Diane E. Wirth, *A Challenge to the Critics* (Bountiful, UT: Horizon Publishers, 1986), 55–56.
25. FARMS Research Report, Updated, August 2000. Once More the Horse?
26. Ludwell H. Johnson III, "Men and Elephants in America," *Scientific Monthly* 75 (1952), 220 as quoted by Hugh Nibley, *The Prophetic Book of Mormon* (Salt Lake City and Provo, UT: Deseret Book and Foundation for Ancient Research and Mormon Studies, 1998), 111.
27. Wirth, *A Challenge to the Critics*, 51. Information from Hyatt Verrill and Ruth Verrill, *America's Ancient Civilizations* (New York: G. P. Putnam's Sons, 1953), 132–33.
28. Nibley, *Prophetic Book of Mormon*, 111.
29. Wirth, *A Challenge to the Critics*, 51.
30. Rosenvall and Rosenvall, *A New Approach to Book of Mormon Geography*, 359.
31. Matthew Roper, "Swords and Cimeters in the Book of Mormon," *Journal of Book of Mormon Studies*, vol. 8, no. 1 (Provo, UT: Maxwell Institute, 1999), 34–43, 77–78.
32. Daniel C. Peterson, "Mounting Evidence for the Book of Mormon," *Ensign*, January 2000, 22.
33. See John A. Tvedtnes, "Historical Parallels to the Destruction at the Time of Crucifixion," *Journal of Book of Mormon Studies*, Spring 1994, 176–77, 170–72.
34. William E. Berrett, *The Restored Church* (Salt Lake City: Deseret Book, 1956), 65.
35. See John L. Sorenson, "The Submergence of the City of Jerusalem in the Land of Nephi," *Insights*, vol. 22, no. 4 (2002), http://publications.mi.byu.edu/fullscreen/?pub=1291&index=2 (accessed June 4, 2016).
36. See Benjamin R. Jordan, "Volcanic Destruction in the Book of Mormon: Possible Evidence from Ice Cores," *Journal of Book of Mormon Studies*, vol. 12, no. 1 (2003), 80–87.
37. Dewey Farnsworth, *The Americas Before Columbus* (El Paso, TX: Farnsworth Publishing, 1947), 41.
38. Daniel C. Peterson, *The Book of Mormon and DNA Research* (Provo, UT: The Neal A. Maxwell Institute for Religious Scholarship, 2008).
39. Michael R. Ash, "The Book of Mormon and DNA Research," Foundation for Apologetic Information and Research, 2004.
40. Thomas W. Murphy and Simon Southern, "Genetic Research: A 'Galileo Event' for Mormons," *Anthropology News*, vol. 44, no. 2, February 2003.
41. Gospel Topics Guide - DNA and the Book of Mormon – 2016
42. John L. Sorenson and John W. Welch, "The Sobering Lesson of the Grolier Codex," in John W. Welch and Melvin J. Thorne, eds., *Pressing Forward with the Book of Mormon* (Provo, UT: Foundation for Ancient Research and Mormon Studies, 1999), 296–98.
43. Dallin H. Oaks, "The Historicity of the Book of Mormon," FARMS Banquet Speech, October 29, 1993; emphasis added.

Chapter 18
1. Pratt, Parley P., *The Autobiography of Parley P. Pratt*, (Deseret Book Company, Salt Lake City, 1938), p. 37
2. *The Autobiography of Parley P. Pratt*. p. 298-99.
3. Robert J. Matthews, (Church News, November 2, 1991),
4. Susan Easton Black, Ed., chapter by Richard D. Rust. "Questions Answered," (Expressions of Faith, Testimonies of LDS Scholars, Deseret Book, SLC, 1996), 226.

5. Transcript: Elder Jeffrey R. Holland on the 175th Anniversary of Orson Hyde's Historic Journey, BYU Jerusalem Center, October 27, 2016, http://www.mormonnewsroom.org/article/transcript-elder-holland-return-of-the-jews

6. Victor L. Ludlow, The Scattering and Gathering of Israel: God's Covenant with Abraham Remembered through the Ages in Window of Faith: Latter-day Saint Perspectives on World History. https://rsc.byu.cdu/archived/window-faith-latter-day-saint-perspectives-world-history/scattering-and-gathering-israel

7. Victor L. Ludlow, The Scattering and Gathering of Israel: God's Covenant with Abraham Remembered through the Ages in Window of Faith: Latter-day Saint Perspectives on World History. https://rsc.byu.edu/archived/window-faith-latter-day-saint-perspectives-world-history/scattering-and-gathering-israel

8. D. Todd Christofferson at Library of Congress, "America Reads" and the Book of Mormon, transcript. http://www.mormonnewsroom.org/article/transcript-elder-d-todd-christofferson-library-of-congress

9. John F. Heidenreich, "It Taught Me the Bible," (The Ensign, September 1976), 22.

Chapter 19

1. Jim Morrison, "Real Chills, Evan Hunter, Author," *Spirit*, February 1996, 39.

2. See Noel Reynolds, *Book of Mormon Authorship Revisited: The Evidence for Ancient Origins* (Salt Lake City and Provo, UT: Deseret Book and Foundation for Ancient Research and Mormon Studies, 1997), 145–46.

3. See Reynolds, *Book of Mormon Authorship Revisited*, 255, 263–64.

4. See John L. Sorenson, "When Lehi's Party Arrived in the Land, Did They Find Others There?" *Journal of Book of Mormon Studies*, vol. 1, no. 1 (1992).

5. See Noel Reynolds, "From a Faithful Point of View," *This People*, Spring 1997, 25.

6. See Reynolds, *Book of Mormon Authorship Revisited*, 283, 287.

7. Reynolds, *Book of Mormon Authorship Revisited*, 12.

8. *Insights*, FARMS Update, November 1994 (see original in *BYU Studies*, vol. 33 (1993), 324–25).See also Book of Mormon Central Knowhy #248.

9. Hugh Nibley, *The Prophetic Book of Mormon* (Salt Lake City and Provo, UT: Deseret Book and Foundation for Ancient Research and Mormon Studies, 1989), 225, 227; emphasis added.

10. See Chapter 7 regarding the twenty-four plates of Ether and the history of the Jaredites.

11. See David Rolph Seely, "Chronology, Book of Mormon," in Dennis Largey, *Book of Mormon Reference Companion* (Salt Lake City: Deseret Book, 2003), 196–97.

12. See John P. Pratt, "The Nephite Calendar," *Meridian Magazine,* January 14, 2004. Also reviewed in John P. Pratt, "Book of Mormon Chronology," in Daniel H. Ludlow, ed., *Encyclopaedia of Mormonism*, 4 vols. (New York: Macmillan, 1992), 1:169–71.) Several of the problems some have proposed with Book of Mormon dates are resolved by Pratt in his research on the Nephi calendar model.

13. John W. Welch, "Good and True," in Susan Easton Black, ed., *Expressions of Faith* (Salt Lake City: Deseret Book, 1996), 237.

Chapter 20

1. Brent L. Top, *"The Remarkable Book That Changes Lives,"* Meridian Magazine, January 6, 2004.

2. See Hugh B. Brown, "Profile of a Prophet," general conference talk, October 1967.

3. See Darl Anderson, *Soft Answers to Hard Questions* (Mesa, AZ: Cox Printing, 1992), 55–56.

4. B. H. Roberts, *Defense of the Faith and the Saints* (Provo, UT: Maasai Publishing, 2002), 225–26.

5. "Publications almost without number have appeared denouncing the Book of Mormon as a hoax and a fraud. Most of them have enjoyed briefly the popularity occasioned by curiosity, and then largely been forgotten." See William E. Berrett, *The Restored Church* (Salt Lake City: Deseret Book, 1949), 80.

6. See Noel B. Reynolds, *Book of Mormon Authorship Revisited: The Evidence for Ancient Origins* (Provo, UT: Foundation for Ancient Research and Mormon Studies, 1997), 103.

7. Ted L. Gibbons, "Deseret Blossoms," *LDS Living*, September 6, 2003.

8. See Keith W. Perkins, "Francis W. Kirkham: A 'New witness' for the Book of Mormon," *Ensign*, July 1984, 57.

9. See John W. Welch, "A Book You Can Respect," *Ensign*, September 1977, 48.

10. Hugh Nibley, *The Prophetic Book of Mormon* (Salt Lake City and Provo, UT: Deseret Book and Foundation for Ancient Research and Mormon Studies, 1992), 8:255.

11. Nibley, *Prophetic Book of Mormon*, 128–29.

12. Daniel H. Ludlow, ed., *The Church and Society* (Salt Lake City: Deseret Book, 1992), 20.

13. Nibley, *Prophetic Book of Mormon*, 148.

14. Ludlow, *The Church and Society.*

15. James E. Talmage, *Articles of Faith*, 26th ed. (Salt Lake City: Church of Jesus Christ of Latter-day Saints, 1948), 502.

16. Noel B. Reynolds, Ed., B*ook of Mormon Authorship,* Chapter by Richard Lloyd Anderson, (Bookcraft, Salt Lake City, Utah, 1982) 218–19.

17. See Noel B. Reynolds, "The Authorship of the Book of Mormon," BYU Forum Assembly, May 27, 1997.

18. Robert Brown and Rosemary Brown, *They Lie in Wait to Deceive* (Mesa, AZ: Brownsworth Publishing, 1963), 2:251.
19. Brown and Brown, *They Lie in Wait to Deceive*, 251. Non-Mormon historian Lawrence Foster faulted the Tanners for "twisting" scholarship, resorting to "debaters' ploys," and, in general, demonstrating "lack of balance and perspective." See Terryl L. Givens, *By the Hand of Mormon* (New York: Oxford University Press, 2002), 144. Jerald Tanner died in 2006 of Alzheimer's disease.
20. Nibley, *Prophetic Book of Mormon*, 84. See also 194–201.
21. John W. Welch, "*View of the Hebrews,* 'An Unparallel,'" *Meridian Magazine*, May 16, 2001.
22. See Dennis Lythgoe, "'Lost Books' Is Iconoclastic," *Deseret Morning News*, April 30, 2006.
23. David Bitton, "I Don't Have a Testimony of the History of the Church," 2004 FAIR Conference talk.
24. Glenn L. Pearson, *Moroni's Promise* (Salt Lake City: Bookcraft, 1995), 11–12.
25. Robert Dellenbach, "The Miraculous Translation of the Book of Mormon," *New Era*, June 1996, 6–7.
26. See chapter by Willfred Griggs in Noel B. Reynolds, *Book of Mormon Authorship Revisited*, 77.
27. See Reynolds, *Book of Mormon Authorship Revisited*, 99–100.
28. See Richard Inwood, *Take Heed That Ye Be Not Deceived* (Salt Lake City: R. I. Winwood, 1995)..
29. See Justin Hart, "Winning the Battle and Not Knowing It—*The New Mormon Challenge* Reviewed," *Meridian Magazine*, June 25, 2002. See also Francis Beckwith, Carl Mosser, and Paul Owen, *The New Mormon Challenge* (Grand Rapids, MI: Zondervan Publishing, 2002).
30. Carl Mosser and Paul Owen, "Mormon Apologetic, Scholarship and Evangelical Neglect: Losing the Battle and Not Knowing It?" 1997 Evangelical Theological Society Far West Annual Meeting, April 2, 1997, 2.
31. Gordon B. Hinckley, *Stand a Little Taller* (Salt Lake City: Deseret Book, 2001), 91.
32. Mosser and Owen, "Mormon Apologetic, Scholarship and Evangelical Neglect, Losing the Battle and Not Knowing It?" 2.
33. Joseph Smith, *History of the Church of Jesus Christ of Latter-day Saints*, 7 vols. (Salt Lake City: Deseret Book, 1976), 2:443.
34. Jeffrey R. Holland, "Safety for the Soul," *Ensign*, November 2009, 49.
35. Gordon B. Hinckley, Boston Massachusetts Regional Conference, priesthood session, April 22, 1995, reported in *The Church News*, January 6, 1996, 2.

Chapter 21

1. See David Brooks, "A True Spokesman for Evangelical Christians," *New York Times/The Press Democrat*, December 1, 2004.
2. LeGrand Richards, *A Marvelous Work and a Wonder* (Salt Lake City: Deseret Book, 1976), 55–56.
3. Information describing the Urim and Thummim is given in Chapter 2.
4. Lucy Mack Smith, *History of Joseph Smith by His Mother* (Salt Lake City: Bookcraft, 1979), 119.
5. See William E. Berrett, *The Restored Church* (Salt Lake City: Deseret Book, 1973), 33.
6. "Dr. Mitchell had studied classics; had received medical and scientific training; was a professor of natural history, chemistry, and agriculture at Columbia; and had served as a vice president of Rutgers Medical College. He was recognized as a 'living encyclopedia.'" (Milton V. Backman, "Anthon Transcript," in Dennis L. Largey, ed., *Book of Mormon Reference Companion* [Salt Lake City: Deseret Book, 2003], 64)
7. "What Did Charles Anthon Really Say?" *FARMS Update*, May 1985. Professor Anthon wrote two letters in 1834 and 1841. Both letters deny Martin Harris's account, and both contradict each other. In the first letter, he wrote that he gave Harris a written opinion; but in the second, he denied he had ever been asked to write anything concerning his encounter with him. He was, no doubt, worrying about his prestigious standing among his peers. Also, neither he nor anyone else at that date (except Joseph Smith) could have translated the characters Martin Harris brought to him. Anthon perhaps realized his bluff would be found out. See B. H. Roberts, *Comprehensive History of the Church*, 6 vols. (Salt Lake City: Deseret News Press, 1930), 1:102–108; Richard L. Bushman, *Joseph Smith and the Beginnings of Mormonism* (Champaign, IL: University of Illinois Press, 1988), 87–88; and Milton V. Backman, "Eyewitness Accounts of the Restoration," *Church News*, January 16, 1993.
8. Although the general meaning of *etz* is wood, this could be translated as tree, timber, helve, plank, stalk, staff, stock, gallows—the context determining how the word would be used. It was translated as *wood* in 250 out of 300 uses of *etz* by the Jewish translators. See Keith Meservy, "Ezekiel's Sticks and the Gathering of Israel," *Ensign*, February 1987, 4.
9. See Meservy, "Ezekiel's Sticks and the Gathering of Israel," 4–9.
10. Meservy, "Ezekiel's Sticks and the Gathering of Israel," 24.
11. Meservy, "Ezekiel's Sticks and the Gathering of Israel," 25.
12. Meservy, "Ezekiel's Sticks and the Gathering of Israel," 25.
13. Richards, *A Marvelous Work and a Wonder*, 68.
14. Read Genesis 49:3–38 for the complete blessing.
15. See also Ray Lynn Huntington, "Other Sheep," in Dennis L. Largey, *Book of Mormon Reference Companion* (Salt Lake City: Deseret Book, 2003), 624.

16. Richards, *A Marvelous Work and a Wonder*, 65.
17. George A. Horton Jr., "Prophecies in the Bible about Joseph Smith," *Ensign*, January 1989, 200–219.
18. W. Cleon Skousen, Treasures from the Book of Mormon, 4 vols. (Salt Lake City: Ensign Publishing, 1998), 1:ii–iii.
19. W. Cleon Skousen, *Treasures from the Book of Mormon*, 4 vols. (Salt Lake City: Ensign Publishing, 1998), 1:ii–iii.
20. Yes, it would be easy for someone writing a book to add prophecies about himself or herself; however, it should be apparent to the reader, by now, that it would have been impossible for the poorly educated Joseph Smith to have written such a profound and complex book as the Book of Mormon and to have gotten so many things right..
21. Dennis K. Brown, *Evidences of the True Church* (Bountiful, UT: Horizon Publishers, 2002), 38–39.
22. Monte S. Nyman, "Book Proves Truth of Scriptures—The Restoration of the Plain and Precious Parts: The Book of Helaman," *Church News*, February 8, 1992.
23. Gaye Strathearn and Jacob Moody, "Christ's Interpretation of Isaiah 52's 'My Servant,'" in *Journal of Book of Mormon and Other Restoration Scripture*, vol. 18, no. 1 (2009),13.
24. See Bruce R. McConkie, *Mormon Doctrine* (Salt Lake City: Bookcraft, 1966), 43.
25. See F. Enzio Busche, "Christianity and the Hope of the Future," in *The Prophet and His Work* (Salt Lake City: Deseret Book, 1996), 134–45.
26. Thomas Jefferson, letter to Thomas Whitmore, June 5, 1822, quoted from James A. Haught, ed., *2000 Years of Disbelief: Famous People with the Courage to Doubt* (Amherst, NY: Prometheus Books, 1996).
27. Statement of rejection of formal sectarian organizations and claims, as quoted in William Cullen Bryan t, ed., *Picturesque America* (New York: D. Appleton and Company, 1874), 503. Also, see Richards, *A Marvelous Work and a Wonder*, 29. See also *Funk and Wagnalls New Encyclopedia* (New York: Funk and Wagnalls, 1972), 136–37.
28. H. A. Washington, ed., *The Writings of Thomas Jefferson*, 9 vols. (Washington, DC: Taylor and Maury, 1853–54), 7:210.

Chapter 22

1. See William E. Berrett, *The Restored Church* (Salt Lake City: Deseret Book, 1973), 56–57.
2. Joseph Smith, *History of the Church of Jesus Christ of Latter-day Saints*, 7 vols. (Salt Lake City: Deseret Book, 1976), 1:54–55.
3. Smith, *History of the Church,* 1:54–55.
4. Smith, *History of the Church,* 1:55.
5. Lucy Mack Smith, *The Revised and Enhanced History of Joseph Smith by His Mother*, Scot Facer Proctor and Maurine Jensen Proctor, eds. (Salt Lake City: Deseret Book, 1996), 281.
6. Gordon B. Hinckley, *Truth Restored: A Short History of The Church of Jesus Christ of Latter-day Saints* (Salt Lake City: The Church of Jesus Christ of Latter-day Saints, 2001), 25.
7. B. H. Roberts, *A Comprehensive History of The Church of Jesus Christ of Latter-day Saints*, 6 vols. (Salt Lake City: The Church of Jesus Christ of Latter-day Saints, 1930), 1:147.
8. See Berrett, *The Restored Church*, 74.
9. Richard Lloyd Anderson, "Witnesses of the Book of Mormon," in Dennis L. Largey, ed., *Book of Mormon Reference Companion* (Salt Lake City: Deseret Book, 2003), 789–90.
10. Richard Lloyd Anderson, *Investigating the Book of Mormon Witnesses* (Salt Lake City: Deseret Book, 1981), 56.
11. See Richard Lloyd Anderson, "Book of Mormon Witnesses," Daniel H. Ludlow, ed., 4 vols. *Encyclopedia of Mormonism* (New York: Macmillan Publishing Company, 1992), 1:214.
12. BYU Symposium on Oliver Cowdery, *Insights*, vol. l, no. 26 (2006), 1, 7.
13. Anderson, *Investigating the Book of Mormon Witnesses*, 54.
14. Anderson, *Investigating the Book of Mormon Witnesses*, 53, 42–45.
15. Anderson, *Investigating the Book of Mormon Witnesses*, 63.
16. See Scott H. Faulring, "The Return of Oliver Cowdery," *Ensign*, August 2002, 18.
17. Faulring, "The Return of Oliver Cowdery," Maxwell Institute, 2002.
18. Berrett, *The Restored Church*, 56.
19. Anderson, *Investigating the Book of Mormon Witnesses*, 83–84.
20. Proctor and Proctor, *The Revised and Enhanced History of Joseph Smith by His Mother*, 206.
21. Anderson, *Investigating the Book of Mormon Witnesses*, 68–69.
22. *Church History in the Fulness of Times* (Salt Lake City: LDS Church Educational System, 1993), 187.
23. See Anderson, *Investigating the Book of Mormon Witnesses*, 69.
24. "David Whitmer," in Andrew Jenson, ed., *LDS Biographical Encyclopedia: A Compilation of Biographical Sketches of Prominent Men and Women in the Church of Jesus Christ of Latter-day Saints* (Salt Lake City: Andrew Jenson Printing Company, 1914), 1:263.
25. Proctor and Proctor, *The Revised and Enhanced History of Joseph Smith by His Mother*, 206.
26. See B. H. Roberts, *Defense of the Faith and the Saints* (Provo, UT: Maasai Publishing, 2002), 419.

27. *Doctrine and Covenants Student Manual* (Salt Lake City: Church Educational System, 1981), 33.
28. Anderson, *Investigating the Book of Mormon Witnesses*, 110.
29. Anderson, *Investigating the Book of Mormon Witnesses*, 111.
30. See Dallin H. Oaks, "The Witness: Martin Harris," *Ensign*, May 1999, 37.
31. Oaks, "The Witness: Martin Harris," 37.
32. Berrett, *The Restored Church*, 75–76.
33. Anderson, *Investigating the Book of Mormon Witnesses*, 96–97.
34. Berrett, *The Restored Church*, 76.
35. Doreen Virtue has authored many books about angels and is a firm believer that they communicate with people on earth. See Doreen Virtue, "My Guardian Angel," *Woman's World*, October 8, 2012, 38. Cristy Lane has made "I Believe in Angels" a popular song in the United States. "Touched by an Angel" was a popular TV series for many years, and *Guideposts* publishes a bimonthly magazine titled *Angels on Earth*.
36. "Spirituality in America: God Fearing Americans Put Faith in Angels, Miracles," *Newsweek*, December 14, 2005.
37. See Jeffrey R. Holland, *Brigham Young University, Devotional and Fireside Speeches* (Provo, UT: University Publications, 1987), 33–34.
38. Russell M. Nelson, "A Treasured Testament," *Ensign*, July 1993.
39. See Richard L. Anderson, "Book of Mormon Witnesses," FARMS Book of Mormon Lectures Series, 1994, 16.

Chapter 23

1. William E. Berrett, *The Restored Church* (Salt Lake City: Deseret Book, 1973), 197.
2. Joseph Fielding Smith, "Are You a Mormon?" in *The Life of Joseph F. Smith*, 2nd ed. (Salt Lake City: Deseret Book, 1938), 188–89.
3. See B. H. Roberts, *Comprehensive History of the Church*, 6 vols. (Salt Lake City: Deseret news Press, 1930), 5:560–66. In August 1880 a marble monument was erected over Elder Standing's grave in the Salt Lake City Cemetery. A new thirteen-foot granite replica later replaced that monument and was dedicated on November 3, 2001 (see *Church News*, November 10, 2001, 7). In spite of turbulent beginnings, at the beginning of January 2012, there were 77,948 members of the Church living in Georgia in 15 stakes, 112 wards, and 39 branches, served by three missions and one temple (see *2012 Church Almanac*, 343).
4. See Dean and Tom Hughes, *We'll Bring the World His Truth* (Salt Lake City: Deseret Book, 1995), 30–33.
5. See Truman G. Madsen, *Defender of the Faith: The B. H. Roberts Story* (Salt Lake City: Bookcraft, 1980), 143. Harassment was common, and if the harassers could not stop the Mormons from meeting, they would pound on the doors and windows while hallooing and cursing. If this failed, the homes or buildings would be set on fire. Nine homes were burned during Robert's tenure as mission president. Missionaries were dragged from their lodgings at night and tied to trees, driven into the woods by hounds and kept up all night, beaten with hickory rods and leather straps.
6. Kevin Stoker, *Missionary Moments* (Salt Lake City: Bookcraft, 1989), 27–28.
7. *Church History in the Fulness of Times* (Salt Lake City: The Church of Jesus Christ of Latter-day Saints 1989), 420.
8. See Jeffrey Marsh, "Brigham Young and the Book of Mormon," *Journal of Book of Mormon Studies*, vol. 10, no. 2 (2001), 10.
9. Arnold K. Garr, Donald Q. Cannon, and Richard O. Cowan, *Encyclopedia of Latter-day History* (Salt Lake City: Deseret Book, 2000), 1976.
10. Berrett, *The Restored Church*, 181.
11. Roberts, *Comprehensive History of the Church of Latter-day Saints*, 6: 102-103.
12. *Church History in the Fullness of Times*, 419.
13. *Church History in the Fullness of Times*, 419.
14. Barrett, *The Restored Church*, 181
15. Plural Marriage in Kirkland and Nauvoo, lds.org/topcs/plural-marriage-in-kirkland-and-Nauvoo?Lang+eng)
16. (Oct. 2017 article.). Need to locate.
17. LeGrand Richards, *A Marvelous Work and a Wonder*, (Salt Lake City, Utah, Deseret Book, 1958) 422.
18. Madsen, *Defender of the Faith: The B. H. Roberts Story*, 21.
19. Garr, Cannon, and Cowan, *Encyclopedia of Latter-day Saint History*, 1035.
20. Garr, Cannon, and Cowan, *Encyclopedia of Latter-day Saint History*, 1034.
21. See Madsen, *Defender of the Faith: The B. H. Roberts Story*, 311–12.
22. See John L. Lund, "Leave the Village or Die!" *Ensign*, February 1976, 32–33. In 1988, the Samoa Post Office issued a new postage stamp commemorating the arrival of the first Latter-day Saint missionaries in Samoa one hundred years earlier. The stamp pictured the Apia Samoa Temple, and souvenir sheets

carried a quotation from the Book of Mormon: "Great are the promises of the Lord unto them who are upon the isles of the sea" (2 Nephi 10:21). See "Samoan Stamp Honors First LDS Missionaries," *Ensign*, August 1988, 80.

23. See Sheri L. Dew, *Ezra Taft Benson, A Biography* (Salt Lake City: Deseret Book, 1987).
24. See Grant Salisbury and Warren K. Leffler, "A Church Service in Soviet Russia," *U.S. News and World Report*, vol. 47, no. 17, October 26, 1959, 76–77.
25. See Robert Brown and Rosemary Brown, *They Lie in Wait to Deceive* (Mesa, AZ: Brownsworth, 1995), 4:229–30.
26. *Out of Obscurity*, The 29th Annual Sidney B. Sperry Symposium (Salt Lake City: Deseret Book, 2000), 53–62.
27. "President Ezra Taft Benson: A Sure Voice of Faith," *Ensign*, July 1994, 8–42.
28. Dew, *Ezra Taft Benson, A Biography*, 195, 339, 350.
29. Dew, *Ezra Taft Benson, A Biography*, 480.
30. *The Church News*, November 23, 1991, 4.
31. *The Church News*, August 12, 2000, 13.
32. See Laura Harper, "Serving Where She Stands: Julia Mavimbela in Soweto," *This People*, Winter 1998, 28–32.
33. *The Church News*, August 12, 2000, 13.
34. Shellie M. Frey, *Winning Spirit, An Inside Look at LDS Sports Heroes* (Provo, UT: Brigham Young University Press, 1997), 69.
35. Frey, *Winning Spirit*, 69.
36. Bobby Ross Jr., "Murphy Preaches a Powerful Sermon," *The Daily Oklahoman*, April 26, 2001.
37. See Val Hale, "aw C'mon," *This People*, October 1985, 25.
38. Hale, "aw C'mon," 25. Dale baptized Curtis Patton.
39. Pioneers in Every Land, 30.
40. *2004 Church almanac*, The Church of Jesus Christ of Latter-day Saints, Salt Lake City, Utah, 589.
41. See Bruce A. van Orden, D. Brent Smith, and Everett Smith, Jr., *Pioneers in Every Land*, (Bookcraft, Salt Lake City, Utah, *1997)33*.
42. See Dick Davis and Duane Hiatt, (*New Era*, February 1974).9.
43. News of the Church," *The Ensign, February 1974*), 72.
44. *Pioneers in Every Land*, 30.
45. *Pioneers in Every Land*, 31
46. "Former Y. Basketball Star is Deputy Ambassador," (*Church News* Sept. 26, 1992) 5.
47. *Pioneers in Every Land*, 32-3.
48. *Pioneers in Every Land*, 35.
49. See Shaun D. Stahle, "National Hero," (Church News, January 21, 2006), 8-10.
50. "National Hero," 10.
51. See Rebecca M. Taylor, "Heroes and Heroines: —Kim Ho Jik—Korean Pioneer," *Friend*, April 1997,44.
52. See Denny Roy, "Kim Ho Jik: Korean Pioneer," *The Ensign*, July 1988, 19; and *Church News*, October 25, 2016.
53. From the journal of Scott Anderson and *The Ensign*, November 1973, 93. The author's cousin, Richard Rawson, served as a missionary in Germany during this time and said he "spent many pleasant hours with her, teaching the Gospel to Catholic Priests and parishioners." He also said he and his companion, both 6' 2" tall, almost had to jog to keep up with 4' 9" Sister Specht.
54. See Maurine Proctor, "Ahmad S. Corbitt—Lighting the Fire Within," *Meridian Magazine*, February 10, 2006.
55. Via Sikahema, "Two Contrasting Stories on LDS Priesthood in the News," *Deseret News*, March 2, 2012.
56. "New Mission Presidents," *Church News*, March 16, 2014.
57. Robert L. Millet, *Getting at the Truth* (Salt Lake City: Deseret Book, 2004), 63. (From Bruce R. McConkie, *New Revelation on the Priesthood* [Salt Lake City: Deseret Book, 1981], 132.)
58. See Marjorie Wall Folsom, *Golden Harvest in Ghana* (Bountiful, UT: Horizon Publishers, 1989), 161–62.
59. Hundreds of converted people waiting to be baptized, who had never met a "Mormon," contradicts critics' baseless charge that Mormons "brainwash their converts."
60. See Randall N. Mabey and Gordon T. Allred, *Brother to Brother* (Salt Lake City: Bookcraft, 1984), 58–61.
61. *The Church of Jesus Christ of Latter-day Saints Membership Statistics, December 2017.* Wikipedia.

Chaper 24

1. See Gene R. Cook, "Moroni's Promise," *Ensign*, April 1994, 12–15.
2. See Cook, "Moroni's Promise."
3. See Cook, "Moroni's Promise."
4. Floyd C. McElveen, *God's Word: Final, Infallible and Forever* (Grand Rapids, MI, 1985), 139–42.
5. Darl Anderson, *Soft Answers to Hard Questions* (Mesa, AZ: Cox Printing, 1992), 48.

6. Hugh B. Brown, "Profile of a Prophet," October General Conference, 1967.
7. Davis Bitton, "B. H. Roberts and Book of Mormon Scholarship," *Journal of Book of Mormon Studies*, vol.8, no. 2 (2002), 87.
8. Introduction to the Book of Mormon, last two paragraphs.
9. See Brent L. Top, "The Book That Changes Lives," *Meridian Magazine*, January 6, 2004.
10. Jay E. Jensen, "Why We Ask People to Read the Book of Mormon," *Ensign*, August 1984, 20.

Chapter 25

1. See Gordon B. Hinckley, *Truth Restored: A Short History of The Church of Jesus Christ of Latter-day Saints* (Salt Lake City: Shadow Mountain, 1979), 30.
2. Officially, there is no "Mormon Church." "Mormon" is a nickname given to the Church because of the Book of Mormon and the prophet Mormon who abridged ancient records from which the book was translated. Individuals are called "Mormons," but they are members of The Church of Jesus Christ of Latter-day Saints.
3. G. Homer Durham, ed., *Discourses of Wilford Woodruff* (Salt Lake City: Bookcraft, 1946), 38.
4. See Carrie A. Moore, "LDS Church Called Fastest-Growing Church During '90s," *Deseret News*, September 17, 2002.
5. See Valerie Housley, "LDS Church Second-fastest Growing Religion in the Nation," *Daily Universe*, August 1, 2006, according to a study in the 2006 *Yearbook of American and Canadian Churches*.
6. See Jay M. Todd, "Historic Milestone Achieved: More Non-English-Speaking Members Now Than English-Speaking," *Ensign*, September 2000, 76.
7. "LDS Church Now Ranks 4th Largest in U.S.," *Deseret Morning News*, March 10, 2007.
8. William J. Hamblin and Daniel C. Peterson, "The Popes' Division," *Meridian Magazine,* June 2, 20003.
9. *Out of Obscurity: The LDS Church in the Twentieth Century*, The 29th annual Sidney B. Sperry Symposium (Salt Lake City: Deseret Book, 2000), 4.
10. See Michael R. Leonard, "Prophet Tells Executives about Church," *Church News*, November 18, 1995, 12.
11. Gordon B. Hinckley, "What Are People Asking About Us?" *Ensign*, November 1998, 78.
12. Stephen W Gibson, *From Clergy to Convert* (Salt Lake City: Bookcraft, 1988, 245).
13. See Lucy Mack Smith, *The Revised and Enhanced History of Joseph Smith by His Mother*, Scot Facer Proctor and Maurine Proctor, eds. (Salt Lake City: Deseret Book, 1996), 223–26, 244–47. (The author is a descendant of Susannah Young, Brigham's sister, and therefore one of the thousands.)
14. See Joseph Giacalone, "Growing into the Church," *Ensign*, June 1984, 64–65.
15. See Isaac Swartzberg, "A Jewish Attorney Finds the Messiah," *Ensign*, December 1972, 63.
16. See Gabriel Kelphala Sesay, "Book of Mormon Stories," *Ensign*, October 1992, 27.
17. See Stephen W. Gibson, *From Clergy to Convert* (Salt Lake City: Bookcraft, 1988), 61–66.
18. LeGrand Richards, *A Marvelous Work and a Wonder* (Salt Lake City: Deseret Book, 1976). This book came from an outline titled "The Message of Mormonism," which Elder Richards developed while serving as president of the Southern States Mission, 1934–1937. It gives an overview of the beliefs of The Church of Jesus Christ of Latter-day Saints and has been instrumental in the conversion of countless persons, including many ministers. Richards was called as an Apostle in 1952. He died in 1983 at the age of ninety-six.
19. See Gibson, *From Clergy to Convert*, 40–46.
20. See Richard Tice, "How Rare a Possession," *Ensign*, January 1988, 20.
21. See Vincenzo di Francesca, "I Will Not Burn the Book!" *Ensign*, January 1988, 18–21. An award-winning movie, *How Rare a Possession*, was produced about Francesca's experiences and can be seen on the Internet. https://www.youtube.com/watch?v=D7-3ftN9Y2o
22. See Hartman Rector and Connie Rector, *No More Strangers* (Salt Lake City: Bookcraft, 1973), 1:82–89.
23. See Rector and Rector, *No More Strangers*, 4:6–12. Former Church President David O. McKay had admonished Church members "to flood the earth with the Book of Mormon."
24. See Rector and Rector, *No More Strangers*, 4:92–99.
25. Excerpts from "Georgia Atlanta Mission Conversion Survey," by Scott J. Giaimo, received at mission office April 28, 1998.
26. See Rector and Rector, *No More Strangers*, 2:104–109.
27. See Janae P. Miller, "To Some It Is Given," *Ensign*, January 1992, 30–31.
28. J. Carlos Martin Clari, Testimony translated from Spanish
29. Many Authors, *Why I Believe*, Bookcraft, Salt Lake City, Utah, 2002) 31-5.
30. See Leo P. Talbot, "Bless Those Elders," *Ensign*, March 1983, 65.

Chapter 26

1. Joseph Fielding McConkie, "Seventeen Points," *Harvester*, Scotland Edinburgh Mission, August 1990.
2. Shaun D. Stahle, "Solitary Samuel," *Church News*, April 2, 2005.
3. Arnold K. Garr, "Samuel H. Smith," in *Encyclopedia of Latter-day Saint History* (Salt Lake City: Deseret Book, 2000), 1138.

4. Joseph Smith, *History of the Church of Jesus Christ of Latter-day Saints*, 7 vols. (Salt Lake City: Deseret Book, 1976), Introduction by B. H. Roberts, 4:xxxi–xxxii.

5. Ague involves "a fever (as malaria) marked by paroxysms of chills, fever, and sweating that recur at regular intervals." See *Merriam-Webster's Collegiate Dictionary*, 11th ed. (Springfield, MA: Merriam-Webster, 2004), s.v. "ague."

6. See *Our Heritage: A Brief History of The Church of Jesus Christ of Latter-day Saints* (Salt Lake City: The Church of Jesus Christ of Latter-day Saints, 1996), 56–57.

7. See Fred E. Woods, "Seagoing Saints," *Ensign*, September 2001, 54–60. See also Conway B. Sonne, "Sail to Zion," *Ensign*, July 1991, 7–14.

8. Stahle, "Solitary Samuel."

9. William E. Berrett, *The Restored Church* (Salt Lake City: Deseret Book, 1961), 153.

10. See Wilford Woodruff, *Leaves From My Journal* (Salt Lake City: Juvenile Instructor Office, 1881), 7–8.

11. Berrett, *The Restored Church*, 131.

12. . . . See Woodruff, *Leaves From My Journal*, 97–99.

13. John L. Hart, "Missionary Milestone: 500,000th is Called," *Church News*, May 4, 1991, 3, 7.

14. "Missionary Program," http://www.mormonnewsroom.org/topic/missionary-program (accessed June 6, 2016).

15. Boyd K. Packer, "Agency and Control," *Ensign*, May 1983, 6.

16. As of January, 2017.

17. Gordon B. Hinckley, "My Testimony," *Ensign*, November 1993, 52.

18. Gordon B. Hinckley, "The Miracle of Faith," *Ensign*, May 2001, 68–69.

19. Anugrath Komar, "Why Are Mormons Rising in Business, Politics?" *The Christian Post*, July 25, 2011.

20. Laury Livsey, "The MTC Experience," *New Era*, June 2000, 28–46.

21. Tom Thorkelson to *60 Minutes*, April 8, 1996, as related by Sheri Dew, *No Doubt About It* (Salt Lake City: Deseret Book, 2001), 196–97.

22. From conversations with Renee, the author's friend in Atlanta, Georgia.

23. See Jeff Benedict, *The Mormon Way of Doing Business* (New York: Warner Business Books, 2007), 1, 4, 6.

24. Jeff Benedict, "Faith, Flight Plan Guide JetBlue Boss. Other CEOs Need his Humility," *Boston Herald*, March 5, 2007.

25. Benedict, *The Mormon Way of Doing Business*, 7, 9.

26. Benedict, *The Mormon Way of Doing Business*, 10-12. Clark stunned Harvard by giving up his prestigious position as Dean of their business school to become President of Brigham Young University–Idaho in 2005.

27. Ted Walsh, "Utah Native Named as the World's Top Management Guru. Gives Emotional Speech," *Deseret News*, November 25, 2013.

28. Benedict, *The Mormon Way of Doing Business*, 19–20.

29. See David Ramsey, "Air Forces Gray out of Africa, onto the Field," *The Gazette*, Colorado Springs, Colorado, August 24, 2003, 35.

30. See H. Wells Meeks, "I've Been Waiting for You," *Ensign*, April 1992, 49. These two missionaries were assigned to other locations before the baptisms took place but were happy with the end results.

31. Michael Otterson, "Why I Won't Be Seeing the Book of Mormon Musical, (January 2017. http://www.mormonnewsroom.org/article/on-faith-blog-why-i-wont-be-seeing-the-book-of-mormon-musical

32. "Former Missionaries Connect with People They Served," *Meridian Magazine*, August 1, 2007.

33. "Former Missionaries Connect with People They Served."

34. Mitt and Ann Romney and 50 others, *Why I Believe* (Salt Lake City: Bookcraft, 2002), 288–89.

35. Mark M. Trunnell, "Good-bye, Italy—con Amor," *Ensign*, August 1998, 45.

36. This happened in the Georgia Atlanta Mission where the author and her husband also served with the missionaries, Elder John Montgomery of Payson, Utah, and Elder Travis Heap of St. Johns, Arizona.

37. Arnold Gurr of Parowan, Utah, uncle of the author, was another one of those sent from Germany where he was serving as a missionary and ended up back in Germany as a soldier.

38. See Kris McKay, *No Greater Love* (Salt Lake City: Deseret Book, 1982), 1–5. In time of war, disobeying a direct command from an officer is an offense that may be punishable by death.

39. See Frank Millward, "Eight Missionaries Missed Voyage on Titanic," *Deseret News*, July 24, 2008.

40. See Lee Davidson, *Ensign*, August 1998, 74. See also "Missionary Slayings Very Rare in LDS Church," *Deseret Morning News*, January 5, 2006.

41. See "Brandon J. Miller, "I Needed a Blessing," *Ensign*, September 2001, 64–65.

42. See Graeme MacPherson, "Johnstone Missionaries Stabbed," *Johnstone and Linwood Gazette*, Scotland, October 10, 2001, 1.

43. Maurine Jensen Proctor, "Missing," *Meridian Magazine*, August 7, 2002. In 2013 a movie, The Saratov Approach, was made about their harrowing experience.

44. See Michael Kohn, "Religion in the News," *Washington Post*, August 3, 2001.

45. See Janine S. Creager, "To Welcome the World . . . Sister Missionaries Stroll Temple Square," *Salt Lake Tribune,* January 11, 2007.
46. Personal interview with Dr. Hamilton, who is a brother-in-law to the author.
47. See Genelle Pugmire, "Instant Messengers – LDS Church Introduces New Online Services for Missionaries, *Daily Herald,* March 8, 2018.
48. LeGrand Richards, *A Marvelous Work and a Wonder* (Salt Lake City: Deseret Book, 1976), 246.
49. See John L. Hart, "'Keystone' Vital in Missionary Work," *The Church News,* January 4, 1992.

Chapter 27

1. From a speech given by Henry A. Wallace at the New York Times Book Fair, November 5, 1937, "Where the Book of Mormon Went to Press," *Ensign,* February 1989, 44.
2. Hugh B. Brown, *Continuing the Quest* (Salt Lake City: Deseret Book, 1961), 285.
3. Robert B. Downs, "25 Books That Changed America," *Times Mirror,* New York (1970), 51.
4. See Jerome Kramer, "20 Books That Changed America," *Book Magazine,* July/August 2003, www.bookmagazine.com/issue29.
5. *Parade Magazine,* December 29, 1961, and *Amazon,* May 2014.
6. Richard Eyre, Linda Eyre, and Saren Eyre Loosli, *Empty Nest Parenting: Adjusting Your Stewardship as Your Children Leave Home* (Salt Lake City: Bookcraft, 2002).
7. Jon Meacham and Elise Soukup, "Solid, Strong, True," *Newsweek,* October 17, 2005.
8. See Chapter 10 regarding temples—where families can be sealed together forever.
9. In 2001, ten Latter-day Saint mothers were chosen for each category, and in 2002, a total of nineteen were chosen. See *Church News,* May 12, 2001, and *Church News,* May 11, 2002.
10. "Winning on the Homefront, News of the Church," *Ensign,* July 1979, 78. (The ads have been discontinued).
11. Joe Bauman, "LDS Have Largest Families in U.S.," *Deseret Morning News,* February 26, 2008.
12. Bill Dedman, "Proportion of Married Americans Drops Slightly in New Census," *Globe,* May 5, 2002. The age of first marriages for men in Utah is twenty-three and for women twenty-one. The national age for men is twenty-seven and for women twenty-five, according to a report from The National Marriage Project at Rutgers State University in New Jersey. See Brooke Adams, "Men Delaying Marriage—Except in Utah," *Salt Lake Tribune,* July 3, 2002. Those who are married or attend church regularly report being the happiest with life, according to a Gallup poll. (See "Survey Shows Married People Tend to be Happier," *Focus on the Family,* January 16, 2008.
13. Carol Soelberg, "Birth Dearth: The Family Is a 'Natural Good for Economic Development,'" United Families International, July 31, 2007.
14. See Morgan Jacobson, "Utah Tops for Charity, Volunteering," *Deseret News,* December 9, 2015.
15. See Lois M. Collins, "Volunteer Pinnacle," *Deseret News,* June 10, 2010.
16. Carrie A. Moore, "Games, LDS Church Influenced Each Other," *Deseret News,* March 16, 2002.
17. See Gary Lawrence, "Riordan Can Learn from the Mormons," *L.A. Times,* March 17, 2002.
18. See Carrie A. Moore, *Deseret News,* March 16, 2002, quoting Rodney Stark, a long time professor of sociology at the University of Washington.
19. Yonat Shimron, "Mormon Teens Cope Best," Newsobserver.com, March 13, 2005.
20. Poll: "U.S. Religious Knowledge Survey," Pew Research Center on Religion and Public Life, September 28, 2010.
21. Laurie Goldstein, "Utah Tops Religion Survey," *New York Times,* September 18, 2002.
22. Frank Newport, "Provo-Orem, Utah Is Most Religious U.S. Area," Gallup, March 29, 2001, http://www.gallup.com/poll/161543/provo-orem-utah-religious-metro-area.aspx (accessed June 7, 2016).
23. David J. Marianno Jr., "Special Children Changed My Life," *Church News,* September 1, 1988.
24. Robert F. Bennett, *Why I Believe* (Salt Lake City: Bookcraft, 2002), 58–59.
25. Gerald Davis and Norma Davis, "Behind the Wall—The Church in Eastern Germany," *Ensign,* April 1991.
26. Thomas S. Monson, "Thanks Be to God," *Ensign,* May 1989, 50.
27. "Mormons Reflect Christianity in Lifestyle," *Meridian Magazine,* April 24, 2007.
28. Sheri Dew, *No Doubt About It* (Salt Lake City: Deseret Book, 2001), 96.
29. Stan Albrecht and Tim Heaton, "Education Increases Religious Activity," Review of Religious Research, 1984, *Meridian Magazine,* March 6, 2002.
30. Kelsey Dallas, "Pew Report: Do college campuses put students' faith at risk?" (*Deseret News,* April 28, 2017).
31. See Mark W. Cannon, "Latter-day Saints and Science," *Meridian Magazine,* March 2002.
32. Henry Eyring, "Mormons and Science," *LDS Living,* October 2008.
33. Genaro C. Armas, "Utahans Are Schooled More Than Average," Associated Press, March 28, 2005.
34. See Nancy Zuckerbrod, "Utah the Only State in U.S. without a 'Dropout Factory,'" *Deseret Morning News,* October 30, 2007.

35. See Jennifer Toomer-Cook, "Utah Girls Most Likely to Graduate," *Deseret Morning News*, October 31, 2007.
36. "History of BYU," http://yfacts.byu.edu/Article?id=137 (accessed June 7, 2016).
37. "BYU Most Popular University, Says US News and World Report," *Church News*, January 29, 2011, 2.
38. "BYU Is an American Original," *Deseret Morning News*, September 6, 2003, and Brigham Young University 2011 brochure.
39. "BYU Gives Most Bang for Buck Review Says," *Princeton Review* and *Deseret Morning News*, March 29, 2006.
40. See Tad Walch, "5 LDS Grads Make List of World's 50 Best Management Thinkers," *Deseret News*, January 4, 2016.
41. "Top 10 Stone-Sober Schools: BYU Takes the Honor 18th Year in a Row," *Princeton Review*, August 8, 2015.
42. "BYU Safest College Campus," *Church News*, January 17, 2016.
43. "BYU and Empower Playgrounds Install Electricity-Generating Merry-Go-Round in Ghana, Brigham Young University News Release, June 17, 2008. See also http://www.empowerplaygrounds.org/history/ (accessed June 7, 2016.)
44. See Viviane Vo-Duc, "BYU Students Making Prostheses," *Deseret News*, June 14, 2011.
45. See Rachel Lowry, "Y Engineering Professors Find Solutions to Chronic Back Pain," *The Deseret News*, June 17, 2012. The professors are Anton Bowden, Larry Howell, and Peter Halverson.
46. See Chase Larson, "BYU Students Build Drill for Finding Ground Water," *Deseret News*, April 12, 2011.
47. Danielle Christensen, "BYU Well Brings Water to 23 Countries" *Deseret News*, September 18, 2017. "Inspiring Engineering," President's Report, Winter 2017-18.
48. "BYU Movies Mark Twenty-fifth Year," *Ensign*, September 1978, 79.
49. See David Mortimer, "BYU Animation: A Work of Collaboration," *Church News*, August 14, 2010; Terry Toone, "Animated BYU Film Wins Emmy," *Deseret News*, April 17, 2011; and Tori Ackerman, "3 BYU Student Films Win 5 Student Emmys," *Deseret News*, April 6, 2012.
50. See Grace Leong, "BYU's Marriott School Ranked No.1," *Daily Herald*, September 18, 2007.
51. "Forbes Says BYU MBA among Best Returns," *Deseret News*, August 16, 2011.
52. "The Gift of Gab," *BYU Magazine*, Fall 2002, 14. See also Sarah Jane Weaver, "BYU's Multilingual Campus," *Church News*, February 2, 2002, 3.
53. See Sarah Jane Weaver, "BYU Leads Middle East Center," *Church News*, August 24, 2002, 4.
54. Weaver, "BYU Leads Middle East Center," 3.
55. See Sarah Jane Weaver, "A Place of Miracles, Polynesian Cultural Center Attracts Millions," *Deseret News*, December 4, 2010, 6–7.
56. See Ray Grass, "40 Years Later," *Church News*, April 19, 2003, 8–9.
57. See Conning Meyers, "Polynesian Cultural Center, Cultural Feast-Student Lifeline," *BYU Magazine*, Spring 2001, 37.
58. LDS Newsroom, 17 October, 2011, Salt Lake City, Utah; Talk by John J. Carmack, Sons of the Utah Pioneers, May 18, 2017.
59. See Sarah Lou Weaver, "BYU Pathway Worldwide" (*Church News*, February 12, 2017)
60. Doctrine and Covenants 89 contains the full revelation.
61. James B. Allen and Glen M. Leonard, *The Story of the Latter-day Saints* (Salt Lake City: Deseret Book, 1976), 527.
62. Mark W. Cannon and Danielle Stockton, "Decades of Proof Show Word of Wisdom Works," *Deseret News/Mormon Times*, April 12, 2010.
63. 1997 Sesquicentennial Tour, Salt Lake Mormon Tabernacle Choir program booklet.
64. Trent Toone, "Tabernacle Choir Joins American Classical Music Hall of Fame, *Deseret News*, February 27, 2015.
65. "Mormon Tabernacle Choir Program Turns 4000," *A Cappella News*, May 2, 2006.
66. See R. Scott Lloyd, "Recording Career Reaches Landmark," *Church News*, June, 19 2010.
67. Doug Robinson, "Tabernacle Choir Has Been a Shining Star at Games," *Deseret News*, March 2002.
68. See Sarah Jane Weaver, "In 75 Years, Institute Grows from 25 Students to 316,000," *Church News*, May 5, 2001, 7, 13.
69. See "First Time Charming for Miss Junior Teen," *Church News*, April 3, 2004, 15.
70. See Jason Swenson, "Coffin Project Saves Children's Lives," *Church News*, September 27, 2003, 6.
71. See Darla Isackson, "The Overwhelmed Women and the Feminist Movement," *Meridian Magazine*, July 26, 2014.
72. *Church News*, February 9, 2002, 7, quoting from the *Vancouver Sun*, January 5, 2002 issue.
73. Utah, according to "Charitable Statistics at the Urban Institute" leads the nation in charitable contributions, giving 4.9 percent of adjusted gross income. In Texas where 85 percent claim a religious identity, they give only 1.9%. See Cathy Lynn Grossman and Anthony DeBarros, "Irreligious Not Charitable," *USA Today*, March 6, 2002.

74. See Gerry Avant, "Lifting Hearts and Souls," *Church News*, April 27, 1996, 8.
75. See Sarah Jane Weaver, "New Central Storehouse Opens in S.L.," *Deseret News*, January 27, 2012.
76. Susan Whitney, "Caring for Others Not Limited by Denomination," *Deseret Morning News*, July 15, 2006, E2. See also Gerry Avant, "Church Welfare Program" *Church News*, April 16, 2011.
77. Tad Walch, "Elder Holland Speaks Before UK Parliament," *Deseret News*, June 11, 2015.
78. See Lee Davidson, "Church Welfare Is Role Model for Public Assistance Reform," *Deseret News*, February 11, 1992. Quoted in *Church News*, February 15, 1992, 3.
79. R. Scott Lloyd, JustServe.Org:, Connecting volunteers with community needs, *LDS Church News,* March 29, 2018.
80. See Art Rascon, *On Assignment: The Stories Behind the Stories* (American Fork, UT: Covenant Communications, 1998), 136–37.
81. "Director of the World Food Program Lauds Church's Humanitarian Efforts," *Ensign*, October 2004, 73.
82. LeGrand Richards, *A Marvelous Work and a Wonder* (Salt Lake City: Deseret Book, 1950), 436.
83. Gordon B. Hinckley, "The Gospel Makes Bad Men Good and Good Men Better," *Ensign*, November 1976, 96.
84. Sheri L. Dew, *Ezra Taft Benson: A Biography* (Salt Lake City: Deseret Book, 1987), 339.
85. "Who Said It?" *LDS Living*, May/June, 2004, 10.
86. Wayne Holst, "America's Prophet Left Mixed Legacy," *Toronto Star*, January 4, 2003. Robert Remini also states, "By 2050, the Latter-day Saints will likely rank among the top five Christian denominations in the United States." (That comment must be a typo as the Church was already number four in 2003.)
87. John F. Kennedy, speech in Salt Lake City Tabernacle, Salt Lake City, September 26, 1963.

Chapter 28

1. Lucy Mack Smith, *The Revised and Enhanced History of Joseph Smith by His Mother*, Scot Facer Proctor and Maurine Jensen Proctor, eds. (Salt Lake City: Deseret Book, 1996), 130–34.
2. Smith, *The Revised and Enhanced History of Joseph Smith by His Mother*, 239, 243.
3. Smith, *The Revised and Enhanced History of Joseph Smith by His Mother*, 238–43.
4. Smith, *The Revised and Enhanced History of Joseph Smith by His Mother*, 207–12.
5. See *Our Heritage: A Brief History of The Church of Jesus Christ of Latter-day Saints* (Salt Lake City: The Church of Jesus Christ of Latter-day Saints, 1996), 18–19.
6. Doctrine and Covenants 95:8. See Arnold K. Garr, Donald Q. Cannon, and Richard O. Cowan, *Encyclopedia of Latter-day Saint History* (Salt Lake City: Deseret Book, 2000), 623.
7. See William E. Berrett, *The Restored Church* (Salt Lake City: Deseret Book, 1973), 125–27.
8. Hubert Howe Bancroft, *History of Utah, 1540–1886* (San Francisco: The History Company, 1889), 112.
9. See Berrett, *The Restored Church*, 116–17.
10. Berrett, *The Restored Church*, 78.
11. See Leonard J. Arrington and Davis Bitton, *The Mormon Experience* (New York: Vintage Books/Random House, 1980), 146.
12. See Berrett, *The Restored Church*, 116.
13. Berrett, *The Restored Church*, 116.
14. "Nibley Counters World's Perception of Prophets' Role," *FARMS Insights*, July 2000, 4.
15. These revelations, along with future ones, eventually became The Doctrine and Covenants of The Church of Jesus Christ of Latter-day Saints, which is accepted as scripture by the Church. The first edition was published in 1835. Subsequent revelations were, and are, added to later editions. Only twenty-six or twenty-seven copies of these original "Book of Commandments" have since surfaced. A copy, even though incomplete, sold for $200,000 in 2001, and another, also in 2001, sold for $391,000 at Christie's auction in New York City.
16. See *Our Heritage*, 40–41.
17. Joseph Smith, *History of The Church of Jesus Christ of Latter-day Saints*, 7 vols. (Salt Lake City, Deseret Book, 1976), 1:390–91.
18. See Ivan J. Barrett, *Joseph Smith and the Restoration: A History of the LDS Church to 1846* (Provo, UT: Brigham Young University Press, 1967), 255.
19. 00000*Our Heritage*, 42.
20. See *Our Heritage*, 42–43.
21. See Smith, *History of the Church*, 6:431, footnote.
22. Berrett, *The Restored Church*, 120.
23. B. H. Roberts, *A Comprehensive History of The Church of Jesus Christ of Latter-day Saints*, 6 vols. (Salt Lake City: Deseret News Press, 1930), 1:344.
24. See *Our Heritage*, 27–28.
25. *Our Heritage*, 44.
26. *Our Heritage*, 44–45.
27. Karl Ricks Anderson, *Joseph's Kirtland* (Salt Lake City: Deseret Book, 1989), 206.

327

28. See *Our Heritage*, 36. The Kirtland Temple is owned by the Community of Christ, whose headquarters are in Independence, Missouri. They are a branch of the Latter-day restoration movement along with The Church of Jesus Christ of Latt000er-day Saints. The Community of Christ was formerly known as the Reorganized Church of Jesus Christ of Latter Day Saints, but in 2000, they changed their name to Community of Christ.

29. Smith, *The Revised and Enhanced History of Joseph Smith by His Mother*, 58.

30. Smith, *History of the Church*, 4:29.

31. See Berrett, *The Restored Church*, 138.

32. Berrett, *The Restored Church*, 138.

33. Berrett, *The Restored Church*, 138–39.

34. Berrett, *The Restored Church*, 139.

35. Smith, *History of the Church*, 4:31.

36. Smith, *History of the Church*, 3:158–59.

37. Smith, *History of the Church*, 3:158, 161–64.

38. See *Our Heritage*, 45–47.

39. See James B. Allen and Glen M. Leonard, *The Story of the Latter-day Saints* (Salt Lake City: Deseret Book, 1976), 105.

40. See *Our Heritage*, 47. After 138 years, this order of "extermination or expulsion" of the Mormons from Missouri was finally rescinded. In 1976, the 200th anniversary of the United States, Governor Christopher S. Bond of Missouri said, after rescinding the decree, "Governor Boggs' order clearly contravened the rights to life, liberty, property, and religious freedom as guaranteed by the Constitution of the United States, as well as the Constitution of the State of Missouri." See "Extermination Order Rescinded," *Ensign*, September 1976, 95.

41. See *Our Heritage, 47*.

42. See Berrett, *The Restored Church*, 141.

43. See B. H. Roberts, *The Missouri Persecutions* (Provo, UT: Maasai Publishing, 2001), 201.

44. Allen and Leonard, *The Story of the Latter-day Saints*, 127–28.

45. See Darla Jackson, "The Haunting Message of Haun's Mill," *Meridian Magazine*, September 14, 2007.

46. See Berrett, *The Restored Church*, 143.

47. Roberts, *Comprehensive History of the Church*, 1:488.

48. Roberts, *Comprehensive History of the Church*, 3:193.

49. Smith, *History of Joseph Smith by His Mother* (Salt Lake City: Bookcraft, 1979), 290–91.

50. See Berrett, *The Restored Church*, 144.

51. Parley P. Pratt, *Autobiography of Parley P. Pratt* (Salt Lake City: Deseret Book, 1950), 190–91.

52. Smith, *History of the Church*, 1:488. His communication was dated November 29, 1838. (Documents, etc., published by the Missouri Legislature, p. 94).

53. Smith *History of the Church*, 3:191.

54. See Gracia N. Jones, "My Great-Great-Grandmother Emma Hale," *Ensign*, August 1992, 33.

55. See J. Christopher Conkling, *A Joseph Smith Chronology* (Salt Lake City: Deseret Book, 1979), 129. Among the precious papers Emma carried was Joseph's inspired revision of the Bible.

56. Roberts, *Comprehensive History of the Church*, 2:41.

57. Pratt, *Autobiography of Parley P. Pratt*, 285–86.

58. See Allen and Leonard, *The Story of the Latter-day Saints*, 140–41.

59. "Mormon Tabernacle Choir Says Thank You to Quincy, Illinois," *Nauvoo Internet News*, June 28, 2002, and *Webmaster*, May 30, 2002.

60. Jeffery W. Walker, "Mormon Findings in Caldwell and Daviess Counties and the Mormon Conflict of 1838: New Findings and New Understandings," *BYU Studies*, vol. 45, no. 1, 2008.

61. Berrett, *The Restored Church*, 145.

62. See Roberts, *The Missouri Persecutions*, 241–43.

63. What comprised the town of Commerce? Joseph Smith said, "When I made the purchase of [property from] White and Gilland, there was one stone house, three frame houses, and two block houses, which constituted the whole city of Commerce." See Roberts, *Comprehensive History of the Church*, 2:8–9.

64. Allen and Leonard, *The Story of the Latter-day Saints*, 144–45.

65. Dan Jones, *History of the Latter-day Saints, from Their Establishment in the Year 1823, to the Time When Three Hundred 000Thousand of Them Were Exiled from America Because of Their Religion in the Year 1846*, published in Welsh in 1847, facsimile translation by Ronald D. Dennis, *Welsh Mormon Facsimile Translations* (Salt Lake City: Deseret Book, 2001), 68–70.

66. Smith, *History of the Church*, 5:85.

67. Deborah Gertz Husar, "Mormon Exodus Highlights Nauvoo's Place in History," *Herald-Wig*, Nauvoo, Illinois, January 28, 2000.

68. See Husar, "Mormon Exodus Highlights Nauvoo's Place in History," January 28, 2007.

69. Carrie A. Moore, "Nauvoo Temple," *Deseret News*, May 2, 2002. The author and her husband were among the thousands of descendants who attended the dedication.

70. See Berrett, *The Restored Church*, 215–16, 18–21.
71. Berrett, *The Restored Church*, 221.
72. From a speech before the Historical Society of Philadelphia, March 26, 1850.
73. Smith, *The Revised and Enhanced History of Joseph Smith by His Mother*, 460–61.
74. See Jones, "My Great-Great-Grandmother Emma Hale," 31–39.
75. Garr, Cannon, and Cowan, *Encyclopedia of Latter-day Saint History*, 1113.
76. Garr, Cannon, and Cowan, *Encyclopedia of Latter-day Saint History*, 818–19.
77. Jones, *History of the Latter-day Saints*, 100–102.
78. See Jones, *History of the Latter-day Saints*, 100–102.
79. *The Pioneer Trail*, Church Pioneer Sesquicentennial Celebration pamphlet (Salt Lake City: Church of Jesus Christ of Latter-day Saints, 1980).
80. See Susan Easton Black, "I Have a Question," *Ensign*, July 1998, 41.
81. See *Church History in the Fulness of Times* (Salt Lake City: Church of Jesus Christ of Latter-day Saints, 1993), 393.
82. William G. Hartley, *Church News*, March 9, 1996, 7.
83. Craig T. Neises, "Nauvoo Schools Pass Over Mormons," *The Hawk Eye*, Burlington, Illinois, May 9, 2002.
84. Bruce R. McConkie, *Ensign*, January 1973, 37. Also quoted in *The Bruce R. McConkie Story: Reflections of a Son* (Salt Lake City: Deseret Book, 2003), 431.
85. John A. Widtsoe, *Discourses of Brigham Young* (Salt Lake City: Deseret Book, 1946), 348–49.

Chapter 29

1. Hugh B. Brown, "Profile of a Prophet," General Conference Talk, October 1967.
2. Joseph Smith, *History of The Church of Jesus Christ of Latter-day Saints,* 7 vols. (Salt Lake City, Deseret Book, 1976), 1:19.
3. Lucy Mack Smith, *The Revised and Enhanced History of Joseph Smith by His Mother*, Scot Facer Proctor and Maurine Proctor, eds. (Salt Lake City: Deseret Book, 1996), 93–94.
4. Gordon A. Madsen, "Joseph Smith's 1826 Trial: The Legal Setting," *BYU Studies*, Spring 1990, 93; also, *Ensign*, June 1994, 24.
5. See Truman Madsen, *Joseph Smith the Prophet* (Salt Lake City: Bookcraft, 1989), 35–36.
6. See Karl Ricks Anderson, *Joseph Smith's Kirtland* (Salt Lake City: Deseret Book, 1989), 38.
7. See Hugh Nibley, *Prophetic Book of Mormon* (Salt Lake City: Deseret Book, 1989), 241.
8. John Schroeder, "Religious Competition," *Article VI Blog*, February 20, 2009.
9. Smith, *History of the Church*, 1:94.
10. See Smith, *History of the Church*, 1:89–91.
11. See Smith, *History of the Church*, 1:92–96.
12. See Smith, *History of the Church*, 1:97.
13. Joseph and Emma had ten children. Five died as infants: Alvin, died the same day, 1828; Thaddeus and Louisa, twins, died the same day, 1831; Joseph Murdock Smith, adopted twin, died at eleven months because of exposure caused by the mob at Hiram, Ohio, 1831–1832; and Don Carlos, fourteen months, 1840–1841. The other children were: Julia Murdock (adopted twin), 1831–1880; Joseph III, 1832–1914; Frederick, 1836–1862; Alexander, 1838–1909; and David Hyrum, 1844–1904. (See Smith, *The Revised and Enhanced History of Joseph Smith by His Mother*, 475. (The book reports eleven children, one a stillborn son, but that has since been found not to be true.)
14. See Anderson, *Joseph Smith's Kirtland*, 32–34.
15. Smith, *History of the Church*, 1:264–65.
16. Smith, *History of the Church*, 1:31–32.
17. See William E. Berrett, *The Restored Church* (Salt Lake City: Deseret Book, 1973), 133–36. Also, Anderson, *Joseph Smith's Kirtland*, 236.
18. See Anderson, *Joseph Smith's Kirtland*, 206, 235. Also, *The Revised and Enhanced History of Joseph Smith by His Mother*, 248. (This was in January 1838.)
19. Parley P. Pratt, *Autobiography of Parley P. Pratt* (Salt Lake City: Deseret Book, 1938), 187.
20. Smith, *History of the Church*, 3:190–91.
21. Smith, *History of the Church*, 3:190–91 footnote.
22. Smith, *History of the Church*, 3:193.
23. See Smith, *History of the Church*, 3:202–13.
24. "Highlights in the Prophet's Life," *Ensign*, June 1994, 28. Those imprisoned with Joseph and Hyrum were Lyman Wight, Caleb Baldwin, Alexander McRae, and Sidney Rigdon. See Berrett, *The Restored Church*, 146.
25. See Berrett, *The Restored Church*, 143–47.
26. See Madsen, *Joseph Smith the Prophet*, 57.
27. Smith, *History of the Church*, 3:420.
28. Smith, *History of the Church*, 3:421.

29. See *Our Heritage: A Brief History of The Church of Jesus Christ of Latter-day Saints* (Salt Lake City: The Church of Jesus Christ of Latter-day Saints, 1996), 52.

30. Smith, *History of the Church*, 4:4, 35. Church leaders Edward Partridge, Brigham Young, Heber C. Kimball, and others petitioned the state legislature, asking for a full investigation of the Missouri troubles. The state debated it and, after the Saints had completely left Missouri, approved the $2,000. See J. Christopher Conkling, *A Joseph Smith Chronology* (Salt Lake City: Deseret Book, 1979), 127.

31. B. H. Roberts, *A Comprehensive History of The Church of Jesus Christ of Latter-day Saints*, 6 vols. (Salt Lake City: Deseret News Press, 1930), 2:53.

32. See *Our Heritage, 53.*

33. "Highlights in the Prophet's Life," *Ensign*, June 1994, 28.

34. Roberts, *A Comprehensive History of the Church*, 2:226–27.

35. Roberts, *A Comprehensive History of the Church*, 2:47.

36. Roberts, *A Comprehensive History of the Church*, 2:144–45.

37. *Church History in the Fulness of Times* (Salt Lake City: Church of Jesus Christ of Latter-day Saints, 1993), 63–68.

38. "Nauvoo Expositor Was a Conspirators' Tool to Destroy Joseph Smith," *Church News*, August 22, 2001, 15.

39. See Ted Gibbons, *The Road to Carthage* (Provo, UT: Maasai, 2001), 60.

40. Gibbons, *The Road to Carthage*, 67–68.

41. *Church History in the Fulness of Times*, 275.

42. Roberts, *A Comprehensive History of the Church*, 2:229.

43. Roberts, *A Comprehensive History of the Church*, 2:235.

44. *Church History in the Fulness of Times*, 274–75.

45. *Church History in the Fulness of Times*, 276.

46. Smith, *History of the Church*, 6:546.

47. *Our Heritage*, 63.

48. One of the "friends," was James Guymon, great-great-grandfather of the author. "He was a personal friend of the Prophet Joseph and ate supper with him the night before he left for Carthage. He was a member of the Nauvoo Legion. At the time of the martyrdom, James and families lived on a farm in Hancock County, Illinois, the same county as Nauvoo. He went into his house and sat down with his head in his hands and cried like his heart would break. The children asked why he was crying, and he said, 'They have murdered the Prophet Joseph.'" (Clara Guymon Boyer, *Overall History of the Guymon Family*, unpublished.) The Guymons were among those who were driven out, crossed the plains, and settled in Utah.

49. *Church History in the Fulness of Times*, 277.

50. Smith, *History of the Church*, 6:546.

51. Joseph Fielding Smith, *Teachings of the Prophet Joseph Smith* (Salt Lake City: Deseret News Press, 1938), 313.

52. Smith, *History of the Church*, 6:552.

53. See John L. Hart, "Glimpse of Past Captured by Nauvoo Document," *Church News*, January 7, 2006. The written order from Governor Ford was in the possession of Wilford Woodruff for many years and was taken west with him. It remained in the family after his death in 1898. It was eventually sold to a private collector of Church artifacts, Brent Ashworth, in Provo, Utah, in 1968 and is believed to be the third-to-last signature of Joseph Smith.

54. Smith, *History of the Church*, 6:552–64.

55. Smith, *History of the Church*, 6:569–85.

56. John Taylor, *Witness to the Martyrdom: John Taylor's Personal Account of the Last Days of the Prophet Joseph Smith* (Salt Lake City: Deseret Book, 1999), 70.

57. Smith, *History of the Church*, 586–601. Dan Jones, a native of Wales, left on his first mission to Wales on December 6, 1844, accompanied by his wife and others, including Wilford Woodruff. By the next year, he was assigned to preside over the missionary efforts in all of Wales. By the end of his first mission, there were nearly four thousand Saints in Wales, 249 of whom departed with him for the Salt Lake Valley when he left Wales in 1849. See Ronald D. Dennis, "Dan Jones, Welshman: Taking the Gospel Home," *Ensign*, April 1987, 50–56.

58. See Ronald K. Esplin, "God Will Protect Me until My Work Is Done," *Ensign*, August 1989, 20.

59. See Smith, *History of the Church*, 6:606–608.

60. See Joseph L. Lyon and David W. Lyon, "Physical Evidence at Carthage Jail and What It Reveals about the Assassination of Joseph and Hyrum Smith," *BYU Studies*, vol. 46, no. 4, (2008), 36, 44.

61. See Reed Blake, "Martyrdom at Carthage," *Ensign*, June 1984, 36.

62. See Smith, *History of the Church*, 6:619–21.

63. Smith, *History of the Church*, 6:623.

64. See John Taylor, *Witness to the Martyrdom: John Taylor's Personal Account of the Last Days of the Prophet*

Joseph Smith (Salt Lake City, Deseret Book, 1999), 105.

65. See Smith, *History of the Church*, 7:114–15.
66. See Smith, *History of the Church*, 6:626–27.
67. See Smith, *The Revised and Enhanced History of Joseph Smith by His Mother*, 457.
68. Smith, *The Revised and Enhanced History of Joseph Smith by His Mother*, 287, 459.
69. See Larry C. Porter, "How Did the U.S. Press React When Joseph and Hyrum Were Murdered?" *Ensign*, April 1984, 22–23.
70. See Smith, *History of the Church*, 6:629–30.
71. See Smith, *History of the Church*, 2:322.
72. Smith, *History of the Church*, 2:328, 331.
73. See Smith, *History of the Church*, 7:422.
74. Gibbons, *The Road to Carthage*, 42, 45–60, 53–54, 58, 110.
75. Smith, *The Revised and Enhanced History of Joseph Smith by His Mother*, 460. The others were Joseph Smith Sr., Joseph Smith Jr., Hyrum Smith, Samuel Smith, and Samuel's wife, Mary Bailey Smith.
76. *Our Heritage*, 65.
77. See Smith, *History of the Church*, 6:602–606.
78. Smith, *History of the Church*, 6:187–88.
79. See James B. Allen and Glen M. Leonard, *The Story of the Latter-day Saints* (Salt Lake City: Deseret Book, 1976).
80. Roberts, *A Comprehensive History of the Church*, 2:209.
81. See Madsen, *Joseph Smith the Prophet*, 61.
82. *See Church History in the Fulness of Times*, 273.
83. Spencer W. Kimball, "Conference Report," April 1955, 96. (From *Teachings of the Presidents of the Church—Spencer W. Kimball* [Salt Lake City: The Church of Jesus Christ of Latter-day Saints, 2007], 234.)

Chapter 30

1. See Lucy Mack Smith, *The Revised and Enhanced History of Joseph Smith by His Mother*, Scot Facer Proctor and Maurine Jensen Proctor, eds. (Salt Lake City: Deseret Book, 1996), 137.
2. See Joseph Smith, *History of the Church of Jesus Christ of Latter-day* Saints, 7 vols. (Salt Lake City, Deseret Book, 1976), 1:18.
3. See Smith, *History of the Church*, 1:18.
4. William E. Berrett, *The Restored Church* (Salt Lake City: Deseret Book, 1961), 29.
5. See *Church History in the Fulness of Time* (Salt Lake City: Church of Jesus Christ of Latter-day Saints, 1993), 45.
6. Smith, *History off the Church*, 1:19.
7. See *Teachings of the Presidents of the Church—John Taylor"* (Salt Lake City: Church of Jesus Christ of Latter-day Saints, 2001), 83–84.
8. See Smith, *History of the Church*, 1:19.
9. Kenneth W. Godfrey, "A New Prophet and a New Scripture," *Ensign*, January 1988.
10. See *Church History in the Fulness of Times*, 46. This house eventually burned, leaving only the foundation. The Church of Jesus Christ of Latter-day Saints rebuilt it on its original site and dedicated it in September 2015. The Church also rebuilt Emma's parents' home across the road, including a small chapel and visitors' center.
11. See Smith, *The Revised and Enhanced History of Joseph Smith by His Mother*, 161–62.
12. *History of the Church in the Fulness of Times*, 47–49.
13. Smith, *History of the Church*, 1:47.
14. *Church History in the Fulness of Times*, 54.
15. Smith, *History of the Church*, 1:35, 44.
16. See *Church History in the Fulness of Times*, 53.
17. See Smith, *The Revised and Enhanced History of Joseph Smith by His Mother*, 192.
18. Smith, *The Revised and Enhanced History of Joseph Smith by His Mother*, 192–96. The Whitmer family was later baptized and became close friends with Joseph.
19. *Church History in the Fulness of Time*, 56–57.
20. See Smith, *The Revised and Enhanced History of Joseph Smith by His Mother*, 195.
21. See *Church History in the Fulness of Times*, 57–58.
22. Richard L. Bushman, "The Recovery of the Book of Mormon," in Noel B. Reynolds, ed. *Book of Mormon Authorship Revisited* (Provo, UT: Foundation for Ancient Research and Mormon Studies, 1997), 32.
23. Smith, *The Revised and Enhanced History of Joseph Smith by his Mother*, 197–99.
24. Smith, *The Revised and Enhanced History of Joseph Smith by his Mother*, 203.
25. Smith, *History of the Church*, 1:2 footnote. Joseph mentioned this on May 2, 1838, the day he started writing his history.

26. See *Church History in the Fulness of Times*, 62–65. Grandin was hesitant to take the printing job because his friends had tried to persuade him from doing so.

27. *Church History in the Fulness of Times*, 65.

28. Berrett, *The Restored Church*, 38.

29. *Church History in the Fulness of Times*, 64.

30. *Church History in the Fulness of Times*, 63–66.

31. Smith, *History of the Church*, 1:59.

32. See John W. Welch, "How Long Did it Take to Translate the Book of Mormon?" *Ensign*, January 1988, 46–47.

33. Michael DeGroote, "Seven Wonders of the Book of Mormon," *Mormon Times*, October 19, 2008, 38.

34. Keith W. Merrill in *Why I Believe* (Salt Lake City: Deseret Book, 2002), 231.

35. See Amy Choate, "Joseph Smith Research Gets Top Endorsement," *Deseret Morning News*, August 12, 2004.

36. Berrett, *The Restored Church*, 197. (The 200th anniversary of the birth of Joseph Smith was December 5, 2005.)

37. George Edward Clark, *Why I Believe: 54 Evidences of the Divine Mission of the Prophet Joseph Smith* (Salt Lake City: Bookcraft, 1952), 62.

38. R. Scott Lloyd, "Joseph Smith, Brigham Young Rank First and Third in Magazine's List of Significant Religious Figures," *Deseret News*, January 9, 2015.

39. *Teachings of the Presidents of the Church—John Taylor*, 82–83.

40. Brigham Young, "A Knowledge of God Obtained Only through Obedience to the Principles of Truth," *Journal of Discourses* (London: George Q. Cannon, 1862), 9:332. (See also Berrett, *The Restored Church*, 199).

41. George Q. Cannon, *The Life of Joseph Smith, the Prophet* (Salt Lake City: Juvenile Instructor Office, 1888; reprinted Salt Lake City: Deseret Book, 1986).

42. Amasa Potter, "A Quiet Grove in Old Nauvoo," *Meridian Magazine*, March 6, 2003.

43. See Hugh B. Brown, "Profile of a Prophet," General Conference Talk, October 1967.

44. Berrett, *The Restored Church*, 198. (See also Cannon, *The Life of Joseph Smith*, 198.)

Art Credits

Page 6: Christ Blesses the Nephite Children © Robert Barrett. For more information please visit www.robertbarrett.com

Page 10: First Vision, © Jon McNaughton. McNaughton Fine Art Co. For print information go to www.mcnaughtonnart.com

Page 13: If Father Will Hold Me © Liz Lemon Swindle. Foundation Arts. For print information go to www:foundationarts.com.

Page 20: Joseph Receives the Plates © Robert T. Barrett. For print information go to www:roberttbarrett.com

Page 21: Book of Mormon Artifacts. Courtesy Wikimedia commons; for more information visit www.commons.wikimedia.org

Page 22: Hill Cumorah pageant, Timothy Taggart; photographer; timothyltaggart@gmail.com

Page 27: Nahom Alter. Courtesy Wikimedia commons; for more information visit www.commons.wikimedia.org

Page 32: Joseph Translating the Bible © Liz Lemon For print information go to www.foundationsarts.com

Page 40: By the Gift and Power of God © Anthony Sweat - For contact information go to www.anthonysweat.com

Page 47: Kon Tiki Raft. Courtesy Wikimedia commons; for more information visit www.commons.wikimedia.org

Page 50: Behold Your Little Ones © Del Parsons. For print information go to dparson@delparson.com

Page 55: Words © Lester Yocum. For print information go to les@lesteryocum.com

Page 60: Baptism in Waters of Mormon, © Jorge Cocco. For print information go to www:amielcocco@hotmail.com

Page 61: John the Baptist ordaining Joseph and Oliver. Statue photo by Grace G. Jones

Page 62: Peter, James and John Ordaining Joseph © Liz Lemon Swindle For print information go to www.foundationsarts.com

Page 67: Founding Fathers in St. George Temple. © Glen Hopkinson. For print information go to www:glenhopkinson.com

Page 84: Bring Forth the Records © Robert Barrett. For print information go to www:roberttbarrett.com

Page 92: He is Risen. © Del Parson. For more information go to www.dparson@delparson.com

Page 100: Salt Lake City. Courtesy of Wikimedia commons; for more information visit www.commonswikipedia.org

Page 104: King Benjamin Confers priesthood on Mosiah © Robert T Barrett. For print information go to www.roberttbarrett.com

Page 111: Nephi With His Broken Bow © Jorge Cocco. For more information go to www:amielcocco@hotmail.com

Page 121: Manti Temple, Photo by Grace G. Jones

Page 133: Samuel the Lamanite © Jorge Cocco. For more information go to www:amielcocco@hotmail.com

Page 136: He Called Me by name © Liz Lemon Swindle. For print information go to www.foundationsarts.com

Page 143: Crucifixion of Christ © Liz Lemon Swindle. For print information go to www.foundationarts.com

Page 150: President Gordon B. Hinckley. Courtesy of Wikimedia commons; for more information visit www.commonswikipedia.org

Page 160: Other Sheep © Robert T. Barrett. For print information go to www.roberttbarrett.com

About the Author

Grace Guymon Jones has made extensive contributions to both her church and community since she graduated from Brigham Young University in 1950 where she was editor of the BYU yearbook. In 2001, BYU awarded Grace with a "Special Recognition Alumni Award" in honor of her public and church contributions.

While living in Ukiah, California, Grace served many years as a Public Affairs Director for The Church of Jesus Christ of Latter-day Saints and has published hundreds of articles about the Church. She served as a Stake Public Communications Director for over thirty years, and then for fourteen years, she was the Santa Rosa Region Public Communications Director, an area that included several stakes and extended from the Golden Gate Bridge to the Oregon border. Her diligence was recognized in The Church News, "Her Successes Bring Church into Public View."

Grace wrote and illustrated a weekly column on positive parenting in a local newspaper for several years. Her ideas were later published in a book titled *Family Phrases—What Is Your Child Hearing?* In 1987, this mother of six was selected as "Mother of the Year" by a local newspaper. She also was an elementary school teacher for a short period.

With her husband, Dr. Milton B. Jones, she has served two missions for the Church in Scotland and in Georgia where a son, Richard, was their mission president. Dr. Jones spent his academic career as a professor in the Department of Agronomy and Range Science with the University of California, Davis Campus. Pursuant to his academic position, they have also taken sabbaticals to New Zealand and Brazil. Along with their six children, they have thirty-seven grandchildren and nearly forty great grandchildren. They moved to Provo, Utah, in 2005.

Index

Made in the USA
Columbia, SC
02 June 2019